The Gree

The Greek City

From Homer to Alexander

Edited by

OSWYN MURRAY

and

SIMON PRICE

CLARENDON PRESS · OXFORD

Oxford University Press, Walton Street, Oxford OX2 6DP

Oxford New York Toronto
Delhi Bombay Calcutta Madras Karachi
Kuala Lumpur Singapore Hong Kong Tokyo
Nairobi Dar es Salaam Cape Town
Melbourne Auckland Madrid
and associated companies in
Berlin Ibadan

Oxford is a trade mark of Oxford University Press

Published in the United States by
Oxford University Press Inc., New York

British Library Cataloguing in Publication Data

Data available

Library of Congress Cataloging in Publication Data
The Greek city : from Homer to Alexander / edited by Oswyn Murray and
Simon Price.
Includes bibliographical references.
1. Cities and towns, Ancient—Greece. 2. Cities and towns—
-Greece—History. 3. Municipal government—Greece—History.
4. Greece—History—to 146 B.C. I. Murray, Oswyn.
II. Price, S. R. F.
DF82.G74 1990 938—dc20 89–25574
ISBN 0-19-814791-0

3 5 7 9 10 8 6 4 2

Printed in Great Britain
on acid-free paper by
Biddles Ltd., Guildford and King's Lynn

For Tony Andrewes

Preface

This book originated in the Oxford Ancient History Seminar for Michaelmas and Hilary Terms of the year 1986/7, which was devoted to the Greek City; ten of the chapters began as papers for that occasion, and four are completely new.

Our title reflects that of an Oxford book of an earlier generation, A. H. M. Jones's *The Greek City from Alexander to Justinian*, although we can make no claim to the impact that Jones's work had in pioneering a new field of history. The origins, development, and nature of the classical Greek *polis* have been a central concern in this as in previous generations. Our book therefore offers a series of studies representing the different methodological approaches currently being practised, in order to provide an introduction to the state of the art. Each chapter presents a particular viewpoint, rather than an authoritative survey: we have aimed to stimulate thought, not provide a handbook. The book is intended for the general reader and the student of the social sciences as much as for professional historians of the ancient world; technical language has as far as possible been avoided, and Greek is confined to appendices.

A word on the balance, and on the limitations and omissions in this book. Our focus has been the autonomous Greek city-state or *polis* from its origins in the 'Dark Age' until the point at which it was transformed into a basis for world civilization by the conquests of Alexander the Great, and the subsequent expansion of *polis* institutions throughout the Middle East. We regard the urbanization of the Italian peninsula as an integral part of this earlier process, and have therefore welcomed a contribution from the new school of Italian urban archaeology. We have tried (with only modified success) to prevent our book becoming centred on the single best-known *polis*, Athens. We have sought to lay special emphasis on the relationship between the city and its countryside, and on town planning, because these are subjects which are becoming increasingly prominent. Recent work on the relationship between public and private spheres and on social psychology, particularly within the French tradition, has influenced a number of our contributors.

The most significant omission in our book concerns the relationship between trade and food supply in the economic history of the *polis*; the questions here are important and controversial ones, which have been recently discussed in the collection *Trade in the Ancient Economy*, edited by Peter Garnsey, Keith Hopkins and C. R. Whittaker (London, 1983), and in Peter Garnsey's *Famine and Food Supply in the Graeco-Roman World* (Cambridge, 1988). The other main omission of which we are conscious is the relationship between civic institutions and Greek literature; again that subject deserves a book to itself, and an excellent introduction exists in Simon Goldhill's *Reading Greek Tragedy* (Cambridge, 1986).

Finally we wish to dedicate our collection to the most senior member of our seminar, who missed not a single meeting, and whose wise counsels have continued to guide each generation of Oxford graduates in Greek history for thirty years.

Oxford   OSWYN MURRAY
January 1989   SIMON PRICE

Contents

List of Illustrations

Notes on Contributors

BRUNO D'AGOSTINO is Professor of Ancient History and Archaeology at the Istituto Universitario Orientale, Naples, and editor of *AION*, the journal of that university for ancient history; he is writing a book on the Etruscan city.

MOGENS HERMAN HANSEN is Lecturer in Ancient History at the University of Copenhagen, and the author of many books on Athenian democratic procedure and law, the latest of which is *The Athenian Assembly in the Age of Demosthenes* (Oxford, 1987).

MICHAEL JAMESON is Professor of Ancient History at Stanford University, and co-director of the Southern Argolid Survey.

EMILY KEARNS has taught Greek and Latin literature at Oxford and London, and is the author of *Studies in the Significance of Attic Hero-Cult in the Archaic and Classical Periods* (*BICS* supplement, forthcoming).

DAVID LEWIS is Professor of Ancient History at Oxford University, and author of books on ancient history and epigraphy; his most important recent work has been on the third edition of the public inscriptions of Athens, of which the first volume is *Inscriptiones Graecae* i 1 (Berlin, 1981).

OSWYN MURRAY is a Fellow of Balliol College, Oxford; he is the author of *Early Greece* (Glasgow, 1980), and an editor of *The Oxford History of the Classical World* (Oxford, 1986); he is currently British Academy Research Reader, working on a study of the Greek *symposion*.

LUCIA NIXON is currently teaching classics at the University of New Brunswick (Saint John), and is directing the Sphakia Survey (south-west Crete).

ROBIN OSBORNE is a Fellow of Corpus Christi College, Oxford, and has written *Demos: The Discovery of Classical Attika* (Cambridge, 1985) and *Classical Landscape with Figures* (London, 1987).

SIMON PRICE is a Fellow of Lady Margaret Hall, Oxford. He has published *Rituals and Power: The Roman Imperial Cult in Asia Minor* (Cambridge, 1984), and is now working on the Sphakia Survey.

NICHOLAS PURCELL is a Fellow of St John's College, Oxford, and author (with P. Hordern) of *The Mediterranean World* (Oxford, forthcoming).

OLIVER RACKHAM is a Fellow of Corpus Christi College, Cambridge, and the author of *History of the [British and Irish] Countryside* (London, 1986); he has worked on numerous projects in Greece.

W. G. RUNCIMAN is a Fellow of Trinity College, Cambridge, and is currently writing a three-volume *Treatise on Social Theory*.

PAULINE SCHMITT-PANTEL is Professor of Ancient History at the University of Amiens, and author of *La Cité au banquet*, a major study of public dining in the Greek city to be published by the Ecole française de Rome.

CHRISTIANE SOURVINOU-INWOOD has taught classical archaeology at Oxford and Liverpool; her most recent book is *Studies in Girls' Transition Rites: Aspects of the Arkteia and Age Representation in Attic Iconography* (Athens, 1988).

ANTHONY SNODGRASS is Professor of Classical Archaeology at Cambridge. His most recent book is *An Archaeology of Greece: The Present State and Future Scope of a Discipline* (Berkeley, 1987), and he is the co-director of the Cambridge–Bradford Boeotian Expedition.

List of Abbreviations

Annales (ESC)	*Annales (Économies, Sociétés, Civilizations)*
Ath. Pol.	the Aristotelian *Athenaion Politeia* (*Constitution of Athens*)
BAR	British Archaeological Reports
BCH	*Bulletin de Correspondance Hellénique*
BSA	*Annual of the British School at Athens*
CID	G. Rougemont, *Corpus des inscriptions de Delphes: i. Lois sacrées et règlements religieux* (Paris, 1977)
CQ	*Classical Quarterly*
FGrHist	F. Jacoby, *Fragmente der griechischen Historiker* (1923–)
GRBS	*Greek, Roman and Byzantine Studies*
HSCP	*Harvard Studies in Classical Philology*
IG	*Inscriptiones Graecae*
IK	*Inschriften griechischer Städte aus Kleinasien*
JHS	*Journal of Hellenic Studies*
JRS	*Journal of Roman Studies*
LSAM	F. Sokolowski, *Lois sacrées de l'Asie mineure* (Paris, 1955)
LSCG	id., *Lois sacrées des cités grecques* (Paris, 1969)
LSCGS	id., *Lois sacrées des cités grecques. Supplement* (Paris, 1962)
ML	R. Meiggs and D. M. Lewis, *A Selection of Greek Historical Inscriptions to the End of the Fifth Century BC* (Oxford, 1969)
PCPS	*Proceedings of the Cambridge Philological Society*
REA	*Revue des études anciennes*
SEG	*Supplementum epigraphicum Graecum*
Tod	M. N. Tod, *Greek Historical Inscriptions* (Oxford, i², 1946, ii, 1948)
ZPE	*Zeitschrift für Papyrologie und Epigraphik*

Abbreviations for classical authors and works usually follow the conventions of *The Oxford Classical Dictionary*.

I

Cities of Reason

OSWYN MURRAY

> The *polis*, properly speaking, is not the city-state in its physical location; it is the organization of the people as it arises out of acting and speaking together, and its true space lies between people living together for this purpose, no matter where they happen to be.
>
> (Hannah Arendt, *The Human Condition* [Chicago, 1958], p. 198)

BERTRAND RUSSELL describes a puzzling feature of the mentality of apes.[1] Their ability to think rationally was in his day investigated through a series of experiments in which the monkey was put inside a cage and presented with a banana just out of reach; in order to obtain the banana he had to perform some simple logical task, like fitting two sticks together, pulling a string, or pressing a catch. The reward triggered off a learning response which enabled the experimenter to build up more and more complicated variants of the primitive task, with the monkey learning as it went along.

The odd thing about such experiments was that the monkeys behaved differently according to who observed them:

Since the idea of the paper was to provoke discussion as widely as possible, it was earlier published in *Archives Européennes de Sociologie—European Journal of Sociology*, 28 (1987), 325–46, and is republished with the editors' permission; that version contained a number of important comments by M. H. Hansen (pp. 341–5), which are not repeated here: instead where necessary I have modified my comments to take account of them. The paper was written to initiate the Oxford seminar on the Greek city in 1986–7; I am grateful for the response of my audience then, and later at an undergraduate discussion group in King's College, Cambridge. Particular thanks to Eric de Dampierre, Simon Goldhill, Mogens Herman Hansen, John Henderson, Andrew Lintott, Geoffrey Lloyd, Steven Lukes, Martin Ostwald, Simon Price, and Garry Runciman for help.

[1] *An Outline of Philosophy* (London, 1927), ch. 3. I owe the exact reference for this story, which I had remembered from my undergraduate reading thirty years ago, to the indefatigable curiosity of Mogens Herman Hansen.

Animals studied by Americans rush about frantically, with an incredible display of hustle and pep, and at last achieve the desired result by chance. Animals observed by Germans sit still and think, and at last evolve the solution out of their inner consciousness. To the plain man, such as the present writer, this situation is discouraging.

Russell's conclusion was not so much the simple one that the observer affects the interpretation of results, but the more significant point that the character of the experiment itself is predetermined by the mental attitudes of the experimenter:

I observe, however, that the type of problem which a man naturally sets to an animal depends upon his own philosophy, and that this probably accounts for the differences in the results. The animal responds to one type of problem in one way and to another in another; therefore the results obtained by different investigators, though different, are not incompatible. But it remains necessary to remember that no one investigator is to be trusted to give a survey of the whole field.

Thus Germans both had a low opinion of the mentality of apes and believed in rule-oriented activity as an essential ingredient of rationality; they therefore designed experiments of such simplicity that even the most stupid ape could solve them, but only in accordance with the rules. The ape was therefore quietly confident, performed the task, and proved to the German's satisfaction that the German was wrong: the ape possessed true 'insight'. Americans on the other hand were more optimistic about the intelligence of apes, and tended to devise experiments which would stretch the capabilities of even the most gifted monkey; they also placed a high value on free expression as an element of rationality. The average monkey therefore became emotionally disturbed on experiment days, and learned quickly that the only way to obtain results was to rush around banging everything in sight—thus proving to the American's satisfaction that it was all a matter of chance, and the American was wrong. Both groups were inclined to accept the results of their experiments precisely because they con-founded their expectations; but in fact it was the expectations which had determined the results.

This form of national response to the phenomena is familiar to anyone who has studied attempts to characterize the Greek *polis*. To the Germans the *polis* can only be described in a handbook of constitutional law; the French *polis* is a form of Holy Communion; the English *polis* is a historical accident; while the American *polis* combines the practices of a Mafia convention with the principles of justice and individual freedom. Traditional assumptions and expectations predetermine the results, even when they appear to conflict with established views; when predictions are falsified, we are all the more ready to accept the conclusions uncritically. This predetermination of results operates both through theory and through method: the empiricist is revealed merely as someone who does not bother to investigate his own bias.

But perhaps the Greek historian has a worse problem than the behavioural psychologist, who can take the relationship between monkeys and bananas as fixed, and merely has to determine what counts as intelligent behaviour. The historian of the *polis* not only has to define what counts as rational political behaviour; he also has to establish the limits of the factual. To give an example which I shall return to later, is political myth evidence of political rationality or irrationality, and how is it to be related to rhetoric on the one hand and logical argument on the other? The answers to such questions concerning the field of evidence to a large extent determine the result of any enquiry into the rationality of the *polis*.

The problem of the observer is also crucial, at two levels. Firstly, the ancient observer: our most self-conscious and systematic students of the *polis*, Thucydides and Aristotle, present such a coherent picture of its workings that it is very tempting to deny them any status as evidence, and to claim that their views are too well formed to be capable of representing the views of those who lived in and operated under the system. But how did their views differ from the common view? Certainly they were more systematic; and that is likely to imply that they were selective in their presentation of the evidence, thus denying us the chance of testing the theories which have influenced the selection. The same problem arises with less sophisticated mythic representations: the Spartan myth, for instance, was a collective representation which, though it influenced reality, did not wholly correspond to it. And even when such representations falsify reality, one may still ask whether they are not necessary to it: how far was it necessary to the functioning of the *polis* that it should perceive itself as a rationally ordered society? The real problem of the Spartan myth may be, not that it is a myth, but that it is (at least in the first instance) a foreign myth, a myth of otherness (*altérité*).

Secondly, we as observers are in the business of making models, of understanding through systematization; we characterize our societies as tribal societies, nomadic societies, or city-states. In the interests of system we accept or reject evidence because it conforms to other evidence: we do not believe in the untidiness of reality. Worse, we use our models to create evidence; we extrapolate from what we think to be fact by rational argument to further 'facts'. There is, too, a complex relationship between model and argument from analogy: the concept of a warrior society allows transference of individual phenomena from one historical society to another across continents and centuries. There are a number of senses in which the more complete, the more coherent a picture of any aspect of society is, the more false it is likely to be, or at least the more certain that it is the construct of a single observer; for the coherence of any society is a coherence which belongs to the observer rather than the society. Such criticisms remain a basic worry when we try to analyse any picture that seems to us to make sense.

I would suggest that the solution to such problems of relativity does not lie in adopting or discovering a single methodology, held for whatever reason to be proven or neutral or scientific, but rather in attempting to combine as many different styles of approach as possible in a spirit of cautious optimism: as Russell said, 'it remains necessary to remember that no one investigator is to be trusted to give a survey of the whole field'. Then if conflicting methodologies result in conflicting conclusions, that is not surprising, and we must resign ourselves to Russell's paradox; but if, by some extraordinary chance, conflicting methodologies reach congruent conclusions, perhaps we are on the way to establishing that the phenomena exist independently of the observer.

The problem that I wish to discuss is framed in the question, how rational was the Greek *polis*? It is a traditional question, in which the lines of battle were set up in the nineteenth century, when historians first became aware of the potential otherness of the societies they were investigating: *The Ancient City* of Fustel de Coulanges (1864) can still stand as the starting point for such an enquiry. In considering recent contributions to this debate (which seems to have revived significantly in the 1980s), I am struck by the extent to which answers to the question remain, for all their technical sophistication, within two long-established and almost national traditions.

The first of these is Anglo-Saxon in its sphere of influence, but owes what intellectual coherence it possesses to Max Weber's characterization of the Greek city, notably in chapter VI of *Economy and Society*. The idea that Greek society was the first to be politically self-conscious, to separate out the first principles of state organization and of political discourse, from those general traditional skills of community life, such as success in military or religious affairs, or ability to create and administer.rules, is still widely taken for granted in the Anglo-Saxon world. And most of us would agree that this particular 'invention of politics' led to that establishment of the centrality of the political discourse which characterizes western civilization, and its obsession with the separation of spheres of activity in accordance with what Weber called 'formal rationality'. On this analysis the Greeks remain of fundamental importance to us, because they explain our world view.[2]

The alternative tradition is holistic in its approach. It has often been seen as attempting to emphasize the primitiveness of Greek society, to claim that it represents an early and irretrievable stage in the development of society towards its present state; I am not sure that this is a necessary part of such theories, however tempting it may be to believe that social systems get more complex and become more differentiated through history. To me the essential characteristic of this approach, which is associated with the tradition of Émile Durkheim, is the claim that there is no absolute divide between different spheres of activity, public and private: the political institutions of the ancient city are to be understood in terms of the totality of

---

[2] For this evolutionary element in Weber's analysis of rationalism, see W. Schluchter, *The Rise of Western Rationalism: Max Weber's Developmental History* (1979, Eng. trans., Berkeley, 1981).

forms of social interaction. Moreover, if any aspect of ancient society is to be given prominence, it should be the religious, not the political; for in Durkheimian theory, at the beginning 'religion pervades everything; all that is social is religious: the two words are synonymous'.[3] This approach, which privileges religion, and (as its especial mode of discourse) myth, has produced much of the most important recent work on the Greek city.

The problem is that both these opposed styles of social explanation appear to have positive heuristic value when applied to the same society; but we still wish to ask, which has the greater validity, and for what purposes? One type of synthesis between these two general schools, which is sometimes attempted, seems to me unattractive. It would of course be easy to suggest that two different entities are being described: on the one hand the archaic *polis*, which should be analysed in holistic terms, as a city of 'mechanical solidarity', where the collective consciousness was both highly religious, and concrete and specific, and where primitive types of rule and social ritualization were dominant; on the other hand the classical city (perhaps of the fourth century rather than the fifth), in which the various forms of social interaction had become differentiated, and a separate sphere of the political is identifiable.

I do not think this distinction is helpful for two reasons. Firstly it is based on one of the most dubious and insidious of all nineteenth-century postulates, the idea of social development from the primitive and religious towards the complex and secular: it implies too strong a developmental Darwinian model. Secondly (and I think this is an empirical objection) it is desperately hard to locate the shift in consciousness implied by this idea of the transformation of the Greek *polis*, at any meaningful point in the history of the classical age. There was, I believe, a change in political consciousness at Athens in the period around 400 BC, which is reflected in the transition from customary to constitutional democracy, and relates to the development from an oral to a literate culture; but I do not think that literacy will serve to explain a transition (to use Durkheimian terminology) from mechanical solidarity to organic solidarity, and a decline in the collective consciousness.

[3] *The Division of Labour in Society* (Eng. trans., London, 1984), p. 119.

The question, how rational was the *polis* seems to be in fact not one but two questions; and it is significant that these two questions correspond to some extent to the two ways of looking at Greek society which I have outlined. We may ask in the first instance, how coherent was Greek thought about political life, how systematic? That is the sort of question which is familiar to anthropologists, where the coherence of a system of beliefs is held to be a form of rationality, regardless of the truth or falsehood, or the external functional status in terms of success or failure, of the beliefs.[4] In this sense religions or forms of magic may be held to be more rational than isolated but correct medical and scientific beliefs, because they belong to a system; it has recently been increasingly emphasized, for instance, that Greek astrology and Greek magic are organized on principles at least as rational as Greek science and Greek medicine.[5] This criterion is of course fully compatible with a Durkheimian emphasis on the collective consciousness as a unified belief system.

But we may also ask, and particularly of the Greeks, whose systems of thought and values are the origins of our own, how far the Greeks had achieved the separation of politics from other spheres in the Weberian sense, whether and how far there was an independent type of discourse about politics; and a positive answer to this question, a claim that the *polis* was rational in this sense, would appear to argue against the holistic view.

However, it is not mere confusion to lump together these two questions, because, though not identical, they are clearly connected. In terms of historical development or causation, the coherence of a particular set of beliefs is a prerequisite of the recognition that those beliefs could be separated; and

[4] There has recently been much discussion about the general validity of such coherence theories of rationality, which has pointed to the resulting problems of comparability between cultures and the difficulty of determining criteria for an overall definition of rationality (see Bryan R. Wilson (ed.), *Rationality* (Oxford, 1970); Martin Hollis and Steven Lukes (eds.), *Rationality and Relativism* (Oxford 1982). But whatever the difficulties in a wider context, for the Greek world the criterion of coherence does not raise insoluble problems of relativism for us, because of the genetic relationship between their modes of thought and ours.

[5] See the gradual shift in the views of G. E. R. Lloyd, through *Magic, Reason and Experience* (Cambridge, 1979), *Science, Folklore and Ideology* (Cambridge, 1983), and *The Revolutions of Wisdom* (Berkeley, 1988).

contrarily, the ability to separate them may indeed be a consequence of the fact that they are or have become central to the collective consciousness.

There are two areas of Greek history where recent work sheds light on these questions of rationality; they are, on the one hand, the development of the political and social structures of the *polis*, and, on the other, the various types of political discourse found within it.

One of the most striking aspects of Greek political life is the importance of institutional change or 'reform' in both the archaic and classical periods: for the earlier history, indeed, it is easier to study the changes than the normal workings of the system, as the author of the Aristotelian *Constitution of Athens* recognized. All social systems are to some extent functional, and change is often for a reason. It is not, therefore, odd if we can understand the purpose of political reform; but, from a Durkheimian point of view, it is perhaps odd if the system becomes progressively more logical, more coherent, as it reforms itself—since change away from the original state of mechanical solidarity ought often to lead to greater incoherence, rather than greater systematization, as new criteria of organization are introduced without the old ones being wholly abandoned. A classical example of such change towards incoherence would be the history of reform at Rome in almost any sphere, from politics to religion to law: the new was superimposed on the old, and nothing was ever discarded.[6]

Again our own experience of political reform would lead us to find it odd if the *effect* of reforms should turn out regularly to be consonant with their purpose: in our experience change has a tendency to create problems as often as it solves them. Even if we were to attribute this to the greater complexity of modern society, it would still argue enormous powers of discernment on the part of allegedly primitive ancient Greek reformers, if they succeeded in obtaining a high level of intended results.

Thus if we can detect an increasing degree of coherence in a society through its reforms, and if the principles governing the

---

[6] Cf. the view of Cato, expounded in Cic. *Rep*. 2.1.2: 'Our commonwealth was the product not of one genius but of many; it was formed not in the life of one man but over many centuries and many generations.'

social system become clearer through change, then we may say that the society itself displays a high degree of rationality, not merely in the sense of internal coherence, but also in the sense of a self-conscious recognition of the reasons for change and the consequences of institutional reform.

The Spartan system is known to us only in mythic form and from the outside: it is portrayed by a succession of non-Spartan observers as an ideal construct, heavily contaminated with the typical anthropological failings, of emphasis on its otherness, its difference from the norm, and of its conformity to a system; there are basic problems in the observer status of almost everything we think we know about Sparta. As a consequence, we cannot date or follow the development of the Spartan progress towards a distinctive *politeia* or socio-political system. We can, however, say that, in its essential structures, it was a creation of the archaic age, for it belongs to the age of the hoplite or heavy-armed warrior fighting in mass formation: it is the classic example of Weber's description of the ancient *polis* as 'a guild of warriors'.[7] As such, it would never have been conceived and established (though it may have continued to be perfected) in the classical period. It can therefore serve as an example of archaic rationality in political institutions.

It is clear that this rationality operated through the transformation of existing institutions. The basis of the society may be found in practices of commensality widespread in the warrior groups of early Greece and elsewhere, and apparently (if we can trust the Cretan parallels) already at an early date linked to land tenure in at least some Dorian communities. The conquest of neighbouring Messenia allowed the institutional universalization of such practices, to create a community where all members could be warriors. The evolution of the Spartan educational system, the *agoge* (on whatever base it was built) substituted the age-class principle for the family until adulthood, when a male peer-group structure took over. The aim of this state concern for the continuous training of young male members of the community (unparalleled in any other Greek city) was the creation of a specific warrior type of mentality. There seems also to be good evidence that the great

---

[7] *Economy and Society*, ch. 16. v. 6: Eng. trans., p. 1359.

religious festivals of the Spartans, the Karneia and the Gymno-
paidia, were transformed to act as supporters of the system.

When, therefore, we refer to anthropological parallels like
the Zulus, as has been done since at least the days of W. S.
Ferguson and Henri Jeanmaire,[8] we are not, I think, asserting
that the Spartan system should be interpreted as characteristic
of a primitive tribal society. Often we are merely pointing to
the inevitable parallels between societies organized on age-class
principles, or societies whose main purpose is the maintenance
of *la fonction guerrière*. Even if we wish to assert the primitive
origins of many aspects of Spartan society, we must still admit
that in structure Spartan society is functional in all its aspects—and moreover, since it has undergone conscious transformation, that it is intentionally functional and therefore
rationally designed. That is what I meant a few years ago in
describing Spartan society with the term borrowed from Lévi-
Strauss, as 'pseudo-archaic':[9] the so-called archaic features
have been transformed or invented in accordance with a
rational goal. Plato and Aristotle were therefore right to see the
Spartan system as designed to create in its members the single
virtue of *andreia* or disciplined courage, and so as a model for
the theoretical utopias that they wished to build. Political
theory began, not with these fourth-century philosophical
constructs, but with archaic Sparta. And we should take good
note of the barriers which this archaic rationality was able to
overcome: two of the most fundamental forces according to
anthropological theory have been subverted and reformed in
the service of the state—kinship and religion. Already the *polis*
has achieved complete control over what are normally
regarded as essential features of a primitive society.

This same rationality of the *polis* seems to me to emerge from
the work of the Danish scholar, M. H. Hansen, on fourth-
century Athenian political institutions.[10] Until recently it was
perhaps possible to believe that the Athenian democracy could

---

[8] H. Jeanmaire, 'La Cryptie lacédémonienne', *Revue des Études Grecques*, 26 (1913),
12–20; *Couroi et Courètes* (Lille, 1939); W. S. Ferguson, 'The Zulus and the Spartans: A
Comparison of their Military Systems', *Harvard African Studies*, 2 (1918), 197–234: see
now B. Bernardi, *Age Class Systems* (Cambridge, 1985).

[9] *Early Greece* (Glasgow, 1980), ch. 10.

[10] *The Athenian Ecclesia: A Collection of Articles 1976–83* (Copenhagen, 1983); *The
Athenian Assembly in the Age of Demosthenes* (Oxford, 1987).

be explained on the comfortably English principles of Bagehot, in historical terms as the result of a long, idiosyncratic, and largely fortuitous series of changes, which had as their consequence a citizen assembly which was by chance a model of democracy, both absolute and sovereign. Even so it was already noticeable how systematic were the interrelations between various separate aspects of Athenian public life: the relation between the appointment of all officials by lot for only a year, and the principles of collegiality and fragmentation of responsibility among the boards of officials, the rules for accountability and so on, were not accidental developments but part of a coherent system.[11]

The work of Hansen has, first of all, given us a set of facts on which to operate, by establishing the fundamental distinction between the oral customary democracy of fifth-century Athens, and the written formal constitution of the fourth century. It thus becomes possible to discuss the political dimensions of that second great transition from oral to literate culture around the year 400 BC. But more important for my present purposes is the demonstration that the fourth-century democracy was not just a jumble of traditional practices inherited from an age of imperialism, which happened to work well enough: it was a self-conscious and elaborate system of checks and balances, involving two (not one) major centres of decision-making, and establishing a basic distinction between law (*nomos*) and decree (*psephisma*), which is one of the great breakthroughs in the history of jurisprudence. Moreover, although this restored democracy was static in its main lines, it was also capable of continuous minor adjustments through the fourth century, demonstrating that the Athenian *demos* was consciously concerned with the continual renewal and perfection of the political system.

It might still be possible to claim that Athens and Sparta

[11] This was recognized by Aristotle, *Politics* 6. 1: Athenian democracy was based on the principles of freedom to rule and to be ruled, freedom to act as one pleased, and absolute equality in political rights. The coherence of the legal framework which embodied these principles is revealed by the description of the constitution in the second part of the Aristotelian *Constitution of Athens* (chs. 42–69), which reflects the organization of the actual lawcode: see P. J. Rhodes, *A Commentary on the Aristotelian Athenaion Politeia* (Oxford, 1981), pp. 30–7. Among modern writers see especially the classic analysis of J. W. Headlam, *Election by Lot at Athens* (Cambridge, 1891 and 1933).

were unique; but they were also uniquely different, and the two
phenomena we have looked at occurred some two centuries
apart. It might also be possible to say that Sparta is after all
only a theorist's construct of the fourth century; but at least it is
an ancient construct. Athens on the other hand is definitely not
a theorist's construct in the same sense: it is a late twentieth-
century discovery, which owes nothing to Plato and Aristotle,
who ignored it, and which was apparently never idealized by
contemporaries (not even by Isocrates) sufficiently for its
details to be systematically analysed.[12] Maybe we are wrong
about the rationality of both these societies; but if so we must
be wrong for different reasons in each case.

The problem of the rationalization of political institutions in
the archaic period is illuminated by two French studies published in 1976.[13] Independently F. Bourriot and D. Roussel
succeeded in demonstrating that there were at least severe
difficulties in believing in a continuity from pre-state to *polis*
social systems: this belief had rested on the apparent survival of
institutions with names which seemed to reflect a tribal past of
primitive kinship organizations, such as *phyle* (clan), *phratria*
(the sole survivor in Greek of the common Indo-European root
behind 'brother' and similar words in many languages), and
genos (family). But institutions with these names in the classical
period just did not behave like the religious-based kinship
groups of a hypothetical tribal past; further they were found
only in *polis* societies, and not (as far as can be seen) among the
surviving tribal Greek communities organized by *ethnos*. Certainly these names might correspond to the names belonging to
earlier forms of organization, but the institutions themselves
were wholly different; and their characters were determined,
not by any hypothetical past function or primitive survival, but
by their present function within the social order of the *polis*.

---

[12] The 'ancestral constitution' of the 'Solonian democracy' hypothesized by late
fifth- and fourth-century politicians and orators is perhaps the closest approach to a
contemporary interpretation of Athenian democracy; but it is explicitly retrojected
(see M. H. Hansen, 'Solonian Democracy in Fourth Century Athens', forthcoming).
Aristotle's account in the *Politics* (above, n. 11), like that in the *Constitution of Athens*,
ignores the developments at the end of the fifth century.

[13] F. Bourriot, *Recherches sur la nature du genos: Étude d'histoire sociale Athénienne—périodes
archaïque et classique* (Lille, 1976); D. Roussel, *Tribu et cité* (Paris, 1976).

Explanations of the *polis* which rested on the hypothesis of continuity from alleged tribal origins to the developed urban community were shown to be at least seriously defective; and this included most attempts to explain the origins of the *polis*, from the ancient theories of the pupils of Aristotle, to the great nineteenth-century theories of Grote, Fustel de Coulanges, Maine, Morgan (and therefore Marx and Engels), with all their followers in the present century. Only Weber seemed to stand apart, with his unheeded warning that 'it does not follow, therefore, that the Greek *polis* was actually or originally a tribal or lineage state, but that ethnic fictions were a sign of the rather low degree of rationalization of Greek political life'.[14]

The explanation for this paradoxical phenomenon of linguistic survival and institutional innovation must lie in the extraordinary and apparently widespread changes during the sixth century, which involved the reorganization of the citizen body. This was such a radical transformation of pre-state forms that it amounted to the creation of wholly new types of social division. The process is most clearly attested with the *phylai*. From Kleisthenes of Sikyon in the early sixth century, to Cyrene in the middle of the century and Kleisthenes of Athens at its end, the numbers, membership, and social functions of the *phylai* are in play, manipulated by men for the purposes of social reform, as if the existing *phylai* had no embedded function within the system. Scattered instances in other cities, like the change from three to eight *phylai* at Corinth, belong to the same period, and show that this was a well-recognized way of resolving various types of political conflict in the high archaic period.

For detailed information about smaller social units we are confined to Sparta and Athens. It is obvious that the changes introduced by Kleisthenes at Athens involved a basic rethinking of the functions of social institutions at all levels, and a high degree of rationality in developing a new system of interrelated units; the facts that the names appear traditional, and that appeal is made to religious sanction, should not obscure the

---

[14] *Economy and Society*, ch. 5, section ii, Eng. trans., p. 389.

radical nature of this experiment in restructuring the entire citizen body.[15]

For the sake of being controversial, let me take one example, Kleisthenes' reform of the Athenian *phratriai*. These appear to be a typical pre-state form of social grouping: by analogy with other Greek cities, they may well have once been aristocratic warrior organizations under the control of particular aristocratic kinship groups (*gennetai*).[16] But in the classical period they show no sign of this possible origin. Every citizen belongs to a phratry; membership of the phratry is prior to membership of the citizen body; for a legitimate Athenian male belongs to one even before conception, in that his father's legal betrothal is witnessed by members of the phratry. Presentation of the young child to the group by his relatives at a formal sacrifice is the first public recognition of his legitimacy; he is again presented at adolescence, and his name is entered on the phratry register. In practical terms, membership of the phratry and participation in its cult acts were the direct channel of mediation between family and community; to the individual in the classical period the phratry was more important than any other single group organization, and the ultimate proof of citizenship was not in fact inscription on the citizen list kept by the local demes, but acceptance by fellow *phrateres*.

The phratry had existed in the seventh century, for its members were invoked in Drakon's homicide law in the third instance, after family and kin;[17] but that does not of course necessarily imply that it was then universal in Athenian society. A law of uncertain date and meaning regulates entry to the phratries, and implies different social levels within the phratry, which therefore suggests the widening of its membership at some point.[18] More striking is the fact that the classical

---

[15] This point was well made by P. Lévêque and P. Vidal-Naquet, *Clisthène l'Athénien: Essai sur la représentation de l'espace et du temps dans la pensée grecque de la fin du VIe siècle à la morte de Platon* (Paris, 1964), despite the fact that 'one reviewer considers that the book has practically nothing of historical importance to tell about Cleisthenes'. The evidence has been transformed by the researches of J. S. Traill, *The Political Organization of Attica: A Study of the Demes, Trittyes, and Phylai, and their Representation in the Athenian Council*, *Hesperia*, suppl. XIV (1975).

[16] So for instance A. Andrewes, 'Philochorus on Phratries', *JHS* 81 (1961), 1–15.

[17] C. W. Fornara, *Archaic Times to the End of the Peloponnesian War* (Translated Documents of Greece and Rome, vol. 1, Baltimore, 1977), no. 15.

[18] Philochorus, in *FGrHist* no. 328 F 35a.

phratries are universal and standard: they all worship the same two gods, Zeus Phratrios and Athena Phratria, and have the same rituals on the same feast days. They may make individual regulations, but they are under the control of the state, and must therefore in their classical form be the consequence of a conscious reorganization by the state. This deliberate remodelling of an apparently earlier institution and its ritual framework is a characteristic example of the archaic mode of reform. It is explicitly attributed to Kleisthenes by Aristotle, who shows its close connection with Kleisthenes' other reforms:

> A democracy like this will find useful such institutions as were employed by Kleisthenes at Athens when he wished to increase the power of the democracy, and by the party setting up the democracy at Cyrene; different *phylai* and *phratriai* must be created, outnumbering the old ones, and the celebrations of private religious rites must be grouped together into a small number of public celebrations, and every device must be employed to make all the people as much as possible intermingled with one another, and to break up the previously existing associations.
>
> (Aristotle, *Politics* 6, 1319ᵇ)

Of course there is an ambiguity here, since Aristotle is referring both to Athens and to Cyrene. It is typical of the power of modern theory to determine historical fact that the majority of historians reject this coherent account, which is supported by consideration of the later functions of the phratry, and prefer the bald statement of the generally derivative Aristotelian compilation on the *Constitution of Athens* that 'Kleisthenes allowed the *gene*, the *phratriai* and the priesthoods each to remain with their traditional functions' (21. 6). It is much more comfortable to believe in the primitiveness of an institution so bound up with the family and religion. But even if the reform is not a reform of Kleisthenes, it remains true that the classical Athenian *phratria* has no effective relationship with the sort of *phratria* which might be thought to have existed before the reforms. The classical institution is post-Kleisthenic, and therefore Kleisthenic in spirit if not in fact.

The later existence of institutions with names reflecting pre-state forms cannot, then, be taken as evidence of substantive continuity; for the identity in nomenclature often disguises a

series of conscious changes which have in many cases completely transformed the institutions. This argues either an
exceptionally low degree of embedding for such institutions in
the social and religious rituals of the early *polis*, or an exceptionally high degree of rationality, in the willingness to trans-
form traditional institutions in the service of social and political reform. To rephrase Max Weber,[19] these ethnic fictions
reflect, not the low degree of rationalization of Greek political
life, but the very early date at which it occurred; just as Hesiod
expressed the relationships between abstract political concepts
in terms of genealogies, so the archaic age borrowed the
language of a tribal past to describe a rationally articulated
future.

I turn from political structures to political discourse: how did
the Greeks argue in public debate on political issues? Direct
evidence exists only for the fourth century at Athens, although
other forms of evidence make it possible to discuss the practice
of fifth-century Athens; and there is a considerable body of
theory from both fifth and fourth centuries on how one should
(or should not) persuade.

It is a surprising fact that no serious study of the logic of (for
instance) Demosthenes exists, or of the rationality of his
premises: 'an article or book entitled "Demosthenes as a
Political Thinker" has yet to appear'.[20] Sir Kenneth Dover in
his *Greek Popular Morality* (Oxford, 1974) discusses certain basic
moral and religious attitudes expressed by the orators and
undoubtedly shared with their voting audience. But he does
not tackle the question of the rationality of the arguments put
forward in individual speeches; and most other discussions are
concerned with their conformity to supposed rules of rhetoric
or persuasion, rather than their logical status. It is Aristotle in
his *Rhetoric* who points the way to a whole new field of research.
I will merely state an impression, gained from reading the
political oratory of Athens, and reinforced by the way that
modern historians so often find it easy to argue on the same
level for or against the views of ancient orators, that the mode
of discourse displayed by the fourth-century orator-politicians

[19] Above, p. 13.
[20] Hugo Montgomery, *The Way to Chaeronea* (Oslo, 1983), p. 15.

of Athens is a rational mode of discourse. It is not just that the influence of the classical tradition ensures that our politicians proceed from the same type of premiss and argue in the same way; rather these starting-points and methods are rational in both the senses defined before, of belonging to a coherent system of shared assumptions and methods of argument even when these lead to opposed conclusions, and of constituting a separate form of discourse, consciously distinguished from questions of religion, and (I would add) of history. It is surprising how much of the argumentation employed by Demosthenes and his opponents is argumentation about expediency, danger, cost, and likely results, and how little concerns religious duty, taboos, ritual purity, and so on. It is perhaps less surprising how close the psychological assumptions of Demosthenes are to our own, in questions such as patriotism and the persuasiveness of emotional response: but that too represents a system of values with a certain constancy in the political sphere, as Aristotle emphasized.

The case of history is especially important. In *The Invention of Athens*, Nicole Loraux has shown for one area of classical oratory, the public funeral oration, how history in the orators is recollected as myth; its truth is unimportant.[21] In the oratory of advice rather than of praise, the past is even less central; it serves merely to decorate or support arguments which are themselves based on rational calculation; and it is accordingly altered or invented just as freely as Plato alters or invents it to serve his philosophical ends. As historians we may deplore this, but we must recognize that it is an essentially rational procedure, far more rational than the bastard mixture of history and calculation that passes for political argument in modern assemblies.[22]

There are various ways of tracing this conception of a rational civic discourse back in time: one would be to extra-

[21] Paris, 1981, Eng. trans., Harvard, 1986. On this topic see also M. Nouhaud, *L'Utilisation de l'histoire par les orateurs attiques* (Paris, 1982).

[22] In his comments on this paragraph (*European Journal of Sociology*, 28 (1987), 342–3) M. H. Hansen suggests that I underestimate the importance of the past in fourth-century Athenian political rhetoric. But my point is that a situation in which the needs of the present wholly determine the vision of the past is one in which the past does not affect political decisions. The relationship between the *constitution* and history is of course more complex. It was not until the age of Lycurgus that the vision of the past was sufficiently autonomous to determine the decisions of the present.

polate from the modes of argument used in tragedy, and even comedy, to the political sphere. But I want to concentrate on myth in order to move towards a conclusion. Myth has had a privileged status in modern work on Greek history, because it appears to bridge the gap between a primitive reified mode of thought and the abstractness which is held to be characteristic of reason. Political myth in Greece is at least as old as Hesiod in the late eighth century, who offers a remarkable range of types of myth expressing political ideas. And recently Simon Goldhill has demonstrated how pervasive the political discourse is in Greek myth, in *Reading Greek Tragedy* (Cambridge, 1986), his fascinating development of the ideas of the Parisian school of Jean-Pierre Vernant. In this account, Greek myth, as it is represented in tragedy, is far more interested in the civic consciousness than in religion: Attic tragedy is essentially *polis*-centred, and the festival of which it is a part is one whose public political significance is at least as important as its religious aspects. The specific stories presented, and the way that they are told, reflect problems of the conflict between political discourse and other possible areas of discourse, connected with family, religious powers, or the demands of the individual. The presupposition behind Attic tragedy is the centrality of the *polis* as social institution; and the problems with which tragedy deals are the problems which result from this centrality.

Tragedy is part of the civic consciousness, and yet serves to emphasize its ambiguities and dangers. Here we have a typical use of ritual, the playing out of the conflict between religious or 'pre-state' forces and the *polis*, in a festival created and maintained by the *polis*. But I would emphasize that, even in denying the absolute validity of the demands of the *polis*, tragic myth is performing one of the normal roles of myth in mediating conflicts; and it is important that the focus of this mediation is the preoccupations of the *polis*. A society whose public presentation of myth is a presentation so related to the concerns of the body politic is a fundamentally political society. Athenian tragic myth is political, not religious myth.

It is from this standpoint that I want finally to ask, in what sense is the Greek city a city of reason? So far I may seem to

have leaned rather heavily towards a Weberian and moderniz-
ing interpretation of the Greeks as rational beings like ourselves. But that is an illusion.

I believe that the holistic approach of Durkheim is essentially the right one.[23] But the rationality of the Greeks does not
depend on the fact that they have separated out an area of
political discourse from the starting-point of an undifferen-
tiated religious consciousness. On the contrary, it seems to me
clear that political activity was basic to Greek society; it did not
have to struggle to birth, and it became highly developed in
Greece, because it had always been the central organizing
principle. The mistake that Durkheim made was in universaliz-
ing the principle of religion, and asserting that the collective
consciousness could always and everywhere be identified in
origin with the religion of a society. The *polis* as a rational form
of political organization is the expression of the collective
consciousness of the Greeks.

The concept of collective consciousness is itself, I believe, a
useful one; so too are many of the attributes that Durkheim
assigned to it: that it permeates all other relationships, that it is
ultimately socially determined, that it is expressed and maintained through ritual, that it is a representation or restructuring of reality—all these claims will help us to understand
various aspects of Greek political life and of the structure of the
polis. If we regard the *polis* as the characteristic expression of
the collective consciousness of the Greeks, we can see how it is
that the *polis* dominates religion and the family and gentile
structures, rituals of death, military organization and rites of
commensality; we can understand how it is that the political
life of the city develops as a set of ritual practices concerned
with decision-making, why tradition counts and is yet manipulated as a rational tradition. Such a viewpoint explains why
there are no significant aspects of Greek culture which appear
independent of its political structures, in contrast to other
societies, which may be organized around different centres such
as religion or warfare, or which may have a more complex
polyvalent structure. Even the intellectual ordering of internal
and external reality in philosophy, medicine, and science

---

[23] See Appendix, below, pp. 22–3.

reflects the political order. The Greek city is a city of reason because the Greek man is a political animal from Homer onwards: we may trace the development; but this development represents, not a change of nature from one type of social organization to another, but the rational evolution of a system whose basic character did not change.

There is of course an obvious response to such a claim, which may indeed appear to be an objection: why were the Greeks different, or when did this difference arise? These are questions of fundamental importance, which were already being raised by Jean-Pierre Vernant in 1962, in the context of the decipherment of Linear B;[24] more recent writers have seemed to evade the issue, perhaps because no definite answer can be given: it may well be disputed whether 'the origins of Greek thought' are to be found in the organization of the Mycenean palace economy, in the confrontation with Semitic culture during the early archaic period, or in a process of self-definition related to internal change. It is not my purpose to answer this question, but rather to reinstate it by characterizing the *polis* as it existed in the historical period. And I readily concede that this weakness in my analysis is a consequence of its adherence to a Weberian comparativist perspective, with its unwillingness to equate the claims of evolutionism with the laws of historical explanation.

One purpose in emphasizing the Durkheimian holistic approach is that it avoids the trap of believing that the Greeks were like ourselves. There is an essential difference between Greek and modern attitudes to politics, which has nothing to do with the fact that their systems were small and simple face-to-face systems, whereas ours are large, complex, and anonymous. It reflects rather a difference in our perception of the function of politics, which is the result of a fundamental reinterpretation of the theoretical principles behind political institutions in the age of Macchiavelli and Hobbes. For us, politics is the study of forms of domination and control, of organization for effective action, and of conflict between power groups, or their reconciliation with the interests of the whole. These groups are often permanent and institutionalized; they

---

[24] *Les Origines de la pensée grecque* (Paris, 1962; Eng. trans. *The Origins of Greek Thought* (London, 1982)).

have a history from which we cannot escape. Our politics is therefore about conflict and compromise in a historical situation which prevents us from acting rationally: we cannot escape the irrational force of history.

For the Greeks, on the other hand, the immediate aim of politics and political institutions was to discover or to aid in the creation of a general will to action, and to express that general will in an ordered ritual.[25] Politics was concerned with the whole, the community (*koinonia*) was paramount: the purpose of politics was unity, not compromise.[26] That is why the concept of *eunomia* (good order) dominates the early history of the *polis*, and it is also why the emergence of class conflict was so destructive to the *polis*. *Stasis*, political faction, which to us is a natural political state, was to the Greeks a terrifying phenomenon incompatible with the possibility of civic life, a *nosos*, a disease as foul as the Great Plague at Athens itself, which corrupted language, faith, honour, all that made politics possible, and which was analysed in these terms in the great passage of Thucydides in book 3. 82–3 about the consequences of party strife. Once factions arise, the *polis* has no defence, and the rationality of the Greeks disintegrates into an anarchy of word and action.

So I believe it is true that the Greek city, though rational, is fundamentally different from any modern organization. But in all this I can see no reason for discussing it in terms of a tribal or traditional society, as normally conceived. Indeed the *polis* is a good deal less tribal than our own political societies; its discourse is more logical, its potentiality for change is more constant and less erratic. Its structures contain no such glaring conceptual inconsistencies as a House of Lords, or the idea of a Constitution which can be altered only by reinterpretation of the intentions of Founding Fathers dead for two hundred years. No wonder that George Grote found himself more at home in the Athenian assembly than in the gathering of tribal elders which was and is the House of Commons, with its lost rituals, and its language dominated by dead or dying religions

---

[25] The relationship between institutions, ritual, and action is well expressed in the (almost untranslateable) observation of Demosthenes, *Oration* 3. 15: 'Action, posterior in the order of events to speaking and voting, is in its consequences prior and superior.'

[26] So theorists like F. Tönnies who have seen the essence of politics in the expression of the collective will have found much to value in the Greek experience.

and by tribal feuds.[27] In a world which sees the powers of religion and unreason increasing daily in almost every political system, we must admit that it is we who are the primitives. To return to Bertrand Russell, in our attempt to make the Greeks primitive, we have only made them like ourselves.

Appendix

In a future article Hansen intends to develop one particular point that he made in his comments on my original paper, in *Archives Européennes de Sociologie* 28 (1987), 341–5, and I do not wish to anticipate his argument. But in the light of his fundamental objections already made (pp. 343–4) to my interpretation of Athenian society in Durkheimian terms, I should perhaps repeat here the reasons why I do not believe Athens to have been an exceptional Greek city which should be analysed in terms different from those used for Sparta and other cities.

The personal *eleutheria* which the Athenian citizen enjoyed as part of the values of Athenian democracy, 'to live as one pleases' (*Zen hos bouletai tis*), is different in kind from the modern liberal conception of the freedom of the individual. In his classic essay of 1819, 'De la liberté des anciens comparée à celle des modernes', Benjamin Constant argued for the incompatibility of ancient and modern ideas of liberty, although he was prepared to admit that Athens was an exception. Rather than accept this modification of a general view which I believe to be correct, I would prefer to analyse all Greek cities according to the same principles, and to explain the growth of individualism at Athens in terms of the complexity and conflicting nature of social constraints in a developed *polis*: the freedom of the individual Athenian was not an absolute freedom, but a form of interstitial freedom compatible with the holistic analysis offered above. It is this type of freedom which I tried to describe in my chapter on 'Life and Society in Classical Greece' in the *Oxford History of the Classical World*:

[27] 'A mild and philosophical man, possessing the highest order of moral and intellectual endowments; but wanting something which for need of a better phrase I shall call *devil*. He is too abstract in his tone of reasoning and does not aim to influence others by any proof excepting that of ratiocination' (Richard Cobden, quoted in John Morley, *The Life of Richard Cobden* (London, 1906), pp. 136–7).

The developed Greek city was a network of associations: as Aristotle saw, it was such associations which created the sense of community, of belonging, which was an essential feature of the *polis*: the ties of kinship by blood were matched with multiple forms of political and religious and social groupings, and of companionship for a purpose, whether it be voyaging or drinking or burial . . .

In such a world it might be argued that multiple ties limited the freedom of the individual, and there is certainly an important sense in which the conception of the individual apart from the community is absent from Greek thought: the freedom of the Greeks is public, externalized in speech and action. This freedom derives precisely from the fact that the same man belongs to a deme, a phratry, a family, a group of relatives, a religious association: and, living in this world of conflicting groups and social duties, he possesses the freedom to choose between their demands, and so to escape any particular form of dominant social patterning. It is this which explains the amazing creativity and freedom of thought of classical Athens: the freedom which results from belonging in many places is no less a freedom than that which results from belonging nowhere, and which creates a society united only in its neuroses.

(*Oxford History of the Classical World* (Oxford, 1986), pp. 209–10)

Bibliography

in chronological order

SOME CLASSIC WORKS

CONSTANT, B., 'De la liberté des anciens comparée à celle des modernes' (1819), printed in *De la liberté chez les modernes; Écrits politiques*, ed. M. Gauchet (Paris, 1980).

FUSTEL DE COULANGES, N. D., *The Ancient City* (1864; Eng. trans., 1874, reprinted Baltimore, 1980).

MORGAN, L. H., *Ancient Society* (New York, 1877).

DURKHEIM, E., *The Division of Labour in Society* (1893, 1902; Eng. trans., London, 1984).

—— *The Elementary Forms of Religious Life* (1912; Eng. trans., London, 1915).

WEBER, M., *Economy and Society* (1922; 5th German edn., 1976; Eng. trans., Berkeley, 1968).

SOME RELEVANT MODERN WORKS

ARENDT, H., *The Human Condition* (Chicago, 1958).
LEVI-STRAUSS, C., *Structural Anthropology* (1958; Eng. trans., New York, 1963).
BALANDIER, G., *Political Anthropology* (1967; Eng. trans., Harmondsworth, 1970).
FORTES, M., *Kinship and the Social Order: The legacy of L. H. Morgan* (London, 1969).
MOMIGLIANO, A., 'La città antica di Fustel de Coulanges' (1970), reprinted in *Quarto contributo alla storia degli studi classici e del mondo antico* (Rome, 1975), pp. 159–78; English trans. in *Essays in Ancient and Modern Historiography* (Oxford, 1977), pp. 325–43.
WILSON, B. (ed.), *Rationality* (Oxford, 1970).
LUKES, S., *Emile Durkheim* (Harmondsworth, 1973).
SCHLUCHTER, W., *The Rise of Western Rationalism: Max Weber's Developmental History* (1979; Eng. trans., Berkeley, 1981).
HOLLIS, M. and LUKES, S. (eds.), *Rationality and Relativism* (Oxford, 1982).
BERNARDI, B., *Age Class Systems* (1984; Eng. trans., Cambridge, 1985).
MANN, J. M., *Sources of Social Power*, 1. *A History of Power from the beginning to* A.D. *1760* (Cambridge, 1986).
SAHLINS, M., *Islands of History* (Chicago, 1986).

THE *POLIS*: RECENT WORKS

VERNANT, J.-P., *Les Origines de la pensée grecque* (Paris, 1962; Eng. trans., *The Origins of Greek Thought*, London, 1982).
FINLEY, M. I., 'Sparta and Spartan Society' (1968), in *Economy and Society in Ancient Greece* (London, 1981), pp. 24–40.
VERNANT, J.-P., and VIDAL-NAQUET, P., *Mythe et tragédie en Grèce ancienne* (Paris, 1972; Eng. trans., *Tragedy and Myth in Ancient Greece*, Brighton, 1981).
DOVER, K. J., *Greek Popular Morality in the Time of Plato and Aristotle* (Oxford, 1974).
ROUSSEL, D., *Tribu et Cité* (Paris, 1976).
BOURRIOT, F., *Recherches sur la nature du genos: Étude d'histoire sociale Athénienne—périodes archaique et classique* (Lille, 1976).
SNODGRASS, A. M., *Archaeology and the Rise of the Greek State* (Cambridge, 1977).
HUMPHREYS, S. C., *Anthropology and the Greeks* (London, 1978).
LLOYD, G. E. R., *Magic, Reason and Experience: Studies in the Origin and Development of Greek Science* (Cambridge, 1979).

AMPOLO, C. (ed.), *La città antica* (Bari–Rome, 1980).

BAECHLER, J., 'Les Origines de la démocratie grecque', *Archives Européennes de Sociologie*, 21 (1980), 223–84.

MEIER, C., *Die Entstehung des Politischen bei den Griechen* (Frankfurt, 1980).

LORAUX, N., *L'Invention d'Athènes* (Paris, 1981; Eng. trans., *The Invention of Athens*, Cambridge, Mass., 1986).

RUNCIMAN, W. G., 'Origins of States: The Case of Archaic Greece', *Comparative Studies in Society and History* 24 (1982), 351–77.

FINLEY, M. I., *Politics in the Ancient World* (Cambridge, 1983).

HANSEN, M. H., *The Athenian Ecclesia: A Collection of Articles 1976–83* (Copenhagen, 1983).

HUMPHREYS, S. C., *The Family, Women and Death* (London, 1983).

LLOYD, G. E. R., *Science, Folklore and Ideology: Studies in the Life Sciences in Ancient Greece* (Cambridge, 1983).

WELWEI, K. W., *Die Griechische Polis: Verfassung und Gesellschaft in archaischer und klassischer Zeit* (Stuttgart, 1983).

HANSEN, M. H., *Die athenische Volksversammlung im Zeitalter des Demosthenes* (Konstanz, 1984; revised English edn., *The Athenian Assembly in the Age of Demosthenes*, Oxford, 1987).

MEIER, C., *Introduction à l'anthropologie politique de l'antiquité classique* (Paris, 1984).

POLIGNAC, F. DE, *La Naissance de la cité grecque* (Paris, 1984).

RAHE, P. A., 'The Primacy of Politics in Classical Greece', *American Historical Review*, 89 (1984), 266–93.

GAWANTKA, W., *Die sogenannte Polis: Entstehung, Geschichte und Kritik der modernen althistorischen Grundbegriffe der griechische Staat, die griechische Staatsidee, die Polis* (Stuttgart, 1985).

BLEICKEN, J., *Die Athenische Demokratie* (Paderborn, 1986).

GOLDHILL, S., *Reading Greek Tragedy* (Cambridge, 1986).

STARR, C. G., *Individual and Community: The Rise of the Greek Polis 800–500 BC* (New York, 1986).

VERNANT, J.-P., and VIDAL-NAQUET, P., *Mythe et Tragédie 2* (Paris, 1986).

OSBORNE, R., *Classical Landscape with Figures: the Ancient Greek City and its Countryside* (London, 1987).

FARRAR, C., *The Origins of Democratic Thinking: The Invention of Politics in Classical Athens* (Cambridge, 1988).

GILLI, G. A., *Origini dell'eguaglianza: ricerche sociologiche sull'antica Grecia* (Turin, 1988).

LLOYD, G. E. R., *The Revolutions of Wisdom* (Berkeley, 1988).

MURRAY, O., 'Greek Forms of Government', *Civilization of the Ancient Mediterranean: Greece and Rome*, ed. M. Grant and R. Kitzinger, (New York, 1988), pp. 439–86.

A
The City in Mediterranean History

2

Mobility and the *Polis*

NICHOLAS PURCELL

> [To Periander] the greatest miracle of his lifetime, as the
> Corinthians say (and the Lesbians agree), was the bring-
> ing of Arion the Methymnaean safe to Taenarum on a
> dolphin. He was a lyre-player second to none of those who
> lived then.
>
> (Herodotus 1. 23–4)

ARION of Methymna, the inventor of the song called dithy-
ramb, is not perhaps the most obvious figure to choose as an
emblem of early Greek history; but he may begin to seem more
representative if the tentative suggestions of this rather general
paper are plausible. The singer from Lesbos in the eastern
Aegean who voyaged via Corinth, where he resided for some
time, to take part in many competitive festivals in the cities of
the Ionian and Tyrrhenian coastlands is an apt symbol of
personal mobility and of ease of communications. On a more
mythic level his delivery from the widest sea of the Mediterranean by the sea god's dolphin, and voyage to Cape Tae-
narum which turned seafaring into miracle, may be set as
illustration and counterpoint to all that we frequently repeat of
the horrors of storm, piracy, shipwreck, and being eaten by
fishes, and of the awe felt for the sea by the Greeks and
Romans. In stories like these, paradeigmatic or exemplary
narratives meet ones which were regarded as literally factual;
systems of explanation which depend on the supernatural jostle
with those which prefer to leave it aside: they should not be
ignored by the historian of the early Greek world.

I am very grateful to the editors of the volume for constructive criticism of this essay: it
has gained from their disagreements with some of its arguments. The notes that follow
aim to illustrate and support the text; they do not aim at providing a full bibliography,
and have usually not referred to the standard synthetic accounts.

This account is an exploration of the phenomenon of movement. It begins from the perspective of long-term Mediterranean history, in which the nature and density of contacts between one part of the coastlands of this landlocked sea and another have been very prominent objects of investigation.[1] What kind of contacts existed?

Section I faces the main cases for limited mobility and attempts to criticize them. In section II the underlying cause of mobility is approached, and linked with the ecology of the Mediterranean environment. Section III examines how it is that those basically ecological circumstances promote human mobility. Section IV elaborates the effects of this model on the economy of the Mediterranean world: ecology is seen at work in the redistribution of material goods of various kinds and the mobility which goes with it. Section V, finally, traces some of the cultural and social effects of the model on the world of the *polis*.

The account must be highly selective, and cannot avoid schematism. The archaeological evidence for the contacts between one part of the Mediterranean and another is so copious that a survey of that alone would be far beyond the scope of the paper. The point is to explore how mobility can work and what its effects can be. Parallels and illustrations are taken from a broad time-span. If they can be shown to be irrelevant to all or a part of the period covered here, for the most part the first half of the first millennium BC, then our picture is so much the clearer. But in the construction of a model like this for so remote a period, a degree of synthesis of material from different periods is inevitable.

It may be helpful also to say a word about the scholarly context of what is attempted here. The quantitative and qualitative leaps in archaeological research in the Mediterranean over the last thirty years have made possible the elaboration of approaches to ancient history which develop the early initiatives made by the pioneers of fieldwork in the region. What follows therefore has been formed to an extent by the legacy of Ramsay, Myres, Woolley, Blakeway, and Dunbabin, but is also offered as a contribution to the debate about

---

[1] The classic discussion is Fernand Braudel, *The Mediterranean and the Mediterranean World in the Age of Philip II* (Eng. trans., London, 1972), pp. 42–7.

cultural interchange which is currently being promoted by
Italian and French scholars. This debate by no means under-
values the contribution to be made by the study of the literary
sources, but has left to one side increasingly the approaches
which privilege those sources at the expense of the study of
what is to be found in the Mediterranean itself. It is
approaches of that kind that have tended to produce or
encourage the opinions which are criticized in this paper.

1. 'SMALL GREECE'?

Extremum porro nullius posse videtur/esse nisi ultra sit
quod finiat

> (Lucretius 1. 960–1: 'It appears that there can be no
> boundary to anything unless there is something to bound
> it too')

Many historians of early Greece have begun the task of
explaining the economic, social, and political history of the
'historical' period after the eighth century by assuming the
existence before then of an introverted and isolated ethnic
community (accidentally distributed across a rather topographically variegated stretch of the Mediterranean basin)
operating at the end of the 'Dark Ages' in a kind of vacuum in
which horizons were narrow, and everything small, limited,
primitive.[2] This 'small Greece' approach seems almost a kind
of 'early Man' *mythos*, as the Greeks themselves would have
called it, a constructed account serving an explanatory purpose, in this case to outline an original simplicity as a counterpoint to the sophistication which was to follow. To explain how
this came about, this *mythos* demands a sudden widening of the
range of contacts, which brought revolutionary change, as the
Greeks rapidly discovered the world around them, 'met' the
Phoenicians, 'opened up' the Black Sea, all in a kind of
precursor of the conventional view of the late medieval voyages
of discovery. This remarkable view (which has the Greeks
literally unable to enter the Black Sea until they have been

---

[2] For a recent example, Chester G. Starr, *The Economic and Social Growth of Early
Greece* (New York, 1986).

through the necessary revolution) needs defending, rather than simply serving as a latent background assumption.[3] The purpose of this account is to do the opposite, to outline some reasons for inclining towards the other end of the spectrum and assessing overall mobility and consciousness of the world as high throughout the first half of the first millennium BC.

The popularity of 'small Greece' approaches may be the result of various tendencies. Fondness for unilinear progressivism is one: humanity is on the upward road, and the steps by which we ascend can be identified in the historical record. In fact no rule of history entails that if there were dense maritime contacts in the fourth century BC there were fewer in the fifth and still fewer in the sixth. But among the concepts which help the progressivist view have been an eighth-century revolution, ending primitive underdevelopment, and the 'Argo mentality' in which the keels of the early voyagers must break wholly uncharted waters.

Second, the alleged Greek fear of seafaring. This is a simple case of taking the negative remarks of the tradition, from Hesiod and the *Odyssey* to the scenes of shipwrecked sailors being eaten by fish on early vases, to be somehow normative for that society: the Greeks frequently expressed their dread of the sea, therefore they stayed away from it. In fact, of course, no one bothers to express their dread of something with which they are not compelled to be frequently in contact. As for the intellectual and technological wherewithal, a modern seaman's resource like the *Mediterranean Pilot* is not the only basis for navigation in these waters. The work of social anthropologists on other societies shows how complex traditional systems of conceptual space among seafarers can be, and how the arts of navigation can rest on intellectual foundations quite different from those which have formed the mainstream of the geographical tradition. An understanding of the winds and currents of the sea and a conceptualization of coastal features does not depend on compasses and charts. The antiquity of the *periplous*, the written catalogue of coastal features taken in

---

[3] Rhys Carpenter, 'The Greek Penetration of the Black Sea', *AJArch*. 57 (1948), 1–10.

order, which existed from the sixth century onwards, may be taken as a case in point.[4]

Third, it has long been clear that lack of interest in the rest of the Mediterranean and Levantine world has promoted the 'small Greece' view. In 1910 Myres already denounced the inadequacy of the generally available atlas maps of Greece, ancient or modern, for excluding the neighbouring lands.[5] There has been no improvement. Illustrating the proximity of Cyrenaica to Crete, for example, requires a map of the whole Mediterranean from the selection available in modern classical atlases. Greek historians often either ignore the remainder of the Mediterranean or, more commonly, overemphasize the Greek/ non-Greek divide. A recent discussion has said of the settlement at Al Mina in Syria 'the site has little or nothing to do with the great movement of Greek colonization, and is only one of many that attest the close contacts between Greeks and Phoenicians'.[6] Here the density of contacts is indeed noted, but the residual disjunction is still apparent. For the 'great movement' is indissolubly linked to the 'close contacts', and is part of a single transformation of Mediterranean relations in which the societies of the Mediterranean seaboard were all involved, to an extent which makes Greek and Phoenician hard to distinguish, especially on the basis of artefacts. For the western Mediterranean the truth has been perceived and well expressed in recent years: the 'Western Mediterranean ... [was] a fantastic cauldron of expanding cultures and commerces'; and it follows that 'in the study of the currents of expansion in the West, Hellenocentrism can be no longer admissible'.[7] So too in the East, but even earlier than the eighth and seventh centuries BC.

Fourth, the archaeology which should have done most to overcome regional and chronological barriers has been divided

[4] For the Greek attitude to the sea, Albin Lesky, *Thalatta* (Vienna, 1947); for navigation, Charles Frake, 'Cognitive Maps of Time and Tide', *Man*, 20 (1985), 254– 70, and Alfred Gell, 'How to Read a Map: Remarks on the Practical Logic of Navigation', *Man*, 20 (1985), 271–86.

[5] John L. Myres, *Geographical History in Greek Lands* (Oxford, 1954), pp. 114–15.

[6] A. J. Graham, 'The Historical Interpretation of Al Mina', *Dialogues d'histoire ancienne*, 12 (1986), 51–65.

[7] Jean-Paul Morel, 'Greek Colonization in Italy and the West (Problems of Evidence and Interpretation)', T. Hackens, N. D. Holloway, R. Ross Holloway (eds.), *Crossroads of the Mediterranean* (Louvain, 1983), pp. 123–61, a very important article (quotations at pp. 150 and 148 respectively).

against itself. Decline, the unfavourable contrast of the 'Dark Age' with the civilizations of the second millennium BC and of historical Greece, has occupied too prominent a position. The dwindling of numbers of, and material wealth in, recoverable sites in peninsular Greece is overemphasized. Neither of these in fact entails demographic decline or narrower cultural horizons even locally, but they lose still more significance when compared with a broader chronological view of the Mediterranean: a view into which a new site like Lefkandi, revealing a *koine* of contacts across the sea of some complexity already in the tenth century, fits well.[8] The continuities are at last being triumphantly attested, overwhelmingly by the formerly shadowy eighth century, now brightly illuminated by archaeology as a time of great cultural interchange, but also for the preceding epoch.[9] It helps to argue positively from what is found towards whatever system makes sense of the evidence, as is done in the archaeology of the Bronze and Iron Ages elsewhere, rather than by taking a constructed acme of civilization as a point of reference and measuring by how much what you have found seems to fall short of it.[10]

There are no doubt other factors at work, and counter-considerations to be advanced. But a more general argument against the 'small Greece' view can be proposed, that of the epigraph to this section. What, Lucretius asks, in the case of the Universe, given a coherent and homogeneous entity, can we say about its limits?

What, therefore, we must ask of the Hellenic world of our period, was actually Hellenic about it? What made it cohere? These obvious questions are so huge that they have been shunned: always on the fringe of vision they recede or dissolve when looked at directly. But in order to attempt the exercise,

---

[8] For Lefkandi, Mervyn Popham (ed.), *Lefkandi* i (London, 1980).

[9] For continuities, Thyrza R. Smith, *Mycenaean Trade and Interaction in the West Central Mediterranean, 1600–1000* B.C. (Oxford, 1987); for the example of sites like Broglio di Trebisacce near Sybaris, *Cahiers Centre Jean Bérard* viii: *Ricerche sulla protostoria della Sibaritide*, 2. For the eighth century as a whole, J. N. Coldstream, in R. Hägg (ed.), *The Greek Renaissance of the Eighth Century* B.C.: *Tradition and Innovation* (Stockholm, 1983), pp. 17–25 (and on continuity with earlier periods, ibid. 208–10). Also C. Dehl, 'Cronologia e diffusione della ceramica corinzia dell' VIII s. a. C. in Italia', *Arch. Class* 1983 (1986), 186–7.

[10] Cf. below, n. 26.

let us advance three possible kinds of homogeneity for the sake of argument.

Most people would think first of linguistic coherence, perhaps connecting it consciously or not with genetic ethnicity (despite our total ignorance of patterns of genetic ethnicity at any point of ancient history). The second is likely to be cultural coherence, whether at the level of material culture, institutions, or ideas. Reflection, of course, reveals that the first is contingent on the second: linguistic coherence across wide geographical separation is itself a cultural phenomenon; more significantly, we should be ignorant of the linguistic coherence if it were not for the preservation of localizable documents, and the inscriptions and oral and written literary texts of the eighth century and later are of course a very specialized and coherent cultural product. So let us leave homogeneity of utterance as our first phenomenon of Hellenism.

The utterances relate closely to a material culture which is well known to us from archaeology, as well as from the documents themselves; it is the material expression of a complex stratified society distinguished by a great elaboration of the physical accoutrements of the rituals of warfare and relaxation. It makes sense, from this point of view, to regard the Hellenic world as the world of the oil-bottle and the hoplite-corslet, the enveloping helmet, and the wine-strainer. Where these things are found it is not rash to assume a connection with the milieu defined by our first homogeneity. And the great contribution of modern archaeology has been to demonstrate precisely how widespread across the Mediterranean basin is this association of types of artefact.

For the third type of coherence, it may be useful to look at the interaction of humankind with the landscape, with physical space. The documents of the first approach and the material remains of the second help us build up a picture of a human landscape which we take for granted, but which is the third type of cultural coherence alluded to above; nucleated settlements (villages or *poleis*) scattered across a region so as to make possible the differentiated extraction of livelihood from a wide range of productive opportunities. With this goes something rarer and more important; a sense of the unity of the landscape as a collection of cells, of equipollent divisions of

space (*chorai*, the territories of *poleis* and other similar tracts)
which combine to form a conceptual collectivity—in its largest
development a notion of the inhabited world itself, called from
at least the fourth century BC just that, the *oikoumene*. The
earliest clear expression of this vision of the world is in the
Catalogue of the Ships in Book Two of the Iliad, and it is not to
be taken for granted. It requires explanation. We may draw
the analogy of the regularity of the settled landscape of south-
east Britain after the Saxon conquest. Here too a degree of
conceptual and institutional homogeneity across wide distances
demands a special explanation, and matches the circumstances
of violent 'barbarian invasion' as little as the Greek concept of
the landscape of *poleis* (or other settlements) does the conventional view of a disruptive Dark Age.[11]

These homogeneities—and no doubt many others are to be
found—help our argument in two ways. First, it is extremely
hard to see how they could become established without considerable movement within the Greek world; and second, they
actually also entail contact with the world beyond.

'It appears that there can be no boundary to anything unless
there is something beyond to bound it too'. Lucretius illustrates
his famous proof (quoted above) of the infinity of the Universe
by referring to the contemporary problem of defining the
extent of the Roman world. With our homogeneities we have
precisely the same difficulty. All the lines of enquiry taken in
the previous paragraphs raised the question of what lay
beyond; against what did these characteristics serve to define
the Hellenic? The enquiry must with inevitable logic take us
out from the involuted approach which looks only into the
Greek world; the answer to the question must be found among
the visibly different neighbouring milieux of the Levant, of
Egypt, of Anatolia or Thrace, of the peoples (*not* 'native'
peoples, a useless and indeed often pernicious qualification) of
the Italian peninsula or Libyan litoral.

Now that in turn entails that we must examine the nature of
the interface between the Hellenic and the non-Hellenic; the

[11] Robin Osborne, *Classical Landscape with Figures: The Ancient Greek City and its
Countryside* (London, 1987); for the Saxons in Britain, J. N. L. Myres, *The English
Settlements* (Oxford, 1986). On cultural horizons and notions of space, Roger Dion,
Aspects politiques de la géographie antique (Paris, 1977).

argument so far suggests that it is in that zone of contact that the answer to questions about the nature of the Greek world itself will be found. In other words a 'small Greece' approach to the history of the period is to be ruled out on logical grounds. The whole process of self-definition and the promotion of the three distinctively Hellenic homogeneities entails contact, and the scale and complexity of the Hellenic phenomenon suggest that those contacts were intricate and frequent and intense. How frequent? Neither the literary nor even, despite recent advances, the archaeological evidence seems to offer much hope of quantification.

Faced with a similar lack of statistics, Roman social and economic historians are increasingly adopting a technique of hypothetical quantification.[12] In the absence of statistical evidence we may still outline the limits of the possible. Where the evidence is particularly patchy this may be combined with a counterfactual enquiry in asking questions to which the answers will never be forthcoming, but which make us sensitive to the anatomy of the problem. So we may imagine a kind of index of cultural homogeneity, allowing a calculation of the first kind to be made along the lines of 'what is the minimum average number of annual sailings between one city and another to promote similar religious architecture in both?'; and 'what density of traffic can be postulated to account for the spread of more or less canonical temple design across the whole Greek Mediterranean?'. The fact that such an index is an impossibility does not deprive it of usefulness in building models. More specifically we may enquire what if there were only 114 ships longer than 20 feet in the whole Mediterranean in 850 BC? What if there were 8,670? How many native Greek-speakers ever travelled more than 20 kilometres from where they were born in the seventh century BC? Was it 2 per cent of the group? Or 25 per cent? or 50 per cent? Such questions have real answers although they are unverifiable. A spectrum of possibilities can be imagined and we can say at what end we would expect the answer to lie, and why. It is essential to call the spectrum into existence, however, and not allow the nugatory quantities of anecdotal evidence to lead us

[12] See now Willem Jongman, *The Economy and Society of Pompeii* (Amsterdam, 1988).

surreptitiously to prejudge the issue and take minimum answers to the questions which I have just posed. Why on earth should ancient Mediterranean seafaring be statistically proportional to numbers of allusions to sea journeys in Herodotus?

In order to arrive at some educated assessment of this kind, we must now put into practice the conclusion of the argument and turn to the relations of the homogeneous world of the Greeks with what was beyond. The object is to see if any pattern other than random encounter can be traced in these contacts; if it can, then we may be on the way to explaining how it came about that they were dense enough to promote the homogeneities which we examined.

II. THE EAST AS SOURCE OF MOVEMENT

The grand Assyrian vacuum-cleaner was assisted in its task of ruling the world by the gnomes of Byblos

(Larsen)

For orientalists the most prominent phenomenon of this half-millennium is the expansion to unprecedented size of the systems of controlled exploitation of far-flung resources in the Neo-Assyrian and Neo-Babylonian empires, extraordinary structures of management and exploitation which exerted a very strong economic and social influence on the peoples of the whole of western Asia, and which did much to shape the later Achaemenid Persian Empire. The debate about the economic nature of the system of requisitioning, which is in full swing, is one of the most stimulating in the field of ancient economic history. Many of the details are so uncertain as to obstruct the process of modelling what went on within the system, but the effect on societies marginal to the world of the Fertile Crescent is less controversial. It is this effect that Mogens Larsen whimsically calls the 'grand Assyrian vacuum-cleaner'.[13]

Basically the effects of the need to meet the constantly

[13] Mogens T. Larsen, in M. T. Larsen (ed.), *Power and Propaganda* (= *Mesopotamia*, Studies in Assyriology 7, Copenhagen, 1979); M. Helter, *Goods, Prices and the Organisation of Trade in Ugarit* (Wiesbaden, 1978); see also Morris Silver, *Economic Structures of the Ancient Near East* (London, 1985), to be used with caution.

increasing demands of the requisitioning system, which was the central structure and manifestation of Assyrian power, was to intensify in each society the means of producing a local surplus, whatever these had been. A general increase in the 'kinetic energy' of local productive systems is found, and a lubrication of mobility and material and people. On the periphery, miniature versions of the central system are created which pass on the dynamic effect of the power of the empire to their own dependencies and spheres of influence. Such subsidiary centres of intensification, owing their dynamism and power ultimately to the powers of the Fertile Crescent, have been recognised in Lydia and in Egypt. Naturally the degree of political allegiance which accompanied the experience of transformation by the economic pull of Nineveh or Babylon was very variable. The response to the widening influence did not have to be peaceable: the war effort of those who opposed the political power of the East was as much the work of the 'vacuum-cleaner' as the mustering of materials and manpower by those who supported it.

Waxing and waning requisitioning systems had long been a factor in promoting or discouraging surplus production in the landlocked Levant.[14] The rhythms of land transport or riverine communications were well-established, and the precursors of the great power-structures of the first millennium had turned their backs on the different world of the sea.[15] Now a significant threshold was crossed, and the people of the coastal strip of the east Mediterranean were drawn into the requisitioning network, and their waterborne redistribution system was galvanized like those of so many landlocked societies in the Fertile Crescent—positively, in response to demands for tribute of various kinds, and negatively, in compensation for losses of resources through aggression. The Levantine coast had a distinctively Mediterranean human geography, a chain of interlocking ecologies connected by coastal shipping. The effect of the pressures towards intensification on such a system

[14] For interesting views on the theory of centre and periphery, and discussion of the early Mesopotamian state of affairs, Michael Rowlands, Mogens Larsen, Kristian Kristiansen (eds.), *Centre and Periphery in the Ancient World* (Cambridge, 1987).

[15] Robert B. Revere ' "No man's coast": ports of trade in the East Mediterranean', in Karl Polanyi, Conrad Arensberg, and Harry Pearson (eds.), *Trade and Market in the Early Empires* (Chicago, 1987), pp. 38–63.

was to lead those who used it to extend the number of
microregions bound into the redistributive pattern, by extending the range of communications. Phoenician ships, in plainer
words, went further more often in pursuit of increasingly
valued resources. On land such an effect had been limited by
the inertia of friction: at sea the limitations were vastly less.
The concrete result was the phenomenon which we know as the
Phoenician expansion, the foundation of Gades and Carthage,
the development of the Phoenician *koine* across the Mediterranean which we are coming to understand better and better
from archaeological evidence, above all from the south coast of
Spain and from Sardinia.[16] In the end, when the effect had
developed to its greatest and most formal extent, we see the
Phoenician fleet itself as a military resource made available to
the Persian power. It is hard to resist the temptation to
attribute to the same background change of circumstances the
vigorous movements of Aegean Hellenes across the same sea by
the same routes, which we predicate of the eighth and seventh
centuries and which create the milieu of the *apoikia* (Greek
colony).

The Aegean coastlands and South Anatolian coast, which
had come to be the geographical centre of the cultural homogeneities of Hellenism which we discussed in the last section,
formed a cluster of interlocking regions much more complex
than the Levantine coast, but equally interdependent. The
redistribution of resources, to which we will return in Section
IV, had taken place for many centuries through the medium of
coastwise voyaging, *cabotage* as it is conveniently known. But as
the distribution of large quantities of material with Aegean
connections in the west Mediterranean in the Mycenaean
period shows, many voyages were much longer; the commodities of distant origin at Lefkandi confirm this in the middle of
the gap between the Mycenaeans and the Greek *apoikiai*. It was
natural that such an ecology should respond very rapidly to the

---

[16] Hans-Georg Niemeyer (ed.), *Phönizier im Western* (Mainz, 1982); especially pp.
5 ff. (S. Moscati, 'L'espansione fenicia nel Mediterraneo occidentale'); pp. 261 ff. (J.
M. Coldstream, 'Greeks and Phoenicians in the Aegean'); pp. 277 ff. (G. Buchner, 'Die
Beziehungen zwischen der euböischen Kolonie Pithekoussai und dem nordwestsemitis-
chen Mittelmeerraum' with excellent discussion); pp. 377 ff. (B. B. Shefton, 'Greeks . . .
in the South of the Iberian peninsula'). Also *Atti del primo congresso intermazionale di studi
fenici e punici* (3 vols, Rome, 1983).

intensified pull that was transmitted westwards by shipowners and crews from the Levantine ports. That response is the visible expansion of the range and complexity of seafaring involving the Aegean world, and linking it with societies to east and west in ever more elaborate ways, which we perceive in the eighth century BC.

This development and its Phoenician precursor have proved hard to explain. Analogies with economic growth in more recent periods have rightly been criticized. Intensification of production without real growth still needs an outside explanation of some kind. This is where the growth of the powers of the Fertile Crescent comes to the rescue. Instead of leaving it dangling without visible cause, the extraordinary pull exerted by the new powers of the East may be invoked as the source of a new dynamism which went far beyond what was needed to supply even the voracious demands of the empires.

It is important that the movements brought about by demands of the expanding power structures of the East were intensifications of ones which already existed. The new ecology whose rationale was the supplying of imperial requirements was only a very large and integrated version of systems of immemorial age. Interdependence of resources, and the systematic exploitation of scattered opportunities through movements, are basic human survival strategies. There is no real reason to assume that in human history the settled cultivator is the norm. Stability is not the base, the usual state from which mobility departs. We must clear our minds of the illusory permanence of peasants. In south-west Europe throughout this period we can perceive relatively large-scale movements of human groups. Linguistically there seems to have been little difference between the last arrivals before the dawn of history and their immediate successors whom the development of a more exclusive social system denied access to the southernmost coastlands ('although the Greeks were unaware of the fact, the Macedones were themselves an examples of that Greek-speaking expansion which planted islands at many places on the Mediterranean coasts').[17] The movement of people across the

[17] Nicholas G. L. Hammond, *A History of Macedonia* i (Oxford, 1972), pp. 440–1. Also *Migrations and Invasions in Greece and Adjacent Areas* (Park Ridge, N.J., 1976). Compare now Snodgrass (n. 22), pp. 188–90, for Dark Age mobility.

Aegean to Chalcidice and to the coast of Ionia was indeed a part of this process of settlement. This was compared by the later Greeks to the more recent establishment, further from the Aegean, of *apoikiai*, and the arrival of new groups in the north of Greece was rationalized in terms of familiar forms of intercommunity aggression (which we have still further obscured by using the term invasion). The Greeks saw many points of contact between this period of early mobility and the *polis*-based present.

Modern thought, however, has been keen to make a sharp separation between them, using familiar terms such as diaspora, migration, expansion which carefully remove any purposive colour, but unfortunately in doing so leave the terms so bland that they are of little explicative value. For many modern authors these movements were primitive, prehistoric; they were an aimless *Völkerwanderung* (wandering of peoples), casual and random nomadism. Hence they can be easily disjoined from the experience of the later civilizations. Views are, however, now changing: progressivism and primitivism are more widely questioned, and attention has moved away from the ideal unit of *mythos*-type explanation, a single subsistence household or nomad family plus small groups of animals. Instead of autonomous enterprises and isolated producers, the object of attention is now whole ecological systems which exploit varied resources in highly complex and flexible ways, and which maintain large and ramified social groups. Mobility has often been part of the flexible ecological response: nomads are now seen as pastoralists engaged with a wide range of environments and so much involved with others exploiting adjacent riches in different ways, whether they are hunter-gatherers or arable cultivators, as to be regarded as in some senses a part of the same society: which is not to obscure the fact that the symbiosis need not, unfortunately, be peaceable.[18]

[18] Marshall Sahlins, *Stone Age Economics* (Chicago, 1974); Andrew Sherratt, 'Mobile Resources; Settlement and Exchange in Early Agricultural Europe', in Colin Renfrew and S. Shennan (eds.), *Ranking, Resource and Exchange* (Cambridge, 1982). For a good application in the historical period Pierre Toubert, *Les Structures du Latium medieval; Le Latium méridional et la Sabine du IX< siècle à la fin du XIII< siècle* (Paris, 1973). For pastoralism see e.g. Olivier Aurenche (ed.), *Nomades et sédentaires, perspectives ethnoarcheologiques* (1984), esp. R. Jamo; C. R. Whittaker (ed.), *Pastoral Economies in Classical Antiquity* (*PCPS*, suppl. 14; Cambridge, 1988); and Brent D. Shaw 'Water and Society in the Ancient Maghreb', *Ant. Afr.* 20 (1984), 121–3.

Within these societies, the competition for shares of the resource-base, and the tensions generated in its management, create very varied social, institutional, political responses. The well-known hydraulic civilizations of Wittfogel (in which the origins of centralized power are sought in the co-operative effort needed to increase production through large-scale management of water resources) are a case in point: but similar analyses can be made of much more recent systems: one very helpful recent study, for example, has shown how much of the working of the kingdom of Naples between the sixteenth and nineteenth centuries was founded on managing the antagonism between the pastoral and arable agricultural production systems.[19] For our period, such understanding can help us to analyse mobility in the Mediterranean world in ways which avoid the primitivist assumption, when applied to the pastoral societies of the Balkan and other Mediterranean peninsulas, or to the maritime movements of the world of the *apoikia*. Most importantly, it can be applied to the ecological management-systems of the states of the Fertile Crescent.

So the changes of the ninth and eighth centuries may be fitted in to both the basic ecological background of human relations with the environment and the specific forms which ecological systems in the Fertile Crescent developed at that time. They can be related to structures of mobility which are very long-lasting, and so we can begin to perceive continuities which united prehistoric and historic events, and thus diminish the effect of the artificial divide of the 'beginning of history'. We can also begin to examine ways in which the ecological foundations affected the social and political organization of the societies involved. The Levantine power structures were shaped by their requisitioning systems; in the Mediterranean world, too, networks of dependence and allegiance, obligations and services, shaped the bare movements of what was valued. We can see this in the patterns of alliance and friendship and loyalty in the Homeric poems; the relations of *apoikiai* and *metropoleis*, as they come into being from the end of the eighth century may be regarded as another example. What makes

---

[19] John A. Marino, *Pastoral Economics in the Kingdom of Naples* (Baltimore, 1988). The classic work of K. Wittfogel is *Oriental Despotism: A Comparative Study of Total Power* (New Haven, 1957).

these political responses to material redistribution so varied and important was that the movements were not just the transference of commodities, though that had its place, as we shall see below in section IV. The most important resource was the one most intimately involved in human society, the human resource itself. Central to understanding both the worlds of the East and the Mediterranean ecology is *manpower*.

III. THE HUMAN RESOURCE

Javan, Tubal and Meshech traded the persons of men
and vessels of brass in thy markets

(Ezekiel 27: 13)

The starting point in the discussion of the human resource must be the fact of its relative scarcity. Little can be said for certain about the demographic history of this period, and we cannot discuss even that fully here. Three things only need to be stressed.

First, comparative demography enables us to make estimates of conditions in the ancient Mediterranean: these were very unconducive to rapid population growth by demographic increase.[20] Life expectancy figures are low, and simply reproducing populations at the same level will not have been easy in all circumstances. Since it is likely that overall populations did increase—gradually—we may assume that conditions of mild demographic felicity existed in many communities, at various favourable times; but that the places and reasons in which a community experienced demographic decline would have been familiar to most people. Moreover, nearly half of the population would usually be below—in classical terms—ephebic age; in ancient Greece a lower proportion of the population would

---

[20] For ancient Greek demography Mogens H. Hansen, *Demography and Democracy: The Number of Athenian Citizens in the Fourth Century* B.C. (Herning, 1986) is now central. Some important generalities in Bruce V. Frier, 'Roman Life Expectancy, Ulpian's Evidence', *HSCP* 86 (1982), 213–51. Applying this to archaic Greece, Chester Starr, *The Economic and Social Growth of Early Greece* (New York, 1977), pp. 40–6; Hägg (n. 9), pp. 210–12. See also the important recent account of Ian Morris, *Burial and Ancient Society: The Rise of the Greek City-State* (Cambridge, 1987).

therefore have been available for fully qualified adult male roles like fighting than is the case in some societies.

Second, this tendency to underpopulation crisis is clearly visible in the *mentalité* of Greeks and Romans as presented to us by the literary tradition.[21] Pressure on resources, another common theme, is not to be attributed to demographic growth without the best of evidence. The variability of the resource base, and the pressures of the horizontal mobility of populations (as we are about to see) are more likely causes of this kind of crisis. Demographic growth (that is, two people having three surviving children, for several generations) is not the *deus ex machina* in historical explanation that some have made it. The famous instances of 'overpopulation' causing emigration are more plausibly to be attributed to resource fluctuations or to increase in community size through immigration than to demographic increase (and that is all that the famous passage of advice about *apoikiai* in Plato's *Laws* 4. 707 D–708 D means).

In particular, strain on élite resources, whether the 'élite' is an aristocracy of a few dozen families or an exclusive citizenship of several thousand males, may be the perceived problem: actual demographic increase among the rich, upward social mobility, accommodation in various ways of mobile élite members from other communities, escalation in the resources needed for satisfactory display, these may all bring this about, without our needing to predicate an anomalous general demographic boom of the human population all told. After all, no Greek city which was 'constrained' to send out an *apoikia* ever chose instead to abandon its slaves. Population boom as a factor in the changes in the archaeological record, and in Greek culture in general in the eighth and seventh centuries BC, after a recent vogue, has now rightly been reassessed against considerations like those advanced here.[22]

Third, as has already been hinted, it is unhelpful to discuss the population history of the ancient world in terms of fragmented sealed societies at the mercy of their own

---

[21] L. Gallo, 'Popolosità e scarsità di popolazione: Contributo allo studio di un topos', *Ann Sc. Norm. Pisa* 10 (1980), 1233 ff.

[22] Boom advanced by Anthony Snodgrass, *Archaic Greece* (London, 1979); see now J. McK. Camp 'A Drought in the Late Eighth Century B.C. ?', *Hesperia*, 48 (1979), 397–411; Morris (n. 20); Hansen (n. 20).

demographic conditions. 'The population of Argos' as it is visible to us in literary and in archaeological terms is more a social than a demographic phenomenon. Just as in Attica, evidence which seemed to suggest a boom in the population actually reflects new social structures which redistribute existing populations and make them archaeologically visible in new ways, so in many cases phenomena which look demographic are those of mobility and changing social definition. The real demography—the patterns of procreation—is invisible, and not socially or topographically constrained. Real demographic history demands an extensive understanding of the contribution of those who are socially marginal (understanding by this the place in generation-to-generation procreation patterns of the variously dubious in status, not simply of the rather specific concept of 'illegitimacy'), which are largely absent from our evidence; and in those phenomena the consequences of mobility play an important part.

Not by accident; for the conditions outlined made it obvious that people, above all adult males, were a precious resource which could be deployed, if available, creatively for the various magnification of the deployer. The circumstance of mercenary service is the most obvious case, responsible for the individual mobility of tens of thousands of men during the seventh and sixth centuries. This extraordinary phenomenon deserves more than a relatively minor place in the history of the time. The *nostoi* of these soldiers trained, experienced, equipped, enriched, were as potentially fertile for change as the mythological home-comings from an earlier eastern war of the poems with which they were entertained. Their world is dimly reflected in the lyric tradition—Archilochus in the north Aegean, Antimenidas in the Levant, Hybrias the Cretan—and more explicitly in Herodotus and in the evidence from Egypt, which reminds us that we are not dealing with a wholly Hellenic phenomenon, as we might have expected from the previous section. The Anatolian peoples, especially the Karians, were as involved in these currents of mobility as the Greeks.[23] The vast complexity of the results of this process can

---

[23] J. D. Ray, 'The Carian Inscriptions from Egypt', *J. Egyptian Archaeology*, 68 (1982), 181–98.

only be seen in the odd glimpses of the inexplicable, like the curious presence of 'Samians of the Aeschrionian *phyle*' in an oasis in the middle of the Libyan desert (Herodotus 3. 26).

Directly connected are the wholesale population movements of the eastern empires. Long-distance relocation of whole communities in underpopulated areas was a favourite strategy, and one which, in Persian lands, caused the Greeks of the later period considerable anxiety—though it was one which, interestingly, in the *apoikia* world of Sicily, the Deinomenid tyrants of the fifth century were keen to use.[24] We regularly call these resettlements, in Assyrian Cappadocia, for example, colonization; and the comparison with a Greek *apoikia* is not so far-fetched. The Greeks were aware of the habits of their neighbours, as in Phocylides' famous comparison of the *polis* well-founded on a rock with the folly of Nineveh (*Sententiae* 4); the rulers of societies immediately to their east, intermediate links in the chain of power, used similar techniques, as with the Lydian settlements of Alyatta in Bithynia or Adramyttium; against the general background of mobility, their stories of their own origins, the constant shifts of nearby peoples like the Cimmerians and Scythians, we can set their own plans to shift whole communities, the evacuation of Phocaea and the intended emigration of the Ionians. They feared mass-deportation by the Persians because, to the people who invented and practised *apoikia* in its developed form, it was all too familiar. And in Cyrene or at Syracuse, the growth of the urban community can only have been achieved (as Herodotus saw in the general Greek context, 1. 58) by the creative politics of management of the human resource, incorporating the populations indigenous to the area as well as those who came by in the swirl of Mediterranean movements.

In this context the Greeks can to some extent be seen as purveyors of people; through maritime communications available manpower would be gathered efficiently from where it was available. We do not have to assume significant demographic growth in any individual community; the effect is the better deployment of available resources, intensification, in

[24] J. N. Postgate, *Taxation and Conscription in the Neo-Assyrian Empire* (Rome, 1974); Bustenay Oded, *Mass Deportations and Deportees in the Neo-Assyrian Empire* (Wiesbaden, 1979).

other words, of the sort which we envisaged as a general
response to new political demands. It is not surprising that in
the Mediterranean world of the period we also find prominent
the other form of people-deployment which we usually call
slavery. Slavery is one among many institutions developed to
manage the human resource in the context of primary production, above all of foodstuffs. It too must be seen against the
background of the relative scarcity of the resource of human
power, and taken alongside various other forms of dependence
and social control which arise out of the circumstances of
deploying labour. The developed legal institution of slavery
and the consolidation of the one great barrier between slave
and free, with the phenomenon of manumission which through
crossing it defines it, are later outgrowths of these earlier
practices. We need retroject to the archaic period neither the
inexorable precision of later chattel slavery and its law nor the
formal rigidity of enslavement versus manumission. The institutions of labour control were far more fluid, and social
mobility in both directions over generations need not have
been punctuated by such institutionalized and visible moments
of transition of status.[25] Dark Age and archaic slavery is about
the relocation of people; it is a demographic phenomenon of
great importance. The life history of Eumaeus (*Odyssey* 15.
402) and Solon's concern (fr. 24) to restore to Attica the far-
wandering enslaved, who no longer speak Attic, are key texts.
What we need to ask is 'what became of the descendants of
people like this?' The easy assumption that such low-status
groups can be disregarded demographically is either unrealistic, if it is thought that they can be effectively rendered
wholly unprocreative through total social control, or élitist, if it
considers such outsiders insignificant to social analysis. Because
the demographic effect of the incorporation of the unfree takes
more than one generation it is one of the aspects of 'illegitimacy' (in the broad sense outlined above) which is largely
invisible: it is excluded by male élite citizen-centred concepts of
demography. But we must insist on asking how many town

[25] The work of Moses Finley in this area is basic: see e.g. 'Land, Debt and the Man
of Property', in B. D. Shaw and R. P. Saller (eds.), *Economy and Society in Ancient Greece*
(1981), pp. 62 ff. For a recent application, T. Gallant, 'Agricultural Systems, Land
Tenure and the Reforms of Solon', *BSA* 77 (1982), 111–24.

councillors in the cities of the Aegean in 600 BC had had an unfree great grandmother; and how far from the town was such a person likely to have come from.

The collocation in the epigraph to this section of the metalware with slaves in Ezekiel's Tyre reminds us that there is a close connection between the 'commercial' movements of slaves and exchanges of other commodities. We will find that the redistribution of resources according to patterns of dearth and glut, which is essentially what we have been saying of ancient population movement, is characteristic also of these other movements.

IV. ECOLOGY AND ECONOMY

Like my father and yours, you great dolt Perses, who sailed and sailed in ships in pursuit of a decent livelihood

(Hesiod, *Works and Days* 633-4)

It must never be forgotten that the Mediterranean world is a cellular whole composed of scores of thousands of physically differentiated microregions. But just as those cells were not helpful to the demographer, so the economic historian too takes them as isolated and discrete only at peril. The local ecologies have separable identities; but they continually interact, and interdependence is set up by the very fact of the relatively high degree of differentiation between one microregion and another.

Take Herodotus on Thera again: his narrative (4. 150-9) of the crisis that prompted the *apoikia* which eventually became Cyrene illustrates well the character of a Mediterranean microregion. We are not presented with the Malthusian crisis of a sealed locality undergoing demographic boom, but with a crisis imagined as caused by particular local physical circumstances: seven years of severe precipitation shortfall. The tale illustrates also the way in which such crises were related to the extent of the citizen community; and the Odyssean vagueness of the geography, which introduces also the voyage of Kolaios, is part of the *mythos*-style. The *mythos* is about a new world being called into existence to redress the balance of the old, and serves to explain the later interaction of Cyrene with the Aegean world. The relationship required by the availability— at a price—of cereal surpluses which could resolve local food crises is reduced to its simplest terms, and those terms are explained by a narrative of the dramatic events which brought them about, retrojected to a world in which time and topography take on an idealized simplicity. Behind it we see clearly the redistributive process by which the ecologies of other regions are brought into play to remedy local dearth, and the fact of the mobility which this exchange generates.

The existence and working of this redistributive process has been explored most effectively over the last years by prehistoric archaeologists, who have made it the foundation of sophisticated models of the development of cultural systems and their economic foundations. The growth of these networks, binding together productive regions and fostering cultural homogeneity across ecological divides, can be seen even in landlocked· central Europe: it is still more spectacular when the medium of interchange is the comparatively frictionless sea. The model which has been elaborated for the experience of the Aegean island of Melos, in particular, showing how its economic and social history interacted from very early times with neighbouring islands and the Aegean coastlands, is one which should be reduplicated, *mutatis mutandis*, across the whole Mediterranean.[26]

One significant result is that estimates of the resources available to communities with access to the sea must be raised above the carrying capacity of the local ecology. A recent study of Aegina has outlined the gap, already considerable by the sixth century, between the minimum nutritional needs of a guessable population and the maximum possible nutritional yield of the island environment.[27] We see the impact of these extensive redistribution systems in the sequence of agricultural and alimentary revolutions which popularize in different zones

[26] For the networks in central Europe, Michael Rowlands, 'Conceptualising the European Bronze and Early Iron Ages', in John Bintliff (ed.), *European Social Evolution: Archaeological Perspectives* (Bradford, 1984), pp. 147–56; Sherratt (n. 18). The application to Melos is Colin Renfrew and M. Wagstaff, *An Island Polity* (Cambridge, 1982); with Guy D. R. Sanders, 'Reassessing Ancient Populations', *BSA* 79 (1984), 251–62.

[27] T. J. Figueira, *Aegina* (Salem, 1981); also Oswyn Murray, *Early Greece* (Glasgow, 1980), pp. 211–12.

the large-scale production of new cereals, or olive oil, or wine during the archaic and classical periods. For our argument a still more important consequence is that whole communities can come to rely on the 'invisible' proceeds of carrying out the redistribution: in more modern terms, they are surviving on the proceeds of being middlemen, a strategy which brought prosperity in the early modern period to agriculturally relatively insignificant communities like Leonidi in the Peloponnese or Paros (and which indeed in a sense, therefore, historically underlies the modern Greek merchant marine). Such communities, and Aegina is a likely ancient example, are of the highest importance in understanding mobility in the Mediterranean (though oddly that phenomenon somewhat weakens arguments about minimum nutritional requirement, in that mobile Aeginetans will have been somewhat independent of the resource base of the island).

By chance, and from a later period, we have a vignette of a community much smaller and more wretched than Aegina, but equally surviving on the fact of redistribution. Between it and Aegina may be imagined the whole range of places which could to some extent, greater or less, engage with the possibility of disposing of glut and meeting crises in this way. Anthedon, on the east Boeotian coast, is known to us from a fragment of a Hellenistic writer who is concerned not with scientific geography but with comic, piquant, theatrical scene-setting: the assumptions are none the less instructive.[28] The territory produces little in the way of cereals, but a quantity of wine: the inhabitants, however, are principally fishermen, living picturesquely among salt and seaweed in huts on the beach. Now nutritionally this is indeed a precarious existence; but the account does not suggest that we are dealing with a subsistence economy in which each producer aims only at satisfying household needs. It can be argued that fish was too dear to be a staple for the poor; but conversely, this high price (which reflects redistribution to the élites of a relatively wide area) is what kept the Anthedonians alive as their fishes' flesh could not have done. Fish-pickle and—still more luxurious—purple dye, indeed, are the particular products mentioned; but a similar case could be made for their choice of viticulture over cereal culture. Finally, their role as waterborne distributors is reinforced by the statement that they functioned as boat builders and, most importantly, as ferrymen.

The theatrical misery of Anthedon reminds us that the redistribution postulated in this analysis is a general tendency, an averaging process with many failures. That it allows, in general, Mediterranean populations, which would otherwise be critically vulnerable to local dearth, to rise above local ecologies' carrying capacity does not entail felicity or eliminate hardship—or even disaster. The Anthedonians were wretched, but they could not have *existed* without the demands and resources of people far beyond their boundaries. Despite its particular inadequacies, redistribution of this kind, and the mobility which it entailed, formed in macro-historical terms a major causative factor.

The Anthedonians, and probably Hesiod's father, may have depended on what we might risk calling trade.[29] But the phenomenon of redistribution extends far further. The coexistence of agricultural and hunter-gatherer responses at Anthedon reminds us of the variety of means of exploiting Mediterranean ecologies to the full, and that that could involve a good deal of straightforward movement. The transhumant pastoralist, who engages with a whole range of ecologies and participates in 'the annual interplay of sedentary and pastoral existence'[30] is not so unlike the coastwise *caboteur* (for the term, above p. 40) who exchanges the surpluses of his ports of call. But if redistribution creates the middleman, and feeds him, it does not necessarily do so against a background of peaceful, regulated exchange. Violence is equally characteristic; and pirates, brigands, the Samian aristocrats who practised the regularized plundering called *sule*, as well as military powers

---

[29] Alfonso Mele, *Il commercio greco arcaico: prexis ed emporie* (Naples, 1979); cf. S. C. Humphreys, 'Homo Politicus and Homo Economicus: War and Trade in the Economy of Archaic and Classical Greece', in *Anthropology and the Greeks* (London, 1978), pp. 159–74.

[30] The phrase is that of R. Jamo, in Aurenche (n. 18).

making more or less legitimate demands, all these fit in to the model as well as the early trader.[31]

This is why there is no problem in setting a model which stresses redistributive mobility alongside a social value system in which fair commodity exchange was sneered at. The Hellenic aristocrat was, as the nautical element in the art of the period shows, fully involved in the world of Mediterranean mobility.[32] Indeed the obligations of aristocratic status relations expressed through the gift and its accompanying systems of favours are a principal motive force, and one analogous to the gravitational pull of the powers of the East.[33] The networks of homage and obligation and loyalty did far more than market forces to modulate this kind of distributive system. In other periods of Mediterranean history too, social obligation can be found playing an important part in stimulating production and assisting redistribution.[34] After all it is likely to have been through inter-élite communications that the information which made redistribution effective was disseminated.

In this the figures known to the Greeks as *demiourgoi* (craftsmen, state artisans) had an important part to play. Our symbol Arion the singer is not irrelevant; a less mythic case is the fascinating 'Phoenicizer', or scribe (*poinikastas*) whom a Cretan city can be seen tempting to desist from his mobility at the beginning of the fifth century, offering rich honours to win his skills for their exclusive benefit.[35] These mobile persons—and the mercenary or ambassador belongs alongside the trader, the pirate and the *demiourgos*—provide the basis of the interactivity of the ancient Mediterranean. They convey and process

[31] For the Tyrrhenians cf. the studies of M. Giuffrida Gentile, *La pirateria tirrenica, momenti e fortuna = Kokalos* Suppl. 6 (Rome, 1983), and Michael Gras, *Trafics tyrrhéniens archaïques* (Rome, 1985). On conditions promoting brigandage, for the Roman example, Brent D. Shaw, 'Bandits in the Roman Empire', *Past and Present*, 105 (1984), 3–52.

[32] S. C. Humphreys (n. 29), esp. pp. 164–9.

[33] Gabriel Herman, *Ritualised Friendship and the Greek City* (Cambridge, 1987), pp. 82–8.

[34] For the sixth century AD, Eveline Patlagean, *Pauvreté économique et pauvreté sociale à Byzance* (Paris, 1977); for the change in the eleventh century AD by which, with the separation of military from other economic endeavours, gift and commodity also drew apart, Georges Duby *The Early Growth of the European Economy* (Ithaca, 1974).

[35] On *demiourgoi*, Marie-Françoise Baslez, *L' Étranger dans la Grèce antique* (Paris, 1984); for the Cretan scribe, Georges Daux, 'Le Contrat du travail du scribe Spensithios', *BCH* 97 (1973), 31–46.

materials, like the wandering metallurgists of the end of the second millennium whose ingots and metalmaking equipment were found recently in a wreck off the Levantine coast at Haifa.[36] The maritime world of Mentes the Taphian (*Odyssey* 1. 179–86), the Homeric seafarer whose boat was laden with ingots of iron, did not depend on structures of industry or support on shore, but functioned from the sea. Despite all the disruption of the late second millennium the shape of metal ingot used in this milieu, the famous 'ox-hide', and the marks with which it was calibrated, show a continuity that covers a millennium down to the fourth century BC.[37] This is the world of contacts which exists to be expanded and exploited in the changing circumstances of the first millennium, the pattern of currents in which the new tracer-dye of the aristocratic paraphernalia of the age can be seen circulating—the bronzes of the great sanctuaries from so wide a range of provenances, the goods of the orientalizing movement like the ivories at the sanctuary of Hera in Samos which reflect the movements of men like Kolaios or Sostratos.[38] But the great expansion of this kind of material in the archaeological record is not a sign of the creation of the currents of redistribution, just of their intensification and of their use in new ways.[39]

V. MOBILITY AND THE GREEKS

> PRAXITHEA. (In Athens) we are not a people brought from elsewhere, but we grew from the ground itself. The other cities, however are distributed all in the same way as the throw of the dice, and one community is drawn out of another.
>
> (Euripides, *Erechtheus* fr. 50 Austin, 7–10)

For most inhabitants of the ancient Mediterranean world, being 'brought from elsewhere' (*epaktos*), or 'in the state of

---

[36] E. Galili, N. Schmueli, Michael Artzy, 'Bronze Age Ship's Cargo of Copper and Tin', *IJ Nautical Archaeology*, 15 (1986), 25–37.

[37] See P. A. Gianfrotta and P. Pomey, *Archeologia subacquea* (Milan, 1980); anchors show a similar degree of uniformity across the maritime *Koine*.

[38] For the bronzes the best synthesis is Claude Rolley, 'Les bronzes grecs: recherches récentes', *Rev. Arch.* 1985, pp. 255–96. On ivories Brigitte Fryer Schauenburg, 'Kolaios und die westphönizischen Elfenbein', *Madrider Mitteilungen*, 7 (1966), 80–108.

[39] Ian Morris, 'Gift and Commodity in Archaic Greece', *Man*, 21 (1986), 1–17.

being derived from another place' (*eisagogimos*), were as familiar as Praxithea alleges. For Herodotus, the whole Greek race was 'one which had been extremely given to migration' (1. 56). For Thucydides likewise, mobility and stability are basic to the interpretation of the Greek past (1. 2). He makes a complex series of oppositions, between wandering peoples on the land and the ease of communication which goes with commerce, between productive and unproductive terrain, as well as between movement and its absence. For him Athens' autochthony is the product of poverty; wealth and communications, especially waterborne ones, are intimately linked. Less fluid societies do not need such precise terms for these concepts in their vocabularies, which is one reason for the length of this exposition. Euripides is expressive in more than conceptual concision; likening mobility to the unpredictable outcomes of the throws in the game of *pessoi*, the quintessence of the random, he sums up its whole dangerous, haphazard nature— terribly risky, utterly uncertain, but full of real and imagined opportunities for success. Gambling could hardly be an apter metaphor for the crazy compulsiveness of the all-embracing quest for *biotos*, livelihood.

By the fifth century the language had come to express sharply the effect of the conditions which we have been examining. *Pari passu* the social institutions of the Greeks were moulded by mobility too. Most remarkable among the communities 'drawn out of one another' the formal idea of the *apoikia* developed. The whole complex legal and ideological system of *apoikia* and *metropolis* constitutes an epiphenomenon on mobility, a rationalization in specific circumstances—strategy or resource subsidization or the resolution of domestic dispute— of participation in the perennial currents of Mediterranean communications, currents whose kinetic energy depended on ecology, whether within the Mediterranean basin or involving the greater force of ecologies located beyond, such as the great states of the Levant. Detailed study of the vocabulary involved shows the steady growth in the elaboration of this remarkable Hellenic institutional response, and warns against the easy retrojection to the eighth century of the developed forms.[40] That retrojection helps create a fault line in the eighth century

---

[40] Michael Casevitz, *Le vocabulaire de la colonisation en grec ancien* (Paris, 1985).

which is hard to explain; the truth is a model of much more organic growth over centuries. But of no period is it helpful to use the term 'colonization' (a coinage in this sense of Edmund Burke in 1770 made common currency in English parlance, as in ancient history, by George Grote in 1849). The ethnic presumptuousness and false sense of purpose in the term have nothing to do with whatever strange blend of the ideologies of Telemachus and Hesiod's father and Kolaios the Samian might be found among Corinthian vessel-owners off Ortygia in the last decades of the eighth century BC. When the term does emerge, moreover, what could be more expressive of the links which bound the maritime world than the term 'out-home'? It is hard to imagine the Pennsylvania Dutch or Australian transportees using a term so expressive of the closeness of their starting point. In the modern world colonies began as pioneering departures to a fresh start, and ended up as missions of subjection. Neither is right for the opportunistic endeavours of the eighth and seventh centuries, which were located in close contact with the world of home. Archilochus' Thasos, full of the dregs of all the Greeks (fr. 102), is no less typical than distant Massalia.

Like the *apoikia*, the increasing formalization of both guest-friendship and the (as has now been shown) closely related practice of proxeny represent an attempt to neutralize any tendency had by mobility towards the fissiparous.[41] It is indeed the paradox of mobility that it promotes such efforts—the story of Arion is again our symbol—and, through encouraging cultural homogeneity over wide distances, builds wider structures of social interaction. Within each city institutions are formed to regulate the status of the stranger, to an extent which would be unnecessary in less mobile milieux—concepts like 'newcomer' (*epelys*), as opposed to resident (*enoikos*), and the institutionalization of hospitality. It has been seen that these are reflections of archaic life, but in fact, by the same paradox, these institutions are not helpless reflections of '[le] morcellement extreme du monde archaïque' but signs of the systematic overcoming of the separateness risked by widespread mobility.[42]

[41] Herman (n. 33); Christian Marek, *Die Proxenie* (Frankfurt, 1984).
[42] Baslez (n. 35); the quotation is from p. 359.

Praxithea introduces us to a second paradox. The notion of resident citizenship is vastly reinforced by being compared to and seen against the traveller's lack of it. That is seen not just in the newcomer/resident dichotomy but, spectacularly, in the singular practice of *phuge* (exile) and *anastasis* (return), which could only exist in an interdependent world in which there existed beyond the city, counterbalancing citizen rights, the exiled state in which the victim joins a continuum of being a wanderer, a guest, a votary—even on occasion a trader or a *demiourgos*.[43] The whole notion of Greekness, indeed, to return to our earlier problem, can be seen as a reaction against a melting-pot world in which ethnicity was a reassuring and advantageous structure of identity.[44] Athens, because of its political centrality, attracted more of the mobile than many places (though note Aristotle, *Politics* 1326ᵃ18–20 '*poleis* without doubt must contain large numbers of slaves, metics and foreigners'); in insisting on the autochthony of its people it came to develop these tendencies more than other states— creating, among other responses, an exclusive law of citizenship, a developed institution of slavery, and in the status of metic, a unique solution to the problem of aliens.[45] But it would also be plausible, in a similar way, to attribute the advantages which accrued to the *polis* through the development of the politics of cooperation, of concerted decision-making, of shared responsibility, to the world of movement against which these forms of behaviour were defined. The city of reason would not be possible without all the original outside movements on which it turned its back.

We have, moreover, at last perhaps laid the ghost of 'small Greece'. One of the reasons why it proved hard to cope with the picture presented by the homogeneities outlined in section I was that they related not to a compact society but to a world of movements. They were characteristics of people in transit, a culture founded on mobility. The Greeks were not the people to whom the ideas of the east or the metals of the west were

---

[43] Jakob Seibert, *Die politische Fluchtlinge und Verbannten in der griechischer Geschichte* (Darmstadt, 1979).

[44] For the early origins of this, Coldstream, in Hägg (n. 9), stressing that it was the density of intercommunication that made the Greeks 'proud to be parochial'.

[45] Nicole Loraux, *Les Enfants d'Athena* (Paris, 1981; Eng. trans., Harvard, 1986); David Whitehead, *The Ideology of the Athenian Metic* (*PCPS* suppl; Cambridge, 1977).

brought, they were the bringers. No one purveyed the alphabet to the Greek world: alphabetization is to be predicated of the whole milieu in which the Greeks and other Mediterranean peoples of this period moved.[46] The bounded, coherent, homogeneous, enclosed, defined world which was rejected as a model for the earlier period was created during the late sixth and fifth centuries when the Greeks became self-conscious and xenophobic—and nowhere more than in the city of the autochthonous Athenians from which so much of our information comes.

The case for the system which rested on the *mythos* of autochthony seems strong. But in the end involution and exclusiveness of this kind, which was alien to the dominant patterns of Mediterranean social and economic life, alien and actually structurally antagonistic, made it impossible for Athenian institutions to form the basis for really wide social and political institutions. The *polis* in general, we might say, was a cul-de-sac, an unhelpful response to the challenges of the Mediterranean reality, if building large and relatively harmonious and inclusive societies is considered a worthwhile goal. It was elsewhere that a *mythos* about origins was told which was a polar opposite of the Athenian case and indeed hard to parallel in the world of the *polis*. The success that came with the currents of Mediterranean mobility was reserved for the people whose first community of shepherds grew by the addition of vagabonds and runaways, which preyed on more stable and involuted neighbours for the procreative resource, and whose first leaders were reared on the milk of the roving wolf.

[46] Jack Goody, *The Interface between the Written and the Oral* (Cambridge, 1987), pp. 60–1.

3

Military Organization and Social Structure in Archaic Etruria

BRUNO D'AGOSTINO

> They are indeed, perfect enough in their exercises, and
> under very good discipline, wherein I saw no great merit:
> for how should it be otherwise, where every farmer is
> under the command of his own landlord and every citizen
> under that of the principal men in his own city?
>
> (Jonathan Swift, *A Voyage to Brobdingnag*, ch. 8)

THE political and social organization of the Etruscan world is obscure:[1] that is a consequence of the complete loss of those literary texts which we know to have existed, and of the nature of the epigraphic records, which for the most part consist of funerary inscriptions of a formulaic type. For such reasons the archaeological evidence assumes a fundamental importance, and represents our source of knowledge for these aspects of the

This chapter was written at Cambridge in 1987, during a period as Visiting Fellow at Clare Hall, financed by a grant from the Aylwin Cotton Foundation and a travel award from the Italian Consiglio Nazionale delle Ricerche. It was presented and discussed at two seminars held in the Department of Classics at Cambridge and in the series on the Greek city at Oxford. My thanks to all the institutions mentioned, and in particular to my colleagues A. Snodgrass, O. Murray and P. Cartledge for suggestions and criticisms. Naturally any inadequacies and errors are the responsibility of the author.

[1] J. Heurgon, 'L 'État etrusque', *Historia*, 6 (1957), 63 ff.; J. Heurgon, 'Classes et ordres chez les Etrusques', *Recherches sur les structures sociales dans l'antiquité classique—Caen 1969* (Paris, 1970), pp. 28 ff.; M. Torelli, 'Tre studî di storia etrusca', *Dialoghi di Archeologia*, 7 (1974–5), 3 ff.; M. Cristofani, 'Società e istituzioni nell'Italia Preromana', *Popoli e civiltà dell'Italia antica*, 7 (Rome, 1978), pp. 51 ff.; G. Colonna, 'Il lessico istituzionale etrusco e la formazione della città (specialmente in Emilia-Romagna)', *La formazione della città preromana in Emilia-Romagna* (Atti Convegno 1985; Bologna, 1988), pp. 15 ff.

Etruscan world. The situation is made even more complicated by the absence of any political unity, and by the profound difference which existed between the various parts into which this world was divided. From their earliest origins, which can be placed at the start of the ninth century BC,[2] the different cities of Etruria behaved in fact as independent and unconnected political entities, even if the existence of federal magistrates like the *praetor Etruriae* may suggest the existence of some sort of federal link operating at least within certain limits and under particular circumstances. On the other hand the differences which existed between the various areas into which this little world was divided are very marked.

Etruria proper extends on the western side of the Italian peninsula from the River Arno to the River Tiber (Fig. 1):[3] it includes therefore the modern region of Toscana and part of northern Lazio. Within these boundaries the Etruscan territory can be divided into three main areas. The southern coastal area, which played the leading part in the development of Etruscan culture, extends roughly from the Tiber to the River Fiora, and includes centres like Veii, Caere, Tarquinia, and Vulci. The northern area, which contains the chief metal resources of the region, is dominated by centres like Vetulonia, Populonia, and Roselle. Inland Etruria lies along the Apennine mountain range in the river valleys of the Tiber and the Chiana; the most important cities are Volsinii (Orvieto), Chiusi, Perugia, and Arezzo. The distinction between these areas is not only economic and cultural; at times it was transformed into actual political opposition, as happened at the end of the sixth century, when the king of Chiusi, Porsenna, traditionally regarded as the supporter of the Tarquins at Rome, in fact imposed the hegemony of Chiusi and of inland Etruria. From Etruria proper, major expansion

[2] H. Müller Karpe, *Zur Stadtwerdung Roms* (Heidelberg, 1962); A. Guidi, 'An Application of the Rank–Size Rule to Protohistoric Settlements in the Middle Tyrrhenian Area', in C. Malone and S. Stoddart (eds.), *Papers in Italian Archaeology*, iv (BAR International Series, 245) (Oxford, 1985), pp. 217 ff; *id.*, 'Sulle prime fasi dell'urbanizzazione del Lazio protostorico', *Opus*, 1 (1982), 279–89, and the discussion of this article in *Opus*, 2(1983), 423–48. See now G. Colonna, 'Urbanistica e architettura', in *Rasenna: Storia e civiltà degli Etruschi* (Milan, 1986), pp. 371 ff.

[3] T. W. Potter, *The Changing Landscape of South Etruria* (London, 1979): M. Torelli, *Etruria* (Bari, 1980).

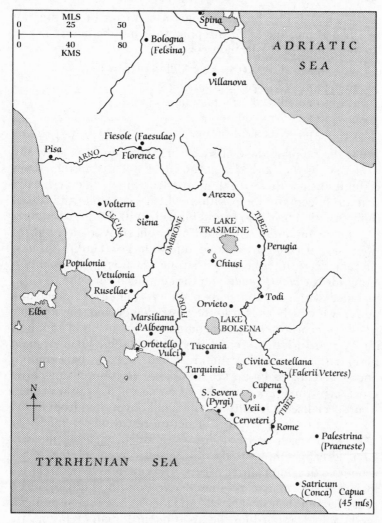

FIG. 1.   Map of Etruria

occurred north-eastwards and southwards. The first included the Po valley, and had its centre at Felsina (Bologna), the second comprised a large part of coastal Campania, with its principal centres at Capua and Pontecagnano.

Chronologically, the development of Etruscan culture can be divided into the following phases during the period before the beginning of the Roman conquest:

900–730 BC   Early Iron age; Villanovan period
730–630 BC   Early Orientalizing
630–550 BC   Late Orientalizing
550–470 BC   Archaic period
470–400 BC   Classical period

From the point of view of social organization, it is generally held that in the Early Iron Age there was a transition from communities with an egalitarian structure to hierarchically organized communities, within which economic and social differentiation began to be established. With Early Orientalizing the communities developed a gentilicial type of organization; they became articulated into enlarged kinship groups, characterized internally by strong economic inequalities: alongside the *princeps gentis* and the gentilicial élite, the *gens* also included within itself a mass of *clientes* and slaves. Economic power was closely related to the possession of land; the stranger could be incorporated in the community by means of adoption into a *gens*. In Late Orientalizing and the subsequent Archaic periods the gentilicial structure faded into the background, and was replaced by an economic organization of timocratic type:[4] economic power was based on personal wealth, derived from specialized agriculture (vines and olives) and from trade. The social basis of this new structure rested on the family or *oikos*, where each *paterfamilias* was an independent agent. As I have already emphasized, this reconstruction of the socio-economic development of Etruria rests essentially on archaeological evidence; its main lines derive from the study of burial practices and their sociological and ideological analysis, using a methodology applied for the first time in Italian prehistory by H. Müller Karpe in his book dedicated to the process of state formation (*Stadtwerdung*) at Rome.[5]

In this analysis the problem of the formation of the city immediately assumes a central position; the influence of the

[4] G. Colonna, 'Basi conoscitive per una storia economica dell'Etruria', *Ann. Ist. It. Numism.* 22 (1975).
[5] Cf. above, n. 2.

Greek model has induced many to postulate in Etruria also the emergence of an entity similar to the Greek *polis*, endowed with a high potential for legal forms and with the ability to create within itself the distinctive status of citizen. For such a type of enquiry the available evidence is scarce and difficult to interpret. But since in the case of the Greek city the study of military organization has been held to have made an important contribution to clarifying these problems, in Etruria too the efforts of scholars have been directed to the study of the literary and archaeological evidence relevant to military organization.[6]

For the Greek world the problem is well known:[7] at a point which is placed between 700 and 650 BC, Greek military organization underwent an important transformation: the outcome of battle was no longer dependent on the duel or hand-to-hand fighting between aristocratic warriors, who gained the field of battle in chariots like the Homeric heroes. Instead the hoplite army emerged, in which every hoplite had standard equipment, characterized by a new and more controllable type of shield, and fought occupying a fixed position within a rigidly ordered formation. The adoption of such an organization has been seen as indicating the arrival of a self-conscious society of equals, in a process of the democratization of society which fits well with the phenomenon of the birth of

---

[6] The problem first raised by H. L. Lorimer, 'The hoplite phalanx, with special reference to the poems of Archilochus and Tyrtaeus', *BSA* 42 (1947), 76–138, was reconsidered in critical terms by A. Momigliano, 'An Interim Report on the Origins of Rome', *JRS* 53 (1963), 95 ff., and by A. Snodgrass in his articles on hoplites (n. 7). On the structure of the Etruscan army, cf. Ch. Saulnier, *L'Armée et la guerre dans le monde étrusco-romain VIII–VI s.* (Paris, 1980); in addition, J. R. Jannot, who is working on the theme 'Les Cités étrusques et la guerre', has presented some of his ideas in a number of lectures.

[7] It is impossible to mention all the contributions to this topic. I will mention only some of the most recent papers: A. M. Snodgrass, 'L'introduzione degli opliti in Grecia e in Italia', *Rivista Storica Italiana* (1965), 434 ff.; id., 'The Hoplite Reform and History', *JHS* 85 (1965), 110–22; M. Detienne, 'La Phalange: Problèmes et controverses', in J.-P. Vernant (ed.), *Problèmes de la guerre en Grèce Ancienne* (Paris–La Haye, 1968), pp. 119–47; P. Vidal-Naquet, 'La Tradition de l'hoplite Athénien', ibid. 161 ff.; P. A. L. Greenhalgh, *Early Greek Warfare* (Cambridge, 1973); P. Cartledge, 'Hoplites and Heroes: Sparta's Contribution to the Technique of Ancient Warfare', *JHS* 97 (1977), 1 ff.; J. Salmon, 'Political Hoplites', ibid. 84 ff.; A. J. Holliday, 'Hoplites and Heresies', *JHS* 102 (1982), 94ff.; J. K. Anderson, 'Hoplites and Heresies: A Note', *JHS* 104 (1984), 52 ff. An extreme position, denying the historical significance of the hoplite reform, has now been presented by I. Morris, *Burial and Ancient Society: the Rise of the Greek City State* (Cambridge, 1987), pp. 196–205.

the *polis*. This interpretative model has been much discussed, especially among English scholars, in the last twenty years. In the context of Etruscan studies, there has been a strong tendency to accept it as an uncontroversial model, with the illusion that it is only necessary to establish, in the iconographic evidence or in the contents of tombs, the occasional appearance of hoplite elements, in order to be able to infer the birth of the democratic *polis*.

In the present chapter I propose to undertake a study of this hypothesis in the light of the different types of evidence available.

From a political and social point of view, the process of state formation comes to an end in Rome with the *comitia centuriata*, instituted by king Servius Tullius towards the middle of the sixth century.[8] This reform coincided with the birth of the hoplite army, with the various social and political implications that different scholars attribute to this event. As is well-known, the tradition handed down by the ancient sources has been widely discussed, and some scholars are inclined to mistrust it, and to maintain that even king Servius Tullius must have been a legendary character.[9] However, I do not hesitate to admit that I believe in the essential lines of the ancient tradition concerning this king and his reform.

These events are of essential interest for the Etruscan world because some Greek authors writing in Roman times[10] stated clearly that the Romans learnt from the Etruscans the tactics of fighting in the hoplite *phalanx*. These sources also maintain that this was the main reason for the initial Etruscan superiority over the Romans, and that only when the Romans took over these new tactics, were they able to defeat the Etruscans. This version of the facts has been so confidently accepted by some modern scholars as to lead to statements such as this: 'the centuriate reform of Servius Tullius was clearly enough caused

---

[8] The massive bibliography on the issue is given in R. Thomsen, *King Servius Tullius* (Gylendal, 1980); cf. also J. Ch. Meyer, *Pre-Republican Rome* (Anal. Inst. Danici suppl. xi; Odense 1983), where a useful bibliography may be found.

[9] Cf. R. Thomsen (n. 8).

[10] Diod. Sic. 23. 2. 1; Ined. Vat., ch. 3; Ath. 6. 273.

by the need for taking over from the Etruscans the superior hoplite tactics'.[11]

But before accepting the ancient tradition handed down by Diodorus we need to scrutinize the Etruscan evidence. In fact, the existence of a hoplite organization in the Etruscan cities gives rise to a series of questions, which were well summarized by A. Momigliano. In his important article of 1963 he wrote: 'how the Etruscans ever managed to combine an army of hoplites with their social structure founded upon a sharp distinction between nobles and *clientes*, I cannot imagine'.[12] As is easily seen, the question concerns the nature of the hoplite organization. Even if it was not identical in the different cities of Greece, there it was in general the expression of a community of equals. But what was it like in Etruria? This is a fundamental question and it must be considered in the light of a general analysis of Etruscan society.

In fact, some attempts have been made in this direction, but they do not answer what seems to be a central question: if Etruscan society reached the level of organization of a Greek *polis*, that should have resulted in a substantial weakening of the gentilicial structure, such as was achieved by Kleisthenes in Athens. But if that happened, how is it that the gentilicial structure re-emerged, though in a new form, in the fourth century? It is a real problem, which has been recognized even by some of those scholars who maintain that an Etruscan *polis* did exist.[13] Indeed the whole historical situation is unclear, and it is worth reconsidering the question of the nature and the character of an Etruscan hoplite army.

Our knowledge of this subject has been substantially increased by P. F. Stary's important contribution,[14] which

---

[11] Cf. R. Thomsen (n. 8), 200.

[12] A. Momigliano (n. 6), 119; cf. A. Snodgrass, *JHS* 85 (1965), 119: 'if the hoplite system could be organised and maintained within an unregenerate oligarchic society in Etruria, by what right can it be assumed that its adoption in Greece had far-reaching and almost immediate consequences?'.

[13] When e.g. G. Colonna describes the growth of a substantial wealthy class which would have given birth to the new city, he cannot help wondering 'whether they are still subject to the formal control of the great *gentes*' and he concludes: 'and the noun *servi* which is still being used to refer to them makes us assume that they were': cf. M. Cristofani (ed.), *Civiltà degli Etruschi* (Milan, 1985), p. 242.

[14] P. Stary, *Zur eisenzeitliche Bewaffnung und Kampfesweise in Mittelitalien (ca. 9 bis 6 Jh.v.Chr.)* (Marburger Studien zur Vor- und Frühgeschichte 3. Mainz, 1981).

must be the starting point for any re-examination of the problem. Stary made a thorough study of all the archaeological evidence relating to armour and fighting techniques, from the typology of weapons to their occurrence in grave contexts and the artistic representations of armed people. His principal conclusions are the following:

towards the end of the eighth century the Etruscans abandoned the armour they had used in the early Iron Age; and, in the period from 725 to 675 BC they also underwent in this field a strong oriental influence. But from the middle of the seventh century a significant change took place: Greek hoplite armour began to dominate. The round Etruscan helmet gave way to the Corinthian; the shield with embossed decoration was superseded by the hoplite shield, and also the greaves, the cuirass, the sword and the use of one or more spearheads were borrowed from the Greeks.

We cannot, however, help noting that there are some oddities in this neatly defined picture; the warriors only rarely wear a complete hoplite armour, and in some cases the characteristic hoplite weapons are replaced by the national Etruscan ones, such as the axe and the double-bladed axe, which would scarcely have been suitable for a warrior fighting in a *phalanx*. Moreover, as Stary rightly points out, neither the evidence from the graves nor the representations tell us 'whether the Etruscans were also fighting in a close *phalanx* formation'.

It is impossible here to make a study of all the images which have been collected by Stary, and I shall only offer some comments. In the period of oriental influence the figures of warriors, both in style and also in the typology of their arms, are clearly imitating oriental prototypes as simple decorative patterns, as can be seen on the silver bowl from the Bernardini tomb in Praeneste.[15] In the second part of the seventh and the

---

[15] F. Canciani and F. von Hase, *La tomba Bernardini di Palestrina* (Rome, 1979), pp. 6, 36–7; further examples of oriental imitations are the bronze plaques from Marsiliana d'Albegna: cf. G. Camporeale, 'Su due placche bronzee di Marsiliana', *Stud. Etr.* 35 (1967), 31 ff.; Stary (n. 14), B 7. 9, p. 405, pl. 4.1. The only significant exception is the large round-bodied vase from the Bockhoris tomb in Tarquinia: H. Hencken, *Tarquinia: Villanovans and Early Etruscans* (Cambridge, Mass., 1968), pp. 368 ff., figs. 363–4. This vase, clearly of local tradition, dates to the very beginning of the Orientalizing period, that is to the end of the 8th cent. Its row of Greek hoplites might have been borrowed from a Greek prototype, as can be inferred by comparing it with a contemporary Pithecusan vase: Stary (n. 14), B 1. 19, p. 369, pl. 63.1. A row of Greek hoplites may be seen also in the Plikaśna situla from Chiusi. Cf. M. Martelli, *Stud. Etr.*

beginning of the sixth centuries we find rows of warriors in the sub-Geometric and the earliest Etrusco-Corinthian vases.[16] In general, I believe that these images have been taken from the Corinthian reportory merely as simple decorative patterns; in fact they are only rarely found on other contemporary productions which are less dependent on Corinthian influence. Whether their reception was made easier by the existence of an Etruscan hoplite army is very difficult to say; yet we must admit that images of warriors were by now widespread in Etruscan art, and that this evidence indicates a concern for representations of war.

The most convincing images of an Etruscan army in ordered formation are found on two vases situated at opposite ends of the period under discussion. The first one is the *oinochoe* from Tragliatella near Caere (Fig. 2),[17] a puzzling vase dated about the middle of the seventh century. It has often been compared with the Chigi vase because of its row of seven hoplites, each bearing a round shield and three javelins. The meaning of this

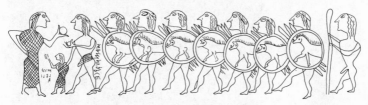

FIG. 2. *Oinochoe* from Tragliatella (P. F. Stary, *Zur Eisenzeitlichen Bewaffnung und Kampfesweise in Mittelitalien* (Mainz, 1981), pl. 9)

41 (1973), 97 ff. G. Camporeale, *Mélanges . . . de l'École Française de Rome*, 99 (1987), 29 f., who suggests that this might be the earliest representation of Etruscan hoplites.

[16] 'Civitavecchia style': Stary (n. 14), B 1. 4, 359, pl. 12; H. B. Walters, *Catalogue of the Greek and Etruscan Vases in the British Museum* i. 2 (London, 1912), pp. 259 ff., H 241, pls. XXII–XXIV. Stary, B1. 3, p. 13. 1; G. Q. Giglioli, *Stud. Etr.* 20 (1948–49), 241 ff., pl. XIII; Stary, B 1. 10–11, p. 195, pl. 10. 1, 3. Close to this group are the vases Stary, B 1. 12–13, p. 395 f., pl. 10. 2, 5. 'Polychrome style': *oinochoe* from Vulci, Stary, B 1. 9, p. 395, pl. 11. 3. *Olpe* in Villa Giulia, Stary, B1. 15, pl. 11. 2; F. Canciani, in M. Moretti (ed.), *Nuove scoperte e acquisizioni in Etruria Meridionale* (Rome, 1975), n. 13, pp. 203 ff.

[17] Stary (n. 14), B 2. 13, p. 397, pl. 9; J. P. Small, 'The Tragliatella *oinochoe*', *Röm. Mitt.* 93 (1986), 63 ff., where the preceding literature is mentioned. I will not discuss here that other puzzling vase, the *oinochoe* by the Bearded Sphinx Painter in Paris, which is now believed to represent an Ilioupersis: cf. F. Zevi, 'Note solla leggenda di Enea in Italia', in *Gli Etruschi a Roma* (Rome, 1981), pp. 145 ff., pl. v a.

frieze is debated; the most recent interpretation is that of J. P. Small, who believes that the whole frieze has a funerary character. In her view the three figures designated by name are the dead woman with her family, while the riders and warriors are engaged in funeral games. Yet, even if this is the case, we are still faced with the fact that the warriors carry hoplite shields and are arranged in an orderly row, just like hoplites.

The other vase, an Etruscan black-figure amphora from Tarquinia (Fig. 3), belongs to the last decade of the sixth century. It shows a row of hoplites armed with round shields and Greek helmets, preceded by a man playing a *salpinx*.[18] As was seen by E. McCartney in 1915, this image recalls the well-known passage of Diodorus (5. 40. 1) where the invention of

FIG. 3. Etruscan black-figure amphora from Tarquinia (P. F. Stary, *Zur Eisenzeitlichen Bewaffnung und Kampfesweise in Mittelitalien* (Mainz, 1981), pl. 22)

[18] E. S. McCartney, 'The Military Indebtedness of Early Rome to Etruria', *Memoirs of the American Academy in Rome* 1 (1915–16), 121 ff., pl. 51. 3; Stary (n. 14), B 6. 9, 406, pl. 22. 1; B. Ginge, *Ceramiche etrusche a figure nere* (Materiali Museo Tarquinia xii Rome, 1987), pp. 51 ff., pl. xxxvi–xxxviii, xcii; N. Spivey, *The Micali Painter and his Followers* (Oxford, 1987), p. 10 n. 35, figs. 6 b, 7 a. On the *salpinx*, cf. P. F. Stary, 'Foreign Elements in Etruscan Arms and Armour: 8th to 3rd Centuries B.C.', *Proceedings of the Prehistoric Society*, 45 (1979), 181 ff.

the *salpinx*, 'very useful for warfare', is attributed to the Tyrrhenians. Yet a boar is running in front of the warriors; and the whole scene might therefore be interpreted as a boar hunt. These vases are too isolated to allow general conclusions to be drawn. However, even if we were to admit that the Etruscans underwent a hoplite military reorganization before the middle of the sixth century, we would still need to understand the exact significance of this in the particular historical situation. It must also be observed that on the various classes of Etruscan figured vases individual warriors or duels are widely represented. With reference to these, Stary points out that even in Greece, where the hoplite *phalanx* certainly existed, duels are common in archaic Attic pottery. He advances the explanation that, as the *phalanx* was not easy to represent, the only possible reference to fighting was an individual duel. And yet the *phalanx* is well-represented on Corinthian vases, such as the Chigi vase. If we always find in the archaic Attic vases scenes of duels between heroes, or of heroes fighting around the body of a fallen warrior, this is rather because the Homeric conception is still dominant in representations relating to the *arete* of the warrior,[19] even if the hoplite *ethos* is far removed from the Homeric one. But this explanation is only possible in the case of Athens because we know from other sources that a hoplite organization already existed. In the case of Etruria, since literary sources are lacking, we have to guess from the archaeological evidence what these images mean; this we can do in two ways: by relating the images either to their iconographical context, when it exists, or to the social context, as far as that may be known from the cemeteries.

In those cases in which the duel is part of a wider scene we get the impression that in the Etruscan images it is clearly related to a heroic way of fighting. I am referring to scenes like that on the bucchero wine jug from Ischia di Castro (Fig. 4), where the heroic duel between hoplites is set between war chariots driven by charioteers.[20] Heroes on chariots also appear

---

[19] A. Schnapp and F. Lissarrague, 'Imagerie des Grecs ou Grèce des imagiers', *Le Temps de la Réflexion*, 2 (1981), 275–97.

[20] Stary (n. 14), B 2. 14, p. 397, pl. 7. 1. M. T. Falconi Amorelli, *Stud. Etr.* 36 (1968), 171, pl. 28. Cf. also the *olpe* by the Painter of the Bearded Sphinx from Vulci; F. Zevi, *Stud. Etr.* 37 (1969), 40, pl. xiv–xv.

FIG. 4. Bucchero *oinochoe* from Ischia di Castro (P. F. Stary, *Zur Eisenzeitlichen Bewaffnung und Kampfesweise in Mittelitalien* (Mainz, 1981), pl. 7)

in hoplite parades on many contemporary monuments.[21] Starting in the second half of the seventh century, this iconographic scheme continues to be widely reproduced until the third quarter of the sixth century BC; it seems to be rooted in an early aristocratic conception preceding the emergence of a true hoplite formation. But on this subject there is more evidence available from tombs.[22]

In Etruria, in tombs dating from the second half of the ninth to the first half of the eighth century, high-ranking people represent themselves as warriors,[23] displaying in their tombs striking bronze armour. In this connection I need mention only tomb 871 from Veii[24] which included a parade helmet with the highest crest ever found in Etruria. And it is the bronze helmet, more than any other item of armour, that reveals the persona-

---

[21] Ostrich egg from the Polledrara tomb in Vulci: Stary (n. 14), B 11. 4–5, 409, pl. 19. 1–2; A. Rathje, 'Five Ostrich Eggs from Vulci', in J. Swaddling (ed.), *Italian Iron Age Artifacts in the British Museum* (London, 1986), pp. 397 ff. Pania *pyxis* from Chiusi: Stary, B 11. 1–2, p. 409, pls. 17, 18. 1. These examples are dated to the second half of the 7th cent., but the scheme is well known in the 6th cent.—cf. e.g. G. Camporeale, *Buccheri a cilindretto di fabbrica orvietana* (Florence, 1972): frieze XXII, pp. 70 ff., pl. XXIV B—and continues to be widely reproduced in the architectural revetments of phase 1, cf. Stary, B 14 A, pp. 415 ff, pl. 34 ff.; it is still found, after the middle of the century, on the stand from Poggio Civitate: Stary, B5. 6, p. 400, pl. 21; P. G. Warden, 'A Decorated Stand from Poggio Civitate (Murlo)', *Röm. Mitt.* 84 (1977), 199 ff.

[22] On the relation between funerary evidence and society, cf. B. d'Agostino, 'Società dei vivi, comunità dei morti: Un rapporto difficile', *Dialoghi di Archeologia*, 3. 1 (1985), 47 ff.

[23] Problems relating to social evolution in Iron Age Etruria have been briefly summarized by B. d'Agostino, 'La formazione dei centri urbani', in M. Cristofani (n. 13), pp. 43 ff.

[24] This tomb is dated to the very end of the first Iron Age (3rd quarter of the 8th cent.), cf. H. Müller Karpe, 'Das Grab 871 von Veji, Grotta Gramiccia', *Prähistorische Bronzefunde* xx. 1 (Munich, 1974), pp. 89 ff.

lity of the dead, and emphasizes his warlike character as the most significant aspect of his funerary image.

In the second half of the eighth century a great transformation occurred. Etruscan society now came to be deeply stratified: economic differences became sharper, and the gentilicial organization that was to be typical of the following century began to emerge. This transformation, already evolving in the indigenous society, was stimulated and hastened by contact with the Greek world.[25] This process took place concurrently with the development of the Orientalizing culture in the late eighth century.

During the Orientalizing period, in the tombs of southern Etruria, interest in the characterization of the dead man as a warrior decreases. This is a long-term phenomeon, and the change was a widespread one, as appears from the analysis conducted by Stary, who explains it as the result of a transformation in burial customs.[26] Certainly this was the case, but the particular way in which the phenomenon occurred is significant. Arms are generally lacking, even in the wealthiest furnishings, though there are a few exceptions among the highest levels of the social élite, such as the warrior buried in the corridor of the Regolini Galassi tomb in Caere, and the owners of some of the so-called princely tombs.[27]

But even in these tombs warlike valour is expressed in a new way, and the ritual which is now reserved for 'princes' has been borrowed, through the mediation of the Euboeans of Cumae, from the Homeric conception as it is expressed in the tombs of high-ranking warriors in Eretria. The sword and the shield, when they occur, are splendid parade weapons. Attention has shifted from signs of warlike valour towards signs of rank and gentilicial continuity. Social status is indicated by the *agalmata*, the splendid cauldrons and vases in bronze and silver, which are hidden in a kind of *thalamos* like the Homeric *keimelia*. The

---

[25] B. d'Agostino, 'I paesi greci di provenienza dei coloni e le loro relazioni con il Mediterraneo occidentale', in *Magna Grecia—Prolegomeni* (Milan, 1985), pp. 43 ff.

[26] Stary (n. 14), p. 29.

[27] On the problems concerning the princely graves of the first half of the 7th cent., cf. B. d'Agostino, 'Grecs et indigènes sur la côte tyrrhenienne au VII siècle', *Annales (ESC)*, 32 (1977), 3 ff.; id., *Tombe principesche dell'Orientalizzante Antico da Pontecagnano, Monumenti . . . dell'Accademia dei Lincei* (Rome) serie misc ii. 1 (1977).

continuity of the *gens* is expressed through a cluster of items characteristic of the hearth, the princely *hestia*. The focus of interest is no longer the single man as warrior, but the gentilicial group, with its links of solidarity and continuity which transcend time. Into this picture we can place the 'princely' tombs of Palestrina, Caere and Pontecagnano, dated between the second quarter and the middle of the seventh century.[28]

As far as attitudes towards the world of warfare are concerned, the situation appears to be somewhat different in northern Etruria, where the most significant place for our purpose is Vetulonia. There too warlike display is restricted to the highest levels of the social élite, but it is more evident and more structured. It is in Vetulonia, which shared with Populonia control of the mining district of Etruria, that there reappears the most striking symbol of warrior valour—the helmet, which is now the rounded Etruria type,[29] quite different from the preceding Iron Age one.

The rounded helmet, in two different types, appears towards the middle of the seventh century on both sides of the Italian peninsula.[30] In fact, its more ancient examples are those found in Vetulonia, in the second pit of the Tomba del Duce, and in

---

[28] Actually, in southern Etruria there were two significant warrior's tombs belonging to the end of the 7th cent.: the Avvolta tomb in Tarquinia: H. Hencken, op. cit., 397 ff., fig. 385 A, and the Campana tomb in Veii: M. Cristofani and F. Zevi, *Arch. Class.* 17 (1965), 1 ff.; A. Seeberg, 'Tomba Campana, Corinth, Veii', *Hamburger Beiträge zur Archäologie*, iii. 2 (1973), 65 ff., the latter being the only tomb in southern Etruria to have yielded a rounded Etruscan helm. However, leaving aside the problems concerning these two tombs, whose furnishings were dispersed and partially lost a long time ago, we must emphasize that in these cases too the signs of the warlike character of the dead are included in a context of exceptionally high level. Thus, here too, the dead had belonged to the highest social élite.

[29] It is the type Stary W 5, cf. P. Stary, in J. Swaddling (n. 21), pp. 25 ff.

[30] The most ancient example of this kind of helmet, which because of its area of distribution might be called 'Vetulonian', was actually found in Rome, in the well-known tomb 94 from the Esquilino cemetery, cf. H. Müller Karpe, *Zur Stadtwerdung Roms* (Heidelberg, 1962), pp. 55, 89, pl. 20. On the chronology of this tomb, cf. id., *Prähistorische Bronzefunde* xx, p. 94. This chamber tomb included equipment typical of an aristocratic warrior; as well as the helmet, there were also a shield, an iron spear, and remains from a chariot. This cluster of items is frequently found in tombs marked by the presence of a helmet in northern Etruria, from the second quarter of the seventh cent. onward. Yet, even if its chronology is disputed, the Esquilino tomb cannot be dated later than the end of the eighth cent. This phenomenon, unique from the point of view of both chronology and area is so far difficult to explain.

tomb 3 at Fabriano,[31] two tombs of uncommon wealth, akin to the contemporaneous 'princely' tombs of southern Etruria and neighbouring areas.

The Tomba del Duce belongs to the class of grave circles marked out by white stones. As was stated by Falchi,[32] the excavator of the necropolis of Vetulonia, in this class of grave circles the chariot and horse furnishings often occur together with helmet, greaves, and iron or bronze spears and spits.

In the circle of the Tomba del Duce, there were five pits.[33] If we consider the items found in them as a whole, we get the image of a coherent system, revealing the complex funerary ideology peculiar to the highest levels of the Vetulonian social *élite*. The *agalmata*, of the same kind as those found in the 'princely' tombs of southern Etruria, are placed together with implements relating to the domestic hearth, sets of vases intended for the consumption of wine and the banquet, and the signs of warlike valour. In the latter category almost all types of weapon are represented: there is a great bronze shield on which rests a rounded helmet, a bronze spear-head, spits, knives, and axe. There is no sword, which seems to have been replaced by the axe, according to an Etruscan fashion known also from representations on gravestones. But the most important feature, characterizing this grave and other warrior graves which include a helmet, is the two-wheeled chariot pulled by two horses, which in contexts like those in Vetulonia may be confidently interpreted as a war-chariot.[34]

The Tomba del Duce is certainly the best preserved and best-known of the Vetulonian examples of its type. But, apart from this, other graves of the same site have also yielded rich furnishings characteristic of a member of the social élite, and

---

[31] Stary (n. 14), W 5. 1; W 6. pp. 11–12. Tomba del Duce: I. Falchi, *Not. Scav.* (1887), 477 ff., still very useful; G. Camporeale, *La tomba del Duce* (Florence, 1967). Tomb 3 from Fabriano: P. Marconi, *Monumenti . . . dell'Accademia dei Lincei* (Rome), 35 (1933), 339 ff.

[32] I. Falchi, *Not. Scav.* (1892), 384.

[33] Unfortunately, the interpretation of the Tomba del Duce is not clear: within the circular compound of white stones there were five pits, each containing a large number of grave goods closely related to those found in the princely tombs in southern Etruria and Campania, and it is impossible to know whether this furnishing belonged to a single person.

[34] Stary (n. 14), p. 129.

which include helmet, arms, and chariot. All these graves are clearly related to the heroic conception of war, according to which the warrior goes to the battle-field on his chariot, to contend with the enemy in a duel to the death.

In fact, as was pointed out by Stary, after the middle of the seventh century a substantial change occurs in the type of armour, and the essential elements of Greek hoplite armour spread all over Etruria. The most significant example of this change is the Tomba dei Flabelli di Bronzo in Populonia.[35] It is reported that the tomb contained four people, including a woman. Amongst the four helmets that were found, three are Corinthian,[36] and the other items of armour are also of Greek type, as are the three pairs of greaves. In this case, the exhibition of armour that is as close as possible to Greek hoplite armour goes nevertheless together with the signs of a strong gentilicial tradition and high-ranking social position.

The situation was almost the same at the end of the century, as can be seen from the tomb at Casaglia near Pisa,[37] a high dome-shaped chamber that, with its monumental appearance, shows in an effective way the power of the gentilicial group. Though the tomb was found already robbed, nevertheless it has preserved the essential features characterizing the furnishing of a wealthy warrior. The armour has a mixed character: the helmet is of the rounded Etruscan type,[38] while the two pairs of greaves are of Greek type; there were also two shield-bosses, two spear-heads, and probably a cuirass. Even from the few elements which were left it is possible to recognize that the furnishing was very rich; in fact it included some bronze chalices and wine jugs.

This evidence, which could easily be increased, indicates that in northern Etruria, the display of hoplite armour is restricted to the 'princes'. The image which is committed to these tombs emphasizes the high rank of the dead, his gentilicial condition, and enhances the distance which separates him from the class of *clientes* and serfs.

From the analysis of the preceding evidence we cannot

[35] A. Minto, 'Le ultime scoperte archeologiche di Populonia', *Monumenti ... dell'Accademia dei Lincei* (Rome), 34 (1931), 289 ff.

[36] Stary (n. 14), W 13. 7, 12, 20.

[37] P. Mingazzini, 'La tomba a tholos di Casaglia', *Stud. Etr.* 8 (1934), 59 ff.

[38] Stary (n. 14), W 5. 20.

arrive at the image of a hoplite society; yet it can hardly be denied that, in northern Etruria, the Etruscan aristocracy assumes, in the seventh century, a war-like character. Moreover, the same situation is found on the Adriatic coast and in other regions of northern Italy. Looking at the tombs of these aristocratic warriors, I cannot help thinking of Frederiksen's view of the new wave of Etruscan colonization during the Archaic period: he argued some years ago[39] that this was due to the enterprise of aristocratic chieftains. In fact we know at present of several tombs in Capua, in northern Campania, and in the interior of southern Italy, where Etruscan luxury goods, like the so-called Rhodian wine-jug, are found together with Greek hoplite armour. Often these tombs include objects connected with the hearth, which emphasizes the aristocratic status of the owners. All this evidence seems consistent with Frederiksen's theory.

As for our inquiry, to the information obtained from the tombs we may add that from gravestones. In Etruria, figured gravestones in the Archaic and Classical periods are restricted to northern Etruria. The first monument relevant to the present research, the gravestone of Aule Feluske (Fig. 5),[40] is bound up in a particular way with the evidence already considered. In fact it was found by Falchi in a grave circle in Vetulonia.[41] The circle was a very large one, and had previously been robbed. But it still included some 'sherds of clay vases and great carved handles', which inclines us to date the tomb to the second half of the seventh century. The engraved image is that of a warrior armed in the Greek way, with a hoplite shield and a Corinthian helmet; but his weapon, a double-bladed axe, is a typical Etruscan implement and would have scarcely been suited to a warrior fighting in a *phalanx*.

The social position of Aule Feluske is clearly indicated by being buried in a grave circle. Moreover, further evidence can be obtained from the funerary inscription,[42] which is the most ancient as yet found in Etruria. Its text is rather unusual in the

---

[39] M. Frederiksen, 'The Etruscans in Campania', in D. Ridgway and F. Ridgway Serra (eds.), *Italy before the Romans* (London, etc., 1979), pp. 295 ff.

[40] Stary (n. 14), B13. 5, p. 414, pl. 27. 2.

[41] I. Falchi, *Not. Scav.* (1895), 304 f. fig. 18.

[42] Cf. G. Colonna, 'Nome gentilizio e società', *Stud. Etr.* 45 (1977), 175 ff. esp. 189–91).

FIG. 5. Gravestone of Aule Feluske from Vetulonia (P. F. Stary, *Zur Eisenzeitlichen Bewaffnung und Kampfesweise in Mittelitalien* (Mainz, 1981), pl. 227)

complexity of the formula used to designate the dead. In fact, as well as his two names, his father's and mother's names are also mentioned. We feel, in this text, the same attention to familial and gentilicial links that I pointed out in my earlier remarks on grave furnishings of high-ranking people.

Throughout the seventh century the use of gravestones remains exceptional,[43] and a fixed hoplite iconography has not yet been established, although many elements of the hoplite armour have been introduced into the attire of Etruscan aristocratic warriors.

[43] We can quote only two other examples which show figures of warriors, but these are rather in a narrative context: gravestone from Monte Qualandro near Perugia, Stary (n. 14), B 13. 2, p. 414, pl. 52; slab from Tarquinia, Stary, B 13. 4, p. 414, pl. 27. 1. They show two warriors confronting one another, and this image seems to allude to the fate of the aristocratic warrior, who finds his natural *telos* in the act of dying.

Towards the middle of the sixth century, when, after a gap, the use of gravestones reappears, the image of the dead is even more distant from the hoplite, which means that this social category was still absent from people's imagination.[44] The arms are varied, and some of the more characteristic hoplite features, such as the helmet and the shield are almost always absent. The weapons may consist not only of a spear and a sword, in the Greek fashion, but also of an axe and a large knife with curved blade (*machaira*).

During the sixth century substantial changes took place in Etruria. From the end of the preceding century trade, even with remote regions in central and northern Europe, was already undergoing an unprecedented development; new forms of intensive agriculture, like the cultivation of olive-tree and grapevine, were established; Etruscan society began to be based on wealth, assuming a timocratic character.

Substantial evidence of this change is found in the cemeteries: it can be seen in the regular planning of the Crocifisso del Tufo at Orvieto, or in the rows of modular cube-shaped tombs which now encircle the seventh century gentilicial barrows in the Banditaccia necropolis in Caere.[45] The increasing prevalence of the new cube-shaped tombs indicates that the familial *oikos* is now prevailing over the traditional gentilicial structure.

Throughout this general transformation, we would look in vain, in southern Etruria, for any evidence indicating the emergence of a hoplite ideology. In the painted tombs of Tarquinia, hoplites are represented only rarely, and in these few cases they are in general represented as armed dancers (*pyrrhichistai*), in a context of games and competitions, with no reference to notions of warlike valour.[46]

[44] I am referring to the gravestones of Aule Tite and Larth Atarnies from Volterrae: Stary (n. 14), B 13. 6–7, p. 414, pl. 28. 1–2; of Larth Aninies from Faesulae: Stary, B 13. 1, p. 414, pl. 29. 3; those from Laiatico: A. Minto, 'Le stele arcaiche volterrane', in *Scritti Nogara* (Milan, 1937), p. 306 f., pl. XLIII. 1; and Roselle: *Enciclopedia dell'Arte Antica*, s.v. Roselle, 1028, fig. 1132; and the cippus from Montemurlo: Stary, B 13. 12, p. 414.

[45] G. Colonna, 'L'Etruria meridionale interna, dal villanoviano alle tombe rupestri', *Stud. Etr.* 35 (1967, 21 ff.

[46] Cf. G. Camporeale, 'La danza armata in Etruria', *Mélanges . . . de l'École Française de Rome*, 99 (1987), 11–42; N. Spivey, 'The armed dance on Etruscan vases', presented to the international colloquium on ceramics held at Copenhagen in 1987. I am grateful to Dr Spivey for having allowed me to read the text in typescript.

On the other hand, if we review the repertory of scenes favoured by the emerging timocratic élite, we find that they are bound up with the traditional gentilicial ideology.[47] In fact they are still centred on the use of wine and the *komos*, and their general view of the world seems to be far removed from the hoplite ideals of an *arete* illuminated by *nomos* and *sophrosyne*.

New phenomena are admittedly also emerging in the funerary ideology, but they concern southern Etruria only in a marginal way. I am referring to examples like the Warrior's Tomb in Vulci,[48] an individual burial dated to the last quarter of the sixth century BC, belonging to a warrior wearing a complete hoplite armour. The helmet is of Etruscan type,[49] there are a pair of greaves, four spearheads and the iron blade of a sword. The furnishing is very significant indeed: it includes bronze vessels and Attic figured vases. These items compose a homogeneous whole linked to wine drinking. Everything in the tomb is strictly related to Greek ideals, and the picture is completed by a Panathenaic amphora, which also introduces an allusion to athletic activities.

As the typical signs of the gentilicial conception are here lacking, M. Torelli argues that this tomb offers the image of an Etruscan hoplite who did not belong to the gentilicial class,[50] as is the case in general for Greek hoplites. This is possibly true, and yet the deceased was a high-ranking man, as appears from the luxury goods included in the furniture; the same conclusions can be drawn from the hoplite tombs dating from the end of the sixth and the fifth centuries in Vulci itself and in inland Etruria (Bomarzo, Todi).[51] As can be seen, even in a period when the image of the hoplite can be recognized from the funerary evidence, it always appears to be linked to high-ranking people, that is to chieftains rather than simple hoplites.

However, in the inland area as in northern Etruria, the situation seems to be evolving in a different way, as can be seen

---

[47] B. d'Agostino, 'L'immagine, la pittura e la tomba nell'Etruria arcaica', *Prospettiva*, 32 (Jan. 1983), 2 ff.

[48] P. Baglioni, in M. Cristofani (n. 13), p. 248, no. 9.8 and 300 ff., no. 11.21, where the previous bibliography may be found.

[49] Stary (n. 14), W 11. 2.

[50] M. Torelli, *Dialoghi di Archeologia* 4–5 (1970–1), 92 f.; 8.1 (1974–5), 15 n. 31.

[51] M. Martelli, in M. Cristofani (ed.), *Gli Etruschi in Maremma* (Milan, 1981), pp. 253 ff., ead., in *Pittura etrusca a Orvieto* (Rome, 1982), 66.

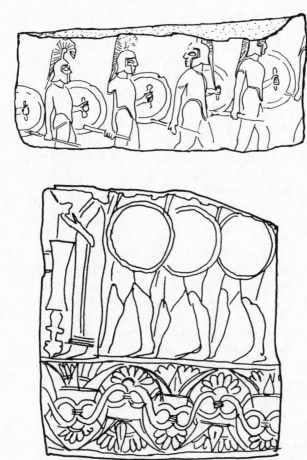

FIG. 6. Funerary base from Chiusi (J.-R. Jannot, *Les Reliefs archaïques de Chiusi* (Rome, 1984), nos. 68, 70)

from gravestones. The earliest representation of hoplites in funerary sculpture is found on the round base from Poggio Gaiella near Chiusi (Fig. 6): it shows a row of hoplites assisting in the *prothesis*. Furthermore, in the funerary reliefs of the late Archaic and early Classical period from Chiusi, images of hoplites seem to be more frequent and significant.[52] At Orvieto

---

[52] J. R. Jannot, *Les reliefs archaïques de Chiusi* (Rome, 1984). The reliefs from Poggio Gaiella are the nos. 2–3 of his class A.

and in the region of Faesulae,[53] a significant production of gravestones and *cippi* developed towards the end of the sixth and in the first half of the fifth centuries. The image of the hoplite seems to be finally fixed in a definite iconography, very close to the Greek one. Unfortunately, there is no evidence concerning the burials to which the gravestones belonged, but—particularly for the series of the gravestones from Faesulae—the analysis of representations offers hardly any allusion to an aristocratic ideology; the principal concern seems to have been that of showing that the deceased belonged to an accepted social type. Therefore, I would guess that these gravestones did not belong to 'chieftains' but to true hoplites.

This in my opinion is the situation, as revealed by the archaeological evidence; we can now try to come to some conclusions.

As we saw at the beginning, some Greek sources of the Roman period stated that Etruscans knew not only hoplite armour, but also the particular military tactics associated with it, and did so even before the Romans borrowed it from them. And yet, when Dionysius (9. 5. 4) describes the Etruscan army preparing to fight with the Romans at Veii about 460 BC, he says: 'The enemy's army . . . was both large and valiant . . . for the most influential men (*oi dynatotatoi*) from all Tyrrhenia had joined them with their dependants (*tous eauton penestas*)'. Therefore this army is 'harmonious' (*homonoousan*), and we can guess that it might look like a *phalanx*.

I believe that the shaping of the army on the model of the *phalanx* took place in Rome together with the institution of the *comitia centuriata*. All these events, timocratic reform, renewal of the voting system, adoption of a new military tactic, are strictly interrelated, and can be ascribed to Servius Tullius. The reform of the *comitia* and the institution of classes based on income (*census*) were strongly influential in shaping the army and the political structure.

---

[53] Orvieto: H. Mühlestein, *Die Kunst der Etrusker* (Berlin, 1929), figs. 215, 233–5; F. Nicosia, *Stud. Etr.* 34 (1966), 163, pl. xxiv b–c; Fiesole; F. Magi, 'Stele e cippi fiesolani', *Stud. Etr.* 6 (1932), 11 ff.; 7 (1933), 59 ff.; 8 (1934), 407 ff.; id., 'Nuova stele fiesolana', *Arch. Class.* 10 (1958), 201 ff.; P. Bocci, 'Una nuova stele fiesolana', *Boll Arte*, 4th ser. 48 (1963), 207 ff.; F. Nicosia, 'Due nuovi cippi fiesolani', *Stud. Etr.* 34 (1966), 149 ff. The stele from Montaione, F. Nicosia, *Stud. Etr.* 35 (1967), 516 ff., a gravestone of the same type as the stele from Volterra, seems to belong to this group.

Certainly, it would be ingenuous to believe that Servius' reform gave birth to some kind of democracy. We learn from the ancient sources that, in the *comitia centuriata*, the voting system was organized in such a way as to restrict the real power to the wealthiest people. Nevertheless, it seems that at this period the distinction between aristocrats and *plebs* was not so clearly marked as it was later in the early Republic: there seems not to have been a substantial discrepancy between the real society and the juridical definition of social relations.

The situation was different in Etruria: here too a timocratic evolution took place: a new wealthy class grew up, but the new situation was never completely ratified by a new definition of juridical relations. Rather, its birth was overshadowed by the traditional gentilicial establishment. The real economic power was in new hands, but political and social power remained firmly in the hands of the old gentilicial structure. Social hierarchy restricted these *novi homines* to the condition of *etera*, an Etruscan word which has been thought to convey the same meaning as the Latin *clientes*; it does at least indicate a condition of subjection, even if not so strongly as the Etruscan *lautni*. This social hierarchy bore heavily upon the structure of the army, and prevented the birth of a hoplite *ethos* based on the premiss that everyone had the same political standing, and that each man was risking his life for his own land.

In Etruria, until the third quarter of the sixth century, we are rather in a phase that might be described as the 'gentilicial hoplitic army'. As has been pointed out by Detienne for the Greek world,[54] in this phase preceding the growth of the true hoplitic organization, the gentilicial élite arrived on the battlefield in their own chariots, a practice we have already seen in several Etruscan representations. They owned the parade armour which would be buried with them. In the meantime we can hypothesize that the simple Etruscan hoplite did not provide his own armour, which was supplied to him by the *gens*.

Both in Rome and in Etruria the gentilicial army was made up of bands: in Rome and in Latium they still survived as an archaic heritage at the start of the fifth century, as can be seen in the well-known episode of the Fabii, and as is suggested by

[54] M. Detienne, 'La phalange—Problèmes et Controverses', in J.-P. Vernant (ed.), *Problèmes de la guerre* (Paris, 1968), pp. 119ff.

the *lapis Satricanus*.[55] In the case of the Fabii, we know from Servius (on *Aeneid* 6. 845) that they 'trecenti sex fuerunt de una familia, qui ... coniurati cum servis et clientibus suis contra Veientes dimicarent'. In the *lapis Satricanus*, the archaic Latin inscription recently discovered in the Volscian sanctuary, there is a mention of *sodales* of Publius Valerius and his *gens*. The noun *sodales* has been interpreted as the evidence of a gentilicial band, akin to the already-mentioned Fabian army.

In Rome, however, the structure of the army had been reshaped by the reform of the *comitia centuriata*. The Etruscan army, as we learn from Dionysius, was ordered and looked just like a hoplitic formation. In fact, central power was very strong in Etruscan cities, and—until the fourth century BC—there is never any mention of internal social unrest.

During the second half of the sixth century the situation probably took a different turn in central and northern Etruria; in this area there is some indication that a military class was emerging, but the evidence is too scanty to enable us to understand the conditions under which it developed. We can only point out that in this very period Chiusi began to be dominant, and was able to undertake the expedition of Porsenna. Moreover, from the end of the century the Etruscan cities situated in the Tiber valley and in northern Etruria had the upper hand in relations with the Po valley and Campania.

Apart from this particular development, if we look in general at the organization of the army in Etruria, it does not seem surprising that, with this kind of hoplite army, there was a general absence of the hoplite image from Etruria, and particularly from its southern area, despite the fact that it seems to have been the more advanced in many ways. In comparison with Greek *poleis*, the Etruscan city remained only partially realized, and when confronted with the Roman conquest, was ready to start singing its 'Recessional' and to revert to its traditional agricultural economy.

[55] C. M. Stibbe (ed.), *Lapis satricanus* (Gravenhage, 1980).

B

The Geography of the City

4

Ancient Landscapes

OLIVER RACKHAM

WHAT did Ancient Greece look like? The Abbé Barthélémy, writing in the 1780s,[1] thought he knew: it was like Marie-Antoinette's France, with heroes spearing the boar in noble forests and nymphs swimming in crystal fountains. From this popular writer, and his scientist contemporary Sonnini,[2] derives the traditional theory that Greece has gone to the bad since classical times. The forests, we are told, have been felled and burnt and the remains grazed to create the prickly-oak 'scrub' that the modern visitor sees. The soil, no longer under the magic protection of the trees, has washed away into the plains or the sea; the fountains have dried up; and some say that the very climate has been degraded. These changes are supposed to be progressive and irreversible, so that mischief done in the age of railways has been added to that done by Turks, Venetians, and Byzantines. This theory makes excellent sense and is still very much alive: it is the basis for a recent television programme, *The First Eden*, as well as for many scholarly publications. But is it true?

Landscape history generates fallacies more than almost any other branch of learning. In England these fallacies add up to a complete rival version: a pseudo-history which is consistent and logical, is believed in by farmers, schoolteachers, and

The fieldwork on which this paper is based was done when I took part in archaeological surveys and projects in Boeotia, Laconia, the Nemea Valley, Macedonia (Grevenà), and Crete (Myrtos, Khania, Vrokastro, and Sphakia). I have received much help from directors and colleagues in these projects. Mr A. T. Grove gave me insights into climate and its consequences. Robin Osborne and Lucia Nixon kindly answered many questions. I am especially indebted to the enthusiastic collaboration of Jennifer Moody, and to her wide knowledge of archaeology and of plants.

[1] J. J. Barthélémy, *Voyage du jeune Anacharsis en Grèce* (Paris, 1788).

[2] C. S. Sonnini, *Voyage en Grèce et en Turquie fait par ordre de Louis XVI* (Paris, An IX (1801)).

cabinet ministers, but has no connection with what really happened.[3] In Greece we see the same kinds of evidence being treated in the same way that has generated the pseudo-history of England. In this chapter I warn the reader against repeating these errors and set out the kinds of evidence now available, before summarizing the little that can be said with confidence about what ancient Greece looked like.

There are two great obstacles to our ever knowing the history of the Greek countryside with the same degree of certainty as that of England. English landscape history is the sum of the individual histories of thousands of woods, hedges, fields, meadows, moors, and so on, each of which can (with luck) be traced down the centuries in the documents. Many of them are still extant, and it is possible to combine their historical, archaeological and vegetational evidence. We can recognize a moat, or a hedge, or a boundary bank in a wood as being within a particular range of dates, and by a process analogous to archaeological stratigraphy we can establish that undated features must be earlier or later than it.[4] Even in the best-documented sites (e.g. Hayley Wood, Hatfield Forest) fieldwork discovers aspects of land-use that are not recorded in writing.[5] In Greece this is very rarely possible: because of the tradition of fragmented land-holding, parcels of land are very small and seldom have proper names. We cannot identify a feature mentioned in a document and see what is there today. The second obstacle is that we are separated from the classical Greek landscape by a great gulf of time: well over a thousand empty years with almost no relevant written record to show how the landcape was developing. Archaeological survey bridges this gulf but for our purposes is severely limited: much of the material cannot be closely dated, and relates chiefly to settlement and only at second hand to the landscape as such.

I hope that in future it will be possible to overcome some of these limitations, but up till now the study of the Greek

[3] O. Rackham, 'The Countryside: History and Pseudo-history', *The Historian*, 14 (1987), 13–17.

[4] O. Rackham, *The History of the [British and Irish] Countryside* (London, 1986); T. Williamson, 'Sites in the Landscape: Approaches to the Post-Roman Settlement of S.E. England', *Archaeological Review, Cambridge*, 4 (1986), 51–64.

[5] O. Rackham, *Hayley Wood: Its History and Ecology* (Cambs & Isle of Ely Naturalists' Trust, Cambridge, 1975); id., *The Last Forest* (London, 1988).

countryside lacks the detail that would give it solidity. It is difficult to resist being forced into the kind of generalization that time and detailed study have shown to be pseudo-historical in England.

GREECE TODAY AND YESTERDAY

The classical Greeks did not create their cultural landscape: they inherited it from their archaic and Geometric predecessors, and adapted it, doubtless incompletely, to their own activities and requirements. This was part of a process continuing from the earliest civilization until now. To escape from Barthélémy's error we must compare classical Greece with its aboriginal and its modern equivalent. By 'aboriginal' I mean Greece at the end of the Mesolithic period, just before civilized mankind had begun to convert it from a wholly wild to a cultural landscape.

For a modern comparison, Greece today is unsuitable, because in the 1980s too many transitions are happening at once: mechanization, rural depopulation, the retreat of agriculture from the more difficult terrain, abandonment of terraces, and increasing woodland. A better comparison is with the late nineteenth century, when the country was generally more stable, although some of these changes had already begun. I shall compare classical Greece with Greece in the late Victorian age, as depicted by Edward Lear, described by Philippson and Frazer,[6] and photographed by Gerola.[7] The Greece of Yesterday (as I shall call it following Anthony Snodgrass)[8] was a distinctly more arid-looking country than today. In three important respects it was like classical Greece but unlike Greece in the age of tractors. Greece then had cattle almost everywhere; it had fens, almost all of them now destroyed and made into ordinary farmland; and cereals were

---

[6] A. Philippson, *Der Peloponnes* (Berlin, 1892); id., 'Der Kopaïs-See in Griechenland und seine Umgebung', *Zeitschrift der Gesellschaft für Erdkunde*, 29 (1894), 1–90; id., *Die griechischen Landschaften* (Frankfurt-am-Main, 1951–9); J. G. Frazer, *Pausanias' Description of Greece*, 6 vols (London, 1898).

[7] e.g. G. Gerola, *Monumenti veneti nell'Isola di Creta*, 4 vols. (Venice, 1905–32).

[8] A. Snodgrass, *An Archaeology of Greece* (Berkeley, 1987).

grown in every part of the country, instead of being almost confined to the plains as they have now become.[9]

The environment

Lowland Greece has a Mediterranean-type climate, with hot dry summers and warm wet winters. Winter is now the main growing season; frosts are uncommon in most places.

But the climate is not simple. Modern Greece is sharply divided into a wet side and a dry side; the boundary follows roughly the contour of 750 millimetres mean annual rainfall (Fig. 7). The wet side is relatively well vegetated. The dry side is semi-arid, and lack of moisture is the chief constraint on wild vegetation and cultivated crops. Rainfall varies widely from year to year; it is not uncommon for one season to have three times the rainfall of another. A drought in one part of Greece may coincide with an average season in another. Most of the important *poleis* of ancient Greece—Athens, Sparta, Thebes, Argos, Corinth, Aegina, Knossos, and so on—were on what is now the dry side. They would have been profoundly affected by any change in rainfall in a way comparable to what has happened in the recent history of the Sahel on the other side of the Sahara. (Plate I.)

Change or stability of climate is (or should be) one of the central questions to be asked of ancient Greece. The pollen record shows that Greece had been distinctly wetter in earlier periods, but by the classical period the climate seems not to have been very different from what it is now.[10] The written record of climate is meagre—ancient writers took it for granted—and no decisive answer is likely ever to be extracted. Peter Garnsey, in his exhaustive analysis of scarcity in the ancient world, shows that, while lean years were frequent,

[9] V. Raulin, 'Description physique de l'île de Crète', *Actes de la Société linnéenne de Bordeaux*, 22 (1859), 307–426 (pp. 411, 419).

[10] O. Rackham, 'Land-Use and the Native Vegetation of Greece', in M. Bell and S. Limbrey (eds.), *Archaeological Aspects of Woodland Ecology* (BAR International Series, Oxford, 1982), pp. 177–98; id., 'Observations on the Historical Ecology of Boeotia', *BSA* 78 (1983), 291–351; J. A. Moody, O. Rackham, J. Rapp, 'Paleoenvironmental Studies of the Akrotiri Peninsula, Crete: Pollen Cores from Tersana and Limnes', *J. Field Archaeol.* forthcoming; J. A. Moody, '*The Environmental and Cultural Prehistory of the Khania Region of West Crete*', Ph.D. thesis, University of Minnesota (1987).

FIG. 7. Map of Greece. The thick line divides the dry (east) side of Greece from the wet (west) side.

actual famine was rare unless caused by war.[11] This suggests
that crop yields, and therefore rainfall, may have been rather
less precarious than they were on the dry side of Greece in the
mid-twentieth century. Another scrap of information is that
the ancient hunter had to deal with frost, snow-lie, and even
snowdrifts, which seem to have been less rare in Greece than
they are today.[12]

Vegetation, soils, and land-use may have been permanently
affected by runs of wet and dry years, or by single great storms
or frosts, of which no direct record is preserved. From time to
time weather or climate are proposed as explanations for such
events as the fall of Mycenaean civilization.[13] Such a simple
(but untestable) explanation of the archaeological record is
now out of fashion, but recent events in Africa remind us how
drastic can be the consequences of a temporary change from a
semi-arid to an arid climate.

The geology of Greece is very variable, but for our purposes
can be divided into three zones. The *plains* are basins filled with
silts and other alluvial materials washed off the hills in periods
of erosion. These are easily cultivable unless marshy. The *soft
hills* are a huge extent of marls, schists, volcanic lavas, and
other rocks which can be rendered cultivable by terracing. The
hard rocks, such as hard limestone which forms most of the
mountains of classical Greece, are not cultivable and are
covered in wild vegetation; if ever they had soil, they have lost
most of it by erosion.

In contrast with the rest of Europe, including other Mediterranean countries, there is little altitudinal zonation in the area
covered by classical Greece. There are really only three belts.
At low and middle altitudes the natural vegetation is dominated by deciduous and evergreen trees, undershrubs, and
grasses, which occupy different habitats determined by climate
and geology but hardly by altitude. As we ascend, these drop
out one by one—for example the olive at 600 to 800 metres—
but the landscape remains of much the same character until
about 900 metres, where it changes abruptly to the conifer belt

[11] P. Garnsey, *Famine and Food Supply in the Graeco-Roman World* (Cambridge, 1988).
[12] Xenophon, *Kynegetikos* 4. 9.
[13] R. Carpenter, *Discontinuity in Greek Civilization* (Cambridge, 1966); R. A. Bryson
and T. J. Murray, *Climates of Hunger* (Wisconsin, 1977), ch. 1.

of the higher mountains. The highest trees are normally at 1700 to 2000 metres, above which is a treeless belt of alpine plants, remote and small in extent and seldom written about by the ancients. Only northward from Thessaly, beyond the limits of Greece in the classical period, is there a more complex zonation, in which deciduous trees tend to grow above the evergreen instead of at the same altitudes.

Ancient, like modern, Greeks never discovered how to live with alpine snow. Year-round settlements were very rare above 900 metres.

Cultivated plants

Much of Greek farming and cuisine now depend on plants unknown to the ancients. Tomato, potato, maize, tobacco, egg-plant, prickly-pear, and *Agave americana* were all brought from the Americas in the Turkish period. Oranges and probably chestnuts came in Roman times; water-melons and okra are a more recent Asian introduction.

The introduction of cultivated plants began in the Neolithic and included most of the staple crops of ancient agriculture— although some of the wild progenitors from which cereals have been derived (e.g. *Aegilops speltoides*) are wild grasses in Greece today. The olive may be native to Greece, although if so it was much less widespread in aboriginal times than it became as a cultivated tree in classical times or today.

The classical Greeks are said to have introduced a number of cultivated plants. These included two fodder crops: *cytisus*, which was apparently giant medick, *Medicago arborea*, said to have been originally an endemic plant of Kythnos island, and its sister lucerne, *M. sativa*.[14] The carob, which has no proper Greek name, seems to have been brought from Palestine early in this period. These are among the many legumes then grown—the only group of cultivated plants at which the ancient Greeks excelled.[15]

There are also now many introduced wild plants, especially weeds of cultivation. A remarkable example is *Oxalis pes-caprae*

---

[14] Pliny, *Natural History* 13. 134; 43. 144.
[15] S. Hodkinson, 'Animal Husbandry in the Greek *polis*', in C. R. Whittaker (ed.), *Pastoral Economies in Classical Antiquity* (*PCPS*, suppl. 14; Cambridge, 1988), pp. 35–74.

from South Africa, a plant which is encouraged by ploughing and weedkilling, now so common in the cultivated parts of Crete that it has altered the whole colour of the island as seen from a satellite in spring.

The ancients had some cultivated plants which are now seldom seen: for example the Biblical sycomore or 'fig-mulberry', *Ficus sycomorus*, introduced from Palestine in the classical period, and several legumes. Nevertheless, the ancient Greeks seem to us to have had a curiously monotonous diet, amazingly over-dependent on cereals[16] and not making full use even of such alternatives as there were. Why do they seem to have eaten so little fish? How, keeping animals, did they eat so little meat? Why were olives (then as now) appreciated chiefly for oil rather than for eating? Why were figs not a staple crop?

METHODS AND FALLACIES IN ECOLOGICAL HISTORY

There are other actors in this theatre besides Man

The history of the countryside is not to be confused with the history of country *folk*, nor with the history of what people have *said* about the countryside.[17] Other branches of history deal with human actions and motives, but landscape history is just as much about human default. Much of it is not to do with persons at all, but with plants and animals and with the environment. An account of the classical Greek landscape must begin with a study of how the modern Greek landscape functions. Unless we take into account the behaviour of plants and animals, mountains, and the climate, we shall write pseudo-history.

Sudden and gradual changes

In some places classical Greece was very different from the Greece of Yesterday. A famous example is Thermopylae, where even the mountains and the sea have altered to such a

---

[16] L. Foxhall and H. A. Forbes, 'Σιτομετρεία: The Role of Grain as a Staple Food in Classical Antiquity', *Chiron*, 12 (1982), 41–90.

[17] Rackham (n. 3).

degree that the ancient battles cannot be understood in terms of the modern topography. The story here is very complex, and even now is not fully elucidated: it involves (or may involve) changes in the general level of the oceans, local uplifting of the land, the effects of changes in both climate and land-use, and deliberate engineering works.[18] Not all these changes have happened everywhere.

Greece is a tectonically active country, one of the points at which Africa is burrowing under Europe. The effects of earthquakes and fault-movements are most dramatically obvious along the coast—one example being the ancient harbour at Phalasarna in west Crete, now 5 metres above sea-level.[19] But similar movements occur all over the landscape and make it unstable. The mountains are altered not only by earthquakes but are also rotted from within by percolating water dissolving the limestone. From time to time, even within the span of human history, collapses and mud-slides occur, or springs disappear through underground streams finding deeper fissures. Because the mountains are still being raised, erosion is an inherent property of the landscape, and is not necessarily due to human action. Most of the better cultivable soils in Greece have been created through past erosion, and would not otherwise exist.

Most changes in Greece are episodic rather than continuous. The landscape may locally be altered overnight by a landslide or (as I witnessed in Crete on 23 September 1986) by the fall of half a year's rain in 36 hours. But even processes which might be continuous, such as the deposit of alluvium or the growth of trees, often are not: one infers that they have occurred at various times in the past, but may not be able to point to them occurring now.

Trees are not destroyed for ever

More than half of Greece is covered with natural vegetation: even in cultivated terrain, wild plants persist in terrace walls,

[18] J. C. Kraft, G. Rapp, G. J. Szemler, C. Tziavos, and E. W. Kase, 'The Pass at Thermopylae, Greece', *J. Field Archeol.* 14 (1987), 181–98.
[19] T. A. B. Spratt, *Travels and Researches in Crete* (London, 1865), ii. 232; E. Hadjidaki, 'Preliminary Report of Excavations at the Harbour of Phalasarna in West Crete', *A. J. Arch.* 92 (1988), 463–79.

baulks, and hedges. But all the natural vegetation (with the important exception of cliffs) has been modified by centuries of grazing, burning, and woodcutting. Plants react to these operations in different ways which have to be studied in order to understand the landscape. Grazing and burning have gone on since long before Greece had human inhabitants, and plants have adaptations to them.

For example, the commonest Greek wild plant is prickly-oak, *prínos*, *Quercus coccifera*. This oak burns fairly easily, and goats will eat its foliage, but neither burning, grazing, nor felling kill it: it sprouts from the stump. Depending on the amount of burning, grazing, or woodcutting, it can be anything from a carpet of bitten shoots, less than 5 centimetres high, to a giant oak-tree. If browsing stops, the bitten shoots grow into bushes; at 60 centimetres they start to produce pollen and acorns; and if further left alone they grow into big oaks.

Adaptations of one kind or another are possessed by all Greek wild plants except those which grow only on cliffs. Aleppo pine, *Pinus halepensis*, although easily killed by burning is encouraged to germinate from the heated seed, to such an extent that it is widely regarded as a fire-dependent tree.[20]

Goats are not necessarily bad

Browsing animals are not indiscriminate destroyers of vegetation, but each kind has definite likes and dislikes. In general, goats do not mind harsh textures, but dislike strong flavours. In Crete I have watched them devouring spiny plants such as prickly-oak and thistles, but ignoring the distasteful cypress and pine. Over the millennia, therefore, browsing animals will not only have reduced trees to bushes, but will have favoured those species which they dislike. What we now think of as the typical evergreen character of Mediterranean trees is, in part, the result of animals having preferred, and eliminated, the deciduous species.

Natural vegetation and the importance of roots

Prickly-oak is one among many common Greek plants which can be either trees or shrubs, according to how often they are

[20] Rackham, 'Boeotia' (n. 10), 308.

grazed, burnt or cut; others include phillyrea, arbutus, and laurel. In their shrubby form these constitute the familiar patchy, mainly evergreen *maquis (macchia)* of the uncultivated hillsides. The intervals between the *maquis* patches are occupied by different kinds of *phrygana* composed of undershrubs such as sage, thyme, and *Cistus* species—aromatic bushes which are not potential trees. Among the *phrygana* are patches of *steppe* composed of grasses, orchids, bulbous and other herbaceous plants.[21] (Plate I)

What grows where is determined chiefly by moisture. On the wet side of Greece *maquis* predominates; on the dry side, *phrygana* and steppe. No less important than rainfall is the amount of moisture retained by the different rocks, and whether or not roots can penetrate the rocks to get at it. As a result of recent road-cutting, we can now see that many an apparently barren landscape is in fact a closed plant community: the bushes may be widely spaced above ground, but their huge root systems completely fill the space available below ground. Some rocks such as marls may be 'barren' when under wild vegetation, because tree-roots cannot get into them, but may make quite good cultivated land when the surface layer has been broken up.

When grazing, burning, and woodcutting cease for a few years, shrubs grow back into trees, and *maquis* becomes woodland. Trees such as pines and deciduous oaks also grow from seed to invade abandoned farmland. Greece is full of potential trees, waiting to take over the landscape when given a chance. But that is not to say that the natural vegetation, in the present climate, would be dense forest. Trees can grow only up to the limit set by moisture and the space available for their roots. Only where there is now continuous *maquis*, with no *phrygana* or steppe, could there be continuous forest.

Those who write about the destruction of forest in Greece should define carefully what they mean by 'forest' and by 'destruction'. They should not assume that the aboriginal forest would necessarily have produced good timber. Prickly-oak and other Greek trees tend to be short, hard, crooked, and intractable. It is likely that trees suitable for big buildings or ships have always been hard to come by.

[21] Rackham, 'Boeotia' (n. 10).

The written record needs to be looked at critically

Sonnini's theory was based, of necessity, almost entirely on his interpretation of classical authors. It is a weakness of the theory that it is still argued along much the same lines despite all the evidence that has come from other directions over the last 200 years. Sonnini probably supposed that the classical period came near the beginning of the development of the cultural landscape, instead of being nearly three-quarters of the way through, as we now know it to be.

Ancient authors rarely tell us what Greece looked like, for they assumed that their readers would know. There is scattered information on land-use in literary and epigraphic sources, from which Robin Osborne has constructed a learned and ingenious account of Greek (chiefly Athenian) farming practices.[22] But even this is an account of land-*use*, not of the landscape itself, which the sources take for granted.

Where ancient authors do appear to let fall scraps of information, these have to be looked at critically. Literary or philosophical authors are more concerned to get their scansion or philosophy right than to give accurate details of things that were only of background interest. Often the information is not at first hand, and may already have been corrupted or over-generalized before it reached the author. Some of it may be merely proverbial, like the modern, untrue, platitude that Greece has a crystal-clear atmosphere. Every author on defor-estation and erosion quotes (or misquotes) a famous passage in Plato, *Critias* 111, without mentioning that it occurs in a work of fiction and was probably not written as history at all.

Soldiers and hunters are more useful sources, for their lives depended on having an eye for landscape. In the *Cynegetica*, Xenophon (or pseudo-Xenophon) hunts the hare, or on grander occasions hart or boar, in a land divided into moun-tains (*ore*) and tillage (*ergai*), a land of rocks, thickets, and occasional woods: a land indistinguishable from the Greece of Yesterday. He looks for the boar not in noble forests but in oak-groves, depressions, roughs, meadows, fens, and waters (*dryma, anke, trachea, orgades, hele, hydata*)—precisely where wild swine

[22] R. Osborne, *Classical Landscape with Figures: The Ancient Greek City and its Countryside* (London, 1987).

I Landscape zones on the dry side of Greece, near Thebes. The nearer hills, of soft rock, are speckled with a mosaic of maquis (dark bushes), phrygana and steppe. The maquis is both taller and denser at the foot of the slope, where the soils retain more moisture, despite being more exposed to browsing from the adjacent goat-fold. Behind lies the anciently-cultivated Teneric Plain. In the distance is the hard limestone of Mount Sphinx, generally very arid but with a wood on its lower slope where there is a patch of deeper soil.

Mavrommáti, July 1980

II The desert.
Near Zakro, E. Crete, September 1986

III The jungle (planes, deciduous oaks, arbutus).
Alônes, north of Mount Kryoneritis, W. Crete, April 1988

IV Crystal fountains (bordered by planes, reeds, and the occasional alder).
River Eurotas above Sparta, August 1984

lived in nineteenth-century Greece, or in Provence today. It is not woods that one misses in the modern Greek landscape, but the meadows and fens.

Ancient writers occasionally give us scraps of information specific enough to compare with what is there now. Pausanias, though he lies outside our period, was a most useful topographer. He mentions, for example, an oakwood called Skotitas, in a remote part of the Parnon mountains; the spot can be precisely identified, and the wood is still there.[23] Theophrastus tells us a good deal about where trees and other plants grew, although not necessarily at first hand. He describes in detail the remarkable Copais basin in Boeotia, with its great reedbeds.[24] More detailed still is the vision by Hermas, the first- or second-century AD divine, of the twelve contrasted mountains of Arcadia, and the trees, plants, and animals growing and living on each of them.[25] It reads remarkably like the different mountains of Arcadia today. Since the literary Arcadia is mainly a Renaissance creation,[26] it seems that it was indeed the geographical Arcadia that Hermas had in mind.

In Greek, as in English, landscape history there is a consistent tendency to exaggerate the woodland of the past, and to assume that every wood mentioned must necessarily be a *large* wood by modern standards. Crete's hackneyed reputation as a very wooded island appears to depend on a single word in Strabo, who says that the island was *daseia*.[27] This word, which means just 'wooded', is commonly mistranslated 'thickly wooded'. What it means depends entirely on Strabo's standard of comparison: modern Crete would be described as a 'wooded' island by an Arab but not by a Finn. A related fallacy forms the basis of a recent paper by J. D. Hughes, who has collected an impressive list of ancient allusions to tree-felling, and infers that 'classical authors noted deforestation which they believed to be widespread and severe'.[28] Unfortunately authors,

---

[23] *Description of Greece*, 3. 10. 6; O. Rackham, 'Observations on the Historical Ecology of Laconia', forthcoming.

[24] *Historia plantarum* 4. 10. 7 ff.

[25] *Shepherd* 9. 1.

[26] J. P. Mahaffy, *Rambles in Greece*, 2nd edn. (London, 1907), pp. 290–3.

[27] *Geography* 10. 4.

[28] J. D. Hughes, 'How the Ancients Viewed Deforestation', *J. Field Archaeol.* 10 (1983), 437–45.

especially literary authors, notice sudden changes like felling, but do not put on record the gradual, unnoticed growth of new trees. Even if everything that Hughes's authors said were true, it would have been perfectly possible for the classical period, like the twentieth century, to have been a time of net increase of trees.

Modern writers tend also to play down the landscape of the present. Von Trotta-Treyden, for example, wrote in 1916 that 'Crete today is almost woodless'; he had evidently not read the pages devoted by Trevor-Battye, who travelled the island in 1909, to enumerating the woods of Crete.[29]

Literary evidence has gradually been supplemented by epigraphical, especially inscriptions dealing with trade or the movement of timber.[30] The boundaries of *poleis* were defined by perambulations, going from object to object round the landscape. Similar documents for Anglo-Saxon England are of the greatest value in telling us exactly what was where,[31] but the Greek perambulations tend to be rather banal and perfunctory. However, the second-century BC bounds of Delphi tell us (which we would not otherwise know) that even the heights of Mount Parnassos were carefully divided among states.[32] The Hellenistic bounds of Lato in east Crete show that the Skinavria and Kritsa mountains could not have been very different in appearance from what they were in modern times: they were dominated by rocks, as they were 'Yesterday', rather than by trees, as they are becoming today.[33]

The peril of generalization

Greece is a hugely varied country. The island of Crete has some of the most arid terrain in Europe along its south coast, grading into desert in the east (Plate II). In the inland west it has a high

---

[29] H. von Trotta-Treyden, 'Die Entwaldung in den Mittelmeerländern', *Petermanns geographische Mitteilungen*, 62 (1916), 248–53, 286–92; A. Trevor-Battye, *Camping in Crete* (London, 1913).

[30] R. Meiggs, *Trees and Timber in the Ancient Mediterranean World* (Oxford, 1982).

[31] Rackham (n. 4).

[32] Osborne (n. 22), p. 51.

[33] H. van Effenterre and M. Bougrat, 'Les frontières de Lato', Κρητικὰ Χρονικὰ, 21 (1969), 9–53.

rainfall and water-retaining schist soils—a land of rushing streams and waterfalls even in high summer, of deciduous oaks and ancient pollard chestnut trees, of irrigated terrace gardens, having such drought-sensitive plants as primrose and even royal fern (Plate III). 'Welsh Crete' and the 'European Sahara' (which approach within less than 10 kilometres of each other) are two extremes in a range of landscapes worthy of a whole continent.

These differences depend on climate and soils; something like them would already have been there in classical times. It is therefore not legitimate to take scraps of evidence from different parts of the island and to expect them to add up to a landscape history of Crete. We must assume (until the contrary is proven) that each Cretan landscape, and still more each Greek landscape, has its own separate history. We must further take into account the tendency for different groups of people to create different cultural landscapes out of what looks like much the same natural environment. The landscapes of physically and biologically similar parts of ancient Greece may well have differed from each other as radically as Cambridgeshire differs from Essex in England.

POLLEN ANALYSIS AND THE ABORIGINAL LANDSCAPE

A completely independent source of evidence are the pollen grains shed by plants in antiquity, which in permanently wet places are preserved and can be recovered and identified. We find a lake, fen, or bog in which a stratified deposit builds up from year to year; we take a core of sediment, and (after suitable preparation) identify and count the pollen grains under the microscope; and we reserve samples for radiocarbon dating.

In Greece suitable deposits are now rare because of the destruction of fens; but they are not as rare as we once thought. So far there have been published eight pollen diagrams for the mainland of classical Greece (and several others from further

north) and three for Crete.[34] My colleagues Drs Margaret
Atherden and Jennifer Moody have found and are working on
six more sites. However, many of these deposits have lost their
top layers or are difficult to date. They therefore tell us less
about the classical period directly than about the prehistoric
landscape out of which the classical one developed.

Another difficulty is that many important Greek plants,
including most undershrubs, are insect-pollinated and shed
little pollen, and so are under-represented in the pollen record.
Different plants may produce indistinguishable pollens: for
example it is difficult to separate the pollens of cereals from
wild grasses or from the reeds which often fringe the wet basins
where pollen collects. It is possible (but difficult) to distinguish
the pollens of deciduous from evergreen oaks, but not to
separate the different species of oak. And because trees and
shrubs are often of the same species, one cannot tell *maquis*
from woodland: a prickly-oak bush 60 centimetres high produces the same pollen as a prickly-oak tree 25 metres high.

Despite these limitations, pollen analysis tells us (which we
would not know from any other source) that the pre-Neolithic
landscape of Greece was very different from the modern
natural vegetation. It was then much more wooded, particularly with deciduous trees, including north European species
like birch and lime. Even so, woodland was not continuous,
especially in the south: all the pollen diagrams contain evidence
of steppe plants (which do not flower in the shade) as well as
trees. But *phrygana* was very local and contributed much less to
the landscape than today. This points to the climate being less
arid than it is now, though not wet enough for trees to be
continuous on all soils.

---

[34] M. C. Sheehan, '*The postglacial vegetational history of the Argolid Peninsula, Greece*',
Ph.D. thesis, Indiana (1979); J. R. A. Greig and J. Turner, 'Some Pollen Diagrams
from Greece and their Archaeological Significance', *J. Archaeol. Science*, 1 (1974), 177–
94 (see also Rackham, 'Boeotia'; (n. 10)); S. Bottema, 'Pollen Analytical Investigations
in Thessaly', *Palaeohistoria*, 21 (1979), 20–39; id., 'Palynological Investigations on
Crete', *Rev. Palaeobotany and Palynology*, 31 (1980), 193–217; id., 'Palynological Investigations in Greece with Special Reference to Pollen as an Indicator of Human Activity',
Palaeohistoria 24 (1982), 251–89; H. E. Wright, 'Vegetation History', in W. A.
McDonald and G. Rapp (eds.), *The Minnesota Messenia Expedition* (Minneapolis, 1972),
pp. 188–99; J. A. Moody and others (n. 10).

THE LANDSCAPE AND THE *POLIS*—HOW MUCH DO WE KNOW?

The classical and the aboriginal landscapes

In general the Greece of classical times was more like the Greece of Yesterday than aboriginal Greece.[35] Most of the big changes had already taken place in the Bronze or Iron Age. The plains, unless marshy, were already cultivated; indeed attempts had long been made, as in the Copais basin, to extend cultivation into the marshes. Woodland was scarce and mainly in the mountains. By classical times the countryside was fully used: perambulations show that even the mountains were carefully demarcated between city-states and were full of minor place-names.

The profound changes since the early Neolithic are partly attributable to the climate becoming more arid, and partly to human activity. North European trees had disappeared long before the classical period, except for occasional survivals in the damp microclimate of north-facing cliffs and on the banks of cold rivers like the Eurotas (Plate IV). The plains and soft hills, which would have been the habitat for deciduous oaks, had nearly all been made into farmland (in the twentieth century the farmland has retreated even here sufficiently to allow some deciduous trees to return). On the hard rocks most of the original mosaic of woodland and steppe had been transformed into something like the present mosaic of *maquis*, *phrygana*, and steppe.

There is hardly a scrap of evidence as to changes in the Greek landscape during the classical period—for example, woods which existed early in the period but not at its end, or *vice versa*.

Cities and ecological zones

Any one place in Greece has access to up to six ecological zones: plains, cultivable hill-slopes, uncultivable hill-slopes, high

---

[35] Rackham, 'Boeotia' (n. 10); id. (n. 23).

mountains, fens, and sea. The character of any one zone varies with climate, geology, and the use made of it, and may also have varied with time. For example, the boundary between cultivable and uncultivable slopes depends to some extent on how much effort is put into cultivation. The lower limit of high mountain vegetation could well have varied with climate. But it is unlikely that the zones were any less distinct in antiquity than they are now. The most obvious change in the last hundred years has been the destruction of the larger fens, which have been added to the farmland of the plains.

Ancient Greek cities varied hugely in size, territory, and resources. Athens and Sparta, the two giants, each had access to all six zones. But even Athens was far from self-sufficient in either grain or timber;[36] its solvency depended on the mines of Laurion, and therefore, by implication, on setting aside a few per cent of its territory for producing fuel with which to smelt the metals. At the other end of the scale were places like Aegiale, Minos, and Arkesine, the three 'cities' of the barren mountain-isle Amorgos, or Araden and Anopolis, glaring at each other across the chasm of the Aradhena Gorge in southern Crete.

Settlement patterns

Greek literature is notoriously centred on cities, and especially on Athens. In ancient Greece, as in England until this century, many cities had land which was worked from farms within the city.[37] But much of the population lived outside the cities in villages and small towns: for example the 139 *demoi* (corresponding roughly to civil parishes) into which the territory of Athens was officially divided. Archaeological survey indicates that there were smaller settlements still: hamlets and isolated farms, grading into field-houses lived in only seasonally.[38] The rigid organization of most of the Greece of Yesterday, and still more of Greece today, where everyone lives in a village (often, as in modern Boeotia, a big village) in an otherwise empty countryside, would have been unusual. More typically there

[36] Garnsey (n. 11); Meiggs (n. 30). [37] Osborne (n. 22).
[38] Snodgrass (n. 8); Moody (n. 10).

would have been tracts of villages, tracts of hamlets, single farms, and occasional small towns, scattered over the landscape, as can still be seen in west Crete.

The limits of cultivation

Cultivation in modern Greece occupies almost all the plains and extends a variable distance up the hillsides. Usually the hills are terraced, although occasionally (as around Mount Kedros in Crete) fields are ploughed on the slope. In most areas it is clear the cultivation has at one time extended further into the hills than it does now. Much of the retreat of cultivation is very recent, the result of the invention of tractors, but in many places the process began at least a century ago.

We must not assume that what is now the best land in Greece has always been so. As recently as the last century, some of the dry plains were used only for pasturage; but mountains which, though steep, had water-retaining soils could be very prosperous. The most populous part of the Peloponnese was the rugged northern end of the Parnon mountains;[39] the most productive part of Crete was the tangle of remote valleys of Selino in the south-west.[40] As in England, fenland may have been particularly valuable: it provides part of the answer to the puzzle of how the ancient and early modern Greeks managed to keep so many cattle in a seemingly unsuitable climate.

Terracing forms a huge gap in our knowledge of ancient Greece. It should be the key to the development of the Greek landscape to an even greater extent than its counterpart, ridge-and-furrow, is the key to understanding the English landscape.[41] Most modern authors infer that it was practised, since the ancients often cultivated land too steep to plough on the slope, but can give no positive evidence. Ancient authors seem not to mention terracing; although this may mean that it was too commonplace to remark upon, it is odd that there should not be accounts of battles or other events in which terraces played a noteworthy part. Why did not the hare or boar escape by leaping over terraces where Xenophon could only scramble slowly?

[39] Bory de St-Vincent, *Expédition scientifique de Morée* (Paris, 1836).
[40] Raulin (n. 9).   [41] Rackham (n. 4).

An inscription giving details of a lease of land on Amorgos (an island which would hardly be cultivable otherwise) mentions the repair of what seem to be terrace walls.[42] One of Demosthenes' lawsuits about property encroachment mentions what may have been a terrace wall; but it was built, not to create a field, but to prevent a field from being washed away by a diverted watercourse.[43] In many places where there are ruins of terraces abandoned in the last century, there are also much fainter remains of terraces abandoned much longer ago, and occasionally (as in Attica) there is some evidence to associate these with classical farmsteads.[44] At Loutro in SW Crete I have myself found a gigantic olive-tree, which I estimate from its annual rings to be of Hellenistic date, growing in an old terrace-wall. Such scraps of information still constitute our knowledge of this essential clue as to how the ancient Greeks managed their landscape. We know nothing of the history of the various kinds of terrace (braided or stepped, earthen or stone-walled).

The amount of cultivable land is elastic, depending on how much effort is put into making and maintaining terraces. Steeper slopes and shallower soils get progressively more necessary and more difficult to terrace, and grade into the limits of the absolutely uncultivable. Presumably in ancient, as in modern times, variations in population and in pressure on land took the form of advances and retreats of terracing in the less rewarding places. Another gap in our knowledge is the amount of labour represented by the various types of terraces. Is it true, as writers often assume, that terracing was a great burden on a farmer's time and energy? If so, why does no ancient author say so? Or is it that terraces were constructed piecemeal in hours of leisure over many years, and once built needed little maintenance?

In my experience, and that of the archaeological surveys on which I have worked, the great majority of terraces of which

---

[42] T. Homolle, 'Contrats de prêt et de location trouvés à Amorgos', *BCH* 16 (1892), 262–94 (= Dittenberger, *Sylloge*³ 963. 17–20).

[43] 55 (*Against Kallikles*).

[44] J. Bradford, 'Fieldwork on Aerial Discoveries in Attica and Rhodes, II: Ancient Field Systems on Mt. Hymettos, near Athens', *Antiquaries J.* 36 (1956), 172–80; O. Rackham and N. Vernicos, 'On the Ecological History and Future Prospects of the Island of Chalki', in N. S. Margaris (ed.), *Desertification in Southern Europe*, forthcoming.

there are remains could now be cultivated if somebody were to take the trouble to do it: they have not become uncultivable because the land itself has changed. This probably varies from region to region: on some soils and in some climates it may well be true that neglected terraces, or terraces still cultivated but ill-maintained, lose their soil by erosion.[45] In Crete and on other islands we have occasionally found 'ghosts' of terraces from which all soil has disappeared, in circumstances which suggest erosion by wind.

Roads

Whether or not a landscape makes provision for vehicles is one of its essential characteristics, determining not only patterns of trade and the movement of big indivisible objects, but the fabric of the countryside down to small details. A great difference between the Greece of Yesterday and historic England was that in England for centuries almost every farm had had a cart; roads, lanes, holloways, and tracks have dominated the landscape for well over a thousand years. In Greece (except for parts of Macedonia where there were carts and roads[46]) the landscape was organized for mules and donkeys: it was often well organized, with *kalderímia*—built mule-tracks—reaching every settlement, but these had steps in them and were therefore not for vehicles.

In contrast, ancient Greece was, to some extent, a land of wheels. There had been chariots and wagons since the Bronze Age; the distinction between roads that are or are not *hamaxitós*, 'drivable', familiar to the Greek traveller today, goes back to Homer. By the classical period there were words for several types of vehicle and of road, though not so many as the ancient Romans had.[47] Was not a tombstone, with a picture and an epitaph in verse, raised to a pig run over by a wagon?[48] Classical Greek roads are well-known, especially through the

[45] T. H. van Andel and C. Runnels, *Beyond the Acropolis: A Rural Greek Past* (Stanford, 1987).

[46] W. M. Leake, *Travels in Northern Greece* (London, 1835), i. 34.

[47] C. Daremberg and M. E. Saglio, *Dictionnaire des antiquités grecques et romains* (Paris, 1881–1912), entries for *vehiculum, via*.

[48] G. Daux, 'Épitaphe métrique d'un jeune porc, victime d'un accident', *BCH* 94 (1970), 609–18. (I am indebted to Lucia Nixon for this reference.)

grooves cut for the wheels, after the manner of early railways, in steep and rocky places. Column-capitals and other vast loads could be moved by teams of oxen.[49] What is not clear is how far minor roads extended to remote places, or whether every farm normally possessed a cart. As recent experience shows, road-making in Greece is surprisingly easy for a mountainous country, but if there was a comprehensive road system we might expect to find more definite remains of it.

The diversity of Greece

At least some of the different landscapes of Greece existed in classical times. I have shown, for example, that Boeotia already differed from Attica in much the same way as it does today, Attica being much more wooded with pines and other trees, although it produced little usable timber. The boundaries of the Attic and Boeotian landscapes have fluctuated, but the essential differences have not changed, although they do not rest on any obvious differences of climate or soil.[50]

The unevenness of the landscape would have encouraged specialization. Nature has intended Greece to be a land of trade rather than self-sufficiency. Every city had building stone or earth for mud-brick, and pasturage on uncultivable land. Every other resource was uneven in its distribution. Some cities were rich in cultivable plains; in others cultivation, if possible at all, would have demanded terracing. Olives will grow on almost any soil—indeed, like Greek pears, they hardly require soil at all—but the high inland basins of Arcadia would have been too frosty for them. Timber, like minerals, could be got by only a minority of cities from their own territories. It was brought long distances (e.g. from the Black Sea to Athens) and its supply was an important matter of strategy.[51]

To depend on cereals, to the extent that ancient Greece did, makes self-sufficiency difficult. In a good year the yield (minus the seed) can be four times that in a bad year; in order to survive the bad years one must sow enough to produce a

[49] A. Burford, 'Heavy transport in classical antiquity', *Econ. Hist. Rev.* 13 (1960), 1–18.
[50] Rackham, 'Boeotia' (n. 10).
[51] Meiggs (n. 30).

surplus in an average year and a glut in a goodish year.[52] Since bad, average, and goodish years depend chiefly on rainfall fluctuations, which are not synchronized throughout Greece, this encourages people to live by trade. Trade might also be encouraged by the existence of large numbers of smallholders: one way of getting a living from a small area of land is to grow some more valuable crop than grain.[53] Runnels and van Andel have shown that in the Argolid the number of settlements, and by inference the population, waxed and waned at different periods according to whether or not there was access to markets for the crops. The greatest prosperity of this region, when two of its towns reached the rank of *polis*, was from the early fourth to the early third century BC.[54] The possession of a market, indeed, was one of the symbols of the status of a *polis*, and was a privilege as jealously guarded as in medieval England. Athens, for example, apparently allowed only two markets, besides that of the city itself, in the whole of its vast territory.[55]

We have, as yet, little evidence on the important question of how much grazing and browsing took place. Snodgrass argues (from very circumstantial evidence) that Iron Age Greece was predominantly pastoral, with not only goats and sheep but also cattle, which replaced much of the earlier cultivation.[56] It has been claimed that a similar change happened to the Peloponnese in the late Roman period, but this is based on a text of Philostratus,[57] a tendentious oration which is hardly strong enough to bear that interpretation.

In classical Greece, there is abundant evidence from texts and inscriptions for pigs and draught cattle. There was probably already a distinction between the few special 'house' sheep and goats, kept on the farm, and the big flocks which grazed the hills.[58] Mules and donkeys were often used, even as early as

---

[52] P. Garnsey, T. Gallant, and D. Rathbone, 'Thessaly and the Grain Supply of Rome during the Second Century BC', *JRS* 74 (1984), 30–44.

[53] Y. Triantafyllidou-Baladié, 'Dominations étrangères et transformations de l'agriculture crétoise entre le XIVᵉ et le XIXᵉ siècles', *Greek Review of Social Research: Aspects du changement social dans la campagne grecque* (1981), 180–90.

[54] C. Runnels and T. H. van Andel, 'The Evolution of Settlement in the Southern Argolid, Greece: An Economic Explanation', *Hesperia*, 56 (1987), 303–34.

[55] Osborne (n. 22), p. 108.

[56] Snodgrass (n. 8).

[57] *Vita Apollonii* 8.7 (Loeb edn., vol. 2, pp. 336–7).

[58] Hodkinson (n. 15).

Hesiod,[59] for ploughing as well as riding, although the ox (with his horns to act as towbars) would have had an advantage as a draught animal in those days of poor harness design. However, digging was a common alternative to ploughing on farms as well as gardens. Classical Greece, as far as we can tell, seems to have been rather less well-provided with livestock than mid-nineteenth-century Crete, where all but the very poorest rural families had a yoke of oxen and a donkey or two.[60] As then in Crete, horses were not common; however familiar in works of art, in reality they were mainly status symbols and mule-makers.

In many places little of the cultivable land was available for grazing flocks of sheep and goats.[61] Stubble and fallow land, then as now, were used for feeding draught stock and house sheep and goats. When these animals were more numerous they may well have eaten all the stubble and weeds; legumes, indeed, were sometimes specially grown as fodder. *Maquis* and *phrygana* would have had many uses (including coppicing for fuel) but chiefly that of feeding the flock sheep and goats. There is much controversy as to how many the flock animals were, and to what extent they were transhumant or integrated with farming operations. The strategy evidently varied from place to place, depending on the local topography and on what vegetation there was to eat at different seasons. We cannot directly say how intensively the hills were grazed: the texts give a general impression of a landscape a little more vegetated than the Greece of Yesterday and a little less vegetated than Greece today. Still less can we tell whether ancient Greece had the traditions, to be seen today in Macedonia and east Crete, of managing oaks and other wild trees by pollarding and shredding to yield a continuous supply of leaf-fodder.

It might be thought that all Greek cities would at least have tried to live by farming, but even here it is possible to find an exception. On the little gravel fan at the seaward end of the great Gorge of Samarià in Crete stand the copious remains of Tarrha with its Roman glassworks.[62] Tarrha, although a place

[59] *Works and Days*, 816.
[60] Raulin (n. 9), pp. 418–19.
[61] Osborne (n. 22).
[62] G. D. Weinberg, 'Excavations at Tarrha, 1959', *Hesperia*, 29 (1960), 90–108.

of some note, was spectacularly lacking in a hinterland. Immediately behind the town rise cliffs upon cliffs to a height of 2400 metres, plunging into a deep and harbourless sea. Apart from meagre gravel terraces within the gorge itself, there is no possibility of cultivation. There is no way out except by sea or by a very stiff climb. What did Tarrha do for a living? In the Middle Ages its one resource was cypress, a precious timber which, then as now, grew chiefly in and around the gorge.[63] We are tempted to suppose that already in the classical period this city specialized in cypress, a timber known to have been exported from Crete;[64] Theophrastus associates the tree with Tarrha.[65]

A degraded landscape?

The notion that Greece was mismanaged and ruined either during or since classical times is elusive and difficult to substantiate. Whenever ancient authors tell us what was there, what they say is in most instances compatible with the modern topography. For example, it is not true that oaks have vanished from Dodona: there is now (1988) a giant old deciduous oak within 300 metres of the site of the original oracular oak, but guidebook writers have not noticed it. Skotitas is but one instance where Pausanias mentions trees or woodland and there are still trees or woodland today. Less often, as with Pausanias' wood Pontinos, near Lerna,[66] the wood is not there today, and we can be reasonably sure of having looked for it in the right place. But there are also instances where a modern wood seems not to have been there in classical times. A notable example are the great woods of the Taygetos Mountains, which are nowhere mentioned in the numerous ancient sources for the Peloponnese. These woods are extensive and magnificent, and would have formed an important timber resource in ancient Greece. They are known to have increased greatly since the eighteenth century, and I infer that they were not there in classical times.[67]

---

[63] e.g. C. Buondelmonti (1415), *Descriptio Insule Crete*, ed. M.-A. van Spitael (Herakleion, 1981), pp. 115–18.

[64] Meiggs (n. 30). [65] *Historia Plantarum* 2. 1. 2.

[66] Pausanias, *Description of Greece* 2. 37. 1. [67] Rackham (n. 23).

I am sceptical of the belief that Greece had much more soil in classical times than now and has been degraded by erosion through human mismanagement. Greece is indeed a very eroded country; but most of the erosion took place in the Pleistocene or earlier, long before any human impact on the land.[68] Erosion in historic times has happened in some areas but not others: for example, the long series of alluviations described for the Argolid[69] has no parallel in Boeotia. Despite all the research that has been done, no general link has ever been established between the occurrence (in time and space) of erosion and of any particular form of 'mismanagement'. The most spectacularly eroding part of Greece today is southern Macedonia, which is also the least disturbed and most wooded: there are miles of continuous oakwood, and thousands of gullies eating into the woods.

Erosion must be the normal state of a country where the mountains are still being rapidly uplifted. But it is episodic, like many processes in Greece: circumstances favour erosion at some times and in some places but not others.[70] Some rocks are much more erodible than others. Most of Crete and most of Boeotia, in the modern climate, resist all traditional forms of use or misuse; only the bulldozer, vigorously applied, induces them to erode. The southern Argolid, according to van Andel and Runnels, is more precarious; terraces will hold it together, but need to be well maintained. The sandstones and serpentines of south Macedonia crumble and slump of their own accord, and no vegetation will stop them. Trees have no magic power to retain soil: my own observations in recent deluges show that such lowly plants as mosses and lichens are equally protective.

The better one knows modern Greece, the less easy it is to accept that it is degraded from the landscape of classical times. Possibly Barthélémy was not so far wrong after all. There are still noble forests and crystal fountains in many parts of Greece today, and writers who deny it have not looked for them. They

---

[68] O. Rackham, 'Desertification or De-desertification? Questions in the Historical Ecology of Southern Greece and Crete', in Margaris (n. 44).

[69] van Andel and Runnels (n. 45).

[70] J. M. Wagstaff, 'Buried Assumptions: Some Problems in the Interpretation of the "Younger Fill" Raised by Recent Data from Greece', *J. Archaeol. Science*, 8 (1981), 247–64.

are not mentioned in guidebooks: one comes upon them in unexpected places at the end of a long day in the field, like that turquoise pool under tall oleanders in the depths of an arid gorge behind Kalo Chorio in east Crete. Mount Kryoneritis on its accessible south side, facing the Sahara, is a vast, grimly arid limestone mountain, treeless right to the top; but its north face, which few writers have seen, is a cliff more than a kilometre high plunging into a jungle of great oaks and tangled tree-heather, of streams and thick moss and water-loving plants. Such places are awesome by contrast with their surroundings, and one can understand that they were the haunts of gods and heroes in Antiquity. Such things are now few, but maybe even in classical times they were rare and wonderful; the very fact that most woods and springs were sacred to gods and nymphs means that they were not commonplace.

5

Survey Archaeology and the Rural Landscape of the Greek City

ANTHONY SNODGRASS

'FOR all scholars' good intentions the study of the ancient city has remained the study of the town.'[1] This chapter is addressed to those (surely the great majority) who think that this statement is true, and especially to those—still I think a majority—who think that it ought not to be true. Most studies of the *polis* at least pay lip service to the axiom that it formed an indissoluble union between town and countryside but, when and if they move from the abstract level to the physical, they find that they have embarrassingly little to say about the second element in this partnership. I shall not linger here on the reasons for this state of affairs: we can, if we wish, comfort ourselves by laying a good part of the responsibility on the ancient Greeks, first for using such an infuriatingly ambivalent term as *polis*, and secondly because their surviving authors do in fact show an almost exclusive preoccupation with the urban component of the physical make-up of the *polis*, at the expense of the rural.

What can we do, at this late stage, to counteract a bias which can be traced all the way back to antiquity, and which nearly two centuries of organized archaeological work in Greece have only served to reinforce? In a general way, we can take a leaf from the book of other schools of modern classical studies, and adopt approaches from other disciplines. Thus in the present case, it was at first left to non-Classical scholars—most notably, the sociologist Max Weber—to draw attention to the degree of

[1] R. G. Osborne, *Classical Landscape with Figures: The Ancient Greek City and its Countryside* (London, 1987), p. 9.

dependence of the ancient city on agriculture. Weber's insight met with prolonged resistance from within the guild of classicists; but when it eventually won the very widespread acceptance among ancient historians which it now commands, the effect on their work was profound: much valuable work on the agricultural economy and especially its demographic implications has already resulted. On literary classicists, constrained as they are to share the predilections of their chosen ancient authors, the effect has been much less conspicuous. Even if the great majority of these authors themselves owned and worked pieces of farming-land, one would hardly guess as much (at least for the Greeks among them) from their surviving writings.

Equally muted has been the effect on classical archaeologists, until the last few years; and for this there is, I think, a special explanation. It is that the traditional medium of archaeological research, excavation, is in its nature ill-suited to illuminating the rural sector of the ancient world. All the greatest achievements of excavation in the historical periods of ancient Greece and Italy have been associated with urban sites, with the cemeteries that these towns produced, and with the major sanctuaries that either arose within the towns, or themselves grew to the scale of conurbations. The excavator who works in an urban site can be certain of results, even if they do not match in quality, or correspond in period, with what he anticipated. By contrast the ultimate nightmare of the excavator, that of finding quite literally nothing, is a real possibility in a rural context; actual instances, though of course the annals are silent about them, survive in the memory of oral folk-lore among the archaeological fraternity.

In defence of excavation as a source of knowledge of the rural sector, it should be acknowledged that there have been a few outstanding investigations of isolated rural sites. Many archaeologists would also make the further claim that the excavation of a regional centre contributes information on that region as a whole.[2] This argument has a certain instinctive appeal: a capital is after all held to be 'representative' of the country that it controls, in one sense of that word. The trouble

---

[2] See 'The Analysis of Data from Surface Surveys', an exchange of views between R. Hope-Simpson and J. F. Cherry, *J. Field Archaeol.* 11 (1984), 115–20, especially Cherry on p. 119.

is that it is the wrong sense for the purpose under consideration. With the Greek city-state, with its regular verbal identity between the main conurbation and the *polis* as a whole, the temptation to make this semantic slip is all the greater. In ideal conditions, if first the entirety of a city-site were to be excavated, and secondly the entire range of finds were to be recorded, including not only manufactured durables but also more perishable natural commodities, then the claim would have greater substance. As things are, however, the only approximations to the fulfilment of the first condition took place at a time when the second requirement was not yet envisaged; and today financial and political conditions combine to make the first aim an increasingly unrealistic one. Instead, excavators must content themselves with a small sample of the chosen urban site; in terms of representativeness, the best that they can hope for is that the choice of their sample will be determined by scientific criteria rather than (as is more usual) by irrelevant constraints such as the existence of later standing structures or the selective availability of land for purchase.

One natural reaction to this quandary is to abandon the rural sector of urbanized societies, as being archaeologically unapproachable; another, less defensible, is to dismiss it as uninteresting. But a moment's thought will reveal the annihilating effect that either attitude would have on archaeological work in cultures that are not only pre-urban, but sometimes pre-agricultural and even non-sedentary. In all these areas, non-classical archaeology has some impressive past achievements to its credit; but most exciting of all are the very recent results, and the prospects for future ones.[3] Here is a case in point of the desirability of learning from other disciplines, or from other branches of the same discipline. The key to the most successful attainments in these fields has been, above all, a technique of site-location of a kind that has hardly been called on in traditional classical archaeology, together with the scarcely less important dogma that the business of archaeology is the entire material culture of past societies, which itself has a major bearing on what constitutes a 'site'.

[3] For some outstanding examples, see L. R. Binford, *In Pursuit of the Past: Decoding the Archaeological Record* (London, 1983).

Thus we come at last to the topic of archaeological survey. Even when prefixed by 'archaeological', the word 'survey' remains distressingly ambiguous and is uniquely generative of misunderstandings even among professional archaeologists. In the sense in which it was used in the previous paragraph, it need mean no more than a desirable preliminary to later excavation—which is exactly the sense to which many would confine it, descriptively and often prescriptively as well. The idea that a survey, alone and in its own right, can generate worthwhile archaeological results still has to be tirelessly promoted and defended today. In part, this is because some notable surveys have been carried out by those who reject any such idea. In part, too, it arises from the arguable claim that survey is parasitic upon excavation in a different way: namely, that survey archaeologists have constant recourse to knowledge acquired through previous excavations. How else could they date their pottery, recognize a piece of an olive-press, or interpret a fragmentary Doric cornice? As a matter of fact, there is more than one answer to these rhetorical questions—stylistic studies, textual descriptions, and standing monuments have played a part comparable with that of excavation in the understanding of such finds—but let that pass. Supposing that the claim were wholly justified, would it have any bearing on the utility of survey? Would any doctor dismiss diagnosis for being 'parasitic' on anatomy or surgery? In the advance of a discipline, any technique that is developed later is likely to draw on those already established.

But even in those archaeological circles where survey is fully accepted, there is still room for radical disagreement on a further issue: the exact nature of survey to be undertaken. Should a survey cover a smaller but contiguous block of land, or should it proceed by carefully sampling a larger block? If the latter, on what principles should the sample be chosen? Should the survey be concentrated on the period or periods in which its directors have an established interest and competence, or should it deal with all periods? Finally, should it be intensive, to the point of aiming at total coverage of the chosen territory?

The last question is the most important one, and an answer to it determines one's answers to the other questions. When the intensive technique was first tried out in the 1970s, there was room for honest doubt about its value. But enough has resulted from the subsequent decade's work to make only one view tenable today. For one thing, it has been demonstrated[4] that intensive surveys (predictably) find many other sites than 'extensive' ones, which proceed by investigating only the likely site-locations: in some cases, the intensive method yields more than 100 times as many sites per unit of territory. Whatever riposte is offered to this observation, it will have to be a good one to justify a method that can be predicted to miss up to 99 out of any 100 knowable archaeological sites (to say nothing of the others that even the intensive method may miss). In the particular case of the ancient Greek landscape, which has now been shown to have been a populous one (at least at certain periods), and which produces surface material in quantities undreamed of in the areas where the intensive survey technique was pioneered like North America and northern Europe, I think that the need to explore every kind of terrain is absolute.

This finding, if accepted, does not preclude the use of a well-planned sampling technique, though I think it does tip the scales in favour of using what is called a 'stratified' sample: that is, one in which scope is given to pre-existing knowledge about boundaries, preferences of soil-type, and historical evidence generally, rather than allowing purely mathematical factors to determine the locations of the sampled tracts. The finding does also point to an answer to our remaining question, whether to have a selective concentration of period. For intensive survey is a slow, laborious, and taxing technique for everyone involved in it. To invest so much time and labour in a territory, only to dismiss the finds of many of its periods of settlement as being of no direct concern to the project, is an enormous waste of energy. In the same way, the exponents of the older ethic of excavation, who hacked their way impatiently through the post-classical levels of a site in order to get at their chosen

---

[4] See J. F. Cherry, 'Frogs Round the Pond: Perspectives on Current Archaeological Survey Projects in the Mediterranean Region', in D. R. Keller and D. W. Rupp (eds.), *Archaeological Survey in the Mediterranean Area* (Oxford, 1983), pp. 375–416, especially p. 391 and fig. 1.

period, were sentencing themselves to much unproductive labour.

They were also, of course, guilty of permanent destruction of the evidence in question. This brings us to the final justification of survey—what might be loosely called the environmental one. Survey is unlike excavation in that it does not directly involve the destruction of the evidence with which it works. A given stretch of terrain may be re-surveyed, if not indefinitely, then at least several times over, and adequate material can be taken from the surface each time under most conditions. For it is the repetition of the cultivation process, year after year, which provides surface survey with its diagnostic evidence; wherever this continues, and in some cases even where it does not, and natural erosion performs the work instead, this material will continue to appear. Intrinsically, this material is almost always unspectacular: once recorded and analysed, it can be packed away economically, making slight demands on museum storage, and virtually none on exhibition space. This explains its lack of attraction to one kind of archaeological mentality, but in these days of excessive pressure on museum space in Greece, it can be reckoned as a further advantage.

To sum up the generalizations in the first part of this paper: archaeological survey, pioneered in very different conditions and for very different purposes elsewhere, has come to fill a specific need in Mediterranean archaeology. It is uniquely adapted to cope with the long-standing void of relative ignorance in our understanding of the rural territory of the ancient city. In the process of transplantation from the plains of North America and the sparser archaeological landscapes of temperate Europe to the dense palimpsest of Mediterranean settlement, it has inevitably undergone changes: in particular, as it spread first to Italy and then to Greece. After some epoch-making pioneer work at a less intensive level, it was the 1970s which saw the first attempts to apply the total-coverage survey in Greece proper. Pride of place may be given to the Argolid Exploration Project, inaugurated by an American team in 1972 and resumed in 1979–83.[5] The outstanding project of the mid 70s was the Melos survey, which like the Argolid project

[5] See most recently T. H. van Andel and C. Runnels, *Beyond the Acropolis: A Rural Greek Past* (Stanford, 1987).

grew up in association with the excavation of a major site or sites within the territory surveyed.[6] In 1979 came the inauguration of the Cambridge/Bradford Boeotian Expedition, whose work will form the subject of the rest of this paper.[7] The early 1980s saw a proliferation of similar projects, mostly again of Anglo-Saxon initiative, which are not yet fully published: the Megalopolis survey of the University of Sheffield, the Greco-Anglo-American survey in northern Keos and the Nemea Valley Archaeological Project which involved some of the same team, the Methana survey and the Laconia survey of the British School at Athens, and the Strymon Valley project. (This list is a selective one, omitting several undertakings which are either directed at specific periods or less intensive in their coverage.)[8] Between them these projects have involved dozens of researchers, in a number of disciplines besides archaeology, and their existence and concentration of date show that a wave of activity in intensive survey has swept across the scene of Greek archaeology. That such activity is misdirected or unproductive is coming to seem increasingly unlikely.

It is time to turn to specifics, and record some of the experiences of the Boeotian project which I direct jointly with Dr John Bintliff of the University of Bradford. By the time that we took the field in 1979 we had become convinced advocates of an intensive, all-period approach aiming at total coverage. In choosing Boeotia, we are not committing ourselves to the territory of a single *polis*, but rather to that of a loose federation of cities with a slightly qualified degree of independence. In the event, our area of operation within Boeotia was one that quite definitely included parts of the territories of at least two of these cities, since it embraced the urban centres of Thespiai at one extremity and Haliartos at the other (Fig. 8). By ranging from the centres of cities to the borders of their territories we placed ourselves to assemble comparable data for every facet of the classical *polis*, in addition to our findings for other

[6] C. Renfrew and M. Wagstaff (eds.), *An Island Polity: The Archaeology of Exploitation in Melos* (Cambridge, 1982).

[7] For an interim report, see J. L. Bintliff and A. M. Snodgrass, 'The Cambridge/Bradford Boeotian Expedition: The First Four Years', *J. Field Archaeol.* 12 (1985), 123–61.

[8] For an instance of the latter, S. Bommeljé and P. K. Doorn, *Aetolia and the Aetolians: Towards the Interdisciplinary Study of a Greek Region* (Utrecht, 1987).

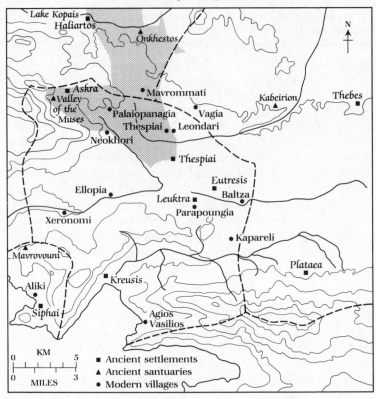

FIG. 8. Map of part of western Boeotia. Stipple shows the area covered by survey in 1979–1986

periods to which such divisions are inapplicable. The account that follows will be highly selective, omitting whole millennia that range from the sparse finds of the Upper Palaeolithic to the surprisingly positive picture of the Turkish period; selective, too, in making little reference to the very detailed patterns of growth and decline, shift and abandonment that emerged from our study of the city-sites themselves, since the main purpose of this chapter is to cast some light on the rural landscape.

First, some overall figures. To date, seven seasons of field-walking and two study sessions have been carried out. In that time, we have covered some forty square kilometres, and it is chastening to reflect that this represents little over 1.5 per cent of the land surface of ancient Boeotia. The area covered forms a single block, if of rather straggling shape, and this means that on strict statistical criteria it has no validity as a sample of Boeotia as a whole. However, we see our findings as complementary to those of the other expeditions working elsewhere on the Greek mainland and islands: it is ancient Greece in its totality that we are combining to sample, and we draw much encouragement from the fact that many of our most important findings for the classical period are being replicated in the results of these other expeditions. Indeed, it will be a matter for specific mention when a finding is *not* so replicated, but seems rather to be pecular to Boeotia.

In these forty square kilometres we have found about 150 sites, maintaining steadily from season to season a frequency of just under four sites per square kilometre. The density is rather high, and already hints at the fact that the great majority of these sites are very small. The figure of 150 of course covers all periods; but the fact is that a large majority of the sites (well over three-quarters) show occupation in the age of the *polis* (more precise specifications will be given presently). Here it is important to mention a subsidiary part of the surveying process which has a bearing on the definition and interpretation of these small sites. From 1980 onwards—that is, in all seasons but the first—we have been systematically recording the density of artefacts over the whole landscape, between, around, and within the sites. This practice has brought into sharp focus two features of the archaeological landscape which would otherwise have remained vague impressions. First, there are whole areas of generally very high and generally very low density of finds in the 'off-site' sector, such that, at times, what would qualify as a 'site' in a 'low' area passes unnoticed, as a stretch of standard 'off-site' density in a 'high' area. In other words, the criterion for defining a 'site' has to be relative to its surrounding level of find-density, and not an absolute one, if absurd results are to be avoided. In case this sounds like a mere piece of sophistry, let me say that, once we tackle the problem of explaining how this scatter of 'off-site' artefacts came to be generated, and why it should vary so greatly in density, we shall thereby also be offering an explanation of the variations in prominence of the actual sites.

The second observation arising from the overall recording of finds will set us on the path towards tackling that problem. It is that, around almost every site, there is a clear 'halo' of finds, whose level of density is decidedly lower than that of the site itself, but equally higher than the standard 'off-site' level of the surrounding area. Typically, it is of a moderately high density in a generally 'low' area, and very high in a generally 'high' area. It usually extends over an area several times larger than the site itself, often on all sides, and regularly extends up-slope as well as down-slope from the site. Figure 9, which shows a

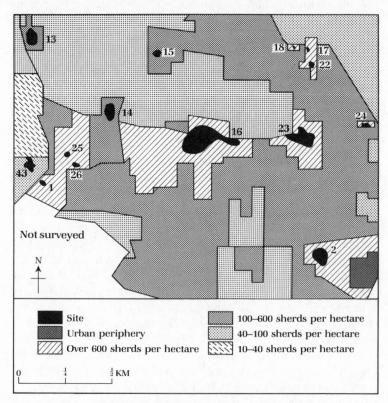

FIG. 9. A sherd density plot. The site of ancient Thespiai lies just off the bottom right-hand corner. In the northern sector, the ground slopes steadily from north to south; in the southern it is virtually level

detail from one of our overall density plots, is taken from an area of generally extremely high density, in the western approaches to the city site of Thespiai itself; it shows a scatter of small rural sites, each with its 'halo', standing out from the unusually high background density. What is the genesis of these haloes? Are they the product of natural processes, geomorphological or climactic, which have eroded or washed the material out from the nucleus of the site? Or are they rather generated by the endlessly repeated human activities of cultivation, with the plough carrying artefacts every year a little more or a little further, down to and beyond the present day? Any of these answers would reduce the archaeological significance of the haloes almost to vanishing point. But fortunately (as we see it) there are some clinching arguments that deny anything more than a minor contributory role to these incidental processes.

First, the observation already made: that the haloes run uphill as well as downhill from their sites, sometimes for fifty or a hundred metres. There is no mechanism whereby weathering could bring about this result, nor can the plough drag small sherds over such distances. Secondly, there is the fact that the background scatter of finds continues where the haloes leave off, often at a far from negligible level of density, and seldom dropping to the zero level. It is too much to believe that every one of these scattered artefacts has got there by means of random subsequent dispersal from the nearest site. Finally, the density of the off-site scatters, the strength of the haloes, and the frequency of the sites themselves are all features that are clearly correlated with each other. Where sites are thin on the ground, individual artefacts in general become correspondingly fewer.

There is one explanation which will answer the facts better than any of those so far considered, and we are inclined to accept it as having played the greatest single part.[9] It is that the activities of cultivation are indeed responsible for the spreading effect: but that these were activities contemporary with the occupation of the sites, and involved fertilizing rather than

---

[9] See J. L. Bintliff and A. M. Snodgrass, 'Off-Site Pottery Distributions: A Regional and Inter-Regional Perspective', *Current Anthropology*, 29 (1988), 506–13.

ploughing operations. The prime fertilizing agent in antiquity was animal manure, collected up from the locations where livestock was stalled or tethered, and then carried out to the fields by cart or on donkey- or mule-back. Since the livestock would normally be kept in or near structures where other activities took place, and since in antiquity many of these other activities involved the use (and therefore the breakage) of pottery, it would be a commonplace thing for rubbish including broken tile and potsherd to be mingled with the manure. When the manure came to be spread on the land, a certain proportion of sherds would go with it: even a single piece in every load of dung, repeated on each journey and augmented by occasional mishaps and deliberate disposals, would be enough to produce the pattern that we see. The relatively high density of the halo around the site itself would have several plausible explanations. Most importantly, there was a common practice of locating very intensive in-field cultivation, of the nature of gardening more often than agriculture, in the immediate vicinity of a town or farm. As far as accidental deposition goes, it is also true that every radial journey must pass through the immediate environs of the centre-point, and that the density of the radii is at its highest there.

If this explanation is adopted, it has some important implications. First, it means that the level of off-site density is an index of agricultural activity, and specifically of contemporary (that is, in this case, ancient) agricultural activity. The general areas of high density are areas of intensive ancient cultivation. Since in many cases these will coincide with areas of similar but later activity, we can see why it is that sites in the low-density area are not only few, but also 'weak', in the sense that their interior density of finds is low: there has not been the same frequency of farming operations over the subsequent centuries to bring their material to the surface. Next, and even more important from the viewpoint of the survey archaeologist's self-confidence, the presence of the haloes serves to confirm the reality of the sites, and indeed to show that they were foci of ancient agricultural operations. We shall see the significance of this last point in a moment.

We had been surveying in Boeotia for some seasons before all these points became clear to us. But meanwhile, virtually every intensive survey in Greece was replicating our main observation about site-distribution: that the scatter of rural sites reached, in the classical period, its highest peak of density at any point in the past, and that the great majority of these classical sites were very small. Not every survey, however, was reporting the same subsidiary features in the pattern: thus, the Nemea Valley Project finds that the haloes are much less distinct, while from the southern Argolid it is even stated that '. . . artifacts occurred for the most part in discrete clusters. . . . Few were found in between; there was little background scatter.'[10] These differences may perhaps in some way relate to the distinctive feature for which, above all, Boeotia was notorious in antiquity, the rustic preoccupations of its inhabitants.

It is time now to face the central question arising from this pattern of classical settlement: the interpretation of the sites and the explanation of their distribution. Let us first tabulate their salient features:

(i) *Small size.* In Boeotia, the typical classical rural site occupied less than one half of a hectare— that is, it measured 70 metres or less across—even after the effects of local dispersal had operated.

(ii) *Frequency.* With an overall density of above three per square kilometre, and an average size as described, it follows that the distance between any two classical sites was frequently of the order of 500 metres, and sometimes much less. They also occurred within this relatively short distance of the major city-sites.

(iii) *Foci of activity.* Almost every site was seen to have formed the centre of a sequence of agricultural operations, which we have identified as being primarily directed at fertilization.

(iv) *Characteristic finds.* These form the most fundamental feature of all, since it is by them that the site is recognized and defined as such. On classical sites, they normally consist of numerous roof-tiles; appreciable quantities of coarse or semi-coarse household pottery; lesser amounts of fine glazed pottery; occasional pieces of cooking ware, burned with use; and occasional pieces of building material.

[10] van Andel and Runnels (n. 5), p. 33.

It is worth mentioning here the interesting cases of a correlation in the *absence*, rather than the presence, of features (iii) and (iv) above. With a very few sites, there was neither the halo that we associate with cultivation, nor any sign of roof-tiles, while the pottery showed an unusual preponderance of fine painted ware. These sites we interpret as rural grave- or cemetery-sites; and their presence in the landscape is not without significance for the interpretation of the very much larger group of 'standard' classical sites.

We are now face to face with the question: what form of rural activity is most consonant with the small size, dense distribution-pattern, and indications of use that these sites present? Our hypothesis about the haloes implies the presence of farm animals, but are the other attributes compatible with structures that were *only* used as animal-shelters? Surely not. These attributes imply at least the intermittent use of the sites for human occupancy. The haloes suggest that they were used as bases from which cultivation was carried out, while the household pottery suggests that they were more than mere barns or implement-sheds. Further, the occasional interleaving of burial locations among these occupation-sites at a distinctly close human attachment to the land, and therefore presumably also to the structures on it.

So far, everything appears to point to one conclusion: our classical rural sites are isolated farmsteads. But no sooner is this hypothesis advanced than it is seen to bristle with difficulties. If these sites represent rural dwellings which were the only residence of the landowner in question, then why did such landowners choose to build them within very close distances of the city (particularly in the case of Thespiai, Fig. 9)? Everything that we know about Greek society, ancient and modern, suggests that the amenities of living in a town or village would be rated far too highly to be sacrificed merely in order to save oneself a ten- or fifteen-minute walk to one's land. Next there is the difficulty about Greek inheritance law—again, both ancient and modern. Since the practices of partible inheritance and dowry tend inexorably to result in the fragmentation of a given family's land-holdings, the construction of a farmstead on any one plot would be a questionable step in the first place, and a diminishing asset with the passage of every generation thereafter. The presumptive preference for living in the town would become a choice with no reasonable alternative.

Somehow, these a priori arguments have to be reconciled with the empirical findings from the evidence. There are at least possible ways out of the impasse. Thus the objection based on partible inheritance is at its weakest in the circumstances of a fresh apportionment of land—an event most familiar from the colonial context (as has been most strikingly confirmed by the survey evidence from Metaponto where, sure enough, rural farmsteads were regularly built[11]), but not an unknown phenomenon in the history of the cities of the Greek homeland. Is it possible that some such step was taken in classical Thespiai, and the other regions of Greece where a similar pattern of settlement is emerging? Again, human occupancy is not synonymous with owner-occupancy: many of these putative farmsteads could have been occupied by the eldest son, bailiff, or slaves of the landowner, without any visible difference in the material evidence. Nor should we exclude the possibility of second homes, expressly recommended by Plato in the *Laws* (745 E 4–5) and later disparaged by Aristotle in the *Politics* ($1265^{b}25$–6) on the grounds that they made life awkward. Both passages date from the general period under discussion, and each in a different way implies that its author was not unfamiliar with the idea of double residence.

The final alternative is to brazen the matter out, and state flatly that at certain periods Boeotians and other Greeks, in contrast to their modern descendants and in default of much other positive evidence to this effect, actually did prefer to reside permanently in farmsteads built on their lands, even when these lay quite close to their city. After all, Brasidas' acceptance into Amphipolis was preceded by his capture of 'the property of those Amphipolitans who were living all over the district' (sc. between the bridge over the River Strymon and the city; Thucydides 4. 103. 5) it is, I think, implied by the phrase 'all over' that they lived in homesteads rather than hamlets or villages. There are also Hellenistic inscriptions from Boeotia, and even from Thespiai itself, which testify to the existence of permanent buildings, of unspecified use but

[11] See e.g. D. Adamesteanu, 'Problèmes de la zone archéologique de Métaponte', *Rev. Arch.* 1967, 3–38, especially p. 26 and fig. 32.

appreciable monetary value, associated with land-holdings in the open country.[12] The history of the study of the ancient Greeks is littered with instances of the overturning of long-established dogmas, and it may be that this is another case in point.

It is at this stage in the argument that critics, and even uncommitted bystanders, invariably ask: 'Surely you must excavate one or more of your rural sites to get the answers?' To us, the belief that excavation would necessarily, or even probably, provide these answers appears ingenuous. We may note that even the admirably-conducted excavation of one such isolated house, above Vari in Attica,[13] did not reveal such farm equipment as would have proved its agricultural use, nor other evidence to determine what was the status of its occupants, nor whether it was their only home. Certain other questions, for example those relating to the size and plan of a small rural structure, would undoubtedly be answered by excavation; but here we can point to the practice of geophysical survey with the electric resistivity meter, which in favourable circumstances can provide an outline plan of buried buildings without disturbing the surface.

I turn now to the question of the distribution of these small sites, tentatively identified as farmsteads, in the classical period. Figure 10 covers the area walked to the end of our 1984 season only, which explains why it contains only just over 100 definite or possible sites of the period, plus nine others designated as 'uncertain' because the relevent evidence is imprecisely dated. The sites shown fall within a fairly long period, from the later Archaic to the early Hellenistic periods, roughly between the limits of 600 and 200 BC. Within this bracket, greater precision is possible in a large number of cases:[14] thus, for example, only a very few of the sites marked can be proved to have been in occupation before the fifth century, while the vast majority show clear proof of habitation in the fourth, which appears to mark the all-time peak of dispersed settlement in this part of Boeotia. This finding, naturally, still falls

[12] The references are collected in my *An Archaeology of Greece: The Present State and Future Scope of a Discipline* (Berkeley, 1987), p. 118 n. 4.

[13] J. E. Jones, A. J. Graham, and L. H. Sackett, 'An Attic Country House below the Cave of Pan at Vari', *BSA* 68 (1973), 355–452, esp. pp. 418–19.

[14] See the period tables in Bintliff and Snodgrass (n. 7), pp. 158–60.

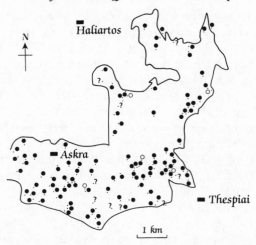

FIG. 10.   Distribution of sites found in 1979–1984. The survey was later extended to include the sites of Haliartos and Thespiai

well short of proving that this large group of sites was actually in *simultaneous* occupation: the difficulty is the acute shortage of imported or otherwise closely dateable pottery: so that, here again, excavation would not necessarily settle the matter.

The distribution shown in Figure 10 is dense, but it is not evenly so. There is a band of almost empty territory running across the middle of the map, roughly in the latitude of Askra. We tentatively identify this as the border-zone between the *chora* of Thespiai and that of Haliartos, two cities that at times pursued sharply contrasting policies. The line roughly coincides with the border as shown in Figure 8, which is based on the placing of this feature by Paul Roesch in his book on Thespiai,[15] even though Roesch himself notes the discovery of Thespian inscriptions (perhaps moved in more recent times) to the north of this line. The line runs closer to Thespiai than to Haliartos, reflecting the fact that the former city had ample territory to the south, whereas that of Haliartos was circumscribed on the north by the shore-line of Lake Copais (now drained). Here, however, our survey has shown that the size of

[15] P. Roesch, *Thespies et la Confédération béotienne* (Paris, 1965), p. 39, map 2, and p. 52 n. 5.

the lake in antiquity was appreciably smaller than in the nineteenth century, prior to the modern drainage. We have surveyed well within the nineteenth-century shore-line, and found that the background scatter disappears only at a line some way north of the shore as it appears in all classical atlases.

Only at one other period does the density of sites even approach that of the classical period, and this is in the 'Late Roman' epoch, a period whose limits are determined by certain classes of plain pottery, whose life is known to have extended from about AD 300 to 600. At that time, many of the actual sites of the classical period were reoccupied, suggesting that the ruined structures could still be rehabilitated, while a few new sites were added. This resettlement, however, is heavily concentrated in the putative Thespian territory; on the land of Haliartos, well under half the number of the classical sites was reoccupied, reflecting the fact that, since its destruction by the Romans long before in 171 BC, Haliartos had effectively ceased to exist as a city. More relevant to our purpose here, however, is the very much lower density of sites at other periods within the lifetime of the *polis*, whether in its independent heyday or in its survival as an administrative unit under the rule of the Hellenistic kingdoms and the earlier Roman empire.

Here I return to chronological sequence, and consider first the interesting pattern of settlement in the formative age of the later Geometric and earlier archaic periods (*c*. 800–600 BC). Today these centuries are widely recognized as having witnessed the rise of the *polis* system. Yet the distribution of sites does little to foreshadow the rural dispersal of the classical period. On Thespian territory, we have only the larger sites of Thespiai and Askra in occupation at this time, plus a very small number (three at the most) of the small outlying sites. But within the area of the actual city of Thespiai, the pattern is interesting: Geometric and earlier archaic sherds are concentrated not in one location, but in three or four, suggesting a cluster of villages rather than an urban nucleus, in a manner recalling Thucydides' description of Sparta (1. 10. 1). Haliartos, however, presents a different picture. In the city itself, Geometric settlement is apparently confined to the area of the later acropolis; but outside, there is a string of small sites, stretching from 500 to 2500 metres away to the east, whose occupation in each case begins not far from 700 BC. Clearly, contrasting patterns of *polis* growth could coexist, even in directly adjacent cities.

This general sparseness of early settlement, with the main centres as yet being few and of modest size, and very limited rural dispersal, suggests a further conclusion about at any rate some parts of Boeotia. The 'take-off' of population-growth, which in many parts of Greece leads to a sudden access of new rural sites, and signs of rapid growth at the major centres, within the eighth century BC, simply did not happen here. No such phenomenon is detectable until some two centuries later, with the evidence already considered for the later archaic and classical periods. Boeotia, on this evidence, developed late; and this may explain why it is not until the fourth century that we hear of its reputation for populousness, and see its fruits in the short-lived Theban hegemony in Greece.

The picture of a relatively late and steep growth to the classical peak is roughly mirrored by the decline that follows. In the later part of the Hellenistic period, the whole process goes into reverse. Of the large sites, Thespiai and Askra both shrink perceptibly in size, while Haliartos (for the historical reason that we have just seen, p. 130) is utterly deserted. Of the small rural sites, something over half are also abandoned at this time, in a few cases for ever, more often for a period several centuries long. The survivors among these rural sites tend to be larger ones. The opening centuries of Roman imperial rule bring no more than the slightest reversal of this decline, and it is not until the remarkable 'Late Roman' revival of the fourth and later centuries that rural settlement recovers; even then this is not fully matched in the main centres, and not at all in Haliartos. There is some literary and epigraphic evidence to substantiate this picture of agricultural depression (and even to suggest some of the reasons for it), which has been rehearsed elsewhere.[16] Our inclusion of the main city-sites within the area of the survey has borne fruit here by showing that the sequence of growth and decline in rural settlement, far from being compensated for it by the cities, is echoed by them: the picture is a total and consistent one.

---

[16] See Bintliff and Snodgrass (n. 7), pp. 145–7.

I turn finally to another conspicuously neglected feature of the Greek rural scene, the *komai* or second-order settlements, which held a dependent status within the territory of a *polis*. They must have been many times more numerous than the actual *poleis*; yet immeasurably fewer of them have been excavated or investigated in detail. Thespiai is altogether exceptional among Greek cities in having three *komai* firmly located with its territory—Askra, Eutresis, and Kreusis—not to mention the extremely controversial case of Leuktra, which may not have been the name of an actual settlement at all. In our survey area, there are a dozen rural sites which comfortably exceed the norm of size, and a range from one to five hectares in extent; in the classical period, at any rate, one would incline to interpret these as hamlets, villages, or in one case a probable sanctuary, rather than as very large farms. But at the end of our 1981 season, we located a site that was larger by a further order of magnitude: originally we reckoned its maximum size at 25 hectares, but intensive coverage of the site has reduced this figure to between 10 and 15 hectares, this peak falling as usual in the later classical period. It lay at an altitude of over 1,500 feet, midway up the Valley of the Muses, and we soon became convinced that it was none other than Askra, the home village of Hesiod (though even he does not unequivocally state that he lived *in* Askra, rather than in a nearby farm).

Once again, the arguments for the identification of the site have been set out by me elsewhere;[17] it should suffice to say here that the literary and epigraphical testimonia, coupled with the absence of any other plausible candidate within the area surveyed, make it difficult to avoid the conclusion that our site is indeed Askra. Hesiod's name was sufficiently closely associated with the place for his bones to be repatriated there, at some time after his death, only for them to be carried off to Orchomenos when (also at an uncertain date) Askra suffered the unreasonably cruel fate of being destroyed by its own *polis*, Thespiai.[18] Whatever the circumstances of this strange episode, it is enough to suggest that Askra was quite a substantial place at the time in question.

---

[17] 'The Site of Askra', in G. Argoud and P. Roesch (eds.), *La Béotie antique* (Colloques internationaux du CNRS, Paris, 1985), pp. 88–95.

[18] See Snodgrass (n. 17), p. 94 for the evidence for this episode.

The reconstruction of Askra's history by means of surface survey presents an obvious contrast, both in method and in the details of the results, with that of another Thespian *kome*, Eutresis, which was the scene of an excavation two generations ago;[19] but the two are alike in having had very interrupted histories. The Early Helladic period sees both sites quite densely settled, but thereafter the parallel breaks down, for Askra shows no sign of occupation for almost a thousand years after the very beginning of the Middle Bronze Age, while Eutresis continued to flourish. After the end of the Bronze Age, however, it is Askra which appears to have recovered first. Pottery of the later Protogeometric period, and of several phases of the ensuing Geometric, is found at Askra, but only in the same limited sector, towards the north-western extremity of the later classical site, as the Early Helladic settlement had occupied. This belated return to the very same location recalls the correspondence that we have observed between the classical Greek and Late Roman Settlements (p. 130); this time, the interval of apparent desertion is even longer, but the likelihood of visible ruins surviving is still considerable.

The small village of Hesiod's lifetime was to prosper for many centuries: the archaic and classical periods see a steady expansion southwards and eastwards, till the settlement bordered on the permanent watercourse that runs southwards to join the main river of the Valley of the Muses. It is possible that Askra, lacking the Mycenaean heritage of Eutresis, felt the need to protect itself with a fortification at some point in this period: round the southern perimeter of the site at its greatest extent, there runs a rather abrupt break of slope, with large blocks visible, embedded in the ground where it temporarily steepens; while within the area of the site itself, we found several worked 'polygonal' blocks, with curving joints between the corners, of a kind known from archaic to fifth-century walls in Boeotia. They seemed too massive to have belonged to house-walls. Outside the settlement to the west another feature was visible: a small enclosure or *temenos*, whose southern and eastern walls, with their junction, partially survive. Inside this the foundations of a rectangular structure can be made out,

---

[19] H. Goldman, *Excavations at Eutresis in Boeotia* (Princeton, 1931).

with four large oblong blocks set on end: these show exactly the same measurement in their long axis, and are clearly re-used. Presumably they were originally orthostats for the walls of a public building, up-ended at some later time to form a crude barricade. We interpret the whole as an extra-mural sanctuary.

In the Hellenistic period Askra begins to show signs of shrinkage, and a falling density of artefacts; but the site is still on too large a scale to be interpreted as another Hellenistic country house, of the kind found by the excavators of Eutresis outside their site. In earlier Roman imperial times, evidence of occupation appears to die away altogether, an observation that is important for the identification of the site, since Pausanias (9. 29. 1) reports that at Askra in his day there was 'a tower and nothing else to remember it by'. The 'Late Roman' era, however, sees a revival at Askra that is as impressive as at any of our sites: the settlement regains most of its former size, and densities are once again very high. Askra survived even the Early Byzantine period (the only epoch, after the opening centuries of the Iron Age, which finds our whole territory almost completely barren of settlements, whether large or small); and it lived on, by now much reduced in scale, through the later Byzantine centuries and the opening years of Turkish rule, before quietly reverting to the vineyard and arable cultivation which cover the site today. All this time, however, the nucleus of the settlement was gradually shifting south-eastwards, to the point where the original Early Helladic settlement and the final Byzantine-Turkish one have no over-lap at all. The occasion for the final desertion of the site may be sought in the reoccupation of another site a short way to the east ('Valley of the Muses 4') which, long deserted, resumes strongly in the seventeenth century of our era and was actually seen in occupation by at least one of the early travellers to Greece.

One other loose end remained to be tied up by the survey: the 'tower' mentioned in the Pausanias passage. There can be little doubt that this is the watch-tower of the fourth century BC which still crowns the hill immediately to the west of Askra, and gives it the name of 'Pyrgaki' today. Indeed, a too literal reading of Pausanias' text had led many earlier authorities to place the site of Askra on the barren, stony summit of this hill,

2,150 feet above sea-level. It now emerges that Pausanias used this tower merely as a loose landmark for the location of Askra. Nevertheless, the hill-top itself did present some interesting features: in the first place, it produced a little Mycenaean pottery, absent from the site below, which hinted that, once before, Askra had suffered desertion by reason of a move elsewhere. In later times, however, from the archaic to the Hellenistic periods, the hill probably served as an acropolis for Askra. There was some pottery from these centuries and, more substantial, the evidence of a wall-circuit enclosing an area of about one-third of a hectare around the fourth century watch-tower. Inasmuch as this fortification had at one point had to be re-aligned to make room for the tower, it could be shown to have been an earlier feature of the site, and its style of masonry is perfectly compatible with an earlier classical date. The size of the fortified enclosure would be appropriate to house the population of a *kome* in an emergency.

Our examination of Askra has, I think, revealed the strengths and weaknesses of survey in approaching a larger settlement; they differ from those which apply in the uncovering of the rural settlement pattern *in extenso*, and the limitations may be rather more apparent here. We have been able to place the site in its local context, that of the settlement and exploitation of the fertile valley in which it lies, at various periods of human history. We have charted the episodes of growth, decline, and shift in the history of the site, in general terms. We can explain its location in terms of water-supply, and general economic base (the finds include wine-jars and bee-hives), and we can detect one industrial activity in the making of pottery: 'kiln-wasters' (mis-fired vessels which would be discarded in the vicinity of the kiln) were found from both Hellenistic and, especially, the Late Roman periods. But we are unable to match the potential of excavation in answering more specific questions: was the settlement walled, and if so when? When did the historically-attested destruction of Askra take place? What exactly was the state of the site in Hesiod's lifetime, or at the moment of Pausanias' visit?

These conflicting thoughts may serve to epitomize the contribution of surface survey to the understanding of the Greek *polis* and its rural territory. Its strength lies in the diffuse nature of its results. As applied to the rural landscape *in extenso*, it is not merely the best, but at present virtually the only systematic source of fresh knowledge. Only the investigation of a sizeable stretch of territory can produce results that are truly representative. Next there is the indispensable function of site-location; and for this, too, a survey of some kind is necessary. Only in the final stage, when the focus narrows to single locations, and the interior of an individual site, does the picture presented by survey become blurred and relatively imprecise. But, for the present, it is the territorial aspect of the Greek city for which we stand in the greatest need of enlightenment; and for the immediate future, it is survey alone that can supply that need.

6

The Size and Resources of Greek Cities

LUCIA NIXON AND SIMON PRICE

MOST Greeks, particularly in the Aegean basin, lived in or were part of cities where political life, as the modern word shows, was based. Our topic is the size and resources of these cities. The data that we are working with, as outlined in section I, are the so-called Athenian tribute lists, which give an idea of allied contributions to the Athenian empire in the second half of the fifth century BC.

Most scholars have used the tribute lists to write the political history of the Athenian empire; we wanted to reverse this perspective and use the lists to examine the nature of the allies themselves. Much of our evidence about ancient Greek politics and urban activity, indeed about nearly all aspects of ancient Greek life, comes from Athens, which in many ways is a peculiar place. It is therefore useful to learn something about the rest of the Greek world during the time of Athenian ascendancy, if only as an alternative to almost inevitable Athenocentrism. We began by asking whether on the basis of the Athenian tribute lists we could say anything about the population sizes of ancient Greek cities, but we soon discovered that there cannot have been a simple relationship between population size and tribute payments. We therefore began to think about the likely criteria for assessment of tribute (section II) and have argued that the lists cast light upon the size and

We first gave this paper in the History Department at Manchester University, and then at the University of Newcastle upon Tyne; in both cases the audiences were extremely constructive. We are also most grateful to Michael Crawford, Chris Howgego, David Lewis, and Oswyn Murray, who commented on a subsequent draft; Amélie Kuhrt provided some valuable guidance. Nixon also wishes to thank Malcolm McGregor, whose graduate seminar introduced her to the Athenian tribute lists.

resources of Athens' allies (sections III and IV are detailed examinations of large and small contributors). The prevalent picture of Greek states is of a series of self-sufficient agricultural units; we wish to offer a corrective to this view (section V).

I

The figures to be analysed here were contributions to the alliance of Athens and her allies, an alliance formed immediately after the Persian Wars. As is well-known, it was more or less a naval alliance, whose aims were to protect Greeks from Persians and to liberate Greeks under Persian domination. It was at the outset an actively belligerent group which needed to maintain a considerable naval force. Allies could provide either ships or money in lieu.[1] The membership of the alliance was predominantly Aegean, as a map of the tribute payers used in our analysis illustrates (Fig. 11). Most of the members were coastal settlements, whose territories were bounded in places by foreign powers (Macedonia in the north; Persia in the east).

Much of our information about the alliance comes from the inscriptions originally set up on the Athenian acropolis and known as the Athenian tribute lists. This name, though conventional, is somewhat inappropriate. The inscriptions do not list the actual payments, but rather the $\frac{1}{60}$ part of each contribution (one *mna* from each talent), the quota reserved for Athena. Thus the tribute payments analysed by scholars of the ancient world are reconstructed by multiplying the sum dedicated to the goddess by 60.

There is an additional reason why the name 'Athenian tribute lists' is misleading. The amount represented by $\frac{1}{60}$ on the inscriptions is certainly not the total revenue received by Athens from her allies. First there was the provision of ships. In

---

[1] For the Delian League/Athenian Empire generally see B. D. Meritt, H. T. Wade-Gery and M. F. McGregor, *The Athenian Tribute Lists*, 4 vols. (Cambridge, Mass., 1939–53); R. Meiggs, *The Athenian Empire* (Oxford, 1972), whose tabulation of tribute payments we have gratefully used; P. J. Rhodes, *The Athenian Empire* (*Greece & Rome* New Surveys, 17; Oxford, 1985), is a helpful introduction; see also M. F. McGregor, *The Athenians and their Empire* (Vancouver, 1987).

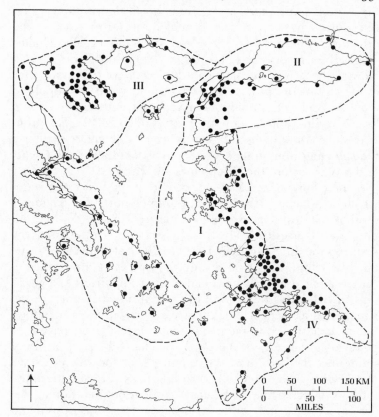

FIG. 11. States paying tribute to Athens, as for 441 BC: dotted lines mark the five assessment districts (adapted from N. J. G. Pounds, *Annals of the Association of American Geographers*, 59 (1969), p. 136, fig. 1)

our period there were still seven states supplying ships (five on Lesbos, plus Chios and Samos, though Samos was to lose her fleet after revolting). As it is likely that one trireme was the equivalent of a talent of tribute, the supply of ten ships by Mytilene in 428 BC 'in accordance with the terms of the alliance' is equivalent to ten talents of tribute.[2] Between them

[2] Thuc. 3. 3. 4. Cf. also the 55 ships of Chios and Lesbos in 440 BC (Thuc. 1. 116. 2, 117. 2) and their 50 ships in 430 BC (2. 56. 2). Athens could produce 100 ships in 440 BC (1. 116). Cf. S. K. Eddy, *Cl. Phil.* 63 (1968), 189-94.

these seven states made a massive contribution to the empire. But quite apart from the provision of ships, some states provided Athens with other goods or money. By chance Thucydides records that the loss of Amphipolis was a great blow to the Athenians 'particularly because of the importance of the city in the provision of ship timbers and the supply of money'. And yet Amphipolis never appeared on the tribute lists. Nor did Samos, made tributary in 439 BC.[3] Income from places like Amphipolis and Samos, from land confiscated from the allies and from other sources may have totalled 200 talents in the years before the Peloponnesian War.[4]

Some scholars have also suggested that the figures for states which do appear on the lists do not represent the full payments of those states; for example, Miletos, Naxos, Sestos, and Potidaia, all assessed below their presumed economic capacity, made up the difference by services to the fleet. Thus they argue that the tribute lists record only the quotas of the surplus of each year's tribute, after expenditure on squadrons and garrisons.[5] If true, this theory would make it impossible to use the tribute lists as evidence for the size and resources of the allies, but in fact the 'low' payments may be explained partly by political circumstances and partly by changes in the wealth of states since the Persian wars (the only period for which we have other evidence as a control). In addition, as at least some of the 'surplus' which came to Athens was spent on maintaining the fleet at Athens, it is difficult to account for the decision to dedicate to Athena only the quota of the 'surplus', rather than a quota of the entire tribute payment. The quota lists thus do provide evidence for the total assessments of those states which appear on them.

We have looked at the figures for the year 441 BC, as they constitute the best preserved set of statistics for a single year, before the Peloponnesian War (54 entries are completely preserved). During the war, there are more completely preserved figures for 429 BC (62), but by then the relative stability of pre-war assessments has ended and it is not safe to supply

---

[3] Thuc. 4. 108. 1; 7. 57. 4.
[4] Thuc. 2. 13. 3; below, p. 164.
[5] A. French, 'The Tribute of the Allies', *Historia*, 21 (1972), 1–20; R. K. Unz, 'The Surplus of the Athenian *phoros*', *GRBS* 26 (1985), 21–42.

figures from other years. The year 441 BC is the second year of the fourth, normally four-year, assessment period (the series began when the treasury was moved from Delos to Athens in 454 BC). When figures for 441 are not preserved we have supplied figures from the same assessment period when possible, or from other periods down to the war, whose overall rate of assessment is the same as the fourth period; doubtful figures have been excluded. There are usable figures for 205 states, out of the 248 states who appear at some time on the lists. The Appendix (below, pp. 166–70) tabulates the sums paid; round brackets indicate that the sum is restored, square brackets that the name of the state is restored, and a combination that both are restored. We have labelled all the figures 'as for 441 BC', because we have used both preserved and supplied figures. As there were 6000 drachmae in a talent 1.3000 means 1½ talents.

The inscriptions record the contributions as ethnics, normally of individual states paying for themselves, but sometimes of individual states or groupings paying for a number of communities; the payments of 'the Milesians' at this time included Leros and Teichioussa, while 'the Keans' paid for all four states on the island. The ancient headings preserved on the stones divide the contributors into five districts: Ionian, Hellespontine, Thraceward, Karian, and Island. It should be noted first that all five districts include islands; the heading Island really means the Cyclades plus Euboea, Aegina, Lemnos, and Imbros. Secondly, we have taken places as they were assessed in 441 BC, so Keos for example counts as one contributor, even though it had four *poleis* (one of which, Koressos, paid separately at least once).

It is clear that the Athenian tribute lists provide an excellent opportunity for some kind of scholarly analysis. After all, they give detailed, if sometimes fragmentary figures for nearly thirty years, which provide a particularly intimate glimpse of the workings of an ancient empire. And yet scholars have generally used these figures to reconstruct only the political history of the empire or the history of individual states. There has been relatively little analysis of the overall pattern of the figures.

Figure 12 tabulates numbers of contributors and amounts paid, in half talents. When Pounds considered the relationship

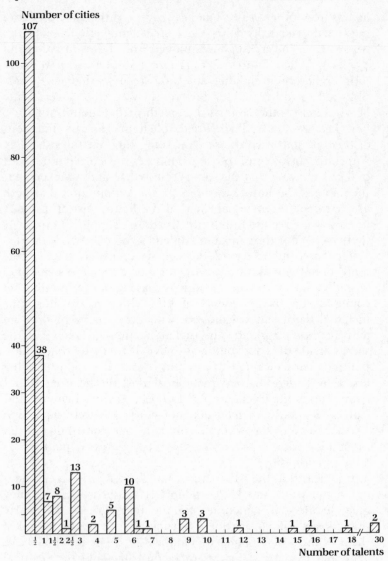

FIG. 12. Range of tribute payments in half talents, as for 441 BC

between contributors and payments, he said that the evidence of the quota lists suggested a truncated primate system, i.e. that the Delian League was dominated by Athens, whose own contributions we do not know, though the implication is that it was massive compared to most payments.[6]

Figure 12 shows that numerically there was a broad base of support for the Delian League; most of the contributors (71 per cent of 205 contributors in 441 BC) paid one talent or less. Though they pay in total only 14 per cent (55 out of 407 T), it is clear that they were important to the League in the sense that they were worth collecting from.

It follows then that 86 per cent of the total revenue for 441 BC is contributed by 29 per cent of the contributors, those paying more than one talent. Hereafter we shall refer to these two groups as 'big spenders' and 'little spenders', with reference both to their level of tribute payments and to their resources. However, the omission of the ship-states and places like Amphipolis means that the balance between big and little spenders was somewhat different from that suggested by the quota lists, and Pounds' 'truncation' should be understood to exclude other cities in addition to Athens.

And now for the figures themselves. Most systems of counting can offer a reasonable degree of precision, but often there will be a certain amount of 'rounding-off' so that some numbers are more important than others. When we are dealing with a monetary system these important numbers can often be predicted from the units of currency. The British decimal currency is based on a pound of 100 pence, with smaller coins of the following fractions: $\frac{1}{100}$ $\frac{1}{50}$ $\frac{1}{20}$ $\frac{1}{10}$ $\frac{1}{5}$ $\frac{1}{2}$; 2, 5, and 10 are important numbers in this system and prices tend to be rounded off in such units. The Greek counting system was not decimal but sexagesimal (with 6000 drachmae to the talent), i.e. based on the much more flexible figure of 60, which is divisible by more numbers than 100 is. Athena's quota of $\frac{1}{60}$ is a strong reminder of this.

Because of the attempts to use the tribute lists in a very

---

[6] N. J. G. Pounds, 'The Urbanization of the Classical World', *Annals of the Association of American Geographers*, 59 (1969), 135–57, pp. 144–5; id., *An Historical Geography of Europe 450 BC–AD 1330* (Cambridge, 1973), pp. 27–36, 60.

precise way, for example to work back to population sizes, one would need to check the assessments to see if they reveal any 'rounding-off'. In Figure 12 there are suggestive peaks at 3 talents and 6 talents, and it is also worth noting that most payments over 6 talents are divisible by 3 and/or 6.

Figure 13 gives a detailed breakdown of assessments of one talent and below. The biggest peak is at $\frac{1}{6}$ of a talent (1000 drachmae); in fact nearly 20 per cent of all contributors pay this amount. There are other, lower peaks at $\frac{1}{3}$, $\frac{1}{2}$, and (lowest of all) $\frac{2}{3}$ of a talent, before a surge up to one talent. This suggests that there was a certain amount of sexagesimal rounding off when assessments were determined. Great caution should therefore be used in trying to correlate these contributions with precise numbers of anything, whether people or commodities. It is better to think in terms of orders of magnitude rather than absolute figures.

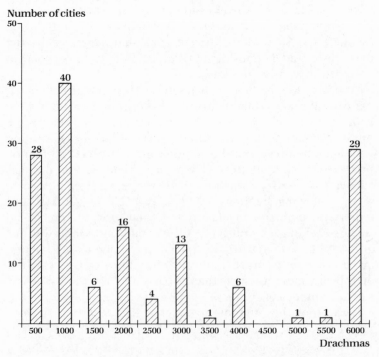

FIG. 13.   Tribute payments up to one talent, as for 441 BC

II

The principles on which the tribute was assessed are not explained in the so-called tribute lists and have to be inferred, partly from the range of tribute payments and partly from external evidence. Any light cast on these principles will enable us to use the tribute lists to sketch some general characteristics of the allies. The Athenians in establishing the original assessments had no Greek models on which to draw; this was the first time that a Greek state had sought to raise revenues on a regular basis from its allies. Within individual Greek states, however, there was a range of taxes both on production and on the sale or movement of goods.[7] In the sixth century Athens herself had a 5 or 10 per cent ($\frac{1}{20}$ or $\frac{1}{10}$) tax on grain production, while at Kyzikos there were (in addition to taxation from which an individual might be granted exemption) taxes on the sale of horses and slaves, a tax on the use of the public scales, a tax on the movement of goods by boat, and a mysterious quarter tax. And the system of taxation in the last quarter of the fourth century is revealed in the treatise ascribed to Aristotle, Book 2 of the *Oeconomicus*. The first part of the book distinguished between royal, satrapal, civic, and personal revenues; about civic revenues it says: 'Here the most important source of revenue is from the peculiar products of the territory, next comes tax from market and points of transit; finally, that from ordinary taxes' (1346[a]). The fourth-century author assumes automatically that states do have revenues at their disposal, drawn from a wide variety of sources. Such taxes, we shall argue, were taken into account by Athens in assessing the level of tribute payments, but the variety of local taxes did not offer a simple principle of assessment.

The obvious non-Greek model was the Persian system.[8] The

[7] H. Francotte, *Les Finances des cités grecques* (Paris, 1909), pp. 11–22, 57–61; A. M. Andreades, *A History of Greek Public Finance* (Cambridge, Mass., 1933), pp. 126–61; A. H. M. Jones, *The Greek City* (Oxford, 1940), pp. 244–6. H. W. Pleket, *Epigraphica* i (Leiden, 1964), gives many of the documents.

[8] F. Altheim and R. Stiehl, *Die aramäische Sprache unter den Achaimeniden* (Frankfurt-am-Main, 1963) i. 109–181; O. Murray, 'ὁ ἀρχαῖος δασμός', *Historia*, 15 (1966), 142–56; C. Tuplin, 'Achaemenid Administration', in I. Carradice (ed.), *Coinage and Administration in the Athenian and Persian Empires* (BAR International Series, 343; Oxford, 1987), pp. 109–66; cf. also the calculations of R. Descat, 'Mnésimachos, Hérodote et le système tributaire achéménide', *REA* 87 (1985), 97–112. Herod. 5. 42. 2 on Ionia.

Persians had after all ruled a fair proportion of the Athenians' allies, and the Persian tribute assessments were known and remained in force through the fifth century. In the Persian empire raising tribute seems to have been the responsibility of individual satraps, who adopted a variety of means, depending in part on the organization of their area. In Ionia after the Ionian revolt the satrap measured the territories of the cities and levied tribute on that basis; that is, the tribute was assessed on cities, which then had to devise their own ways of raising the money. Athens too assessed cities, but the name changed (from *dasmos* to *phoros*) and the basis of the assessment was broadened from the simple extent of a territory.

There are a number of different criteria which the Athenians could have used in assessing tribute payments. The first is population. A study of agricultural yield in one area of the empire, the Chalcidice, argued from modern yields to ancient population size, and from that to the average tribute assessment per head of population, but this argument is based solely on the agricultural potential of the region.[9] The population case has, however, now been argued in more detail: the Athenians, it is suggested, assessed tribute in direct proportion to the number of citizens, which means that one can read off population figures from the tribute payments; 3000 dr. implies 400 adult male citizens (AMC), a talent 800 AMC, and so on.[10] This was indeed the hypothesis which we set out to test in this paper; but we have decided that the assumption of a direct relationship between tribute and population does not work.

Tribute assessments cannot have been proportional to precise figures for total population. Reliable figures even for British history are difficult to obtain. The earliest census in Britain was in 1832; before that figures can only be suggested by extrapolation backwards using parish records as pegs, and

---

[9] Pounds (n. 6). The rate of tribute per square kilometre of land farmed in the Cyclades in 1961 has been calculated: C. Renfrew and M. Wagstaff, *An Island Polity: The Archaeology of Exploitation in Melos* (Cambridge, 1982), p. 280, table 20.2. This shows no stable ratio, and in any case land farmed in 1961 is a very insecure guide to ancient practice.

[10] E. Ruschenbusch, 'Tribut und Bürgerzahl im ersten athenischen Seebund', *ZPE* 53 (1983), 125–43; id., 'Die Bevölkerungszahl Griechenlands im 5. und 4. Jh. v. Chr.', *ZPE* 56 (1984), 55–7; id., 'Die Zahl der griechischen Staaten und Arealgrösse und Bürgerzahl der "Normalpolis"', *ZPE* 59 (1985), 253–63; cf. also id., 'Modell Amorgos', *Hommages à Henri van Effenterre* (Paris, 1984), pp. 265–71.

the process involves an increasing loss of precision.[11] But in the Greek world there were no complete censuses from which we might be able to extrapolate. Even in Athens, whose size might have generated a need for censuses, the only one of which we hear was probably designed to count the number of hoplites, and 'censuses' in other Greek states seem to have been similarly limited in their objectives (adult males for military service).[12] This contrasts with the Roman practice: Augustus in his *Res Gestae* (8. 4) can record that in AD 14 4,937,000 citizens were registered. In the fifth century BC no Greek state could lay claim to such exact counting.

Greek states were, however, able to quantify their potential military forces. From the Homeric Catalogue of Ships (*Iliad* 2. 484–877) to the battles of Lade and Salamis (Herodotus 6. 8; 8. 43 ff.) and beyond, it was possible to identify the naval strength of individual states. States also knew approximately what their total muster of hoplites was, and some, as we saw, even took steps to count the figure precisely. Since the paying of tribute to Athens was originally established as an alternative to supplying ships and their crews, there might be some connection between assessments and the number of adult male citizens. But the connection cannot have been a simple one. Though a talent seems to have been the equivalent in tribute for one trireme, the assessment of the majority of states which paid less than a talent must have been on some other basis. This cannot have been simply population. The range of tribute payments is too large to be in direct proportion to population. They go from 100 dr. up to 18 talents (even if we set aside the 30 T payments of Aegina and Thasos); that is a difference of 1,080 times. If one arbitrarily assigns 30 AMC to the bottom payer, then the top payers have AMC populations of 32,400. And this is plainly absurd. So absurd, in fact, that those who make population the sole criterion for tribute assessments are forced to argue that at least some of the bigger contributors are 'anomalies'; they pay over the odds (as calculated on their populations) because of some special local factors. But the doctrine of 'anomalies' is essentially arbitrary.

[11] E. Wrigley and E. Schofield, *The Population History of England, 1541–1871* (London, 1981), esp. pp. 455–7.

[12] M. H. Hansen, *Demography and Democracy* (Herning, 1986), pp. 28–36. The Athenian 'census' in 322/1 BC counted only those with a certain property qualification.

The second possible basis for assessment was land, which was the criterion used by the Persians in reassessing Ionian tribute after the revolt. But there were no maps for the Athenians to use to establish the areas of individual states, nor is there any evidence for a special (and very time-consuming) survey of civic territories. Indeed a comparison between the amounts paid and the size of territories shows the difficulty of this theory. If one takes the islands without mainland territory, whose extent is thus easy to determine, there is no simple ratio of tribute to area of territory. Two examples will make this clear. Aegina and Thasos both pay 30 talents, and yet the former is 83 and the latter 380 square kilometres. Thasos is nearly five times as big as Aegina and yet pays the same amount of tribute, and the ratio is even worse if Thasos had some mainland territory at this time.[13] Or take Naxos and Paros. Naxos (430 km^2) is just over twice as large as Paros (196 km^2), and yet it is Paros who pays more tribute: 18 talents to Naxos' 6.4000 talents. Paros thus pays more than six times as much tribute as Naxos per square kilometre. The overall range of ratios of drachmas per square kilometre is from Karpathos (6.64) to Aegina (2168.67). Even if one excludes these two extremes, the range is still from Syros (11.76) to Paros (551.02). The basis of Athenian assessments cannot have been the size of territories.

Assessment of the products of the land is, however, much more likely. Since the time of Solon, the Athenians themselves had been accustomed to assess the wealth of individuals in terms of their production of grain (or grain-equivalents). Taxes on agricultural production (e.g. wine, oil, beehives) were widespread, and states also raised taxes on the sale of pasturage rights. That is, there was a great variety of land uses to be taken into account, and in addition the sea was a valuable asset. Iasos, for example, was said to have infertile territory, but to gain great wealth from fishing; and various states sold fishing rights.[14] The quality and variety of land types and of the products of land and sea, rather than simple territorial extent, could be taken into account in tribute assessments.

[13] T. J. Figueira, *Aegina* (Salem, 1981), pp. 38–9, 122–5, notes that Pounds's arguments do not work.
[14] Strabo 14. 658 c; cf. below on Byzantion, pp. 153–4.

Products from under the soil are also important. Some states were blessed with gold or silver mines (cf. below on Thasos), copper mines (Chalcedon), *miltos* (cf. below, on Keos), marble quarries (Thasos, Paros). The high assessments of these and other states can be explained in part by the fact that Athens took into account revenues derived from these natural resources.

States also raised revenues from sales taxes on markets and from taxes at points of transit, especially harbours. By the end of the fifth century harbour taxes were levied everywhere. When in 413 BC the Athenians abandoned tribute and went over to taxing the allies directly, they attempted to impose 5 per cent $(\frac{1}{20})$ harbour dues throughout the empire.[15] Mechanisms for levying harbour dues, probably at the lower rate of 2 per cent $(\frac{1}{50})$, must already have been in place—a measure more appropriate for trading states than for self-sufficient agrarian communities. As most of the allies were on the coast, it is likely that any assessment would have taken this tax into account.

Finally one might mention booty. Raids on rich Persian strongholds were important in the early years of the empire, and booty provided wealth for Athens and her allies down to the mid 460s. But such 'income' was a consequence of the financial structure of the empire and can hardly have formed a basis for tribute assessments; and in any case by the period of the stable empire, with which we are primarily concerned, booty was of little significance.

In short, there was no one criterion underlying the tribute assessments, and any attempt to establish a simple correlation between tribute and population or tribute and agricultural land is doomed to failure. The key, in our view, lies in the concept of resources, a flexible term which covers all the possibilities just discussed.[16] After all, taking a cut of local resources was the best way to maximize tribute income in an

---

[15] Thuc. 7. 28. See further G. E. Bean, *JHS* 74 (1954), 97–105, and H. W. Pleket, *Mnemosyne*, 11 (1958), 128–35.

[16] This is also the argument of H. Schaefer, 'Beiträge zur Geschichte der attischen Symmachie', *Hermes*, 74 (1939), 225–64, reprinted in his *Probleme der alten Geschichte* (Göttingen, 1963), pp. 41–81. The first attempt on these lines was K. J. Beloch, *Griechische Geschichte*, 2nd edn. (Strasburg, 1916) ii.2, pp. 356–71. E. Cavaignac, *Population et capital dans le monde méditerranéen antique* (Strasburg, 1923), p. 39, argued that the tribute corresponded to 10% of landed revenues.

equitable manner. This is indeed exactly the basis on which Aristides is said to have made the first assessment. According to Plutarch (*Aristides* 24. 1), the allies asked Aristides to take into account their territory and their revenues in setting reasonable and feasible levels of tribute. By having both territory and revenues taken into account Athens' allies hoped for a more equitable basis for tribute than that used by Persia. Plutarch, writing almost 600 years later, cannot be pressed too hard, but fortunately his statement is supported by other, better evidence. When the Athenians decided to raise drastically the overall level of tribute in 425/4 BC, the decree of the assembly included the following provision: 'The council shall deliberate in full session and continually in order that the assessment may be effected, unless the people vote otherwise. They shall not assess a smaller tribute for any state than it was previously paying, unless owing to the poverty of the territory they cannot pay more'.[17] 'Poverty of the territory', not 'number of citizens', is conceded as a mitigating factor.

The same principle was at work when the payments of individual states were varied. A state could appeal to an Athenian court to reduce its level of tribute; from 430 BC there was a special court for this purpose. In one case we can see the actual arguments used. Fragments of a speech on behalf of the island of Samothrace happen to survive. The speech argues that the inhabitants had never really wanted to live there, but had ended up on Samothrace after being exiled from Samos in the sixth century. More to the point, 'the island we inhabit, as you can clearly see even from a distance, is steep and rugged. Only a small part of it is useful and workable; the rest is useless, though the island is small.'[18] Similarly when a cleruchy (or settlement of Athenian citizens) was established on the island of Andros in 450 BC, the amount of tribute payable fell from 12 to 6 talents. The number of Andrians remained the same, but their land had been drastically reduced by the confiscation of land for the cleruchs (who did not pay tribute). In other words, their resources had been cut.

---

[17] ML 69. 19–22.

[18] Antiphon fr. 51 Thalheim. *ATL* (n. 1) iii. 77–81, discusses the court, and Meiggs (n. 1), pp. 525–6, summarizes the variations. On the more radical theory of French and Unz see above, p. 140.

Resources formed the basis for tribute assessments because tribute was not a tax but, in principle at least, a payment in place of military (and especially naval) service. The payments had to be related to the military potential of states in terms both of citizen population and of wealth derived from all possible sources. Such wealth consisted not simply in the agricultural production of farmers, but derived from other products of the land and sea, and from the exchange of goods and services both within individual states and between states.

How individual states paid their assessments is an additional and obscure issue. The orthodox view is that the burden of paying tribute fell principally on the rich; in other words, that the conversion of resources into cash had already been carried out by individual members of the state, especially the upper class.[19] The responsibility for collection of tribute fell perhaps on the wealthy men appointed as tribute collectors, but there is hardly any evidence that the wealthy had normally to pay the tribute themselves directly. And in states which provided ships rather than money, we do not know that the ships were financed by the wealthy through a system of trierarchies. It may rather be that at least some states paid tribute out of their own revenues, that is, resources were converted into cash via taxation. If this happened, the burden of tribute payments lay heavy on the rich only indirectly: they contributed a greater proportion of the indirect taxes from sales of their agricultural surplus. From Athens' point of view it did not matter how the tribute was raised, any more than it did to the Persians. Indeed the freedom to choose different means of raising the money was implied by the original autonomy of the allies. But whether the connection between resources and tribute was through the rich or through local taxation, the implication of our hypothesis about resources and revenues is that there is no need to see some or all of the big contributors as anomalies, paying a level of tribute out of proportion to their population. Every state was, in principle, paying in proportion to its resources.

[19] Rhodes (n. 1), p. 37. ML 68 (426 BC) shows that the Athenians ordered cities to appoint local collectors; but the fact that local tribute *collectors*, perhaps forming *synteleiai*, were chosen from the rich (Antiphon frs. 53, 56 Thalheim) does not necessarily support the orthodox view that it was the rich who paid. Thucydides 3. 19 suggests that the rich may have been liable for supplementary payments in wartime.

Let us now move on to more detailed analysis of the states paying tribute. We have divided them into two groups: big spenders paying more than a talent a year, who form 20 per cent of the total, and little spenders paying a talent or less. They will form the subject of the next two sections.

III

According to our hypothesis, the big spenders in the Athenian tribute lists are contributors with a particularly rich resource base, which could be taxed by regular civic taxes. Case studies of three big spenders from three of the five districts of the Athenian empire will give some indication of their available resources and how they were exploited: Thasos (Thraceward district; 30 T); Byzantion (Hellespontine district; 15 T 4300); and Keos (Island district; 4 T).

The island of Thasos was conveniently located in terms of ancient trade routes;[20] with or without its mainland territory, it had a wide range of resources which could have been taxed. Wine and vinegar were important products of the territory; a text of 480/470 BC shows that the trade in both these products was already carefully regulated by the state; by the end of the fifth century very detailed regulations for wine were in force.[21] But the most valuable Thasian products were those of the mines. The gold mines on the mainland, according to Herodotus (6. 46), had yielded 80 T per year; these were lost to Thasos after the revolt of 465. On the island itself, however, there were gold, silver, lead, and copper mines, which also

---

[20] J. Pouilloux, *Recherches sur l'histoire et les cultes de Thasos* i. (Études Thasiennes, iii, Paris, 1954), pp. 10–12.

[21] Text of 480/470 BC: Pouilloux (n. 20), pp. 37–45; cf. stamped amphorae of similar date, *Archaeological Reports for 1987–88*, p. 63. Late fifth-century text: the date of purchase for wine was strictly regulated with respect to the time of the harvest; sales of wine in pithoi were valid only if the pithoi were specially stamped; Thasian ships could not bring 'foreign' wine into the area between Athos and Cape Paxi; wine could be sold only by the vessel, whether large or small (amphora, pithakne, pseudo-pithos), but not in part quantities; wine could not be watered (*IG* XII Supp. 347, 1 and 2, with Pouilloux, pp. 41, 130–1). M. I. Finley offers a critique of some of Pouilloux's other views on Thasian trade in 'Classical Greece', *2nd International Conference on Economic History, 1962* (Paris, 1965), i. 28–32.

yielded a substantial (if lesser) sum. [22] Metal was thus always available for minting, and late archaic coins of Thasos have been found as far away as Egypt, the Levant, and Magna Graecia.[23] No coins were struck between 463 and 435, but the Thasians were still prosperous enough to construct the sanctuary of Soteira and the first version of the theatre in the second half of the fifth century.[24]

Byzantion paid 15.4300 talents, that is 15 plus $\frac{2}{3}$ plus $\frac{1}{20}$.[25] The first ancient author to comment in a general way on the resources of Byzantion is Polybius, who mentions its position (excellent for trade), the fertility of the land, and fishing.[26] An even later source says that gold and copper were locally available (Dionysius Byzantinus, fr. 48); if so, it is even more peculiar that Byzantion did not mint its own coinage until the end of the fifth century.[27] For more information about the

---

[22] Meiggs (n. 2), pp. 570–8. Mines on the island: L. A. Muller, *BCH* supp. 5 (1979), 315–44; J. des Courtils, T. Koželj, and A. Muller, *BCH* 106 (1982), 409–17. The marble quarries at Aliki are said to have been exploited from the sixth century onwards (*Aliki* i (Études Thasiennes, ix; Paris, 1980), p. 125), and therefore count as another product of Thasian territory. But there is no direct evidence that this was a taxable resource. On Thasos generally see R. Osborne, *Classical Landscape with Figures: The Ancient Greek City and its Countryside* (London, 1987), pp. 76, 79–81, 89–92, 104–8.

[23] Pouilloux (n. 20), pp. 51–5.

[24] Gap in coinage: *Guide de Thasos* (Paris, 1968), p. 186. New construction: Y. Grandjean, *Recherches sur l'habitat thasien à l'époque grecque* (Études Thasiennes, xii, Paris, 1988), p. 476.

[25] Cf. S. K. Eddy, 'Some Irregular Amounts of Athenian Tribute', *AJPhil.* 94 (1973), 47–70. He suggests that such irregular amounts, in Attic terms, when divisible by 24 and paid by Hellespontine states, were possibly paid in Kyzikene electrum staters: he does not, however, comment specifically on Byzantion. Cf. also Meiggs (n. 1), pp. 442–3. It is worth noting that some 'regular' amounts from the Hellespont are also divisible by 24: Kyzikos itself nearly always paid 9 T, or 2250 staters. Why 4300 dr. were added to this amount is not clear, but the total then works out to 3939 $\frac{1}{6}$ staters.

[26] J. Dumont, 'La Pêche du thon à Byzance à l'époque hellénistique', *REA* 78/9 (1976/7), 96–119, suggests that by the third century BC fishing was a highly commercialized, professional industry; Athenaeus quotes a poem saying that Byzantion was the mother of tuna, mackerel, and swordfish (3. 116 c). T. Gallant, *A Fisherman's Tale: An Analysis of the Potential Productivity of Fishing in the Ancient World* (Miscellanea Graeca, 7; Ghent, 1985), pp. 35–8, argues that the supposed importance of bluefin tuna in the economy of Byzantion is a particularly good example of how the importance of fishing for ancient economies has been exaggerated. But other parts of the Propontis are known to have been involved in the fishing industry, e.g. the Roman colony at Parion; see J. and L. Robert, *Hellenica*, 9 (1950), 80–97; L. Robert, *Hellenica*, 10 (1955), 272–4. And the late archaic–classical coins of Kyzikos teem with tuna: see H. von Fritze, *Nomisma*, 7 (1912), 1–38, with pls. 4 and 5 (coins of Group III, 475–410 BC).

[27] But O. Davies, *Roman Mines in Europe* (Oxford, 1935), pp. 237–8, says that gold is not likely to occur in the locality, and that he could detect no ancient workings of

resource base we return to the *Oeconomicus*, which discusses political administration in the abstract, as we saw above, and gives a series of specific examples in roughly chronological order. The section on Byzantion relates to the mid fifth century BC. According to the *Oeconomicus* (1346^b), the inhabitants of Byzantion were financially embarrassed and therefore set about raising money, using some familiar methods. For example, they privatized sacred enclosures by selling them off; they sold shop-space for city merchants; they sold the rights for fishing and salt-collecting. They sold permits for conjurors, diviners, and drug-sellers, and they demanded a third of their takings. They established an official city exchange, and forbade any other sale or purchase of currency. Apparently even citizenship could be bought for 30 minas ($\frac{1}{2}$ talent) by those who had only one citizen parent.

Fish and salt count as products of the territory, but all the other examples given here can be classified as new taxes, and regulations for ordinary day-to-day activities. These measures were presumably added to the usual taxes, including harbour dues.

Our third case study is the island of Keos, about one third the size of Thasos.[28] It lies off the coast of Attica, but had no territory there in the classical period. Keos had four *poleis* (usually assessed together) and paid 4 talents; Koressos, when paying separately, paid 2.1500 talents. Koressos, Karthaia and Ioulis all minted their own coins between 480 and 465 (or possibly 450), but only in denominations of less than a

copper there. As for the coins of Byzantion, W. Newskaja, *Byzanz in der klassischen und hellenistischen Epoche* (Leipzig, 1955), p. 51, says that the lack of earlier coins is due to the widespread use of Kyzikene staters, but that minting began at the end of the fifth century BC because of a great increase in Byzantine trade. For the circulation of Kyzikene staters, see M. Laloux, 'La Circulation des monnaies d'électrum de Cyzique', *Revue Belge de Numismatique*, 117 (1971), 31–69; and cf. above, n. 25. E. Schönert-Geiss, *Die Münzeprägung von Byzantion* (Berlin–Amsterdam, 1970), does not discuss the late beginning of Byzantine coinage.

[28] Archaeological surveys on Keos: H. Georgiou and N. Faraklas, 'Ancient Habitation Patterns of Keos', Ἀριάδνη, 3 (1985), 207–66; E. Mantzourani, J. Cherry, and J. Davis, Ἀρχαιολογικὴ ἔρευνα ἐπιφανείας στὴ νῆσο Κέα', Παρουσία, 4 (1986), 189–201; G. Galani, L. Mendoni, and Kh. Papageorgiadou, ''Επιφανειακὴ ἔρευνα στὴν Κέα', Ἀρχαιογνωσία, 3 (1982–4 [1987]), 237–44; L. Mendoni, 'Surface Survey in Kea', Acts of the Aegean Islands Colloquium, Canadian Archaeological Institute at Athens, Athens 1987, to be published as a BAR vol., eds. C. and H. Williams; *Archäologischer Anzeiger* (1987), 728. See also Osborne (n. 22), pp. 60–2.

drachma in value; Koressos alone minted later in the fifth century (*c*.420).[29]

How could such a small island reach this level of prosperity? There are two possibilities, in addition to the usual agricultural ones, which are limited by the island's size. First, Keos was a source of several minerals, notably high quality red ochre (*miltos*), which was used to paint trireme hulls and had pharmaceutical applications as well. A fragmentary inscription from Athens dated to the mid fourth century BC records the restoration of the Athenian monopoly of Kean *miltos*.[30] Thus *miltos* could be described as a 'strategic material' of no small economic importance for the people controlling its distribution.

Second, the island has an excellent double harbour at Vourkari and Korissia in the bay of Aghios Nikolaos.[31] It is perhaps worth noting that both the major Bronze site at Aghia Irini and the only Kean *polis* to pay separately (Koressos) are located around this bay. Thus the wealth of Keos could have come from taxes on *miltos*, a product of its territory, and from harbour dues.

By checking texts such as the *Oeconomicus* we could put together patchy information about the ancient resources of some twenty of our sixty big spenders; but such information is not complete, nor is it consistently reliable for the fifth century. In any case, we wanted an independent way of getting an overall picture of the range of resources for *all* contributors. After all, how real is our division into big spenders of over one talent and little spenders of one talent or less?

Naturally, we thought of material indications that might help us, for example, expensive building projects normally financed with public funds. And indeed, in addition to Athens itself, two contributors built treasuries at Delphi (Poteidaia and Siphnos); at least two had new temples (Ephesos, Samos); and a number had archaic city walls (e.g. Eretria, Paros,

---

[29] E. S. G. Robinson, 'The Athenian Currency Decree and the Coinages of the Allies', *Hesperia*, supp. 8 (1949), 324–40, at p. 329; E. Erxleben, 'Das Münzgesetz des delisch-attischen Seebundes II', *Archiv für Papyrusforschung*, 20 (1970), 66–132, at pp. 71–2.

[30] Tod ii. 162. All of the *miltos* was to go to Athens and only on authorized ships; a 2% tax was levied when it reached Piraeus.

[31] *Admiralty Handbook for Greece* iii (London, 1945), pp. 444–5 and pls. 142–3.

Samothrace, and Thasos). But of course not all sixty big spenders, still less our total of 205 contributors, have been archaeologically investigated by excavation or survey.

There is, however, one class of material evidence which survives well and can be roughly dated, whose provenance can normally be accurately determined, and whose potential usefulness for investigating economic activity has yet to be fully exploited, and that is coinage. Coinage is in fact the only evidence that offers a picture as comprehensive as that of the tribute lists themselves.

The study of fifth-century coinage is not without difficulties. Few of the mints have been comprehensively studied in the past fifty years, and even for these there are very few independent dating criteria. Dates of issues can thus float around two decades or more. The problem is further complicated by the Athenian decree banning (among other things) local coinages.[32] The dating of this decree itself floats between the early 440s and the 420s, and the efforts of numismatists have been directed at dating breaks in minting, in order to date the decree, rather than at the significance of the general pattern of minting. None the less, that such a decree was thought necessary shows at least the symbolic value of local coinage.

If one sidesteps the problem of the decree and the date of interruption (if any) in the allies' coinage, an interesting general picture emerges. Sixty of our 205 allied states issued coins at some point between 480 and 400.[33] The correlation between this list and the levels of tribute payments is very striking. No fewer than forty of the sixty minting states paid more than one talent in tribute; in other words, most of the big spenders (67 per cent) had their own coinage. To this figure could be added four of the seven ship-contributors, who also had their own mints.

Only twenty minting states paid a talent or less, i.e. 14 per cent of the little spenders. Three of them mint only in the first fifteen years of this period. Most of the little spenders made only scanty issues, and only in denominations of less than a drachma. Only the coinage of Neapolis par' Antisaran seems at

---

[32] D. M. Lewis, 'The Athenian coinage decree', in Carradice (n. 8), pp. 53–63.
[33] See Robinson and Erxleben (n. 29). Their evidence has been modified slightly in the light of more recent research.

all substantial. In general the little spenders that do mint produced relatively few coins, of low value.

The mints of the big spenders vary considerably in their output. One way of estimating this is by counting the number of dies used to strike the coins. The figures that follow take into account the survival rate of the coins, and give the hypothetical total number of obverse dies.[34] We have also, for the sake of comparability, converted this hypothetical number into a figure for striking Athenian drachmas (that is, we have multiplied the number of tetradrachm dies by the weight of the coin and divided by the weight of the Athenian drachma). Die studies have been carried out for only a small proportion of the mints in this category, but they seem to show a correlation between the level of tribute payment and the size of coin issues. Abdera (15 T) and Ainos (10 T) struck far more then Teos (6 T) and Knidos (3 T). Abdera gives over 490 dies, Ainos 270, Teos 118, and Knidos 39. For comparison, ship-supplying Samos gives a figure of 140. The bigger the spender, the greater its minting output.

One might object that this is hardly surprising: big spenders had to mint more coins in order to pay the tribute, so that coin issues are not an independent index of local resources. But in fact the absence of mints in some of the big spenders (e.g. Byzantion, 15.4300 T; Perinthos, 10 T) shows that local mints were not necessary for tribute payments. Tribute could be paid either in bullion or in the coinage of another state. The evidence of hoards supports this argument. For example, the plentiful (if largely unpublished) Aeginetan coinage found in hoards shows that much of the coinage went into general

---

[34] For die studies see: J. M. Balcer, 'The Early Silver Coinage of Teos', *Schweizerische Numismatische Rundschau*, 47 (1968), 5–50; J. P. Barron, *The Silver Coins of Samos* (London 1966); H. A. Cahn, *Knidos, die Münzen des sechsten und des fünften Jahrhunderts v. Chr.* (Berlin, 1970); J. M. F. May, *Ainos, its History and Coinage* (London, 1950); May, *The Coinage of Abdera* (London, 1966). Though other methods might prove superior on better data, we have here calculated the die numbers on the method expounded by G. F. Carter, in W. A. Oddy (ed.), *Scientific Studies in Numismatics* (British Museum Occasional Paper, no. 18; London, 1980), pp. 17–29. Coins below a drachma in value have been ignored in the calculations. We have not attempted to calculate the number of *coins* issued, but we hope that dies produced on average roughly the same number of coins. However, output per die may have varied greatly between cities, and depended partly on the size or relief of coins and other technical reasons.

circulation, not into the coffers of Athens. Those states who chose to mint coins did so primarily for their own purposes.

What are we to make of this correlation between large contributions and the presence of mints? Sometimes, especially in Macedonia and Thrace, output is connected with the presence of a mine, but this is only to be expected, since mines were a very important part of local resources.[35] Even more important, some big spenders who did not have their own mines (e.g. Aegina) did mint, and in large issues. But some big spenders, such as Byzantion, used the coinage of other states and thus did not mint their own coins. That is, resources did not necessitate coinage, but coinage does imply local resources, and the general pattern of minting thus permits inferences about the scale of resources of individual minting states. Thus, the allies who issued more than a few coins did have something in common, solid local prosperity often deriving from the full range of resources and revenues available to ancient states. And the big spenders are not anomalies, even the biggest of them. They are big spenders because they have big resources, of various kinds, in various combinations, and therefore constitute a group of their own.

IV

We move on now to consider those who paid a talent or less, some 71 per cent of the total. The chart (Fig. 13) shows three peaks, one at the one talent level, and three more at the bottom of the scale. Thus no fewer than 52 per cent of the total pay half a talent or less, and 33 per cent pay 1000 dr. or less.

Can we say anything about the resources and even population of this category of allies? This is the claim of Ruschenbusch, which we would like to test. Even given our argument about resources as the basis for tribute assessments, it might be possible to establish a correlation with population. Two assumptions would be necessary: first, that the agricultural hinterland of these states is their basic resource; there will be

---

[35] The output of mines may have affected the production of coins even in the Roman imperial period when one would have expected a closer correlation between output and expenditure: G. D. B. Jones, *JRS* 70 (1980), 161–3, on Rio Tinto mines.

revenues from other sources (e.g. harbour dues), but if these are small and vary in proportion to the hinterland, then they could be ignored for this purpose. The second assumption is that equal areas of agricultural hinterland will support the same numbers of people. This is somewhat fragile as yields vary with the fertility of the soil, but perhaps one could hope that the variations can be allowed to average out. If these two assumptions are accepted, then the tribute payments of the lower payers represent *relative* population figures, ranging sixty-fold within this category of spenders.

Can we convert these relative figures into absolute ones? Can we say what size of population it took to pay 1000 dr. of tribute? People have made attempts to do this, which we are about to discuss, but we shall argue that our data do not permit the kind of quantification which has been attempted. There are two main ways in which one might achieve absolute figures: individual ancient references to numbers of citizens, and modern population figures.

First, ancient references. Assembly voting figures might seem an attractive source of information. Decrees inscribed on stone sometimes refer to the number of votes cast in the passing of the decree. For example, a Hellenistic inscription from Keramos in Karia records that 9[5]1 votes were cast in favour, and 44 (or [1]44) against a particular motion.[36] But we are reluctant to make much use of such figures. We have voting figures for only five of the 205 allied states, and for most of those we have only a single figure. How can we tell whether the 1100 votes cast at Keramos represent a typical turn-out, or what proportion of the citizen body they represent? We can at most say that this gives a minimum figure. From only one state, Kolophon, do we have a series of figures, six in all, and their range is worth noting, from 903 to 1,342; the highest figure is almost 40 per cent larger than the smallest.[37] But in any case the figures all come from the Hellenistic period, and by that time the classical city of Kolophon had been abandoned and reoccupied. Thus we cannot use voting figures as absolute pegs for the relative

[36] E. Varinlioğlu (ed.), *Die Inschriften von Keramos, IK* 30 (Bonn, 1986), 9.

[37] W. Blümel (ed.), *Die Inschriften von Iasos, IK* 28 (Bonn, 1985), 81; Hiller von Gaertringen (ed.), *Inschriften von Priene* (Berlin, 1906), 57; L. Robert, *REA* 65 (1963), 307 = *Opera Minora Selecta* iii. 1502; *ZPE* 13 (1974), 113.

sizes of the tribute payers.[38] The other type of ancient references consists of statements about the number of citizens in particular places. Such references are, sadly, very rare, and also rather difficult to interpret. Ruschenbusch has laid much emphasis on the case of Iasos, which he claims had 800 citizens. In fact our sole source does not say this. The historian Diodorus Siculus noted that towards the end of the Peloponnesian War the Spartan Lysander stormed the town and 'put to the sword the males of military age (*hebontas*), 800 in number, and sold the children and women as booty' (13. 104. 7). But those fit and of military age would be only a fraction of the adult males, which could mean that there were 1000 AMC. In any case, we cannot know that Lysander was successful in killing all of this category, nor that the figure for those killed is accurate. Iasos paid one talent to Athens, but we cannot use this piece of evidence to argue that one talent represents 800 AMC.

Secondly, scholars have tried to use modern census data to establish population numbers for ancient city states. In fact the modern figures cannot be used in this simplistic manner. Statistics are available for the island members of the Athenian empire from 1879 onwards (or 1920 or 1922 for some of the eastern islands),[39] but there is no reason to suppose that this period represents the same level of population as in the fifth century BC. Certainly in the fifteenth and sixteenth centuries AD many of the islands were abandoned, and at the start of the nineteenth century their populations were still fairly low. There was growth during that century, but their history in this century is complicated by migration to Athens and emigration from Greece. In any case there is no real correlation between levels of tribute and population in, for example, 1879. The population (in thousands) per talent ranges from 0.38 to 162. Even if one excludes the extremes, the range is from 1 to 6.3.[40]

---

[38] Tribute payments of Teos (6 T) and Abdera (15 T) were in proportion to the quorum of their courts (200 and 500 respectively; D. M. Lewis, *ZPE* 47 (1982), 71–2), but this may be a coincidence. The only other comparable figure, from Thasos, gives 30 T and a quorum of 300.

[39] E. Y. Kolodny, *La Population des îles de la Grèce: Essai de géographie insulaire en Méditerrannée oriental* (Aix-en-Provence, 1974).

[40] Renfrew and Wagstaff (n. 9), p. 277, perform the calculation using population figures for 1961; though their Table 20.2 shows a range of talents per thousand people from 0.18 to 4.22, they assert that this is a 'surprisingly good correlation' (but see above, n. 9). Similarly M. Zahrnt, *Olynth und die Chalkidier* (Munich, 1971), p. 137,

In other words, modern population figures do not establish a reliable basis for estimating ancient populations.

Ruschenbusch argued, on the basis of his population figures, for naval consequences of their size: many states could not man even one trireme, and therefore had always to pay tribute.[41] But on our view his population figures are unreliable, and refer anyway only to citizens (non-citizens could presumably have been used to man a trireme). The real disincentive was cost: if a trireme was the equivalent of a talent in tribute, it was always to the financial advantage of a majority of the allies to contribute money rather than ships.

Is it perhaps possible to suggest any orders of magnitude, rather than precise figures, for the populations of the states paying a talent or less? Unfortunately not, because trying to determine orders of magnitude still presupposes a constant relationship between amounts paid and numbers of people. The little spenders no doubt had small populations, but one cannot quantify them.

This is all rather negative, but we may be able to make some progress on the resources of those states paying a talent or less, though they are difficult to depict as clearly as those of the big spenders; they are among the lesser-known Greek states of the period. One might be tempted to assume that the little spenders fit the model of agricultural self-sufficiency, while the big spenders were anomalous exceptions. But this would be an arbitrary assumption. To take one area, the lower Maeander flood plain, as an example, the five states which pay tribute in this period all fall in the category of little spender: Mydones (Amyzon) 1500 dr.; Parpariotai 1000 dr.; Thasthares 500 dr.; Myessioi 1 T; Prianes (Priene) 1 T. Alinda paid up to 2 T in the first assessment period but then dropped out. A regional study has shown that the first three, inland and upland people, appeared to have few natural resources: the soils of the area are of very low fertility, offering little opportunity for agricultural

argues for a close correlation between tribute payments and population size in the 1960s, but his calculations are faulty; the ratio is not 0.26 to 0.36, but 0.145 to 0.483, which is much less impressive. J. M. Cook, *The Troad* (Oxford, 1973), p. 383, assumes that the census figures of 1940 for the Troad correspond to the fifth-century figures (giving 4000–4500 people per talent of tribute), but this is an arbitrary assumption.

[41] Cf. E. Ruschenbusch, 'Das Machtpotential der Bündner im ersten athenischen Seebund', *ZPE* 53 (1983), 144–8.

exploitation. A temple was, however, built at Amyzon in the early fifth century (to be rebuilt by satrapal money in the fourth century). But Alinda on the lower mountain slopes dominating the fertile lowlands was assessed at the high rate of 2 T. And by contrast the then coastal cities of Myus and Priene enjoyed considerable prosperity in the sixth and early fifth centuries, providing three and twelve ships respectively in the Ionian revolt; Myus also had two temples by the early fifth century. Both states benefited from good agricultural land and from their access to the coast; indeed at that time Myus had a good harbour and was renowned for its fish.[42]

In the fifth century these little spenders on the border of Ionia and Karia give some hint of a range of natural resources, from the poor soils of upland Karia, suitable perhaps for grazing, to the more fertile agricultural land of Alinda, to the coastal sites of Myus and Priene. Obviously, none of the little spenders had major resources like gold or silver mines, but equally they were not all simple farming states. Rather, there was a continuous range of cities and their resources from Thasthara to Thasos.

V

This picture of the size and resources of states has implications for our appreciation of the two main attempts to theorize about the classical Greek state: Plato's *Laws* and Aristotle's *Politics*. Plato's *Laws* are an attempt to produce systematic rules for every aspect of an ideal state, including its size. Plato decided that there should be 5,040 citizens (737 E–738 B; 771 A–C). An odd figure, but chosen by Plato for abstract mathematical reasons: it is the product of multiplying the numbers from one to seven, and is also divisible by eight, nine, ten, and twelve. Plato in certain parts of the *Laws* takes over current practice from Athens or other states; with the number of citizens he is led by theoretical principles to offer a number

[42] R. T. Marchese, *The Lower Maeander Flood Plain: A Regional Settlement Study* (BAR International Series, 292, Oxford, 1986). Unfortunately, both Myus and Priene were ruined in the course of the fifth and fourth centuries by the progradation of the Maeander delta. Priene was refounded on a new site in the mid-fourth century, and Myus was incorporated into Miletos by the end of the third century BC.

much larger than that possible for the majority of tribute payers.

Aristotle in the *Politics* criticizes Plato for suggesting such a large number of citizens: 'We cannot overlook the fact that such a number would require the territory of a Babylon or some other huge country' (1265^a13), and Babylon 'it is said, had been captured for two whole days before some of the inhabitants knew of the fact' (1276^a29), and thus can hardly be counted a real *polis*. Aristotle's own view is that the greatness of a state is not to be measured by the number of citizens. If there are too many people, it can hardly have a true constitution. 'Who can be the general of this excessive population? And who can be their crier, unless he has Stentor's voice?' The optimum size of a *polis* is thus 'the largest population consistent with catering for the needs of a self-sufficient life, but not so large that it cannot be easily surveyed' (1326^{a-b}). As for resources, Aristotle argued that the ideal state should have a territory that produced all kinds of crops and thus ensured a maximum of self-sufficiency; the city itself should be conveniently located for the receipt of crops, of timber, and of any similar raw material for any manufacturing processes the land may possess (1326^b26). But he recognized that his ideal *polis* could not be self-sufficient: 'If these evil consequences [of too many foreigners in the state] can be avoided, it is obviously better both for ensuring an abundance of necessities and for defensive reasons that the state and its territory should have access to the sea ... People must import the things they do not themselves produce, and export those of which they have a surplus' (1327^a18; cf. Plato, *Republic* 370 E–371 A). Indeed in normal states the people might be engaged in all sorts of different work: agriculture, crafts, commerce, buying and selling, the sea (1291^b17). The balance between the different types of employment varied from place to place, but two of his five categories presuppose connections between *poleis*.

The Athenian tribute lists have been described as 'an economic document perhaps without parallel in its scope and geographical precision for any other early empire'.[43] We have analysed data for 205 different states in this paper, but of course this number is only a fraction of the total number of

---

[43] Renfrew and Wagstaff (n. 9), p. 277.

Greek *poleis* at this period. The total number has been esti-
mated at around 700, though not all of these will have existed
in the fifth century.[44] How far is it possible to generalize from
our sample of 205 states to the total number? The first
limitation of the sample is the truncation of important members of the Athenian empire and of Athens herself. The seven
ship-allies of this period and Amphipolis should be added to
the category of big spenders, and Athens' own resources place
her in the same category. Athenian internal revenues at the
time of the outbreak of the war may have been about 400
talents per year, equal to the sum then accruing as tribute,
though less than the 600 talent total which Thucydides esti-
mated as the total revenues of Athens from her allies.[45] Athens
could also raise substantial sums by direct means. In 428 BC an
exceptional capital levy on Athenian citizens raised 200 talents,
and in the fourth century a new property levy could raise 60
talents per year, at a rate of 1 per cent of the 6000 talents of
declared property.[46] Athens in peacetime could raise more than
twice the largest sum contributed by her allies. Her resources
far outstripped those of any of her allies.

Even when the resources of the ship-allies and Athens have
been added to our data, there remains the question of the
representativeness of the sample. Its coverage is mainly
Aegean, and consists mainly of coastal states. The economic
basis of all the allies was a combination of agriculture, other
local resources, and nautical trade.[47] Inland states excluded
from our sample will have been more dependent on their own
local resources, with fewer possibilities for trading connections.[48] Unfortunately, there is no straightforward way of

[44] Ruschenbusch (n. 10); he omits consideration of the Greek states in Asia Minor in
the Roman period, which numbered over 300.

[45] 2. 13. 3, with Xen., *Anabasis* 7. 1. 27.

[46] Thuc. 3. 19. 1. G. E. M. de Ste. Croix, 'Demosthenes' τίμημα and the Athenian
Eisphora in the Fourth Century BC', *Classica et Mediaevalia*, 14 (1953), 30–70. It is not
possible to assess Athens' own input exactly, but she could send an expedition of 100
ships in 440 BC. Expenditure on buildings seems to have been high. The Parthenon, its
cult statue, and the Propylaia may have cost up to 2000 talents: ML pp. 164–5, revising
R. S. Stanier, 'The Cost of the Parthenon', *JHS* 73 (1953), 68–76.

[47] H.-J. Gehrke, *Jenseits von Athen und Sparta: Das dritte Griechenland und seine Staatenwelt*
(Munich, 1986), assumes this in his classification of the resources of Greek states, but
his set of case studies does not generate any general conclusions.

[48] The Akarnanians made peace with Sparta in 388 BC because they knew that since
their cities were inland they could not replace corn destroyed by the Spartan army:
Xen., *Hell.* 4. 7. 1.

assessing the range of resources of states (coastal or inland) which did not pay tribute to Athens. But our observation of a correlation between a high level of tribute payment with the minting of coins could be taken further. Coins offer the only set of data which are both well-preserved and geographically extensive. Analysis of die numbers for states not part of the Athenian empire would bridge the gap between our analysis of the tribute payments and a broader picture of the size and resources of classical Greek states.

The tribute lists are indeed an extraordinary source for understanding the ancient Greek city. At the lower end of the scale, paying a talent or less, were communities with limited resources and fairly small populations. For the bigger spenders one cannot offer population figures, but one can emphasize the range of their resources, from over 1 to 30 talents. This gives a new slant on the Greek city. The study of classical Greek history necessarily focuses on Athens and Sparta, but even when scholars recognize the exceptional nature of these two states, they are too ready to lump together everywhere else as normal states. One can (with Ruschenbusch) produce an ideal type 'normal *polis*', but this concept disguises the range of variation that actually existed.

Averaging out the differences between states creates a false picture of the political and economic relationships between them. The theory of 'peer polity interaction' as applied to archaic Greece is unenlightening. Within a common Greek culture interaction and rivalry did indeed exist, but the individual states were not peers and the theory is thus too crude. The differences of size and resources described here show that there was a hierarchy among *poleis*, although the levels of that hierarchy have not yet been clearly defined.[49] But even a high-ranking *polis* could not ward off the Persians on its own; only if *polis* resources were pooled could the Aegean city states protect

---

[49] A. Snodgrass, 'Interaction by Design: The Greek City State', in C. Renfrew and J. F. Cherry (eds.), *Peer Polity Interaction and Socio-Political Change* (Cambridge, 1986), pp. 47–58, applies the theory; and cf. Gehrke (n. 47). One might rather apply the theory of Early State Modules to the Athenian empire, on which see C. Renfrew, 'Retrospect and Prospect', in J. L. Bintliff (ed.), *Mycenaean Geography* (Cambridge, 1977), pp. 108–21. Central Place Theory, applied to Roman Britain by I. Hodder and M. Hassall, 'The Non-Random Spacing of Romano-British Walled Towns', *Man*, NS 6 (1971), 391–407, is not applicable here. The theory cannot easily be amended to handle the distortions caused by coastal access.

themselves effectively. It is against this background that the concept of political autonomy belongs.

The modern preoccupation with economic self-sufficiency also needs rethinking.[50] Scholars are agreed that the relationship between an urban centre and its countryside is crucial, but the consequent emphasis on individual *poleis* tends to preclude investigation of the economic relationships between states. As the prevalence of harbour taxes shows, inter-state trade was routine and few *poleis* were truly self-sufficient. We should not confuse the Aristotelian ideal of autarky with economic reality. Study of the Athenian tribute lists offers the basis for a rather different picture: the diversity of sources of wealth in the Aegean, the consequent interconnections between states, and the range of sizes and resources of Greek cities.

Appendix

Sums paid in Tribute, as for 441 BC

Round brackets indicate that the amount paid is restored, square brackets that the name of the contributor is restored, and a combination that both are restored. The superscript ᵐ indicates that the city minted coins at some point between 480 and 400 BC.

I. IONIAN DISTRICT

Talents
9	Kumaioi
8	
7	[(Eruthraioi)ᵐ
6	(Ephesioi)ᵐ Teioiᵐ
5	(Milesioi)ᵐ
4	
3	
2	Phokaiesᵐ

---

[50] Thus M. I. Finley, *The Ancient Economy*, 2nd edn. (London, 1985), pp. 123–39, tends to treat states which were not self-sufficient as exceptional.

Talents

1.3000	Kolophonioi^m, (Klazomenioi)^m
1	Nisurioi, (Muessioi), [(Prianes)], (Pugeles), Lebedioi, Hairaioi, Murinaioi, Hessioi^m
5000	
4660	Gargares^m
4000	Oinaioi ex Ikarou, (Polichnaioi), Maiandrioi
3000	Thermaioi ex Ikarou, Marathesioi
2000	Noties
1000	(Isindioi), (Boutheies), Grunees, (Elaiitai)^m, [(Pitanaioi)]^m
500	Dioseritai, (Sidousioi), [(Asturenoi Musoi)]
100	(Pteleousioi), [(Elaiousioi)]

II. HELLESPONTINE DISTRICT

15.4300	Buzantioi
14	
13	
12	Lampsakenoi^m
11	
10	Perinthioi
9	Kuzikenoi^m, Khalkedonioi^m
8	
7	
6	
5	Selumbrianoi^m
4	Abudenoi^m
3	Kebrenioi^m, Prokonnesioi^m
2.5280	Tenedioi^m
2	Arisbaioi
1	Skapsioi^m, Dardanes^m, Cherronesitai
5000	
4000	
3000	[Elaiousioi]
2000	Neandreia, Parianoi^m, Artakenoi
1000	Lamponeia^m, Berusioi hupo te Ide, Sigeies, Perkosioi, Paisenoi, Alopokonnesioi, Kianoi, Astakenoi^m, Didumoteichitai, Daunioteichitai, ?Eurumachitai
500	Gentinioi, [(Palaiperkosioi)], Limnaioi, Madutioi, Sestioi, Priapes, Daskuleion, Turodiza
400	Azeioi
300	Harpagianoi, Neapolis

III. THRACEWARD DISTRICT

Talents

30   Thasioi[m]

15   Abderitai[m]
14
13
12
11
10   [(Ainioi)][m]
9
8

7
6   (Potideatai)[m], (Skionaioi)[m], (Toronaioi)[m], (Samothrakes)[m]
5   (Sermulies)
4
3   Peparethioi, (Akanthioi)[m], (Aineiatai)[m]
2   (Singioi), Spartolioi, (Olunthioi)[m]
1.3000   Maronitai[m]
1   (Aphutaioi)[m], [Dies apo tou Atho], [Thussioi], (Strepsaioi), (Argillioi)
      5000
      4000   Sanaioi, Stolioi, (Mekubernaioi)
      3240   Bergaioi
      3000   (Neapolitai Mendaion apoikoi), (Galepsioi)
      2400   Asseritai
      2000   (Aigantioi), [Olophuxioi], (Skablaioi), [(Dikaia par'Abdera)][m]
      1500   (Ikioi), (Haisonioi)
      1000   [Skiathioi], (Thrambaioi), [Skapsaioi][m], [Pharbelioi], (Phegetioi), [Stagiritai], Neapolis par'Antisaran[m]
       700   (Othorioi)
       500   Sermaioi, Chedrolioi

IV. KARIA

10   Lukioi
9
8

7
6   Lindioi[m], Ielusioi[m], Kameires[m]
5   [(Kooi)][m]

Talents

4	
3	[(Knidioi)]^m, [Phaselitai]^m
2.4200	Kherronesioi^m
2	Kullandioi
1.4000	Halikarnassioi^m
1.3000	Kaludnioi, Astupalaies^m, [Keramioi]
1	Latmioi, Pedases, Iases, [(Suangeles)], (Madnases), [(Kindues)], Hudisses, Kaludnes, Telemessioi
5200	Mulases
4000	
3000	(Peleiatai), [(Termeres)]^m, [(Kares hon Tumnes arkhei)], Kedriatai apo Karias, [(Kaunioi)], Pasandes apo Kaunou, (Telandrioi)
2500	Kasolabes, Huromes
2100	Khalkitores
2000	Pladases, Idumes^m, Kurbissos, Khioi Kares, Khalkeiatai, Krues apo Karias
1500	[(Mudanes)], Siloi
1200	Humisses
1060	Hublisses
1000	Bargulies, Lepsimandioi, Parpariotai, [(Narisbares)], Thudonos, Killares, Erines, [Karpathioi], [Arkesseia], Purnioi, Karbasuandes para Kaunon, Kodapes, Polikhnaioi Kares
500	[(Mundioi)], Karuandes, Pargases, [(Thasthares)], Naxiatai, Auliatai Kares, Brukountioi
400	Kudaies
100	[Pedies en Lindo]

V. ISLAND DISTRICT

30	Aiginetai^m
18	(Parioi)
6.4000	[(Naxioi)]
6	(Andrioi)
5	(Karustioi)^m
4	(Keioi)^m
3	[Eretries]^m, [Khalkides], [(Kuthnioi)], [(Siphnioi)]^m, Hephaisties hoi en Lemno
2	(Tenioi)

Talents
1.3000   Murinaioi en Lemno
1   [(Stures)], [(Seriphioi)], (Mukonioi), Imbrioi
  5000
  4000
  3000   [(Iatai)]
  2000   (Athenai Diades), (Dies apo Kenaiou)
  1000   Grugkhes, Hestiaies, Surioi
   300   [(Rheneies)]

7

Private Space and the Greek City

MICHAEL JAMESON

How space is conceived of and how it is used are artefacts of particular cultures, in much the same way as are relations between the sexes or systems of ritual or of social stratification. Examination of space in this sense can tell us much about the culture as a whole, not least about those aspects which are taken so much for granted that they are rarely expressed verbally. The present essay examines private space, in the form of house and land (*oikia kai chorion*, in the common Greek phrase) as opposed to public space, such as the religious sanctuaries and the secular meeting-places, markets and fortifications of the city-state. In social terms, the distinction between town and country, residence and cultivated land, may be less significant than that between private and public.[1]

For the reconstruction of a balanced picture of space in a historical civilization, the evidence of the surviving texts must be combined with that of the physical remains and with other indications of spatial division and organization. The literary evidence is patchy—we lack, for instance, along with much else, an explicit description of a Greek house; the Roman

[1] For the general approach used here, see Susan Kent (ed.), *Domestic Architecture and the Use of Space: An Interdisciplinary, Cross-Cultural Approach* (Cambridge, forthcoming), to which I have contributed a more detailed article ('Domestic Space in the Greek City-State', ch. 7). Cf. R. J. Lawrence, 'Domestic Space and Society: A Cross-Cultural Study', *Society and History*, 29 (1982), 104–30, for an examination of two contemporary cultures. The study of Greek houses and town plans has received an infusion of rich information and stimulating discussion, together with magnificent graphics, from Wolfram Hoepfner and Ernst-Ludwig Schwandner, and their colleagues, authors of *Haus und Stadt im klassischen Griechenland* (*Wohnen in der klassischen Polis*, i, Munich, 1985). Another recent publication, Fabrizio Pesando, *Oikos e Ktesis: La casa greca in età classica* (Perugia, 1987), completed unfortunately before the appearance of *Haus und Stadt*, gives greater attention to the literary evidence, on which it is imaginative if not always convincing; cf. also his more comprehensive book, *La casa dei Greci* (Milan, 1989).

Vitruvius' account (6. 7) corresponds to no known classical or Hellenistic structure. When we compare what information we have with that from archaeology difficulties emerge. If each type of evidence is given its due and not interpreted so as to conform to the other, they may seem at first sight to contradict each other, but further consideration shows them, rather, to be complementary. Physical remains for the most part do not reveal the use or the social value of the spaces they define, while the texts show distinctions which have no standard physical correlate. On the other hand, regular patterns in the physical ordering of space offer significant information which is obscure or invisible in the texts.

As an example of the problems encountered, let us take the notion, firmly attested in literature, of distinct men's and women's quarters in the private house. With the exception of a single, clearly specialized room (usually referred to in modern discussions as the *andron*), archaeology provides no criteria for assigning different parts of the house to the two genders, and our texts, in turn, provide no indication of a standard location for the two types of space. It is quite arbitrary to mark one or more rooms on a ground plan as male or female.[2] The Greek house was centred on a courtyard and in most cases cannot be divided into a front and back. A second floor was neither universal nor, when it occurred, restricted to use by the women of the household, as is sometimes assumed. Important as the distinction between male and female areas was, it did not affect directly the actual planning and building of houses. We will return to this problem when we examine the house in greater detail.

Private space consists essentially of the agricultural fields in the territory of the *polis* and the houses in compact settlements, whether in the central town of the city-state or in smaller towns

[2] Susan Walker 'Women and Housing in Classical Greece: The Archaeological Evidence', in Averil Cameron and Amélie Kuhrt (eds.), *Images of Women in Antiquity* (London, 1983), pp. 81–91, illustrates male and female quarters from a unique house at Dystos in Euboea which is divided in two by a courtyard. Cf. J. V. Luce, 'The Large House at Dystos in Euboea', *Greece and Rome* 2nd ser., 18 (1971), 143–9, and Th. Wiegand, 'Dystos', *Athenische Mitteilungen* 24 (1899), 458–67. This large house, built exceptionally of stone, as are the other buildings on the steep hill surrounded by a strong fortification wall, has sometimes been interpreted as the residence of the commander of a military garrison. The 5th cent. date, supported by Luce and Wiegand on the basis of the style of the masonry of the fortifications, is not very secure.

and villages. For most periods of antiquity the Greeks preferred to live in such nucleated settlements, even when they were supporting themselves primarily from agriculture. Field surveys of the countryside have confirmed this generalization while showing that in certain, quite limited periods (especially the century or so after about 375 BC in many parts of the Greek world) there were also substantial structures scattered over the countryside; the latter are not accompanied by a diminution of population in nucleated settlements, but were occupied entirely or partly by the same people who maintained homes in the towns or villages.[3]

Very occasionally we have evidence of how the agricultural land was organized by the residents of these settlements through division into regular rectangular and, originally at least, equal lots (Fig. 14). These are the result of the distribution of land for newly founded settlements or of the redistribution of land in old settlements. The implication is that for a time a family farmed a single, unitary property.[4] So too a substantial building in the countryside may indicate that its owner built it on his largest, if not his only, piece of land. But there was a tendency for farmland to become fragmented and for a landowner to possess several plots scattered over the territory of the community. Social, economic, and ecological reasons have all been invoked to account for the phenomenon. In any case, concentrated properties clearly seem to be the

[3] Robin Osborne, *Classical Landscape with Figures: The Ancient Greek City and its Countryside* (London, 1987), esp. ch. 3; M. Jameson, C. Runnels, and T. van Andel, *A Greek Countryside: The Southern Argolid from Prehistory to the Present Day* (Stanford, Ca., forthcoming). A valuable review of the evidence before the beginning of systematic field surveys is given by Jan Pečírka, 'Homestead Farms in Classical and Hellenistic Hellas', in M. I. Finley (ed.), *Problèmes de la terre en Grèce ancienne* (Paris, 1973), pp. 113–47. Cf. above, ch. 5 (Snodgrass).

[4] In the Crimea: M. Dufkova and J. Pečírka, 'Excavations of Farms and Farmhouses in the Chora of Chersonesos in the Crimea', *Eirene*, 8 (1970), 123–74. In Thessaly: F. Salviat and C. Vatin, 'Le Cadastre de Larissa', *BCH* 87 (1974), 247–62, and 'Information sur les recherches en cour', in *Cadastres et espace rural* (Table Ronde de Besançon; Paris, 1983), pp. 309–11. At Metapontion, D. Adamesteanu and C. Vatin, 'L'Arrière pays de Metaponte', *CRAcad Inscr.* 1976, 110–23, and Joe Carter, 'Rural Settlement at Metaponto', in Graeme Barker and Richard Hodges (eds.), *Archaeology and Italian Society* (BAR International Series, 102; Oxford, 1981), pp. 167–78; the presence of divisions producing regular, rectangular lots appears to have been confirmed though there remains some uncertainty as to their shape and size. At Chersonesos and Metapontion, each large allotment had a substantial structure built upon it.

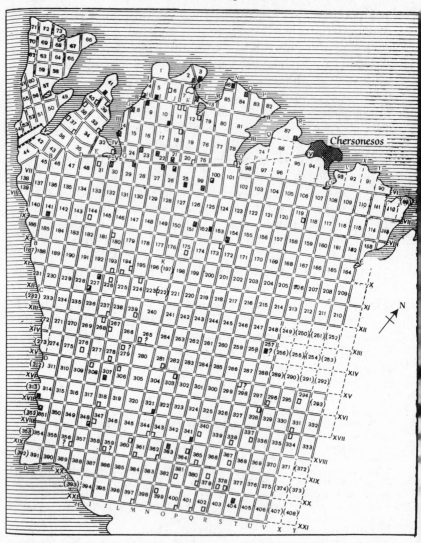

FIG. 14.   Land divisions at Chersonesos in the Crimea (*Akademia Nauk SSSR.
Institut arkheologii. Kratokie soobščeniya* 168 (1981), p. 11. fig. 1). Scale approximately 1:100,000.

exception, the result of political action either in establishing a new community or in restructuring an old.[5]

There seems to have been little social or emotional invest-ment in the family farm or the ancestral estate, and the same is true for the family house. It was the abandonment of a complete way of life, with attachment to ancestral shrines and local communities, as well as the loss of property, that Athe-nians living in the countryside so bitterly regretted when they moved into Athens at the beginning of the Peloponnesian War (Thucydides 2. 16). The particular organization of a family's landed property was determined by economic and other practi-cal considerations, such as proximity to other interests of the household. There were, to be sure, prohibitions on the disposal of land, directed primarily at colonists. But these do not point to a general principle of inalienability or the keeping intact of parcels of land. Their aim was to preserve the initial character of the new settlement—a community of propertied, eco-nomically independent households, each with house and land. Land ownership, the prerogative of citizens, was also a pre-requisite for citizenship in most of the Greek world.[6]

New settlements, like new constitutions, have the great virtue for the historian of making explicit the principles espoused by the community. Initially the principle of equality prevailed. Land in both town and country was divided in uniform rectangles, wherever practical in the broken Mediter-ranean terrain; geometry, literally 'land measurement', was the obvious means to use for equitable division, within towns first for uniform blocks and then for the house plots within the blocks. In both town and country land would seem to have been assigned by lot, as was so much else in the fully developed city-state.

While examples of the pristine division of agricultural land are rare, excavation and the study of aerial photographs since the Second World War have produced a great deal of informa-tion on land division within settlements (Fig. 15). It is now

[5] Osborne (n. 3), pp. 37–40. The phenomenon, together with the preference for nucleated settlements, has been frequently observed in 19th- and 20th-cent. Greece; cf. H. A. Forbes, 'Strategies and Soils: Technology, Production and Environment in the Peninsula of Methana, Greece', Diss., Univ. of Pennsylvania (Ann Arbor, 1982).

[6] Cf. M. I. Finley, 'The Alienability of Land in Ancient Greece', *Eirene*, 7 (1968), 25–32, reprinted in *The Use and Abuse of History* (London, 1974), pp. 153–60.

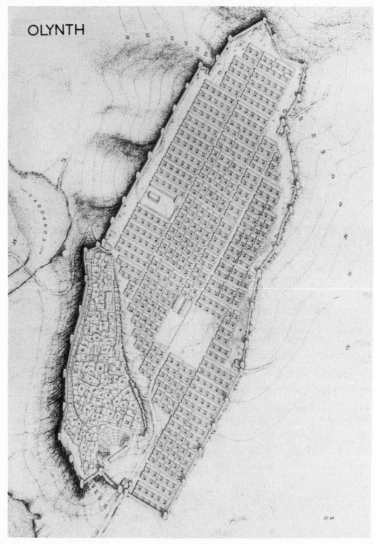

FIG. 15. Reconstruction of the town-plan of Olynthos *c.* 432 BC. The old town is on the south-west side (W. Hoepfner and E.-L. Schwandner, *Haus und Stadt im klassichen Griechenland* (Munich, 1985), fig. 24)

evident that the orthogonal planning of new settlements or rebuilt old settlements was everywhere the norm, in so far as the landscape permitted, from the eighth century BC into the Hellenistic period, and was not confined to new foundations overseas. What is *not* found in these plans throws light on what was regarded as of prime importance. There is no dominating pattern of communications, no axial system oriented to compass points. Sacred or secular public space is included and may be central, but it does not determine the plan of the rest of the town. Uniform blocks of housing take precedence over every other consideration.[7]

Older towns grew haphazardly with houses tightly packed along routes leading to fields, the shore, defensible heights, and sanctuaries outside the settlement; most in time came to be surrounded by a circuit wall. In both orthogonal and unplanned settlements, streets were lined by the continuous outer walls of houses. Space between houses—for privacy, for livestock, or for gardens—was exceptional. As in the countryside, the original uniformity of the plots in orthogonal settlements was often obscured through infringements or purchases of adjoining lots. In planned blocks of the fifth and fourth centuries houses commonly occupied rectangles of 50–60 Greek feet on a side. Olynthos (Fig. 16), Kassope and Priene (built in the late fifth, mid-fourth, and late fourth centuries respectively) show the original divisions; Himera in Sicily and Halieis in the Argolid, for instance, no longer do.[8]

From this brief review of the division of private space we see that agricultural and residential land both partake of the

[7] T. D. Boyd, 'Townplanning in Greece and Rome' in M. Grant and R. Kitzinger (eds.), *Civilizations of the Ancient Mediterranean: Greece and Rome* (New York, 1988) iii. 169–96; Hoepfner and Schwandner (n. 1), esp. ch. 9.

[8] J. W. Graham, in D. M. Robinson and J. W. Graham, *Excavations at Olynthus* viii *The Hellenic House* (The Johns Hopkins University Publications in Archaeology; Baltimore, Md., 1938), and 'Olynthiaka', *Hesperia*, 22 (1953), 196–207, and 23 (1954), 320–46, in the light of which D. M. Robinson, *Excavations at Olynthus*, xii. *Domestic and Public Architecture* (Baltimore, Md., 1946) is to be used. Olynthos, Kassope, and Priene: Hoepfner and Schwandner (n. 1). Himera: N. Bonacasa, *Himera* ii (Rome, 1976). Halieis: T. D. Boyd and W. Rudolph, 'Excavations at Porto Cheli and Vicinity, Preliminary Report IV; The Lower Town of Halieis, 1970–77', *Hesperia* 47 (1978), 327–42; T. D. Boyd and M. H. Jameson, 'Urban and Rural Land Division in Ancient Greece', *Hesperia*, 50 (1981), 327–42. For the insertion of several small houses into the space of one and the combination of two houses into one (producing, exceptionally, two courts) in 3rd-cent. BC Priene, see Hoepfner and Schwandner, pp. 185–6.

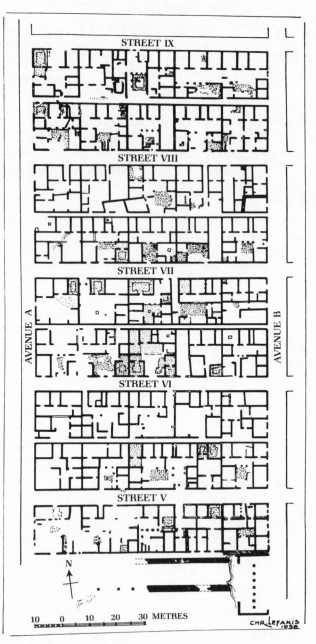

FIG. 16. Plan of blocks of houses at Olynthos (D. M. Robinson, *Excavations at Olynthos* xii. *Domestic and Public Architecture* (Baltimore, Md., 1946), pl. 1)

concept of equal or comparable shares in the resources of the community. Whereas, however, agricultural land is almost infinitely divisible and treated in a purely utilitarian fashion, the house plot may expand or shrink, or even disappear, but so long as it survives it remains a tight nucleus, usually, but not always, within the larger nucleus of a settlement. In fact, the more scattered the landholdings and the other economic and social interests of the household, the more important is the centrally located house where the household concentrates its goods and people, out of sight of all other households. The household, of course, is the familiar basic economic and social unit of Greek society—the *oikos*, composed of a nuclear family augmented whenever money permits with its non-citizen, usually slave, servants (*oiketai*), and the occasional aged or orphaned relative. In effect, private space is *oikos* space, as opposed to *polis* space.[9]

From literature and excavations there has been derived a generally accepted, composite picture of the standard Greek house of the fifth and fourth centuries (Figs 17, 18, and 19). It may be useful, however, to begin with only the archaeological evidence, and then proceed with the help of the texts to examine the various activities carried on in the house, before tackling the more elusive conceptual distinctions. All houses have an interior courtyard and only one. The courtyard is entered either directly from the street or by way of a passage. It is small, being only a little larger than the largest room, and often has a porch supported by posts or columns on one or more sides. Full peristyles seem to be characteristic of the Hellenistic period. While there are many references in texts to an upper floor it is not clear from the remains how common a feature it was. Thanks to the usual construction of rubble and mudbrick, none have survived, except the stone-built towers, which were attached almost exclusively to country houses. It is the court off which open rooms in one or more structures, not the form of any one structure, that is the indispensable feature of the Greek house, no matter what the normal house of the particular town or region may be, nor what historical develop-

---

[9] On this contrast, see S. C. Humphreys, 'Oikos and Polis', in *The Family, Women and Death* (London, 1983), pp. 1–25.

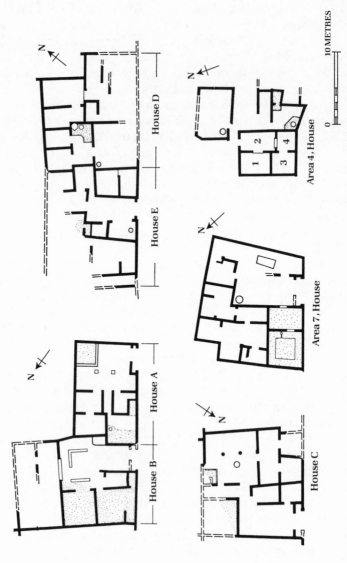

FIG. 17. Houses at Halieis, fourth century BC (T. C. Boyd and W. Rudolph, *Hesperia*, 47 (1978), p. 348, fig. 3)

FIG. 18. Reconstruction of a first-century BC house at Athens (H. A. Thompson and R. E. Wycherley, *The Agora of Athens* (*The Athenian Agora* xiv; Princeton, NJ, 1972), p. 181, fig. 44: courtesy of the American School of Classical Studies at Athens)

ment has led to this result.[10] Although differences in decoration, architectural refinements, and eventually size are discernible, there is no variation of house type that corresponds with

[10] In the complex around the court principal structures of two types are known as *prostas* (which has been derived from an early megaron-type, with a long main room entered through a porch at the short end) and *pastas* (with a broad porch off which open two or more rooms). They are examples of regional traditions, best seen at Priene and Olynthos respectively. See the publications cited above, n. 8.

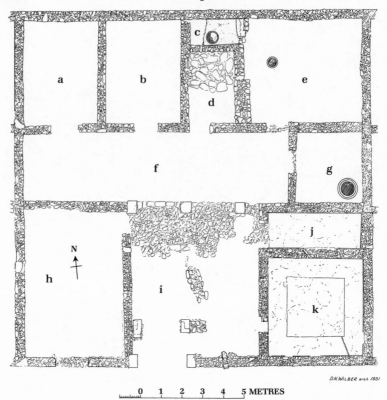

FIG. 19.   Plan of House A vii 4 at Olynthos: the *andron* is in the south-east
corner (D. M. Robinson and J. W. Graham, *Excavations at Olynthos* viii. *The
Hellenic House* (Baltimore, Md., 1938), pl. 100)

economic or social distinctions. The house exemplifies well the
limited range in this respect of most city-state soceties.

The isolated country house, where it is more substantial than
a shack or temporary shelter, reproduces the essential features
of the town house. It is another inturned centre of private
activity focused on the court (*aule*) which, understandably, is
larger than the corresponding space in town. It is likely that the
more important exceptions to the general modesty of classical
housing were to be found in the countryside, away from the

physical constraints of space and perhaps the social constraints of envy.[11]

Judging by the physical remains only the *andron* and some-times a specialized workroom or a storeroom (for processing and storing oil and wine) were distinguished by their construc-tion and permanent equipment. Usually one room is larger than the others but this is not always conspicuous, nor is its position within the house predictable. The uniformly planned blocks of houses in the part of Olynthos built about 432 BC come closest to providing a regular pattern of rooms (Figs. 16 and 19). There a possible kitchen is sometimes connected by a pillared partition to what is usually the largest room, and adjacent to both is a small room (sometimes containing a bathtub), interpreted as providing a flue for smoke from a fire.

That privacy, in effect being invisible to the outside world, was the major aim of these houses is strongly suggested by the remains and is confirmed by literary references to the impro-priety or outrage of intrusion (e.g. Lysias 3. 6, Plutarch, *Moralia* 516 E). The degree to which the barriers erected were affected by gender and in what way the outside world was allowed to enter will be considered shortly. We should note, however, that at the same time that internal privacy was pursued the proximity of other households was not avoided nor buffered by open space. Indeed, in the older city-states the goal that all active citizens should live in town would hardly have been feasible without contiguous construction. But since new towns showed no more interest in greater separation of the units than did the old and sometimes left extensive open areas within the city walls, it looks as if the tight pattern was positively desired. It is interesting that, in addition to any ideological reasons or functional advantages (such as shorten-

---

[11] On Attic houses outside Athens, including isolated country houses, J. E. Jones, 'Town and Country Houses of Attica in Classical Times', in H. Mussche, Paula Spitaels and F. Goemaere de Poesck (eds.), *Thorikos and the Laurion in Archaic and Classical Times* (*Miscellanea Graeca*, i; Ghent, 1975), pp. 63–140; on the evidence from inscrip-tions, R. Osborne, 'Buildings and Residence on the Land in Classical and Hellenistic Greece: the Contribution of Epigraphy', *BSA* 80 (1985), 119–28. There may well have been a few exceptionally large and fine houses even in the classical period which permitted the expression of distinctions absent in the more modest houses known from excavation. Isoc. *Areop.* 52 speaks of the better houses and furnishings being in the countryside and [Xen.] *Ath. Pol.* 2. 10 of the homes of the rich having gymnasia, baths, and changing-rooms.

ing the circuit of the city wall) for its adoption, to Aristotle's eyes the regularity was aesthetically pleasing (*Politics* 7. 10. 4).[12]

A second characteristic of the Greek house was the versatility of its parts. Few rooms reveal a fixed function either in their location or construction and this is not contradicted by the literary evidence which adds details and the names of different rooms. As the composition of the families that occupied the houses changed and the work carried on in the house varied, different arrangements would be made. In Plato's *Protagoras* (315 D) a storeroom has been converted into a guest room for the visiting sophist Prodikos who, lying in bed under layers of sheepskins and coverlets, gives audience to his admirers in its cramped space. At Halieis study of the remains of cooking pottery suggests that at least two adjacent rooms were used at various times, perhaps summer and winter, as a kitchen.[13] Cooking did not require a fixed hearth or heavy equipment. Small charcoal or brushwood fires on the dirt floor or in terracotta or bronze braziers sufficed. Unfortunately there has been as yet little detailed study of the remains in different parts of houses.

The presence of rooms with especially heavy floors is only the most visible indication that the house is also an enclosed working space. Even Athens would not have been a complete exception to the general rule that the majority of Greek towns were the homes of farmers working the surrounding countryside. Euphiletos, the homicidal cuckold of Lysias 1, goes out

[12] Completely contiguous housing was characteristic of the ancient Near-Eastern cities which may have provided a model for the Greeks. In the Greek world archaic Smyrna is our earliest example, aside from the Cretan and island settlements on steep refuge sites, which, however, use a different type of house, without courtyard, facing onto the street, that is, on to public space. Rows of one-room and anteroom, houses of the 7th cent. on a fortified promontory at Vroulia on Rhodes, are anomalous, K. F. Kinch, *Vroulia* (Berlin, 1914). Smyrna: Ekrem Akurgal, *Alt-Smyrna* i. *Wohnschichten und Athenatempel* (Ankara, 1983). Crete: e.g. Kavousi Kastro, G. C. Gesell, L. P. Day, and D. E. Coulson, 'Kavousi 1982–1983: The Kastro', *Hesperia*, 54 (1985), 327–55. Lato: V. Hadjimichali, 'Recherches à Lato, III: Maisons', *BCH* 95 (1971), 169–90; Zagora on Andros, where courtyard houses may also occur: A. Cambitoglou, *Archaeological Museum of Andros: Guide to the Finds from the Excavations of the Geometric Town at Zagora* (Athens, 1981). An early site, apparently with scattered rather than contiguous housing, is Emporio on Chios, J. Boardman, *Greek Emporio: Excavations on Chios, 1952–55* (London, 1967).

[13] Brad Ault, 'The Spatial Distribution of Cooking Pottery at Ancient Halieis', *American Journal of Archaeology*, 91 (1987), 273 (abstract). For two kitchen areas in one house at Olynthos, J. W. Graham, *Hesperia*, 23 (1954), 338–40.

from his house in Athens to his fields. Many town houses were in effect farm houses where supplies and equipment were stored and the products of the farm were processed. Xenophon's Ischomachos does not describe the location of his house but it is certainly the chief respository of the family's equipment and supplies, all of which had to be kept under close control (Xenophon, *Oeconomicus* 9; cf. the locking of the storeroom in Aristophanes, *Thesmophoriazousae* 415–20 and Menander, *Samia* 234–36). Bulky supplies were kept in large pots, sometimes set into the floor. While there was no fixed location for the containers, the heavier supplies, such as water, wine, and oil would not have been kept on an upper floor. The most valuable items were stored in the most secure, interior rooms, which would not normally have been used as living or working areas.[14]

Men's work as well as women's was carried on in the house. At Halieis, located in a major olive-growing region, one out of every six houses seems to have had an oil press, and the press room was the most common specialized room in the house.[15] Many craftsmen and professional men used their homes as their places of business. A single house might serve successively a physician, a smith, a fuller, a carpenter, and a brothel-keeper (a hypothetical case in Aeschines 1. 124). Excavation near the Athenian Agora found the houses of stone- and bronze-workers, judging from the debris, and another was identified by a graffito as that of Simon the cobbler, mentioned by Plato.[16]

In Athens, Olynthos, and Priene, a number of individual rooms adjacent to the street were cut off entirely from the rest of the house and were entered only from the street. These have

[14] In [Dem.] 47. 56 we learn that some furnishings had been kept in an upper room in a tower of a country house where slave girls had barricaded themselves on the appearance of intruders. On the following day when the furnishings had been brought down to replace what had been seized, the intruders reappeared and made off with the replacements as well. The strongly built tower is an exception to the flimsiness of most construction. It was common in those years when the countryside had more substantial houses, but it has also been found in the Attic silver-mining town of Thorikos, where a secure upper floor could be useful. Jones (n. 11), pp. 120–2. On towers of country houses, cf. Pečírka (n. 3), pp. 123–8, and Osborne (n. 3), pp. 63–7.

[15] Information from the Halieis Excavations Publication Committee.

[16] Jones (n. 11), pp. 68–71; H. A. Thompson and R. E. Wycherley, *The Agora of Athens* (*The Athenian Agora*, xiv, Princeton, 1972), pp. 173–85.

been identified as shops, perhaps not only retail shops, barber-shops, and taverns (such as the well-known examples at Pompeii), but also workshops and even warehouses for merchants and peddlers. Existing solely for communication with the outside world and lacking a courtyard and a complex of rooms, they are quite distinct from the private houses out of which they were created, and if the family living in the house operated the adjacent shop, the barrier between the two is all the more striking.[17]

While only some men worked at home, the private house was the workplace of the great majority of all women, the free assisted when they could afford them by female slaves. In addition to the cleaning of the house itself and its contents, the preparation of food and the care of children, their tasks included the processing and preparation of food for storage and the making of clothing and bedding by spinning and weaving. The implements for most women's work were light and portable. Even the upright loom may have been erected and disassembled according to need, if modern practice in the Greek countryside is any guide (the modern loom, however, is horizontal, not vertical and takes up more space). No pattern is discernible in the location of collections of terracotta loom-weights found in houses.[18]

For much of the year food preparation and the working of textiles were probably carried on in the courtyard. The central part of the house including the court was, in effect, women's quarters. The speaker at Lysias 3. 6 implies that in his house the court and the rooms immediately off of it were the women's area; otherwise one would expect him to have dilated on the intruder's progress into the interior of the house (cf. also Plutarch, *Moralia* 516 E). Women and children are breakfasting in the courtyard, of a country or suburban house to be sure, when intruders burst in ([Demosthenes] 47. 55). Since win-

---

[17] John Travlos, *Pictorial Dictionary of Ancient Athens* (London, 1971), p. 393, fig. 505. Thompson and Wycherley (n. 16), pp. 176–78. Hoepfner and Schwandner (n. 1), pp. 72–4, 180–1. However, one of the two shops on a single houseplot at Olynthos, does seem to communicate with the house, Robinson and Graham (n. 8), pp. 97–8.

[18] A room could be referred to as a loom-room (*histeon*). In Menander's *Samia* (228) this is what lay between the living quarters (no doubt on the courtyard) and a locked store-room. It also had stairs leading to an upper storey and a bed on which a baby could be deposited temporarily.

dows were few and small most of the light inside the house came from the courtyard, which acted as an extension of the ground-floor rooms. In the Mediterranean climate, it takes the place of a regular living or workroom, much as the kitchen does in colder climates.

Literature, nonetheless, insists on the physical separation of male and female space. One solution to reconciling the literary information with the actual remains has been to suppose that the upper floor was reserved for women. This will not work. Even if we suppose that most houses had an upper floor, the literary evidence shows it was not regularly the *gynaikonitis*. The son who is prosecuting his stepmother for the murder of his father in Antiphon 1 mentions that a friend of his father's, together with his concubine, stayed in the upstairs of his father's house whenever he came to Athens on business. There is no suggestion that the intruder in Lysias 3 climbed steps to enter the women's quarters. Xenophon mentions bolting the door between men's and women's quarters (*Oeconomicus* 9. 3), which shows clearly that he conceives of them on the same floor.[19]

A revealing passage is the description given by Euphiletos, who is defending himself against a charge of having entrapped and killed his wife's lover (Lysias 1). In his little house he had separate and equivalent men's and women's quarters, downstairs and upstairs respectively. When his wife had a baby, the quarters were switched to spare her the danger of descending the steps at night to wash the child. While one may be suspicious of much in Euphiletos' account, the arrangements must be supposed to have sounded plausible to the judges. The husband's eating, entertaining, and sleeping are contrasted with the wife's and the maid's sleeping; nothing is said of food preparation and other daily work which required access to water and stores on the groundfloor of the house. The terms, *andronitis* and *gynaikonitis*, are used in a restricted sense, and for two areas defined by use, not fixed by the design of the house.[20]

[19] The upper part of the chest in Plato's comparison of the diaphragm to the partition between men's and women's quarters is masculine since it is closer to the spirited parts of the body in the head; clearly he is not thinking of an upper/lower division of the house as corresponding to female and male space (*Timaeus* 69 E–70 A).

[20] Cf. Graham, *Hesperia*, 22 (1953), 199–203, for both terms. On Euphiletos' house, see Gareth Morgan, *Trans. Am. Phil. Assoc.* 112 (1982), 115–23, who, however, supposes

The contrasting men's space, referred to as *andron* and *andronitis* (without distinction of meaning in our texts) is rather more clearly defined. There is a more general sense of men's quarters, and a more restricted sense of a room where guests, always male, are entertained. The broader sense refers to where men spend their time: in Croesus' palace there were weapons on the wall (Herodotus 1. 34. 3); it is where the two usurping Magi are consulting when they are run to earth by the Persian conspirators (Herodotus 3. 77. 3). Any rooms not used for work by the household, nor lived and slept in by the women of the household, could be used by men of the household and their friends. Men's quarters, with the important exception of a single room, were expected to be more rugged than women's. Antisthenes the philosopher was quoted as saying that going from Athens to Sparta was like moving from a *gynaikonitis* to an *andronitis* (Theon, *Progymnasmata* 251 Spengel). The scenes showing respectable women at home on Attic vases suggest attractive surroundings for the upper class at least.[21] Xenophon (*Oeconomicus* 9. 4) has Ischomachos remark on the pleasant decorations of the living quarters for the *anthropoi*. The word might be expected to refer to the family's slaves, and yet the context better suits the household as a whole, perhaps the free women and children attended by the servants.

For the most distinctive room in the Greek house, and in most towns the only one whose architecture reveals a specialized function, scholars have adopted the term *andron* (cf. Xenophon, *Symposium* 1. 4; in Plato's *Symposium* the room is not named). It is clearly identified by its usual cement or pebble floor with a central, rectangular depression; rooms with simpler floors may have served the same function but are less securely identified. Couches on which guests and hosts reclined would have been arranged around the sides of the room. A small antechamber is not uncommon. The room fits the more

that the women, before the baby's birth, would have lived and worked upstairs. If *gynaikonitis* referred only to women's *sleeping* quarters, it would be likely enough that they were on an upper floor, when a house had more than one storey. But the word is not used only in that restricted sense.

[21] See e.g. C. Bérard, 'L'Ordre des femmes', *La Cité des images: Religion et société en Grèce antique* (Lausanne and Paris, 1984), ch. 6.

restricted sense of *andron* and *andronitis*, as the place where hospitality is offered to guests.[22]

A number of details show the extra care and expense bestowed on this room. The windows may be larger and better constructed. A gutter leading from a rectangular, central depression to the street has been found at Olynthos and Halieis, presumably for convenience in washing down the floor. In the latest phase of occupation at Olynthos decorative pebble mosaics were set in the central depression.[23] At Halieis there is a unique example of a curved sideboard of plaster with lion's feet built against a wall.[24] The furnishings are likely to have been the finest in the house. The *kosmos* of the tyrant Polykrates' *andron* was dedicated to Hera after his death (Herodotus 3. 121. 1).

To have such a room was certainly desirable for social prestige, since it appears in all classical towns. It was the one room to which males outside the family had access. Grown women of citizen families are never described as present at the entertainment of strange men. No doubt women of the family would have served the guests if the household had no servants, but most likely the pretensions of having an *andron* meant that the household had slaves as well. Children below a certain age were probably exempt from restrictions: *paidia*, perhaps not only boys, might be summoned to the *deipnon* and fall asleep on the guest's lap (Theophrastus, *Characters* 4. 5).[25]

The superiority of the construction of the *andron* and, probably, of its furnishings may have kept it unused except for formal entertainment, rather like the front parlour of old-fashioned European and American houses. However, the broader sense of *andron* and *andronitis* allows for the accommodation of guests for the night (cf. Aeschylus, *Choephori* 712,

[22] Similar rooms are found in public buildings where they are identified as dining rooms. See e.g. Travlos (n. 17), p. 478, fig. 602, the Pompeion at the Dipylon Gate of Athens.
[23] Hoepfner and Schwandner (n. 1), pp. 58, 266, and 273 n. 123, citing D. Salzmann.
[24] M. H. Jameson, 'Excavations at Porto Cheli and Vicinity, Preliminary Report, i: Halieis, 1962–68', *Hesperia*, 38 (1969), pl. 85 b.
[25] Iphigenia had often sung, presumably as a child, in the 'well-tabled' *androines* of her father, Aesch. *Ag.* 244. Such a scene seems so incongruous for classical Athens that E. Fraenkel (*Aeschylus: Agamemnon* (Oxford, 1950), ad loc.) thought the poet was deliberately adding a Homeric touch, but there is also no Homeric precedent.

androns . . . euxenoi). The *kline* could be used as a bed for sleeping as well as a couch for reclining. When there were no strangers present, or only close kin such as the wife's father or brother, the family may have used the room. But there are no clear indications that this was the case.[26]

Some misconceptions need to be dispelled. One is that the *andron* was always as remote as possible from the women's quarters or at least from the living and working areas of the household. Certainly it is sometimes found just within the entrance, where it would have been convenient to usher guests, whatever the society's ideas about male and female contacts. But there are as many examples of the room being on the far side of the courtyard from the entrance. A location with windows on to the outside seems to have been preferred. The small size and compactness of most of these houses makes the notion of the physical isolation of the *andron* not very realistic. The conceptual separation of this space from the private areas of the house may be all the sharper.

A second misconception, which comes from illustrations on vases of men reclining at *symposia*, is that these rooms were used primarily or exclusively for drinking parties with flute girls and prostitutes. (The *symposia* attended by Sokrates are taken to be exceptionally intellectual.) But although the presence of an *andron* shows some social ambitions, we can hardly suppose that the Attic vases of the fifth century represent the normal use throughout Greece of quite small rooms in modest houses. The vases show an élite ideal, a version of an important archaic aristocratic institution, which was emulated no doubt by those who could on occasion afford it. But much more common would have been the use of these rooms for the many social contacts between the heads of households, out of the glare of public spaces. Farm and business deals, marriage negotiations, politics on the local level and relating to the numerous cult organizations to which Greek men belonged, would have been carried on by means of hospitality in the private house. In a society whose constituent units are households of nuclear

---

[26] Oswyn Murray, while stressing that there is no firm evidence, points out to me that the festival of the Choes at the Anthesteria, which included boys, and the funerary *perideipnon* held at home (D. Kurtz and J. Boardman, *Greek Burial Customs* (London, 1971), p. 146) are plausible occasions for use of the *andron*.

families such contacts play a vital part. The *andron* was an enclave within the largely female space of the private house where representatives of other *oikoi* were admitted.[27] Not every household could boast a special room for entertaining guests. Euphiletos' house may not have had one. He entertains a friend on the upper floor which has become the *andronitis* when the ground floor was made the *gynaikonitis* (Lysias 1. 22). It is also on the upper floor that he takes his supper with his wife, before she slips away to join her lover, and it is there that he sleeps.[28] The flexible use of various small rooms in the Greek house allowed for the accommodation of outsiders without there being a room distinguished either architecturally or even by its permanent furnishings. It remains true that the most common specialized room is the one that serves as the point of contact between the *oikos* and the outside world.

Along with the opposition between male and female and between *oikos* member and outsider, there is the sharp division in Greek society between free and slave. It cannot be correlated with the architecture of the houses that have been excavated. Most houses were too small to have had separate living quarters for slave and free as well as for men and women.[29] Although Xenophon (*Oeconomicus*, 9. 4), when speaking of bolting the door between men's and women's quarters, is only concerned with the objects and the slaves in these rooms, the terms he uses refer everywhere else to quarters occupied by the free, with or without their slaves. The natural inference is that all males, slave and free, slept in the men's quarters, however defined. Within the permitted space, no doubt male servants slept wherever they could find a corner. As for women, Euphiletos' wife and maid slept in the same *gynaikonitis*, consisting probably of more than one room, when the wife was not

---

[27] Much the same conclusion seems to have been reached by Felix Preisshofen (cf. Hoepfner and Schwandner (n. 1), pp. 271–2). On the symposium as an institution, see Oswyn Murray, 'The Greek Symposion in History', in E. Gabba (ed.), *Tria corda: Scritti in onore di Arnaldo Momigliano* (Como, 1983), pp. 257–72.

[28] The newly wed and swiftly cuckolded husband whose humiliation is conjured up at Aristoph. *Thesm.* 477–89 is in bed upstairs with his wife when she leaves him for her tryst. Was it the predictable location of the deceived husband?

[29] In the roomier country house of [Dem.] 47. 56 maid servants have quarters in the tower.

visiting her husband upstairs (Lysias 1). As with living quarters, division by gender took precedence.[30]

Combining the evidence of the physical remains and the texts, we see that the Greek house allowed some minimal specialization of space for entertainment and for work but that the major and very real distinction between female and male space was essentially conceptual and behavioural. Slaves, however, served throughout the house as needed and slept wherever they would be out of harm's way. Their subordination was permanent and complete and not, apparently, defined and reinforced by spatial rules. The house as a whole was the unified domain of the women and men, children and adults, slave and free, who composed the household, but it was especially the domain of women. The stranger was admitted only within limits, physical limits when possible, but conceptual limits always.

Ritual may be expected to reinforce the ideology seen in the design and the use of the house. The Greek house had no separate room for a shrine, and formal, fixed altars were relatively rare.[31] For the world of the Homeric poems the hearth is the focus of social life, whether in a king's hall, a warrior's tent, or a herdsman's hut. In later poetry and cult the symbolism of the physical hearth, serving as altar as well as a source of heat and light, and its personification in the virgin goddess Hestia ('Hearth'), seem to continue the Homeric pattern. Hearth and goddess have been seen as representing and uniting the household, and in particular expressing the internal, female aspect of the house.[32] There are a few specific references to hearths in classical houses. The kinsmen of the dead lover, Euphiletos' victim, evidently claimed that he had reached the hearth and so was a sacrosanct suppliant at an altar when he was killed (Lysias 1. 27). Babies were carried

---

[30] It has been suggested by Eva Keuls (*The Reign of the Phallus: Sexual Politics in Ancient Athens* (New York, 1985), p. 212) that men and women slept in the same bed only to have sex. However, a bedroom for the married couple was probably normal (cf. Theoph. *Char.* 13. 8, 18. 4–5, 19. 5). Pesando (n. 1), pp. 49–50, 59, sees a distinction in rooms for marital and for non-marital coupling.

[31] The best examples are at Olynthos: Robinson and Graham (n. 8), pp. 321–5.

[32] J.-P. Vernant, 'Hestia-Hermes: The Religious Expression of Space and Movement in Ancient Greece', in *Myth and Thought among the Greeks* (London, 1983; a translation of *Myth et pensée chez les grecs*, 2nd edn., Paris, 1969), pp. 127–75.

around the hearth and so accepted into the household in the ceremony of the *amphidromia* (*Souda* s.v.). Slaves were introduced into the house with a shower of dried fruits and nuts (*katachysmata*) at the hearth (Aristophanes, *Plutus* 768 and scholiast).

We need not doubt that the idea of the hearth and its function was alive in classical Greece, but the fact could not have been deduced from the archaeological evidence. Built hearths were found in only seven of 106 houses excavated at Olynthos, two out of seven at Kolophon on the coast of Asia Minor, none at Halieis in the Argolid. At Kassope in northwest Greece, where a 'hearthroom house' is taken to be the basic regional type, they are more common but by no means the rule.[33] The picture is no different for the smaller number of houses excavated elsewhere. Although the neatly cut blocks forming a rectangular hearth were surely attractive to robbers seeking building material, this will not explain the small fraction of excavated houses that had fixed hearths.[34] No circular hearths, thought to be essential for the ideology of the household, are known for any classical house. It is inescapable that by the fourth century BC most Greek houses used portable terracotta braziers or had makeshift fires wherever it was convenient. Household ritual made do with the simplest equipment. The formal entertainment in the *andron*, the point at which the family interacted with the outside world, was interwoven with prayers and libations. Internally the daily consumption of food was accompanied by simple offerings burnt in the household fire (wherever it was lit) and poured on the ground.[35] Portable terracotta altars were known but far from ubiquitous. Finds of miniature cups, such as are found by the thousands in sanctuaries, may point to widespread, simple household rites in the town of Halieis.[36] It is not clear that any of the small terracotta figurines found in sanctuaries and

---

[33] Cf. Robinson and Graham (n. 8), pp. 189–90, 320–1 for Olynthos; Hoepfner and Schwandner (n. 1) pp. 108–12, for Kassope. For Kolophon, L. B. Holland, *Hesperia*, 13 (1944), 91–171.

[34] Cf. Hadjimichalis (n. 12), p. 218.

[35] e.g., Theophr. *ap.* Porph. *De Abst.* 2. 20; Plut. *in Hes.* fr. 79 Bernardakis and *Mor.* 703 D.

[36] Cf. the small 'sacrificial pyres' frequently found in private houses in Athens, R. S. Young, *Hesperia*, 20 (1951), 110–14, and T. L. Shear, *Hesperia*, 42 (1973), 151.

graves were household icons. In Athens there were various forms of a household Zeus, notably Ktesios ('of the goods'), conceived of as a snake that guarded the household's goods, which may sometimes have taken the form of an actual snake living in the storeroom. But the simplest ritual equipment seems to have sufficed for their worship.[37]

Corresponding to the internal symbol of the hearth, it has been supposed that outside the door of an Athenian house there would be a statue of Hermes in the form of a square shaft topped by a head and adorned with genitals.[38] There are also references to an aniconic Apollo Agyieus (Aristophanes, *Thesmophoriazousae* 489) and to Hekate (Aristophanes, *Lysistrata* 64). Archaeology offers little support—neither traces of the statues themselves nor of stone bases have been found in situ, and most of the actual 'herms' known seem to have been public monuments.[39] In part the lack of remains may stem from many figures having been carved from wood.[40] But the main reason is, surely, that we are hearing of an ideal pattern which not all houses could accommodate or afford. The figures protecting the household door correspond to a larger class of powers who watched over entrances.[41] Belief in their efficacy did not require an actual image, and most families probably made do with occasional prayers and libations at the house door. The symbolic pattern was no less important at the gate than it was inside the house in the imagined form of the spirit of the household fire, Hestia.

The archaeological evidence, just because it does not provide

[37] Cf. H. Sjövall, *Zeus im altgriechischen Hauskult* (Lund, 1931). There is little evidence for animal sacrifice in the household courtyard rather than at a shrine. Kephalos, the rich metic, father of Lysias and Polemarchos, was sacrificing in the courtyard of what was no doubt an unusually large and fine house in the Piraeus (at the beginning of Plato, *Rep.*, 328 c). Some animal sacrifice is likely in the more modest house of the man poisoned, along with the father of the speaker of Antiphon 1, after honouring Zeus Ktesios, also in the Piraeus.

[38] Vernant (n. 32).

[39] For a recent discussion of the subject, R. Osborne, 'The Erection and Mutilation of the Hermai', *PCPS* NS 31 (1985), 47–73.

[40] The red figure cup by Epiktetos in Copenhagen (National Museum, 119; J. D. Beazley, *Attic Red-Figure Vase Painters* 75, 59), illustrated in J. Boardman, *Athenian Red Figure Vases: The Archaic Period* (London, 1975), fig. 74, shows a boy cradling a herm in one arm while carving it with his other, an impossible feat if the herm were of stone.

[41] Cf. F. G. Maier, 'Torgötter', in *Eranion: Festschrift für Hildebrecht Hommel* (Tübingen, 1961), pp. 93–104.

confirmation of the physical reality of round hearths and door gods, enables us to appreciate the ideological power of the symbolic figures that defined the classical Greek conception of domestic space. But we have also seen that the archaeological evidence reinforces an aspect of the house that is so basic, and so much taken for granted by the Greeks, that it can be underestimated when we look only at literature. This is the concept of the economic and social independence and privacy of the *oikos*, the household formed around a nuclear family. Furthermore, its simultaneous proximity and isolation vis-à-vis its neighbours is explained by its need to relate to a larger number of such small social units, while being in competition with and suspicious of all others and therefore cloaking its internal workings. At the same time all *oikoi* prized their central location in a compact settlement for the access they gained to the public˙ spaces of government, business and, to a lesser degree, cult. Its economic and social needs explain how the house was used. But we should remember that quite different social systems may use the same type of physical structures. Thus an Athenian house of the fifth century BC and a Byzantine house on the same site have virtually identical plans.[42] The physical environment a society inherits or constructs will set limits on but will not determine the character of the life that goes on within it.

The historical origins of the form of the Greek house would be hard to recover. Here it may be suggested that the classical house on a small scale has the essential features of the archaic aristocratic establishment—complete privacy from the outside world, and a variety of rooms for the work of its inhabitants and ʿfor the social divisions among them, of which those between strangers and household members, and between males and unmarried females were the most important. On a small scale, the private house shows the democratization of aristocratic values, which was in so many ways characteristic of the city-state.

---

[42] Travlos (n. 17), p. 511, fig. 39. In the classical period there is no obvious distinction between the houses of free non-citizens, such as the numerous Athenian metics, and those of the citizen majority. But in this case it is arguable that all shared in a social system and ideology that was more basic than the political organization of the city-state.

C

The Institutions of the City

8

Collective Activities and the Political in the Greek City

PAULINE SCHMITT-PANTEL

THE importance of patterns of behaviour, actions, and collective activities peculiar to social groups is widely recognized among modern historians and in contemporary studies. It is also becoming a preoccupation of research in ancient history.[1] Such studies are not simply a question of rewriting the history of 'everyday life' under another name, that is, discussing collective practices such as hunting, athletic training, and banquets while separating them from their historical context. On the contrary, it is necessary to emphasize the close dependence that exists between such varied observances and the groups that practise them, as well as the particular political system (in this case the *polis*) that created and developed them. In order to avoid the trap of 'static history', we must provide a foundation in the history of the cities for practices that have had no place in the historiography of our discipline until now.[2]

Actions, patterns of behaviour, and collective activities are one means among others for expressing social reality: their study can and must complete traditional social history. But there is more to it than this. Making room for collective activities in general historical explanations can have unexpected consequences: for example, the necessity to ask questions about the content of categories thought to be clearly established, like

---

[1] In speaking of the *symposion*, Murray indicates that his 'studies . . . begin from the activities engaged in by sympotic groups, rather than the composition or functions of such groups': O. Murray, 'Symposion and Männerbund', *Concilium Eirene XVI, Prague 1982* (Prague, n.d.), p. 49.

[2] The 'history of everyday life' as currently undertaken derives from antiquarian methods for collecting facts about life; see A. Momigliano, 'Ancient History and the Antiquarian', *Studies in Historiography* (London, 1966), pp. 1–39.

the category of 'the political'. This is what I wish to do here, by taking banquets as a specific example of collective activity.[3]

In order to avoid repetition, I begin by emphasizing the essential basis for an understanding of the precise form taken by collective activities in the city: the Greek city knows no separation between sacred and profane.[4] Religion is present in all the different levels of social life, and all collective practices have a religious dimension.

In studying the connections between collective practices and the political I would wish on the one hand to emphasize their importance in the functioning of Greek cities in the archaic and classical periods, and on the other to put forward the hypothesis that the status of these practices did not always remain the same.

In the aristocratic Greek city of the archaic period, participation in a set of collective activities is the sign of belonging to the group of citizens, without of course being the only requirement for membership. Thus to participate in sacrifices and banquets, to go on collective hunting expeditions, to belong to the group of ephebes and then to the group of hoplites, to take part in choruses, funerals, and assemblies are all activities peculiar to citizens.[5] These activities form a chain: each is linked to the next. The hierarchy usually established for these communal practices, where greater value is assigned to participation in assemblies and in combat, is in my opinion the result of applying to the archaic world criteria of classification which were formulated for other periods and contexts, particularly those of the classical period. I think on the contrary that these patterns of conduct all have equal value in the archaic city.

[3] Here I reiterate certain points from my article, 'Les pratiques collectives et le politique dans la cité grecque', *Sociabilité, Pouvoirs et Societé*, Actes du colloque de Rouen 24–6 Nov. 1983 (Rouen, 1987), pp. 279–88, but with a broader perspective than that of sociability. For a complete discussion, see P. Schmitt-Pantel, *La Cité au banquet: histoire des repas publics dans les cité grecques* (thèse de doctorat d'état ès lettres, Université de Lyon II, 1987, Ecole française de Rome, forthcoming).

[4] See e.g. J. Pouilloux, *Cultes de Thasos* i (Paris, 1954), p. 241, who emphasizes 'the indecision between sacred and profane peculiar to Greek cities': and J.-P. Vernant, 'Religions grecques, religions antiques', *Religions, histoires, raisons* (Paris, 1979), p. 11.

[5] Many studies emphasize this point in connection with different collective practices, e.g. M. Detienne, *Les Maîtres de vérité dans la Grèce archaïque* (Paris, 1967); A. Brelich, *Paides e Parthenoi* (Rome, 1969); J. Svenbro, *La Parole et le marbre* (Lund, 1975; new edn., *La parola e il marmo*, Turin, 1984); C. Calame, *Les Choeurs de jeunes filles en Grèce archaïque* (Rome, 1977); P. Vidal-Naquet, *The Black Hunter* (Baltimore, 1986).

They are continually interwoven; one pattern leads back to another, presupposes another, is formed with another.[6]

The function of these different patterns of collective behaviour is not simply to bring people together, nor simply to induce festive happiness. What unites them and gives them a common meaning is without doubt the fact that they are the occasion for shared experience. The placing in common of booty, game, sacrificial meat, consecrated wine, and speech inspired by the Muses, precedes in fact the shared experience and the equal distribution among all participants. Access to the shared experience and the equal distribution identifies the man who benefits from it and makes him an equal member of the social group, indeed of the civic group, the *polis*.[7] The man in charge of the *symposion* gives each participant the cup of wine drawn from the common mixing-bowl, and gives each man his turn to speak or to sing, just as the sacrificing priest gives each participant an equal part of the sacrificial victim.[8] Practices like these—common to all and shared by all—constitute an essential part of the common domain (the *koinon*) which characterizes city life.[9] In this sense I would say that they function as civic institutions: to have a share in citizenship is to share in a banquet. But these practices presuppose a society

[6] This equivalence is obvious in the area of representation. By juxtaposing different levels, the image allows one to see, if not a foreshortened version of social life, then at least a summary of the values that define a citizen. For example a banquet scene on an archaic vase can refer simultaneously to various activities (war, hunting, and sacrifice; shared experience and shared speech) as so many ways of expressing membership in the city. See B. Fehr, *Griechische Gelage* (Bonn, 1971); J.-M. Dentzer, *Le Motif du banquet couché dans le Proche-Orient et le monde grec du VIIème au IVème siècle* (Paris, 1982); and P. Schmitt-Pantel and A. Schnapp, 'Image et société en Grèce ancienne: les représentations de la chasse et du banquet', *Rev. Arch.* (1982), 57–74.

[7] For this model of equality see J. Svenbro, 'A Megara Hyblaea: le corps géomètre', *Annales (ESC)*, 37 (1982), 953–64 which cites earlier studies on forms of division.

[8] On the *symposion* see among others M. Vetta (ed.), *Poesia e Simposio nella Grecia antica* (Rome, 1983); O. Murray, 'The Symposion as Social Organization', in R. Hägg (ed.), *The Greek Renaissance of the Eighth Century B.C.: Tradition and Innovation* (Stockholm, 1983), pp. 195–9; id., 'The Greek Symposion in History', in E. Gabba (ed.), *Tria Corda: Scritti in onore di Arnaldo Momigliano* (Como, 1983), pp. 257–72, and O. Murray (ed.), *Sympotica* (papers of a symposium on the *symposion* held in Oxford in 1984), with a bibliography on the subject (forthcoming). See also F. Lissarrague, *Un Flot d'images: Une esthétique du banquet grec* (Paris, 1987). On sacrifice see M. Detienne and J.-P. Vernant, *La Cuisine du sacrifice en pays grec* (Paris, 1979), with bibliography by J. Svenbro.

[9] For the importance of the *koinon* in the *polis*, see L. Gernet, *Anthropologie de la Grèce antique* (Paris, 1968); J.-P. Vernant, *The Origins of Greek Thought* (Ithaca, 1982).

where each man can bring, receive, and exchange his share on an equal basis, where the group is socially homogeneous.

In the archaic city this group is that of the *aristoi*, the best, the rich land-owners: exchange is possible and reciprocity exists only among them. While the *aristoi* alone hold power in the city, there is a complete overlap between these patterns of collective behaviour and citizenship. But when new social strata develop in the city and aspire to citizenship, these practices—to which the new citizens cannot lay claim, through deficiency of wealth—appear to be no more than the privilege of a small minority. This is one of the aspects of the crisis experienced by archaic cities. Attempts to resolve this crisis resulted in a renewal in every area, and a reworking of the structures of cities.[10] I think that this tremendous enterprise of codification, assessment, and rationalization of social connections also affected the collective practices just discussed, which were characteristic of archaic aristocratic cities. The way in which they were handled is different in different cities and depends on the way in which the cities delimit and define the field of the political.

Without going into details, it can be said that in certain cities a large number of archaic communal activities were enshrined in new legislation and in constitutions. If more is known for Sparta than for anywhere else about division into age-sets, the system of collective education, and public meals, this is because they were codified in the age of Lycurgus. Thereafter the *agoge* and the *syssition* are two keystones of Spartan citizenship. Let us take the example of the *syssition*, the daily communal meal of the Spartans. In my view the origins of the *syssition* are not to be found in some tribal practice, nor simply in the organization of the warrior group, nor in kin groups, nor in rural brotherhoods. The *syssition* arose in that attempt to normalize and reorganize the social relations of Sparta known as the 'Lycurgan reforms'; it came about through the desire to fix and regulate the aristocratic practice of the banquet.[11] When the

---

[10] For this analysis see Vernant (n. 9); P. Lévêque and P. Vidal-Naquet, *Clisthène l'Athénien* (Paris, 1964); C. Meier, *Die Entstehung des Politischen bei den Griechen* (Frankfurt-am-Main, 1980).

[11] I agree with Murray in seeing the *syssition* as an institutionalized form of the aristocratic banquet. Our views diverge on the nature of the archaic aristocratic banquet.

banquet became the *syssition* it lost its autonomy along with any possibility of development. But the fact that it was enshrined among the institutions of the city, and had become a built-in mechanism of civic life, proves its importance in the working of the archaic aristocratic city. The same goes for the *andreia* in Cretan cities, and similar types of communal meal in other cities.

The integration of a large number of collective activities through legislation was the act of cities where access to citizenship and thus to political power was restricted to a limited group of citizens. In these cities the political function was diffused through a large number of practices; it was not specialized as it was in Athens in the classical period.

This line was not in fact taken by all Greek cities. In Athens in particular a long process of experiment, selection, precision, and rejection, during which the group of citizens learned to think about social relationships in abstract terms, led to the specialization of certain pre-existing collective practices in the expression of political power.[12] The choice of these practices may result from the fact that they simplified the task of putting this attempt at egalitarian abstraction into concrete form, because they were less directly dependent on a social order which was still inegalitarian. This goes hand in hand with that displacement of authority in the city and enlargement of the citizen body which characterizes Athens at the end of the archaic period. Thereafter only certain collective activities— the assemblies, the law-courts, the magistracies—express common sovereignty and the access to *arche*, political power, at Athens. These activities give the framework of an autonomous domain which we are in the habit of calling the political domain. At Athens political equality is no longer expressed by participation in the banquet, but rather in the assembly.[13]

The question then arises: what is the status of the collective practices which were not retained in the small group of political institutions in this last type of city, in Athens? The elaboration of a new, abstract notion of the political did indeed

[12] See e.g. Meier (n. 10).
[13] See P. Schmitt-Pantel, 'Les Repas au Prytanée et à la Tholos dans l'Athènes classique. *Sitesis, trophè, misthos*: Réflexions sur le mode de nourriture démocratique', *Annali, Istituto orientale di Napoli: Archeologia e storia antica* (1980), 55–68.

develop from earlier social organization. J.-P. Vernant notes that this truly political level is superimposed on kinship, family solidarity, and hierarchical relations of dependence.[14] I would add that it is superimposed on all the collective activities which were occasions for the exercise of citizenship in the archaic city. While the imposition of a political level does not cause these activities to disappear, it does perhaps change their status.

The analyses of numerous historians, whose main focus is the place of the political in the democratic city, could make one think that all forms of collective life (apart from assemblies, law-courts, and magistracies) disappear from the public domain of the city. Thus C. Meier[15] and P. Veyne[16] reduce the public life of the citizen to his participation, to his involvement in political life. Each gives a different explanation of this: Meier appeals to the notion of 'political identity', Veyne to that of 'political militancy'.[17] But they are alike in thinking that all other aspects of citizen life belong to the private domain. In arguing this way, these writers highlight one of the characteristic traits of the mental world of fifth-century Athens: the elaboration of the political field in Athens coexists with a whole discourse on democracy dealing only with matters that seem most suitable for expressing political equality.[18] Thus democratic political discourse says nothing of the existence and the role of communal activities inherited from the archaic period, when other evidence—textual, representational, and archaeological—reminds us of their existence. When political discourse does allude to these activities, as in the funeral oration of

---

[14] Vernant (n. 9).

[15] Meier (n. 10); C. Meier, *Introduction à l'anthropologie politique de l'antiquité classique* (Paris, 1984), p. 30: 'for the majority of citizens the political sphere was the only sphere of their life that lay outside the concrete world of domestic relations, kinship, and the neighbourhood, in addition to small cult associations . . . ; the only sphere in which they did not act only as private persons, the only area in which they took part in some form of public life.'

[16] P. Veyne, 'Critique d'une systématisation: Les *Lois* de Platon et la réalité', *Annales* (*ESC*), 37 (1982), 883–908. See especially p. 885: 'What was then the connection between city and society? It cut each citizen in two: it was more or less like the connection in a modern political party between the member as such and the member as a private person, caught up in the midst of economic forces and social relations.'

[17] For the notion of 'political identity' see Meier (n. 15), who offers several criticisms of P. Veyne's notion of 'political militancy'.

[18] N. Loraux, *The Invention of Athens* (Cambridge, Mass., 1986) studies this discourse, starting with Athenian funeral speeches.

Pericles, it is to describe them as 'recreation for the spirit'.[19]
The silence of this democratic style of discourse should not be
overemphasized, and it is moreover quickly broken: the fourth-
century texts all tend to show how sharing in those specifically
collective forms of social life reinforces the ties of citizenship.
The structures, groups, and associations that support them did
not miraculously reappear in the fourth century to serve as a
basis for the theories of Xenophon, Plato, and Aristotle. They
already existed, creating a very efficient network from the
thiasos to the *hetaireia*, even if political discourse took no account
of them.

Collective activities, it seems to me, were the expression of
the civic community as a whole in archaic cities. Later in
classical Athens they became visible within particular groups.
Cult activity is always present among the various functions of
these groups. They may or may not be integrated into the
institutional subdivisions of the city. Here I give, arranged in
what may seem a somewhat arbitrary fashion, a list of the
categories of groups operating in the city:[20]

(1) groups with more or less official roles as administrative
and political divisions (in Athens, deme, tribe, phratry);

(2) cult associations, groups whose principal function is the
cult of a divinity, a hero, or a dead man (*genos, thiasos, eranos,
orgeon,* and various types of *koinon*);

(3) age-classes, particularly the group of young men;

(4) groups of friends (*philoi*) and companions (it has been
said that the principal function of the *hetaireiai* was of a
political nature, but the notion of political parties was
completely foreign to the classical Greek city).

The importance of these groups for the proper functioning
of the city stems from their intermediate position and their role
as points of contact:[21]

---

[19] Thuc. 2. 38: 'When our work is over, we are in a position to enjoy all kinds of
recreation for our spirits. There are various kinds of contests and sacrifices regularly
throughout the year . . .' (Penguin trans.).

[20] For all these aspects see O. Murray, 'Life and Society in Classical Greece', in J.
Boardman, J. Griffin, and O. Murray (eds.), *The Oxford History of the Classical World*
(Oxford, 1986), pp. 204–33.

[21] See S. Humphreys, *The Family, Women and Death* (London, 1983). In several

(1) They are places for socialization and apprenticeship in political life. Young men become familiar with political conduct, adults are drawn into political practice. The structures of these groups are usually built on the model of the political institutions of the city—assembly, council, president. In a *symposion* the procedures and conventions are those of political life (elections, turn to speak): only the subject matter differs from that of the assembly.

(2) The apprenticeship in civic values (as well as in the rules of the political game) is likewise achieved in these structures, in different ways in different places. Each one is in its own way an instrument of *paideia*.[22]

(3) They are also places where the social order can be expressed: the disparities of fortune, the hierarchies of power. There the tensions, changes and contradictions in social relations—not always detectable in the discourse of political institutions—are more easily perceived.[23]

This rapid classification of the groups, along with a reminder of their importance, is necessary before I go on to emphasize how similar their collective activities are. The places and the actions are the same. The agora, sanctuaries, and gymnasia are the axes of assembly for these groups. Sacrifices, meals with meat, and communal drinking are the major events of their meetings. I call this unity a 'ritual of conviviality' in order to emphasize their composite nature. The ritual in fact includes a series of communal practices whose repetition creates or re-creates the cohesion of the group.

These actions form a structured unity whose components are

articles the author studies the connections that develop between public and private, *oikos* and *polis*, in fifth-century Athens. She shows very clearly that certain places (like the *andron* where the *symposion* took place) and certain collective practices occupied an intermediate position between public and private. She also emphasizes how important such 'bridges' were in Athenian social history.

[22] As M. I. Finley, *Early Greece: The Bronze and Archaic Ages* (London, 1970), p. 30, says: 'By *Paideia* [the Greeks] meant upbringing 'formation' (German *Bildung*), the development of the moral virtues, of the sense of civic responsibility, of mature identification with the community, its traditions and values'.

[23] For example Kimon is the foremost craftsman of Athenian *arche* in the Delian league, but he is also an aristocrat who opens his gardens to everyone and keeps open house for the members of his deme, while fulfilling all the *leitourgiai* assigned to him by the *polis*.

blood sacrifice, the sharing and distribution of the meat, the common cooking of different elements (meat or not), the consumption of the prepared food (properly called the meal); the consecration of the wine; its sharing, distribution, and consumption; the exchange of speeches; songs, games, the *komos*, and dancing.

Not all these components have the same importance at a given time; one or another is sometimes made more prominent during the actual event or in the modes of description. The point of view depends on the nature of the evidence used and the occasion for which this 'ritual of conviviality' is expressed. For example, a religious law promulgated by the city stresses the *thusia* (blood sacrifice) and the redistribution of meat. The account of a *symposion* insists on the speeches that are given during the exchange of cups of wine. A foundation established in memory of a dead man speaks more fully of the meal and of the rank of the participants. The regulations of an association can prescribe any one of these actions. Behind this diversity, the essential point remains: it is this 'ritual of conviviality' that best expresses the union of the members of the group in the classical period. Or to put it another way, it is in the context of the practices connected with 'eating and drinking together under the eyes of the gods' that the ties necessary for social cohesion in the city are reinforced.

This 'ritual of conviviality' is only one practice among others. A similar demonstration could be made using the examples of collective hunting, choruses, or athletic contests. What I want to emphasize here is that, in order to understand what the sense of belonging to the community actually means, it is not sufficient to draw up a catalogue of the groups and their functions in the Greek city; for example, the study of the tribe as an institutional mechanism cannot be separated from the study of the tribe's festival practices. I could give numerous examples of books which dissect artificially that which can only be understood as a whole; but I would rather say that recent books on the subject of the demes make it possible to hope that such methods of analysis are gone forever.[24]

Can it be said that these varied activities belong to the

[24] R. Osborne, *Demos: The Discovery of Classical Attika* (Cambridge, 1985); D. Whitehead, *The Demes of Attica* (Princeton, 1986).

specifically private domain? It seems difficult. The Greek term *idion* means precisely that which is particularly, peculiar to the individual. It often takes in the notion of *oikos*.[25] In general the Greeks connect all collective activities with the common domain; the very term for this association is *koinon* or *koinonia*. Thus the groups that I have been talking about belong to the common domain, which in the democratic city of Athens lies neither in the political sphere (political life is only one of the elements of the common domain), nor in the private domain (*idion*). To put it another way, these collective activities are part of the *koina* which define a city without constituting its political requirements. This is the theoretical position adopted by the political thought of the fourth century when it tries to define what a *politeia* is.

Collective activities consolidate the feeling of belonging to the city: this is the refrain of fourth-century Athenian texts. One famous example is the speech which Xenophon composes for Kleokritos in the context of civil war:[26]

Fellow-citizens, why are you driving us out of the city? Why do you want to kill us? We have never done you any harm. We have shared with you in the most holy religious services, in sacrifices, and in splendid festivals; we have joined in dances with you, gone to school with you, and fought in the army with you, braving together with you the dangers of land and sea in defence of our common safety and freedom. In the name of the gods of our fathers and mothers, of the bonds of kinship and marriage and friendship, which are shared by so many of us on both sides, I beg you to feel some shame in front of gods and men and to give up this sin against your fatherland. Do not give your obedience to those wicked men, the Thirty . . .

The new importance given to communal practices finds an echo in fourth-century political thought, which assigns a different place to political power and to the conditions of citizen life in the characterization of a *politeia*—different, that is, from their place in the fifth century. The place of the *nomoi* becomes more important in the moderate authors of the fourth century.[27]

[25] For the concepts of public and private in the Greek city see Vernant (n. 9); D. Musti, *L'economia in Grecia* (Rome, 1981), and 'Pubblico e privato nella democrazia periclea', *Quaderni Urbinati*, NS 20 (1985), 7–15; Humphreys (n. 21); B. Moore, *Privacy: Studies in Social and Cultural History* (London, 1984).

[26] Xen. *Hell.* 2. 4. 20–1 (Penguin trans.).

[27] On this point see the work of J. Bordes, *Politeia dans la pensée grecque jusqu'à Aristote* (Paris, 1982).

And the *koinon*—the unity both common to all and more inclusive than the political domain alone—is the point of intervention for every legislator concerned with creating a better *politeia*.

The work of Aristotle marks the final development in the thinking on this subject in the classical city. Aristotle theorizes about the place of groups and the activities appropriate for them in the city, and he makes them one of the mainsprings of the community of living well (*he tou eu zen koinonia*) which is the goal of the city. Indeed according to him:

(1) all communities are parts of the political community. They are subordinate to it, the political community having a more general aim. They are simultaneously necessary components for the functioning of the *polis*, and components subject to the domination of the political.[28]

(2) *philia*, the social tie par excellence, maintains the unity of the city. The various collective activities are the work of *philia*. They make communal life possible (*to suzen*) and they are a way of obtaining access to the community of living well, which is a goal of the Aristotelian city.[29]

One of several proofs of the importance of collective practices in the city is Aristotle's way of describing the methods of tyrannical government. He naturally lists:[30]

'Do not allow getting together in messes or clubs, or education or anything of that kind; these are the breeding grounds of independence and self confidence, two things which a tyrant must guard against', and 'Do not allow schools or other gatherings where men pursue learning together, and do everything to ensure that people do not get to know each other well, for such knowledge increases mutual confidence.'

In fourth-century political thought, collective practices are definitively integrated in the conception of city life.

In describing the place of collective activities in archaic cities and then in Athens I have tried to show that the distinction made in classical Athens between political power and the way of life of a citizen could not be made in the same way in an

---

[28] Arist. *Nic. Eth.* 8. 9, 1160ᵃ.
[29] Arist. *Pol.* 3. 9, 1280ᵇ; 2. 4, 1262ᵇ; 1263ᵇ.
[30] Arist. *Pol.* 5. 11, 1313ᵃ, and ᵇ (Penguin trans.).

archaic society. It is there that the difference resides between the status and function of collective practices in an archaic city and their status and function in Athens during the classical period.

In archaic societies collective activities like banquets, hunting, and educational apprenticeships are part of the conception of citizenship. They are not only the way to bring citizens together, to introduce them to one another, and to create ties which are not simply those of the neighbourhood or of kinship; they are also part of a whole set of forms of conduct which makes it possible to distinguish between citizen and non-citizen. In my opinion, they fulfil the role of civic institutions.

The situation is not the same for Athens in the classical period. Now it is only the assemblies, law-courts, and magistracies which are the marks of citizenship.

And when fourth-century political thought reveals in the notion of *politeia* not only that which concerns political power (*arche*) but also the whole set of collective practices, this does not constitute a return to the way in which the archaic city functioned. Henceforth there is a hierarchy established between the *koinoniai* and the *koinonia politike*. The rupture is truly complete. Collective activities have a place in the city, they belong to the common domain, but they are no longer part of the structure of political power; they are simply one aspect of the way of life in a city of this type.

I am suggesting that practices such as communal banquets fulfilled the role of civic institutions and that they characterized the power of citizens in archaic Greek cities (and not only in Sparta and in Cretan cities); and in so doing I am distancing myself from the way in which historians of the archaic period currently present things. Take for example Claude Mossé:[31]

The underlying forms of Greek social organisation stayed the same throughout the history of the *polis*, from Homer to the end of the classical period. The only changes were in the distribution of power to different components, and the criteria of the rights of citizenship.

In other words, the assemblies, law-courts, and magistracies monopolized the expression of political power from the early days of civic life. Development in this area then became a

[31] C. Mossé, *La Grèce archaïque d'Homère à Eschyle* (Paris, 1984).

matter of social access to these institutions, and not their actual structure. The schema proposed strikes me as a projection on to archaic societies of later classifications, worked out by Greeks themselves, and particularly in the fourth century. Now I am not sure that it is necessary to enclose archaic cities in forms of political life that belong to the classical city. A broader, more flexible view of the forms taken by the power of the citizens in archaic society would provide a closer link between the analysis of social transformations (which is the heart of the matter for historians of the archaic period) and speculation on the emergence of a political sphere and of political thought during the archaic period.

In saying this I am simply subjecting archaic collective practices to the general type of analysis which has been carried out in a more abstract way for some time, particularly by J.-P. Vernant.[32] I think that for this area as well it is necessary to determine at what point the emergence of a new conceptual and institutional level in collective life, that is the level of the political, affected the overall functioning of the city. It seems to me that the status of collective activities in archaic societies should be helpful in getting a precise view of the 'rupture that appears between the political and the social order', to use C. Meier's phrase. In addition Meier emphasizes that[33] 'in the archaic period politics and the relations between citizens as citizens did not constitute an independent fact that could be abstracted from social events'.

Yet in order to do this it is necessary to adopt a point of view slightly different from the one that currently prevails among many historians of ancient Greece. That is, it is necessary to try to see the points of contact between areas normally regarded as different, such as the history of institutions, political history, social history, and the history of customs and behaviour. If modern historians of the ancient Greek world seldom ask this type of question, it is largely because the divisions between different ways of doing history remain very powerful in our discipline. For them it is 'unthinkable' that activities such as hunting and banquets, always categorized as snippets of 'daily life', could be put on the same level as the other 'noble'

[32] Since the original publication of Vernant (n. 9), in 1962.
[33] Meier (n. 15).

concerns of history. It will be obvious by now that this is not at all my view!

Anthropology and history encourage us to think differently. Anthropology shows how ineffective our contemporary conception of the political, that is in fact, of political life, is for understanding how radically different, archaic societies worked, in the anthropological sense (and in my opinion this type of analysis is suitable for the archaic Greek city).[34] History of other periods shows that it is by tearing down the barriers between the different historical areas that one can lay claim to the all encompassing ambition that characterizes historical advances.[35]

The activities in which citizens participated in common played a fundamental role in the fashioning and cohesion of the Greek city. No one seriously doubts this. The status of such practices is relatively simple in societies like ours, where the social has a well-defined place somewhere between the state and the individual. But Greek cities knew nothing of such a tripartite division. In the words of L. Gernet, 'the *politeia* is the community of citizens, the social unity itself'.[36] This is why it is difficult to use ideas and concepts worked out for societies that are historically very different (like modern and contemporary societies) for the study of collective activities in the *polis*.

There are, however, two concepts which I think could be useful in assessing the importance of collective activities in the city, as long as methodological caution is exercised: 'sociability', and 'social ritual'. The concept of sociability was developed by the French historian M. Agulhon in his study of eighteenth-century confraternities and associations in Provence; it provides a better way of understanding the ways in which different groups weave the fabric of community in a

[34] The anthropological bibliography on this subject is immense, and the debate on the nature of the political in societies called 'archaic' is still going on. One of the fundamental books is G. Balandier, *Political Anthropology* (Harmondsworth, 1972). There are also two more recent studies: M. Abélès, *Le Lieu du politique* (Paris, 1983), a monograph on the populations of south-west Ethiopia, and P. Rosanvallon, 'Pour une histoire conceptuelle du politique', *Revue de Synthèse*, 107 (1986), 93–105.

[35] Here I refer to the work of F. Braudel. For the particular problem of the history of groups, see M. Agulhon, *Le Cercle dans la France bourgeoise* (Paris, 1977), p. 12.

[36] L. Gernet, 'Les Débuts de l'hellénisme', *Les Grecs sans miracle* (Paris, 1983), p. 43.

city.[37] The concept of social ritual is borrowed from the American historian R. Trexler's study of public life in Renaissance Florence; it stresses actions and the structured unity represented by communal observances.[38] In my opinion, these two concepts are complementary, and they make it possible to describe the function of groups'in the city, and to take account of their structure, their goals, and their forms of collective expression.

Let me now summarize the argument that underlies this article. The status of collective activities is directly connected with the power conferred by citizenship as long as the political is diffused throughout the social organism. But when the political becomes a separate entity, their status changes. In order to characterize this development, I would say that they change from being practices of political power to being social practices. This is to translate into modern terms, and therefore to distort, what the Greek world thought and said rather differently. In order to remain closer to the Greek way of thinking, it would be better to say that collective activities were always part of the common domain (of the *koinon*) in Greek cities. In different periods and cities the common domain might or might not include a political level. Of necessity a study of public banquets must confront the problem of different limits for the public and private domains in different cities and periods, and the problem of defining the political in cities, which also varies. But only a broad investigation of the complete set of Greek collective practices will make it possible to test the validity of such a hypothesis.

Translated by Lucia Nixon

---

[37] M. Agulhon, *Pénitents et Francs-maçons de l'ancienne Provence: Essai sur la sociabilité méridionale* (Paris, 1968); also (n. 35). For an attempt to apply the concept of sociability to the ancient world, see the ancient history papers in the Rouen conference publication (n. 3).

[38] R. C. Trexler, *Public Life in Renaissance Florence* (New York and London, 1980).

9

The Political Powers of the People's Court in Fourth-Century Athens

MOGENS HERMAN HANSEN

OF the Athenian democratic institutions the two most important were the people's assembly (*ekklesia*) and the people's court
(*dikasteria*).[1] In the assembly some 6,000 citizens met 30–40
times every year to make political decisions relating to both
foreign and domestic policy. In the courts panels of 201, 401,
or 501 jurors selected by lot passed judgement in both private
and public actions. The independence of the judiciary in most
modern societies has tempted many historians—implicitly or
explicitly—to draw an analogy and assert that in the Athenian
democracy politics rested with the assembly and jurisdiction
with the courts. A closer examination of the sources, however,
points to a different and much more complicated relation
between the two institutions. The *ekklesia* was sometimes
involved in jurisdiction and, more important, a considerable
number of political decisions were made by the courts.

The purpose of this chapter is to discuss the Athenian courts
as a body of government and their political powers. I shall treat
the following aspects:

(1) were the *dikasteria* a unified and independent body of
government or merely 'judicial committees of the *ekklesia*',
that is 'the *demos* in its judicial capacity'?

(2) How did the *dikasteria* differ from the *ekklesia* in composition, function, and powers?

---

[1] Taking up the observation made by Oswyn Murray in Ch. 1 (pp. 2–3), I confess to
being basically the German type of historian. My monkey (*polis*) is a state and the
banana is the structure of the *polis*, i.e. the political institutions.

(3) How important were the courts compared with the other bodies of government?

(4) Is it possible to isolate the courts' settlement of private disputes from their political jurisdiction?

(5) Which of the powers exercised by the courts were political?

(6) In fourth-century Athens were the *dikasteria* conceived as 'sovereign'?

I

When rendering the term *ta dikasteria*, I have deliberately preferred the singular 'the people's court' to the much commoner plural 'the popular courts',[2] since the first thesis I shall argue is that the Athenians took their *dikasteria* to be a unified body of government, and not just a plurality of law courts to which the people in assembly had delegated some of their judicial powers.

Admittedly, most sources which list and discuss political institutions mention *ta dikasteria* in the plural;[3] and when the singular is used the reference is regularly to a specific *dikasterion* hearing a specific case.[4] Furthermore, the term *dikasterion* is applied not only to the jury courts manned with ordinary Athenians above thirty, but also for example to the homicide courts manned with either *ephetai* or *areopagitai*.[5] Thus, we must ask two simple but basic questions. (1) When the sources, listing democratic institutions, mention *ta dikasteria*, is it legitimate to assume, as we usually do, that the term *dikasteria* denotes the jury courts only, to the exclusion of the Areopagos, the courts manned with *ephetai*, and other law courts? (2) Were

---

[2] Cf. e.g. C. Hignett, *A History of the Athenian Constitution to the End of the Fifth Century* (Oxford, 1952), pp. 216–21; A. H. M. Jones, *Athenian Democracy* (Oxford, 1957), p. 123; V. Ehrenberg, *The Greek State* (London, 1969), pp. 72–4; A. R. W. Harrison, *The Law of Athens* ii (Oxford, 1971), pp. 43 ff.; P. J. Rhodes, 'Athenian Democracy after 403 B.C.', *Class. J.* 75 (1979-80), 315; M. I. Finley, *Democracy Ancient and Modern* (London, 1973), p. 25.

[3] Dem. 24. 2; Aeschin. 1. 91; Arist. *Ath. Pol.* 62. 2; 63. 1; *ML* 69. 49, etc.

[4] Dem. 24. 50 (*nomos*); Dem. 59. 27; Aeschin. 1. 117; Lycurg. 1. 127, etc.

[5] Dem. 23. 63–81 (fifteen occurrences); Lycurg. 1. 12; cf. Lys. 1.39; *Ephetai*: board of 51 judges selected perhaps from the jurors, perhaps from the Areopagitai who are the members of the Council of the Areopagos.

ta dikasteria (in the plural) conceived as a unified body of government to be placed on the same footing as the *ekklesia* and the *boule?*

These are important problems, not often—if ever—discussed, but an examination of the relevant sources suggests an affirmative answer to both questions. In some important passages we do find the singular *dikasterion* denoting the system of *dikasteria*,[6] and not just an individual *dikasterion* appointed for one day to hear a specific case. In numerous passages the plural *ta dikasteria* is juxtaposed with *ho demos* and *he boule* in a way which shows that it denotes the system of *dikasteria*.[7] Occasionally, the term 'Heliaia' is used synonymously with *dikasterion* to denote the system of jury courts.[8] Some passages demonstrate indisputably that the term *dikasteria* usually denotes the popular jury courts only, to the exclusion of other types of court.[9]

The conclusion is that the Athenians regarded their *dikasteria* as a system of jury courts, a unified body of government comparable with other bodies of government as, for example, the *ekklesia* or the *boule*. But this conclusion leads on to the next question: was the people's court really a separate body of government to be contrasted with the people's assembly? Or was the people's court rather the people's assembly in its judicial capacity?

It is often held that the *dikasteria* were the *demos* sitting in judgement. They were a judicial manifestation of the Athenian people.[10] Furthermore, the Solonian Heliaia, introduced around 600 BC, was simply the *ekklesia* transformed into a law court.[11] And in so far as, by Ephialtes' reforms in 462, the

---

[6] *Hesperia*, 43 (1974), 158, line 26 (law on stone); Dem. 24. 54 (law quoted in a forensic speech); Thuc. 8. 68. 1; Dem. 24, 148; Arist. *Pol.* 1282ª34–7.

[7] Dem. 24. 99; 57.56; Arist. *Ath. Pol.* 41. 2, etc.

[8] Dem. 23. 97 (the curse read out to the people by the herald); Dem. 46. 26 (a law quoted in a forensic speech).

[9] Dem. 25. 20; 24. 58; Arist. *Ath. Pol.* 63. 1; Aeschin. 3. 19, etc.

[10] Cf. e.g. E. Meyer, *Einführung in die antike Staatskunde* (Darmstadt, 1968), p. 96: 'particular popular courts, which were simply another form of popular assembly'; E. Will, *Le monde grec et l'orient* (Paris, 1972), p. 456: 'the identity between popular jurisdiction and the Ecclesia derives from three facts'; M. I. Finley (n. 2), p. 27: the *graphe paranomon* gives 'the people, the *demos*, the opportunity to reconsider a decision they had themselves taken'.

[11] Cf. e.g. P. J. Rhodes, *A Commentary on the Aristotelian Athenaion Politeia* (Oxford, 1981), p. 160: 'So Solon's *heliaia* should be a judicial session of the whole assembly.'

dikasteria became separate institutions, they were merely committees of the *ekklesia*[12] and had their powers only by delegation from the people in assembly.[13] In other words, not only the *ekklesia*, but also the *dikasteria* were manifestations of the *demos*.

If this view were correct, it would be a mistake to discuss the political powers of the *dikasteria* and the separation of powers between the *ekklesia* and the *dikasteria*, and I should stop here instead of discussing the difference between institutions which were almost identical. I believe, however, that the traditional view is wrong. Some years ago I collected the evidence and discussed the problem.[14] The sources I adduced all support the following six statements:

(1) The term *demos* has two distinct meanings and uses. When used officially, by the democrats, *demos* means 'the whole of the people' or simply 'the Athenian people'. When used by the philosophers and others who tend to criticize democracy, *demos* usually refers to a social class, and the meaning is 'the common people' or 'the poor' or 'the crowd'.[15]

(2) When *demos* denotes an institution, the reference is invariably to the people's assembly and in hundreds of passages the term *demos* is used synonymously with the term *ekklesia*.[16]

(3) When *demos* denotes an institution it is never used about the *dikasteria*.[17]

---

[12] Cf. e.g. A. W. Gomme, 'The Working of the Athenian Democracy', *More Essays* (Oxford, 1962), p. 188: 'For the dicasteries at Athens were also mass meetings, especially in political trials, with 1000 or more jurors and no skilled judge to guide them—they were judicial committees, as it were, of the assembly.'

[13] Cf. e.g. G. Glotz, *The Greek City* (London, 1929), p. 166: 'The people was also sovereign justiciary. But it delegated judicial powers to those sections of the citizens which sat in the courts.'

[14] M. H. Hansen, '*Demos, Ecclesia* and *Dicasterion* in Classical Athens', *GRBS* 19 (1978), 127–46. Reprinted with addenda in *The Athenian Ecclesia* (Copenhagen, 1983), pp. 139–58 (hereafter *AE*).

[15] For the constitutional sense cf. *AE* (n. 14), 140–3 with nn. 8 (*demos* = the people at large); 10 (*demos* = democracy); 11 (*demos* = the democrats); 12 (*demos* = the Athenian State); 14–18 (*demos* = *ekklesia*). For the social sense (*demos* = the common people) cf. *AE* 151–3 with n. 30.

[16] Some 300 references are listed in *AE* (n. 14), 142–3 nn. 14–18; 151 n. 29 and 152 n. 32. 26 passages are quoted on pp. 144–7.

[17] Cf. *AE* (n. 14), 143–4. The address 'you the people' (*hymeis ho demos*) is never used about the jurors, only about the people in assembly (Dem. 3. 31; Dem. *Ep.* 3. 30).

(4) The term *demos* (denoting the *ekklesia*) is often opposed to the term *dikasteria*.[18]

(5) If we can trust the sources we have, the Solonian Heliaia was a separate institution manned with jurors, and not a judicial session of the *ekklesia*. If we cannot trust our sources, the rest is silence.[19]

(6) In our sources, relating mostly to the fourth century BC, there is nothing to recommend the view that the *dikasteria* were committees of the *ekklesia*, or had their powers only by delegation from the *ekklesia*.[20] Thus the people's court and the people's assembly were separate bodies of government, and consequently it is legitimate to discuss the separation of powers between the people's assembly and the people's court.

My presentation of the evidence has convinced some historians, but it would be an exaggeration to say that it has been generally accepted. There are still adherents of the traditional view who hold that my demonstration of the difference between *demos* and *dikasterion* may be correct in form but is misleading in substance, and that the Athenians were probably not conscious of any opposition between the people's assembly and the people's court.[21] Two arguments in particular are commonly advanced in support of the traditional view: (*a*) in forensic speeches the orators often address the jurors as if they were the people in assembly, and (*b*) although I may be right in maintaining that the *dikasteria* were not a manifestion of the *demos*, it is at least arguable that the jurors manning a *dikasterion* were a cross-section of the people and represented the people. Both observations are correct, but neither disproves my basic position that *demos = ekklesia* and *dikasteria* were separate and sometimes opposed bodies of government.

[18] Dem. 19. 297; 24. 55, 80; 59. 91; Dinarchus 3. 15–16; Pl. *Ep.* 8 365 D; Arist. *Pol.* 1282ᵃ34–7; *Ath. Pol.* 25. 2; 46. 2, etc. Cf. *AE* 151–3.

[19] Arist. *Pol.* 1274ᵃ1; *Ath. Pol.* 7. 3; 9. 1–2. Cf. M. H. Hansen, 'The Athenian Heliaia from Solon to Aristotle', *Classica et Mediaevalia*, 33 (1981–2), 27–39.

[20] Cf. *AE* (n. 14), 155–8; M. H. Hansen, *The Athenian Assembly in the Age of Demosthenes* (Oxford, 1987), pp. 101–4 (hereafter *AA*).

[21] Cf. Rhodes (n. 11), pp. 318, 489, 545; M. Ostwald, *From Popular Sovereignty to the Sovereignty of the Law* (Berkeley and Los Angeles, 1986), pp. 10–11 with n. 29, and 34–5 with n. 131. A reply to Ostwald appears in M. H. Hansen, *The Athenian Ecclesia*, ii (Copenhagen, 1989), pp. 213–18.

Re (a). In the forensic speeches the jurors are frequently styled 'men of Athens', which is the proper form of address to the people in assembly;[22] and an orator often applies a pronoun or a verb in the second person plural in addresses to the jurors even when he refers to a decision actually made by the *ekklesia*. Two examples will suffice: in the speech *Against Aristokrates* Demosthenes tells the jurors that, some years earlier, they were so angry with the general Kephisodotos 'that you deposed the general, and fined him five talents. Indeed, three votes only separated him from being sentenced to death.' Strictly speaking, the *dikasterion* was responsible only for the sentence (passed by *psephophoria*, i.e. by ballot (whereas the deposition (by *apocheirotonia*, i.e. by show of hands) was a decision made by the assembly. Similarly, in Hyperides' speech *For Lykophron* the defendant reminds the jurors of his irreproachable conduct in office and says: 'it was you, gentlemen of the jury, who appointed me first *phylarchos* (squadron leader) and later *hipparchos* (cavalry commander) for Lemnos.' Again, Lykophron was elected, not by a *dikasterion* but by the *demos* at the electional assembly.[23] Now, is this common usage not an indication that the Athenians must have regarded a session of the *dikasterion* as a session of the *demos* like a session of the *ekklesia*? Certainly not, for this line of argument would lead to an identification of the *demos* not only with the *dikasteria* but also with the *boule*. Of the preserved speeches most are written for delivery either in the assembly or in the people's court. But we have a few speeches which were held before the council of five hundred. In the corpus of Demosthenic speeches, for example, the fifty-first oration was delivered in the *boule*. The councillors are addressed not only as 'gentlemen of the council', but also with the phrase 'men of Athens' as if they were attending an *ekklesia*,[24] and the speaker uses the second person plural even when he refers to a decree actually passed by the assembly and not by the *boule*.[25] But, to the best of my knowledge, no historian has

[22] Cf. e.g. Dem. 18. 1; 19. 1; 20. 1; 21. 2; 22. 4; 23. 1; 24. 6; 25. 8; 26. 1. Cf. *AE* (n. 14), 147–8.

[23] Dem. 23. 167; Hyperides 2. 17.

[24] Dem. 51. 3, 8, 12, 22.

[25] Dem. 51. 1, 4; cf. Lys. 16, a speech delivered before the *boule* in which the councillors are addressed as if they had concluded the alliance with Boeotia in 395: Lys. 16. 13, cf. *IG* ii² 14 = Tod ii 101. Cf. furthermore Lys. 16. 6, 20–1; 24. 2; 31. 29.

ventured, on the basis of this evidence, to argue that a meeting of the *boule* was essentially a meeting of the *demos* and that no sharp line should be drawn between the *demos* (= the *ekklesia*) and the *boule*. On the contrary, all ancient historians distinguish the *boule* from the *ekklesia* and discuss to what extent the *boule* may have controlled the *demos*.[26] Consequently, the arguments based on the way jurors are addressed and the use of the second person plural in forensic speeches do not support the view that the jurors were the *demos* sitting in judgement. They demonstrate only that both the *ekklesia* and the *boule* and the *dikasteria* were democratic bodies of government all manned with ordinary Athenians. Many jurors attended the *ekklesia* and served in the *boule*. There was an important overlap in personnel. But there is no basis for obliterating the clear distinction between the three bodies of government attested in all sources.

Re (b). The other line of argument associating the *dikasteria* with the *demos* is based on the idea of representation. Peter Rhodes, for example, when criticizing my interpretation, suggests that the Athenians regarded both courts and assembly as representative in their own way of the *demos* and that the Athenians were not conscious of any opposition between the two institutions.[27] In my opinion, Rhodes is twisting the sources. The assembly was not *representative of* the *demos*; hundreds of sources show that it *was* the *demos* acting as a body of government. A *dikasterion*, on the other hand, was never thought of as an embodiment of the *demos*. The *dikasteria* were rather representative of the *demos*, as Rhodes correctly maintains and as I said more than a decade ago.[28] The idea of representation is apparent in several forensic speeches in which the speaker states that the *dikastai* are assembled to act on behalf of the *demos*.[29] But the idea of representation, i.e. to act or stand for others, implies distinction and not identification. It makes no sense to say that A is representative of B, unless A is

[26] Cf. e.g. P. J. Rhodes, *The Athenian Boule* (Oxford, 1972), pp. 215, 223; W. R. Connor, 'The Athenian Council: Method and Focus in some Recent Scholarship', *Class. J.*, 70 (1974), 32–40.

[27] Rhodes (n. 11), p. 545; Ostwald (n. 21), pp. 34–5 n. 131.

[28] M. H. Hansen, *The Sovereignty of the People's Court in Athens in the Fourth Century B.C. and the Public Action against Unconstitutional Proposals* (Odense, 1974), p. 21.

[29] Cf. e.g. Aeschin. 3. 8; Din. 1. 84; 3. 15–16 (in the last two passages the word *demos* occurs twice, once in the sense 'assembly', and once in the sense 'the Athenian state').

different from B. Furthermore, to represent the Athenian *demos* was not the prerogative of the *dikasteria*. When the *boule* and the *strategoi* took the oath on a treaty concluded with another state, they represented the Athenian *demos*;[30] and similarly, the *epistates ton prytaneon* (the president of the *prytaneis*) may be said to represent the Athenian *demos* for twenty-four hours. But no one would draw the inference that the *bouleutai*, or the *strategoi*, or the *epistates* were in any way an embodiment or manifestation of the *demos*.

In conclusion, the Athenians regarded their *dikasteria* (*a*) as a popular body of government, that is a court manned with jurors to the exclusion of other types of court; (*b*) as a unified body of government and not just a conglomeration of various law courts; (*c*) as an independent body of government and not just 'judicial committees of the *ekklesia*' or 'the *demos* in its judicial capacity'.

II

What I have discussed so far is constitutional terminology and ideology. We must proceed to the more basic question and ask: why did the Athenians distinguish between *demos* and *dikasterion*? Can we point out any substantial difference between the composition of the people's assembly and the people's court which justifies and explains the clear distinction attested in all texts?

The sources provide us with several answers to this question. First, all citizens over twenty were admitted to the *ekklesia*.[31] But the *dikastai* in the people's court were selected by lot from a panel of 6,000 jurors aged thirty or more.[32] In a modern society a body of government manned with citizens over twenty will not be all that different from a body of government manned with citizens over thirty. Not so in ancient Greece. In classical Athens life expectancy at birth was probably about twenty-five

[30] e.g. Dem. 18. 178. Treaties with other states were usually confirmed by an oath which, on behalf of the Athenians, was taken by the *strategoi*, the *hipparchoi*, the *taxiarchoi*, and the *boule*, cf. *IG* ii² 105. 30–4; 111. 17–19, 57 ff.; 116. 14 ff.

[31] *AA* (n. 20), 7 with nn. 48–53.

[32] Arist. *Ath. Pol.* 63. 3; Dem. 24. 151; Cf. J. H. Kroll, *Athenian Bronze Allotment Plates* (Princeton, 1972), pp. 69–90.

years, and the natural population growth did not exceed one half per cent per year. In a population of this type men in their twenties constitute no less than a third of all adult males above twenty.[33] Thus, if some 30,000 adult male citizens were entitled to attend the *ekklesia* on the Pnyx, the number of Athenians eligible for membership of the panel of 6,000 did not exceed 20,000. In other words, every third citizen had restricted political rights. He was old enough to attend the *ekklesia*, to address the *demos*, and to vote on the motions. But he was not old enough to become a juror or to serve as a magistrate either in the council of five hundred or in one of the numerous boards of ten. Thus, the higher age limit for jurors was, demographically, extremely important. But what was the purpose? It is not explicitly stated in any source why the Athenians had a specific age requirement for jurors and magistrates; but it is not difficult to guess the reason.

Almost all Greeks held the view that wisdom and rationality grow in man with the advance of age.[34] The idea is attested in innumerable sources, and I will adduce only a few, all relating to Athenian political institutions. (*a*) The sophist Thrasymachos opens his speech on the ancestral constitution with the following words: 'Athenians, I would have preferred to be a citizen in the good old days, when young men were expected to remain silent, because their participation in debate was unnecessary and their elders managed the state's affairs efficiently.'[35] (*b*) In the opening of the speech *Against Ktesiphon*, Aeschines complains that the Athenians in the *ekklesia* have given up the practice of allowing citizens above fifty to address the people first.[36] Xenophon tells us that Sokrates was called

---

[33] Cf. A. J. Coale and P. Demeny, *Regional Model Life Tables and Stable Populations* (Princeton, 1966); M. H. Hansen, *Demography and Democracy* (Herning, 1985), pp. 9–13. If we choose Model West, mortality level 4 (life expectancy 25 years) and growth rate 0.5%, we find that, of all men aged 18–80+, men aged 18–19 constitute 6.7%, men aged 20–29 constitute 30.5%, and men aged 30–80+ constitute 62.8%. If we choose Model West, mortality level 23 (life expectancy 71 years) and growth rate 0.5% the figures are men 18–19 4.1%, men 20–29 20.0%, 30–80+ 75.9%.

[34] P. Roussel, *Étude sur le principe de l'ancienneté dans le monde hellénique* (Mem. Inst. Nat. de France; Ac. Inscr., 42.2; Paris, 1951), pp. 123–227; K. J. Dover, *Greek Popular Morality in the Time of Plato and Aristotle* (Oxford, 1974), pp. 102–6.

[35] Thrasymachus fr. 1 (Diels–Kranz), fr. 2 (Sauppe).

[36] Aeschin. 1. 23 with the scholia; Aeschin. 4. 3; cf. Herod. 7. 142. 1 and Aeschin. 2. 47. G. T. Griffith, '*Isegoria* in the Assembly at Athens', *Ancient Society and Institutions* (Oxford, 1966), pp. 119–20; *AA* (n. 20), 91 with n. 581.

before the Thirty and instructed by Charikles not to discuss
with Athenians under thirty, since they could not be taken to
be *phronimoi* (prudent) and accordingly were excluded from
membership of the *boule*.[37] (*d*) In fourth-century Athens private
disputes were referred to and often settled by public arbitrators
who were all selected from Athenian citizens in their sixtieth
year (Aristotle, *Ath. Pol.* 53. 4). (*e*) Finally, in Aristophanes'
Wasps the age of the jurors is emphasized and they are called
gerontes (old men). They are in fact the democratic equivalent
of an immemorial feature of human society: the elders of the
community sitting as judges, allegedly because of their greater
experience and wisdom.[38] Conversely, young men are rash and
keen on war and revolution. It is significant that *neoterizein*
(innovate) and *neoterismos* (innovation) are idiomatic Attic
terms for 'making revolution' and 'revolution'.[39] To balance
the youthful spirit of the *ekklesia*, it is only wise to have more
mature men sitting both in the *boule*, which prepared all
business for the *ekklesia*, and in the *dikasteria*, which were
empowered to reconsider and, if necessary, to overrule rash
decisions.

Next, every year all the 6,000 jurors selected by lot had to
take the heliastic oath.[40] So the *dikastai* were sworn, whereas no
oath was ever taken by the citizens who attended the *ekklesia*.
The importance of the heliastic oath is often emphasized in
addresses to the jurors;[41] and in one passage it is explicitly

---

[37] Xen. *Mem.* 1. 2. 35; Stob. *Ecl.* 4. 50. 27; Dem. 22 hyp. 1. 1.

[38] Aristoph. *Wasps* 195, 224; *Knights* 255. K. J. Dover, *Aristophanic Comedy* (Berkeley and Los Angeles, 1972), p. 128. On seniority cf. also: Xen. *Mem.* 3. 5. 15; Dem. 25. 88–9; Thuc. 5. 43. 2; Antiphon 4. 3. 2; Pl. *Laws* 643 D–E; 665 D–E; 755 A; 765 D; 946 A; Arist. *Pol.* 1329ᵃ2–12; 1332ᵇ12–41; *Rhet.* 2. 12 (*neoi*) versus 2. 14 (*akmazontes*); *SEG* IX 1 (Cyrene).

[39] On young persons' inclination to war and revolution, cf. e.g. Thuc. 6. 12–13; 38–40; Eur. *Suppl.* 232–7. *Neoterismos* (innovation, revolution) is connected with the young (*hoi neoi*) in e.g. Pl. *Laws* 798 B–C.

[40] The heliastic oath is an oath taken by the *heliastai*, i.e. the jurors who manned the *heliaia* (cf. above, p. 222). The oath is quoted at Dem. 24. 149–51, but the text is not above suspicion, cf. E. Drerup, 'Ueber die bei den attischen Rednern eingelegten Urkunden', *Neue Jahrbücher für Philologie und Paedagogik* suppl. 24 (1898), 256–64. The oath is reconstructed by M. Fränkel, 'Der attische Heliasteneid', *Hermes*, 13 (1878), 452–66. The oath was taken annually (Isoc. 15. 21) on Mount Ardettos (Harpocration s.v.), cf. Kroll (n. 32), pp. 3–4.

• [41] Andoc. 1. 31; Aeschin. 1. 170; 3. 6, 8, 198; Dem. 18. 249–50; 19. 132. 161, 179; 21. 4; 22. 45–6; 24. 2, 58, 90, 191; Dem. *Ep.* 2. 1; Hyp. 1. 1; Lycurg. 1. 79; Din. 1. 86.

stated that it would be outrageous if a decision made by the sworn *dikastai* in the people's court could be rescinded by the citizens in the *ekklesia*, who had not taken any oath.[42] Today we can sneer at an oath, and as far as I know contemporary students of political systems do not pay attention to the oaths taken by presidents and prime ministers. But I would argue that the taking of a solemn oath mattered more in ancient Athens,[43] and that the heliastic oath constituted an important difference between the *demos* and the *dikastai*.

Two further differences between the *demos* and the *dikasteria* concern the debate in the *ekklesia* and the form of voting used by the *demos*. In both cases the principal source is Aeschines' speech *Against Ktesiphon*. In the introduction Aeschines launches a severe attack on the *ekklesia* and states that the *graphai paranomon* (public actions against unconstitutional proposals) heard by the *dikasteria* are the only effective bulwark of the democratic constitution. The emphasis is on the negative part of the argument. Thus the shortcomings of the *ekklesia* are described in much detail, whereas the corresponding merits of the *dikasteria* are only briefly and generally stated. Nevertheless, whenever Aeschines criticizes assembly procedure, we are asked to conclude *e contrario* that he prefers and approves of the corresponding procedure used by the *dikastai* manning the people's court.

First, voting: Aeschines claims that the *proedroi* who presided over the people and assessed the votes taken by show of hands were often appointed fraudulently and made wrong statements about the outcome of the vote.[44] The implication is that Aeschines prefers voting by ballot as used by the courts. Since the *psephoi* (ballots) were counted, it was a more reliable form of voting which could not so easily be tampered with by the presiding officials. Whether Aeschines' suspicion is justified or not is of no consequence for my argument. My point is that the form of voting used by the *ekklesia* is exposed to criticism and implicitly contrasted with a preferable form of voting applied in the *dikasteria*.

[42] Dem. 24. 78, cf. Lycurg. 1. 79.
[43] Cf. R. Hirzel, *Der Eid* (Leipzig, 1902); Dover (n. 34), pp. 240–50.
[44] Aeschin. 3. 3; cf. *AE* (n. 14), 114. The *proedroi* is a board of nine chairmen of the *ekklesia* and the *boule*, selected by lot for one day.

Next the debate: Aeschines criticizes the chaotic and embarrassing debates which often took place in the *ekklesia*.[45] Again we must infer *e contrario* that debates in the *dikasteria* were believed to be conducted in a more orderly way and did not, to the same degree, baffle and mislead the audience. This view is stated in other sources as well. In the speech *On the False Embassy*, for example, Demosthenes tells his audience that clever politicians, like Kallistratos and Aristophon, had been able to control the *demos* in the *ekklesia*, but never succeeded in being masters of the laws and of the sworn *dikastai*.[46]

In addition to these four constitutional and procedural differences between the *demos* and the *dikasteria* there is a fifth difference which relates to public finances. For attending an ordinary session of the *ekklesia* a citizen received 1 drachma, whereas the jurors obtained only 3 obols per session.[47] These figures are stated in the *Ath. Pol.*, composed in the 330s. On the assumption that assembly pay was the same in the mid-fourth century, and that an *ekklesia* was regularly attended by 6,600 citizens, a session of the *ekklesia* cost the Athenian state 1 talent, whereas a session of a *dikasterion* manned with 500–1,000 jurors could be heard for 250–500 drachmas. Retrenchment, especially in 355 after Athens' defeat in the Social War, inevitably entailed transfer of powers from the *ekklesia* to the *dikasteria*.[48] In the first half of the fourth century, for example, the *ekklesia* had sometimes transformed itself into a law court and heard public actions brought against political leaders. From the 350s onwards, however, all political trials were referred to the *dikasteria*, and the *ekklesia* was deprived of its judicial powers.[49] The Athenian treasury saved money and, at the same time, it adopted one of the reforms recommended by Aristotle in order to change a radical democracy into a more moderate one: to reduce the number of *ekklesiai* and transfer business to the popular courts.[50]

---

[45] Aeschin. 3. 2–8.
[46] Dem. 19. 297.
[47] Arist. *Ath. Pol.* 62. 2.
[48] Cf. *AA* (n. 20), 47, 119–20.
[49] Cf. *AA* (n. 20), 99 with n. 631; 100 nn. 647–8.
[50] Arist. *Pol.* 1320ᵃ22 ff.; *Rhet.* 1411ᵃ28 (with the note by Wartelle in the Budé edn.).

III

In the first section I argued that the *dikasteria*, the people's court, formed a unified and independent body of government. In the second section I tried to explain the Athenians' reasons for distinguishing between the *dikasteria* and the *demos* in assembly. I now turn to the third question: how important were the *dikasteria* for the working of the Athenian democracy compared with the other bodies of government: the *ekklesia*, the *boule*, and the other boards of *archai*?

The prominence of the popular courts is apparent from numerous sources: The Old Oligarch claims that the Athenians are notorious for carrying on more lawsuits than all other Greeks combined; and according to Thucydides the Athenians openly admit the veracity of this statement. In Aristophanes' *Clouds* a pupil of Sokrates places a map before Strepsiades and points out to him on the map where Athens is. But Strepsiades refuses to believe him because he cannot see the law courts on the map. Similarly, in the *Wasps*, the toothless Philokleon uses biting words to demonstrate the powers of the jurors, and the young Bdelykleon can take the sting out of his arguments only by pointing out that the real power rests with the cunning politicians who misuse their eloquence to manipulate the jurors.[51] In the *Politics* Aristotle states that a citizen exercises his political rights primarily by being a *dikastes* and an *ekklesiastes*. He notes, of course, that this applies first and foremost to citizens in a democracy;[52] and accordingly, he (and/or his pupil) concludes the historical description of the Athenian constitution with the following dictum: 'the common people have made themselves masters of everything, and control all things by decrees (*psephismata*) and by courts (*dikasteria*) which are controlled by the common people (the *demos*).'[53] In this condensed sentence a type of decision (*psephismata*) is juxtaposed with a body of government (*dikasteria*). In its full form

[51] [Xen.] *Ath. Pol.* 3. 2, cf. 1. 16–18; Thuc. 1. 77; Aristoph. *Clouds* 206 ff.; *Wasps* 526–729.

[52] Arist. *Pol.* 1275^{a}22–^{b}7.

[53] Arist. *Ath. Pol.* 41.2. On the meaning of *demos* in this passage cf. *AA* (n. 20), 96 with n. 612.

the statement would run as follows: 'the common people have made themselves masters of everything and control all things through *psephismata* [pased in the *ekklesia*] and [by decisions made] by the *dikasteria*.'[54]

Of the six passages I have adduced there is an essential difference between the first four and the last two. The Old Oligarch, Thucydides, and Aristophanes emphasize the importance of the *dikasteria* in connection with the administration of justice in general; whereas in both the Aristotelian passages the courts are mentioned in a constitutional context side by side with the assembly as a body of government of the same importance in the decision-making process as the *ekklesia*. This strikes a modern reader as strange. Admittedly, in traditional descriptions of states and constitutions we are told that in a state there are three branches of government: the legislative, the executive, and the judiciary.[55] This tripartition has been immortalized by Montesquieu in his *De l'esprit des lois* of 1748. But in the famous sixth chapter of the eleventh book, Montesquieu emphasizes that '[the power of] the judiciary is in some measure empty' (168); 'the judgements should be ever identical with the text of the law' (166). Montesquieu does not accord the judicial branch an equal status with the executive and the legislative: 'as we have already observed the national judges are no more than the mouth that pronounces the words of the law, mere passive beings, incapable of moderating either its force or its rigour' (171).[56] Admittedly, some constitutions, as for example the constitution of the United States, assign a political role to the judiciary;[57] but regularly, whenever a state's constitution is described in detail both historians and philosophers and students of political science tend to forget the judiciary. They describe legislation by parliaments and administration by governments, but they have little or nothing to say about the courts apart from the section on the separation of powers,

[54] Precisely the same juxtaposition of *psephismata* and *dikasteria* is found in Aeschin. 2. 178.

[55] Cf. H. Kelsen, *General Theory of Law and State* (Cambridge, Mass., 1946), pp. 269 ff.; M. J. C. Vile, *Constitutionalism and the Separation of Powers* (Oxford, 1967).

[56] Montesquieu, *De l'esprit des lois* (1748), XI. 6; the page references given are to the Garnier edition. Cf. also Vile (n. 55), pp. 86–97.

[57] H. J. Abraham, *The Judiciary: The Supreme Court in the Governmental Process* (7th edn. Boston, 1987).

where the author lists the judiciary as one of the three branches of government and emphasizes 'the independence of the judiciary from control or influence by the political branches of government'.[58]

This traditional truth has become even more apparent during the last decades. In recent years students of political science have stopped speaking of states. The object of their science is now 'political systems'. And of the three traditional branches of government the judiciary has almost completely disappeared. The focus of attention is now on parties and pressure groups, and, in so far as constitutional institutions are discussed, the debate concentrates on the relation between the legislative and the executive.[59] There are exceptions. It is still hard to describe the American Constitution without mentioning the Supreme Court and its judicial review of congressional acts.[60] During the last two decades judicial review has become a formidable check on the legislatures in France and Germany (see n. 114). Similarly, judicial review of laws is prescribed and fairly common in several of the members of the British Commonwealth.[61] But in the United Kingdom itself judicial review of laws is unknown, and impeachment has not been used since 1805.[62] In British constitutional theory the courts are conspicuous by their absence.

Now we ancient historians inevitably apply modern concepts and structures in our analysis of the past. It is my impression that especially British ancient historians tend to underestimate the political powers of the Athenian *dikasteria*; and this is important since, in the last decades, the generally accepted picture of Athenian democracy has been deeply influenced, sometimes almost shaped by British ancient historians. In their typical account of Athenian democracy, the emphasis is on the

---

[58] P. Cane, *An Introduction to Administrative Law* (Oxford, 1986), p. 17.

[59] Cf. e.g. J. Blondel (ed.), *Comparative Government* (London, 1969), pp. 10–20 (on 'political systems', by Almond and Powell), 145–83 (on constitutions, by Loewenstein, Vernay, and Friedrich).

[60] Cf. e.g. W. C. Harvard, *The Government and Politics of the United States* (London, 1965), pp. 43–69: 'The Supreme Court and the Constitution'; J. L. Waltman and K. M. Holland (eds.), *The Political Role of Law Courts in Modern Democracies* (London, 1988), pp. 96–8, 140–4.

[61] K. C. Wheare, *Modern Constitutions* (Oxford, 1966), pp. 100–20: Judicial Interpretation.

[62] The impeachment of Lord Melville for alleged malversation of office.

boule, on the *strategoi*, and on the demagogues. There is very little about the political powers of the *dikasteria*, and in their discussions of the *ekklesia* and the *boule* historians tend to focus on the organization and powers of the *boule*.[63] The unconscious(?) modern parallel is obvious: the *boule* corresponds to the parliament, the *strategoi* to the government, and the demagogues to the politicians. The *ekklesia* has no modern parallel, and the powers of the *dikasteria* in decision-making and politics are unparalleled in Britain. The *ekklesia* and the *dikasteria*, however, are the two institutions which Aristotle singles out as the most important both in democracies in general and in Athenian democracy in particular.[64] All speeches, both symbouleutic and forensic, support the Aristotelian analysis of Athenian democracy. Thus an account of Athenian democracy in the age of Aristotle and Demosthenes ought to give prominence to the *ekklesia* and the *dikasteria*, whereas the sections on the *boule*, the *strategoi*, and the demagogues ought to be cut down and treated in relation to the two basic branches of government.[65]

[63] Cf. e.g. C. Hignett, *A History of the Athenian Constitution to the End of the Fifth Century B.C.* (Oxford, 1952). In the chapter 'Radical Democracy' (pp. 214–51) Hignett correctly distinguishes between 'the three popular bodies, the *ekklesia*, the *boule*, and the *dikasteria*' (p. 215), but on the preceding page he makes the questionable statement that 'in a radical democracy the only body that can be trusted to share power with the *ekklesia* is the popular council' (p. 214). A. H. M. Jones, *Athenian Democracy* (Oxford, 1957): in the chapter 'How Did the Athenian Democracy Work?' Jones devotes less than one page to the *dikasteria* (pp. 123–4), but has much longer sections on the council, the assembly, the *strategoi*, and the *rhetores*. P. J. Rhodes, 'Athenian Democracy after 403 B.C.', *Class J.* 75 (1979–80), 305–23: Rhodes has a fairly long section on the lawcourts (pp. 315–20) where he deals with written documents, arbitrators, payments, and social composition of *dikasteria*, etc. But there is nothing about the political powers of the *dikasteria*. The *graphe paranomon* is mentioned in a footnote only (n. 112) and the reforms of *dokimasia*, *euthynai*, and *eisangelia* are passed over in silence. S. Hornblower, *The Greek World 479–323 B.C.* (London, 1983), 'Athens', pp. 106–26; id., 'Democracy' in *The Oxford History of the Classical World* (Oxford, 1986), pp. 136–41: in both accounts Hornblower treats the demes, the *boule*, the *ekklesia*, the *strategoi*, and the demagogues, but has nothing to say about the *dikasteria*.

[64] Arist. *Pol.* 1273^b–74^a; 1275^{a-b}; *Ath. Pol.* 41. 2, where Aristotle brings his general evaluation of the contemporary Athenian democracy. The account given in ss. 43–68 consists only of scattered notes on individual magistracies (beginning with the *boule*) and on the organization of the *dikasteria*. There is no attempt to assess the relative importance of the institutions described; the account of the *ekklesia* is brought in as a note in the description of the *boule*; there is no mention of *nomothetai*, and only three casual remarks about the Areopagos.

[65] In the description of the *dikasteria* and their relation to the *ekklesia* I have deliberately left out any discussion of the third decision-making body of government in fourth-century Athens, i.e. the *nomothetai*, cf. *AA* (n. 20), p. 97 with n. 617.

IV

Is it possible, within the courts' jurisdiction, to isolate their settlement of private disputes from their political jurisdiction? And were the Athenians aware of any differentiation along such lines? My answer to these questions requires a digression on an important aspect of the Greek *polis*, and as usual most of the evidence we have relates to classical Athens. Sources discussing society regularly contrast the private sphere and the public sphere. What is *idion* is set off against what is *demosion* or *koinon*.[66] The dichotomy of the private and the public is apparent in all aspects of life and society. The *idiotes* is opposed to the *politeuomenos*,[67] the citizens' homes to public buildings,[68] the national interest to private profit,[69] public finance to private means;[70] in political ideology the basic democratic concept liberty (*eleutheria*) is subdivided into a political part— 'ruling and being ruled in turn' (*to en merei archein kai archesthai*)'—and a private part—'live as you like' (*zen hos bouletai tis*).[71] For my topic it is important to note that the private– public dichotomy pervades the entire organization of the administration of justice: the classification of laws, offences, procedures, courts, parties to the case, and penalties to be inflicted. First, the laws of the city are often subdivided into private and public,[72] and the distinction made by the Athenians

[66] *IG* i³ 105. 29; Thuc. 2. 37. 1–2; Eur. *Or.* 765; Aristoph. *Eccl.* 206–8; Xen. *Hell.* 1. 4. 13; Pl. *Rep.* 458 c; Lys. 12. 2 Andoc. 1. 9; Isoc. 7. 30; Dem. 20. 136; Aeschin. 1. 30; Isaeus 7. 30; Lycurg. 1. 3; Din. 2. 8; Hyp. 5.30; Arist. *Pol.* 1329ᵇ35–30ᵃ33; law quoted at Dem. 46. 26.

[67] Dem. 10. 70; 18. 45; 24. 193; 26. 3; 26. 3; 52. 28; *Prooem.* 13. 1; Aeschin. 1. 195; Hyp. 3. 27.

[68] Dem. 3. 25, 29; 13. 30; 21. 17; 23. 207–8; 55. 16; Arist. *Pol.* 1321ᵇ19 ff.

[69] Xen. *Hell.* 1. 4. 13; Dem. 18. 255, 295; 19. 1; 21. 8; Hyp. 1. 39.

[70] Lys. 19. 18; Andoc. 3. 20; Dem. 11. 20; 49. 23; 50. 7, 26–28.

[71] Arist. *Pol.* 1317ᵃ40–ᵇ17; cf. Thuc. 2. 37. 1–2.

[72] Dem. 24. 192–3: 'There are two sorts of problems, men of Athens, with which the laws of all nations are concerned. First, what are the principles under which we associate with one another, have dealings with one another, define the obligations of private life, and, in general, order our social relations? Secondly, what are the duties that every man among us owes to the commonwealth, if he chooses to take part in public life and professes any concern for the state? Now, it is to the advantage of the common people that laws of the former category, laws of private intercourse, shall be distinguished by clemency and humanity. On the other hand, it is to your common advantage that laws of the second class, the laws that govern relations to the state, shall be trenchant and peremptory, because, if they are so, political leaders will not do so

is strikingly similar to our distinction between public and private law.[73] Both in the Greek cities and in modern societies the opposition between public and private law does not correspond to any formal subdivision of the law code, and it is often hard to draw the line between the two spheres. But there can be no denying the fundamental importance of the distinction. Next, in our sources offences are often described as either private or public, and the distinguishing mark is whether the injured party is an individual or the *polis* itself.[74] Third, the offender is brought to trial either as a private individual or as a citizen exercising his political rights.[75] Fourth, legal proceedings are subdivided into public actions (*demosiai dikai*) and private actions (*idiai dikai*).[76] A public action can be brought by any citizen on behalf of the injured person or on behalf of the *polis* itself. A private action can be brought by the injured person only.[77] Fifth, both private and public actions are heard by the people's court, but private actions run for a part of the day only and are heard by panels of 200 or 400 jurors, whereas a public action fills the whole day and is heard by 500 jurors, sometimes even by 1,000 or 1,500 or even more.[78] Finally, the penalties are more severe in cases warranted by public law, whereas leniency—a characteristic of democracy[79]—is recommended in cases regulated by private law.[80] And one penalty, the loss of rights (*atimia*), was exclusively imposed on persons

much harm to the commonalty. Therefore, when he [Timokrates] makes use of this plea, refute it by telling him that he is introducing clemency, not into the laws that benefit you, but into the laws that intimidate political leaders.' Cf. Dem. 18. 210; Aeschin. 1. 195; Pl. *Laws* 734 E–35 A; Arist. *Pol.* 1289ᵃ15–20.

[73] Cane (n. 58), 4: 'Private law might be defined as law regulating the relations of private persons, whether individuals, corporations, or unincorporated associations with one another. This definition suggests that public law concerns the activities of governmental agencies; it regulates relations between governmental agencies and private individuals on the one hand, and between different governmental agencies on the other'.

[74] Dem. 21. 25–8, 32, 44–5; Pl. *Laws* 767 B; Arist. *Rhet.* 1373ᵇ18–24.

[75] Aeschin. 3. 252–3. cf. below n. 85.

[76] Lys. 1. 44; Is. 11. 32; Pl. *Euthyphr.* 2 A; Dem. 22. 25–8; 46. 26 (*nomos*); Arist. *Ath. Pol.* 56. 6. Cf. J. H. Lipsius, *Die attische Recht und Rechtsverfahren* i–iii (Leipzig, 1905–15), pp. 237–62.

[77] Isoc. 20. 2, cf. *GRBS* 22 (1981), 13.

[78] Arist. *Ath. Pol.* 53. 3; 68. 1. Cf. H. Hommel, *Heliaia* (*Philologus*, suppl. 19; 1927), 778–83.

[79] Dem. 22. 51, 24. 24.

[80] Dem. 18. 210; 22. 30–2; 26. 4.

convicted of crimes related to public law.[81] The administration of justice has many different aspects, and the line between public and private was not always drawn precisely in the same place. Some private offences, for example, were redressed by public actions to be brought by any citizen;[82] and conversely, some claims arising out of liturgies were nevertheless considered to be actionable through private actions.[83] It is noticeable, however, that in many sources the administration of justice in the public sphere tends to be identified with the administration of justice in political matters.[84] The Athenians distinguished between public and private law and, correspondingly, between jurisdiction in political and private matters. The clearest delimitation emerges if we focus on the status of the defendant: political trials are actions raised against citizens in their capacity as either magistrates (*archai*), or political leaders (*rhetores*), or ordinary citizens (*politai*) exercising their political rights or performing their civic duties.[85]

V

How important was the political part of the powers exercised by the people's court when balanced against their jurisdiction in private matters? Reading the standard accounts of Athenian law,[86] one gets the impression that the Athenian jurors must have spent most of the court days (which, on my calculation numbered about 150–200)[87] hearing criminal and civil actions raised by private citizens against private citizens and relating to private matters. Then, in addition to hearing all the cases brought by individuals against individuals, the court had some political jurisdiction: especially the *dokimasia* (examination of

[81] Cf. M. H. Hansen, *Apagoge, Endeixis and Ephegesis* (Odense, 1976), p. 74.
[82] In Dem. 21. 32, e.g. the *graphe hybreos* is described as a type of (public) action to be used in the private sphere.
[83] *Skepseis* brought by trierarchs are brought before courts manned with 201 jurors, i.e. they are considered to be private and not public actions, cf. *IG* ii² 1629. 204–17.
[84] Dem. 18. 210; 24. 192–93; 26. 4.
[85] Dem. 22. 30–2; 25. 40; Aeschin. 1. 195; Hyp. 3. 8–9, 27; Din. 1. 99–101.
[86] L. Beauchet, *Histoire du droit privé de la république Athénienne* i–iv (Paris, 1897); Lipsius (n. 76); A. R. W. Harrison, *The Law of Athens* i–ii (Oxford, 1968–71).
[87] M. H. Hansen, 'How Often Did the Athenian *Dicasteria* Meet?', *GRBS* 20 (1979), 243–6.

incoming magistrates), the *euthynai* (audit of magistrates), the *eisangeliai* (impeachments), and the *graphai paranomon* (public actions against unconstitutional proposals), all rather important procedures, but not as time-consuming as the jurisdiction in civil matters. I tend to believe that the *dikasteria* mattered more in political jurisdiction and less in private jurisdiction than often assumed.[88]

To start with, there are important limitations to the courts' jurisdiction in private matters. First, many of the civil cases coming within the jurisdiction of the forty tribe judges (*hoi tettarakonta*) must have been settled by the public arbitrators (*diaitetai*)[89] and thus never reached the courts. Because our sources are forensic speeches delivered before the people's court[90] we tend to assume that most cases were brought before the juries by appeal. But most private actions may well have been settled out of court. Second, with a few exceptions homicide trials were heard by the council of the Areopagos or the *ephetai* (cf. above p. 216), and not by the popular courts.[91] Third, the law prescribed that thieves and robbers caught in the act be arrested, dragged before the Eleven (*hoi hendeka*), and executed without trial if they confessed to their crime.[92] Thus, they were only to be brought before a *dikasterion* if, before the Eleven, they pleaded not guilty.[93]

[88] My view is much more in line with that found in the American handbook on Athenian law: R. J. Bonner and G. Smith, *The Administration of Justice from Homer to Aristotle* i–ii (Chicago, 1930–8), or the view of G. Busolt and H. Swoboda, *Griechische Staatskunde* i–ii (Munich, 1920–6), e.g. pp. 922, 1006–14.

[89] Cf. Harrison (n. 86), ii. 66–8; D. M. MacDowell, *The Law in Classical Athens* (London, 1978), pp. 207–11. Cf. the judicious observations by E. Ruschenbusch, 'Drei Beiträge zur öffentlichen *Diaita* in Athen', *Symposion*, 1982 (Valencia, 1985), pp. 36–7.

[90] Cf. Bonner and Smith (n. 88), ii. 115–16.

[91] Dem. 23. 63–81; Arist. *Ath. Pol.* 57. 2–4. D. M. MacDowell, *Athenian Homicide Law* (Manchester, 1963).

[92] Aeschin. 1. 91, 113; Arist. *Ath. Pol.* 52. 1; Dem. 24. 65. The sources for the *nomos ton kakourgon* (prescribing instant execution without trial of 'felons') are collected and discussed in M. H. Hansen, 'The Prosecution of Homicide in Athens', *GRBS* 22 (1981), 22–6.

[93] In a recent study, '*Akriton Apokteinai*: Execution without Trial in Fourth-Century Athens', *GRBS* 25 (1984), E. M. Carawan has argued that this law must have been a dead letter since 'the accused was not likely to confess if he knew that his life was at stake' (p. 112). This observation is logically correct but psychologically wrong. The history of crime shows that criminals caught red-handed mostly confess regardless of the consequences. Next, in the same study, it has been pointed out that there is not much evidence to show that the law warranting the instant execution of thieves and robbers was often enforced (pp. 116–20 discussing the evidence I presented in *Apagoge*

The jurisdiction connected with politics, on the other hand, was both important and time-consuming. The annual examination (*dokimasia*) of some 700 incoming magistrates (*archai*)[94] in addition to the *dokimasia* of some of the five hundred councillors (*bouleutai*),[95] must have been very laborious—and boring—since the jurors had to vote by ballot on every single candidate no matter whether his candidature had been disputed or not.[96] Thus, quite apart from those cases in which an accusation raised against a candidate resulted in a proper exchange of speeches between prosecutors and candidates, the

[n. 81], cat. nos. 7, 13, 23, 30, and in *Eisangelia* [Odense, 1975], cat. no. 141). True, but it is equally important to note that there is not much evidence either of thieves and robbers being put on trial. The only unquestionable attestation of an *apagoge* for robbery resulting in a hearing before a *dikasterion* is the trial of Agoratos' brother for *lopodysia* (robbery of a cloak), Lys. 13. 67–8; cf. also *Apagoge*, 121 and cat. nos. 6, 18, 30. Trials of kidnappers and robbers are referred to in general in Dem. 4. 47, cf. below p. 237. The Athenians had no police, and most thieves and robbers, if not caught in the act, were probably never caught. Furthermore, it is a fact that we have no forensic speeches and no titles of lost speeches concerning denunciation and arrest for theft or robbery. The reason must be either that the Athenians were more honest than other people, or rather that such cases regularly did not reach the courts and did not leave their mark in the form of a speech. It is true that most thieves and robbers were probably too poor to pay a logographer and too uneducated to compose a speech worth publishing, cf. *Apagoge*, 54. But the persons who were robbed or had their money stolen were often well off and could be expected either to buy a speech from a logographer or to make a memorable speech themselves. Thus the very few attestations of execution without trial are balanced by the equally few attestations of thieves and robbers being put on trial in consequences of their arrest. The silence of our sources seems in fact to support the view that the Athenians may well have done what the law instructed them to do: to redress serious offences against property by instant execution if the offender was caught in the act.

[94] On the number of magistrates cf. M. H. Hansen, 'Seven Hundred *Archai* in Classical Athens', *GRBS* 21 (1980), 151–73.

[95] The *dokimasia* of the (nine) archons and the (five hundred) councillors was conducted both by the (outgoing) *boule* and by the *dikasteria*, Arist. *Ath. Pol.* 45. 3. Whereas double *dokimasia* was obligatory for the archons (Dem. 20. 90), the *dokimasia* of a councillor was probably referred to a *dikasterion* only if the candidate had been rejected by the *boule*, cf. Rhodes (n. 26), pp. 176–8.

[96] The law on *dokimasia* of magistrates was revised in 403/2 (Lys. 26. 9, 20) and is described in some detail in *Ath. Pol.* 55. 2–4 in connection with the description of how the nine archons were selected and appointed, cf. *AE* (n. 14), 189–90. Both the *boule* (Lys. 26. 10) and the *dikasterion* (*Ath. Pol.* 55. 4) had the right to reject a candidate whom nobody had accused. Thus a vote must have been taken on all candidates, both in the *boule* (by show of hands) and in the *dikasterion* (by ballot) (*Ath. Pol.* 55. 4). The obligatory vote applied to the *dokimasia* of both archons (*Ath. Pol*) and *bouleutai* (Lys.) Lysias says (26. 9) that the revised law on *dokimasia* concerned magistrates (in general, not just archons). The reasonable inference is that, in the *dokimasia*, the *dikastai* had to vote on everyone of the *c.* 700 candidates in addition to those *bouleutai* who, having been rejected by the *boule*, had their case referred to a *dikasterion*.

routine *dokimasia* of all other candidates—questions to be answered and the vote to be taken—must have taken more than 200 hours of the available court days in the last month of the year, the equivalent of one *dikasterion* sitting nine hours a day for twenty-two days or even more.

For similar reasons, the audit of all *archai* on the expiration of their office (*euthynai*) must have consumed a considerable amount of the jurors' time in the first month of the new year.[97]

Again, in the course of the year the juries were involved in much administration and routine business which is not often discussed in the conventional accounts of the Athenian *dikasteria*. Let me adduce some examples. Whenever a squadron was sent out, the courts were instructed to hear protests (*skepseis* and *antidoseis*) raised by the trierarchs instructed to launch their ships.[98] Whenever public works were leased by public auction, a section of the people's court had to witness and confirm the sale.[99] And whenever confiscated property was sold at an auction, the Eleven presided over a section of the *dikasterion*.[100]

Less time-consuming, but much more important than the *dokimasia*, were the *euthynai* and the other obligatory procedures, the public actions which were heard by the *dikasteria* only if a citizen took it upon himself to raise the matter and appear for the prosecution. The two most prominent types of political public action were the *eisangelia* (*eis ton demon*) and the *graphe paranomon*, but there were many other types which, in this paper, I will pass over in silence.[101]

---

[97] Arist. *Ath. Pol.* 54. 2; Aeschin. 3. 22–3; Dem. 18. 117; Harpocration and *Lexica Segueriana* s.v. *logistai*. The checking of all accounts must have been more time-consuming than the few and simple questions asked during the *dokimasia*. On the other hand, the jurors hearing the *euthynai* can have voted only on magistrates who had been charged by somebody with misconduct in office. An obligatory vote on a magistrate not accused by anybody would make nonsense; for, in case of conviction, who would know whether the condemned magistrate had to pay the simple or the tenfold fine? And a renewed hearing after a verdict of guilty would be in conflict with the principle *ne bis in eadem*.

[98] Arist. *Ath. Pol.* 61. 1; *IG* ii² 1629. 204–17, cf. Rhodes (n. 11), p. 681.

[99] Public works: *IG* ii² 1669. 8, 18, 21, 38; 1670. 34–5.

[100] Arist. *Ath. Pol.* 52. 1; cf. *Hesperia*, 5 (1936), 393–413, no. 10, ll. 11–12, 115–16; *Hesperia*, 19 (1950), 236–40, no. 14, ll. 45–6.

[101] Other types of public action used exclusively in 'political' trials (but not discussed in this article) are *apophasis, apographe, dokimasia ton rhetoron, probole*, and the following types of *graphe: agraphiou, adikiou, alogiou, bouleuseos* (type 2), *dekasmou, doron, epistatike, katalyseos tou demou, klopes demosion chrematon, nomon me epitedeion theinai, prodosias, proedrike, pseudengraphes, sykophantias*.

The *eisangelia eis ton demon* (denunciation to the people in assembly) was a public action brought against persons charged with treason, attempt to overthrow the democracy, and corruption. It was usually initiated by a denunciation made in the principal assembly (*ekklesia kyria*) which resulted in a decree by which the case was referred to a *dikasterion*. *Eisangeliai* were brought especially against the generals (*strategoi*), and the result was usually a verdict of guilty and a sentence of death.[102]

The *graphe paranomon* was a public action against a *rhetor* who had proposed (and carried) a decree (*psephisma*) that was contrary to the laws in force and/or inexpedient. The action could be brought by any citizen either before or after the *psephisma* had been passed by the people in assembly. The *psephisma* was suspended until the case had been heard by a section of the *dikasteria*. If convicted, the proposer was punished and his *psephisma* annulled.[103]

A collection of all attested occurrences of these two types of public action alone indicates that the control exercised in classical Athens by the people's court over the political leaders was unparalleled in world history.

First the *eisangelia*. In the *First Philippic* Demosthenes has a scornful and despairing remark about the Athenian *strategoi*:

So scandalous is our present system that every general is tried two or three times for his life in your courts, but not one of them dares to risk death in battle against the enemy. No not once. They prefer the doom of a kidnapper or a pickpocket to a fitting death. For malefactors are condemned to the gallows, generals should die on the field of honour.[104]

Demosthenes is no doubt exaggerating, as he often does; but a collection of *eisangeliai* brought against *strategoi* indicates that he is not far from the truth. If we concentrate on the 77 years from the beginning of the Peloponnesian War in 432 to 355 (excluding 404), the sources provide us with the names of 143 generals covering 289 of the 770 *strategiai* to be filled.[105] Out of

---

[102] Cf. J. Tolbert Roberts, *Accountability in Athenian Government* (Wisconsin, 1982); Hansen (n. 94).

[103] Cf. H. J. Wolff, '*Normenkontrolle' und Gesetzesbegriff in der attischen Demokratie* (Heidelberg, 1970); Hansen (n. 28).

[104] Dem. 4. 47 (trans. J. H. Vince).

[105] For the period 432/1–405/4 my count of generals and their terms of office is based on C. W. Fornara, *The Athenian Board of Generals from 501 to 404* (*Historia*, Einzelschrif-

these 143 generals 35 are attested in our sources as having been impeached by *eisangelia*, one of them twice and another three times.[106]

A close examination of the evidence indicates that our fragmentary sources give us information about a fairly random selection of named *strategoi* and a fairly random selection of *eisangeliai* brought against *strategoi*.[107] A simple check disproves the assumption that a significant number of generals are known merely because they were put on trial. Thus the two figures are probably comparable. Since we know that 35 out of 143 known *strategoi* were impeached by *eisangelia*, the presumption is that perfect sources would show that, on average, out of ten generals serving on a board, at least two would sooner or later in the course of their career (when re-elected) be indicted by an *eisangelia eis ton demon*. Furthermore, most of the indicted generals were sentenced to death (often *in absentia*, since many generals preferred to flee Attica before the trial, or never to return to Athens, if the *eisangelia* had been raised in their absence).[108] Moreover, the *eisangelia* was only one of the types of public action brought against generals.[109] Thus the rate of political trials of generals in classical Athens seems to match the

---

ten 16; 1971)—but add Eryximachos 405/4, cf. *P. Ryl.* 489, p. 105. For the period 403/2–355/4 is based on my own updated inventory of *rhetores* and *strategoi* in *The Athenian Ecclesia* ii (n. 21), pp. 34–68. I exclude the oligarchic generals of 411 and the year 404/3 when no democratic generals were appointed. Thus my investigation covers 77 years, not 78. In my *Eisangelia* (n. 93), pp. 60 ff. I presented slightly higher figures (160 generals covering *c.* 300 *strategiai*). The difference is due to the fact that in 1975 I had to base my count of fourth-century generals on the rather sketchy list compiled by Beloch in *Die attische Politik seit Perikles* (Leipzig, 1884), pp. 295–8. A closer inspection of the sources, conducted in 1983, gave some new names of generals, but on the other hand stricter criteria for accepting a military leader as *strategos* combined with the exclusion of broken names have brought the figure down from 160 to 143. In his *Wealth and the Power of Wealth in Classical Athens* (New York, 1981) J. K. Davies lists 140 *strategoi* (plus 4 with a query added); he has no count of *strategiai*.

[106] The names and trials of the 35 generals impeached by *eisangelia* in the period 432–355 are listed in Hansen (n. 93), p. 58 n. 2, cf. n. 16 (35, not 33). Note that in some cases the type of action used may have been an *euthynai* vel sim. and not an *eisangelia eis ton demon*, cf. Hansen (n. 93), pp. 66–7.

[107] For a detailed discussion, cf. Hansen (n. 93), pp. 60–1.

[108] The results of *eisangeliai* against generals are reported in Hansen (n. 93), pp. 63–4 with nn. 44–51. 27 generals were convicted, 5 acquitted, in 3 cases the result is unknown.

[109] For *eisangeliai* against unnamed generals as well as other types of political public action used against generals cf. Hansen (n. 93), pp. 61–3 with nn. 28–43.

French revolution under Robespierre or the Red Army purges under Stalin.[110]

Next, the *graphe paranomon* was the principal weapon used against the *rhetores* in the *ekklesia*. Again, a collection of known applications of the *graphe paranomon*[111] indicates that, on average, the Athenians every month every year instructed a *dikasterion* to hear a *graphe paranomon* and to decide whether a decree of the people was constitutional or not. Thus in the course of their career almost all the prominent political leaders must have been put on trial by a *graphe paranomon*, not just once, but several times.[112] I find it illuminating, in spite of all the important differences, to compare Athens with the modern state in which judicial review of laws matters most.[113] Since 1803 the Supreme Court of the United States has been empowered to strike down any act of congress or portion thereof. In the period 1803–1986 the Supreme Court has exercised judicial review of federal enactments 135 times.[114] Our sources indicate that the Athenian *dikasteria* reached this figure in less than two decades, not in two centuries.

VI

To sum up. The Athenian *dikasteria* exercised a constant control over all *archai* through *dokimasia* and *euthynai*, over the *strategoi* through the *eisangelia*, and over the *rhetores* through the *graphe paranomon*. It was these political powers bestowed on the *dikasteria* and constantly wielded by the *dikastai* which gave rise to the view stated in many fourth-century sources that it was the courts, and not the assembly, that were what we would call

[110] On the French Revolution cf. J. M. Thompson, *The French Revolution* (Oxford, 1962), pp. 494–5. On the Red Army purges cf. D. Thomson, *Europe since Napoleon* (London, 1957), pp. 678–81.

[111] 39 applications are listed in Hansen (n. 28), pp. 28–43. Cat. no. 8, however, should probably be deleted.

[112] The evidence is listed in *AA* (n. 20), 177 nn. 652–3.

[113] The same comparison is made by Bonner and Smith (n. 88), ii. 296.

[114] Cf. Abraham (n. 57), 66–75. In recent years, however, judicial review of laws has risen to Athenian heights both in Germany (constitutional court established in 1949) and in France (constitutional council established in 1958, very active from 1974). In both countries almost every important legislative battle in parliament between the parties will be carried before the constitutional court or council by the losing faction.

the sovereign body of government. The modern concept 'sovereignty', however, is better avoided in an analysis of the Greek *polis*.[115] Thus I prefer to put the statement in Greek and to say that the Athenian *diakasteria* were *kyria tes poleos* (masters of the city) or *kyria tes politeias* (masters of the constitution) or *kyria panton* (masters of everything).[116]

Let us imagine for a moment that we were removed to Athens in the age of Demosthenes and could ask an ordinary Athenian the crucial question: 'who is *kyrios* in Athens?' All sources indicate that the immediate and spontaneous reply would be '*hoi nomoi*, 'the laws'.[117] If asked, however, 'which persons are *kyrioi*?' he would probably say 'the *demos* is *kyrios*',[118] but then he would take the *demos* to mean 'the whole of the people', 'the Athenian people', and not 'the common people' or 'the poor' as Plato or Aristotle would have told us.[119]

Now let us suppose that the interrogation was pushed one step further by the question, 'How and where does the Athenian *demos* exercise its supreme power?' The answer we expect would be 'in the *ekklesia* on the Pnyx where the people meet and make decisions about all important matters'. This is indeed what Aristophanes suggests in his *Knights* by calling the master Demos Pyknites, i.e. 'Mr Demos of Pnyx.[120] It is also the answer found in other fifth-century sources, for example in Antiphon's speeches where he says that 'unproblematical cases are settled by the law (*nomos*) or by the voters in the *ekklesia* who are *kyrioi pases tes politeias*, masters of the constitution.[121] Simi-

---

[115] Cf. *AA* (n. 20), 105–6.

[116] The adjective *kyrios* means 'master of' and in a constitutional context it is used in two different but related meanings: (*a*) competent and (*b*) supreme. In sense (*b*) *kyrios* bears some relation to our concept 'sovereign', especially when it governs an objective genetive, such as *tes poleos* (the state), *tes politeias* (the constitution), or *panton* (everything).

[117] The *nomoi* are *kyrioi*: Dem. 22. 46; 23. 73 (cf. 32, 69, 71, 89); 24. 118; 25. 20–1; Hyp. 3. 5; The *nomoi* save the state and the democratic constitution: Aeschin. 3. 6, 169, 196; Lycurg. 1. 4; fr. 70; Dem. 24. 156, 216. The inseparable connection between *nomoi* and *demokratia* is stressed in: Aeschin. 1. 4 (= 3. 6); 1. 5; 3. 169, 196–8, 202, 233; Dem. 24. 5, 75–6; 25. 20–1; Hyp. 3. 5; Lycurg. 1. 4; fr. 70; Din. 3. 15–16. The rule of law in democratic Athens is also emphasized in Dem. 21. 150, 188, 223–4; 24. 155, 212–14.

[118] Dem. 20. 107; 59. 89.

[119] Cf. e.g. Pl. *Rep.* 565 A–C; Arist. *Ath. Pol.* 9. 1; 41. 2. Documentation in *AE* (n. 14), 141–2, 151–2.

[120] Aristoph. *Knights* 42.

[121] Ant. 3. 1. 1 where the law and the assembly are described as *kyrioi tes politeias*

larly, in Xenophon's description of the Arginusai trial, we learn that the people in the *ekklesia* cry out that it would be outrageous to deprive the *demos* of its supreme power by referring the case to a *dikasterion*.[122] But the step from the supreme *demos* to the supreme *demos* in the *ekklesia* is conspicuously absent from all fourth-century sources.[123] Instead we are told that it is the jurors in the *dikasteria* who are *kyrioi* or *kyrioi panton*.[124] The people's court is set off against the people's assembly and is sometimes singled out, at the expense of the *ekklesia*, as the supreme body of government.[125] Occasionally, the *dikasteria* are even said to be above the laws.[126]

What is the reason for this conspicuous change from the fifth to the fourth century? Let us go back to the first and fundamental statement, 'the *nomoi* are *kyrioi*'. In the fourth century, *nomoi* were no longer made by the *demos* in the *ekklesia*; they were passed by *nomothetai* who were selected by lot from among

(masters of the constitution) so that only doubtful cases are referred to the *dikasteria*, cf. Aristoph. *Wasps* 590–1.

[122] Xen. *Hell.* 1. 7. 12.

[123] In Dem. 3. 30–1 (= 13. 31) it is stated that the *demos* (i.e. the assembly) had *previously* (i.e. in the 5th cent.) been *kyrios panton*.

[124] Dem. 21. 223–4: the *dikastai* are *kyrioi ton en te polei panton*, no matter whether the panel of jurors numbers 200 or 1,000 men. Dem. 24. 118: the *nomoi*, being *kyrioi*, make the *dikastai kyrioi panton*. Dem. 24. 148: Solon restricted the powers of the *boule*, but gave unlimited powers to the *dikasterion* (*kyriotaton hapanton*). Dem. 57. 56: not only the assemblies held in the demes, but also the *boule* and the *demos* are subordinate to the *dikasteria*. Dem. 58. 55: the responsibilities for the harbours in the Piraeus and for the administration in general rests with the *dikastai* who are *kyrioi hapanton*. Aeschin. 3. 20: according to the law, the council of the Areopagos (which is *kyrion ton megiston*) is subordinate to the people's court. Din. 1. 106: it would not be fair if the *dikastai*, who are *kyrioi panton*, reversed the correct decision made by the *demos* and the council of the Areopagos. Arist. *Pol.* 1274ᵃ4–5: Solon is held responsible for having made the people's court *kyrion panton*. Arist. *Ath. Pol.* 9. 1: when the common people (the *demos*) through the courts are invested with the power to make decisions (become *kyrios tes psephou*) they become the master of the constitution (*kyrios tes politeias*).

[125] Dem. 19. 297: many *rhetores* have dominated the assembly (the *demos*), but in the *dikasteria* no *rhetor* has ever succeeded in being superior to the jurors, the laws and the oaths. Dem. 24. 78: who will support a law which overrides a decision made by a *dikasterion* and allows a decision made by the jurors to be reversed by those who have taken no oath? (i.e. the citizens in the *ekklesia*, cf. s. 80). Dem. 59. 91; the *dikasterion* rescinds the decree if the people (i.e. the *ekklesia*) have been persuaded to bestow citizenship on a person unworthy of the honour. Aeschin. 3. 3–5: if the *ekklesia* is paralysed by corruption, democracy is protected only by the *graphe paranomon*. Dem. 57. 56, cf. above, n. 124.

[126] Dem. 24. 73, 78, 152: it would be wrong to pass a law by which the verdicts of the courts were rescinded. Isoc. 20. 22: criminals may show contempt of the laws in force, but never of the verdicts of the courts.

the 6,ooo jurors.[127] Next, and even more important, the Athenians were well aware that laws are invalid unless they are enforced; and the enforcement of the laws is a task incumbent on the *dikasteria*, especially after about 355, when the *ekklesia* was deprived of its right to act as a law court hearing political trials.[128]

So the view that the *dikasteria* were *kyria tes poleos*, or *tes politeias* or *hapanton* is a simple corollary of the basic view that the *nomoi* are *kyrioi*, but have to be enforced, combined with the fact that, in the age of Demosthenes, the *ekklesia* had lost its former powers concerning legislation and jurisdiction.

This conclusion, however, must be accompanied by a discussion of the sources on which it is based. Most of the statements which stress the supremacy of the people's court are made by Demosthenes in forensic speeches. And most of the speeches in question were written for delivery in public actions in which the jurors were asked to confirm or reverse a decision either made by the assembly (a *psephisma* indicted by a *graphe paranomon*)[129] or instigated by the assembly (a *nomos* indicted by a *graphe nomon me epitedeion theinai*, referred by the *ekklesia* to a *dikasterion*).[130] Consequently, we must envisage the possibility that our sources are biassed: the eagerness of the speaker to emphasize the prominence of the courts may be no more than a *captatio benevolentiae* attuned to the composition of the audience. On this view, however, we should expect a political leader just as confidently to emphasize the supremacy of the *ekklesia* in speeches held before the *demos*; and this is certainly not the case. In the *Olynthiacs* and the *Philippics* Demosthenes does not give

---

[127] Cf. D. M. MacDowell, 'Law-Making at Athens in the Fourth Century B.C.', *JHS* 95 (1975), 62–74; M. H. Hansen, '*Nomos* and *Psephisma* in Fourth-Century Athens' and 'Did the Athenian *Ecclesia* Legislate after 403/2 B.C.?', both in *AE* (n. 14), 161–206. P. J. Rhodes, '*Nomothesia* in Fourth-Century Athens', *CQ* 35 (1985), 55–60.

[128] The interdependence of laws and law-courts is most clearly expressed by Demosthenes at 21. 224: 'And what is the strength of the laws? If one of you is wronged and cries aloud will the laws run up and be at his side to assist him? No, they are only written texts and incapable of such action. Wherein then resides their power? In yourselves, if only you support them and make them all-powerful to help him who needs them. So the laws are strong through you, and you through the laws' (translated by J. H. Vince); cf. Aeschin. 1. 36; Dem. 24. 37; Lycurg 1. 4; and also Aeschin. 3. 8; Dem. 22. 46; 26. 8; Isoc. 20. 22.

[129] Dem. 18, *On the Crown*; 22, *Against Androtion*; 23, *Against Aristokrates*; Aeschin. 3, *Against Ktesiphon*.

[130] Dem. 20, *Against Leptines*; 24, *Against Timokrates*.

expression to such respect for the assembly as he does for the courts in his forensic speeches. On the contrary, when addressing the people, he often ventures to scold the *ekklesia* and criticize the *demos*,[131] whereas, in one symbouleutic speech, he even refers to the *dikasteria* as the bulwark of the democracy.[132] And this is not just a Demosthenic idiosyncrasy: criticism of the *demos* can be traced in the (very few) symbouleutic speeches composed by others;[133] and praise of the *dikasteria* is also common in forensic speeches by Aeschines, Lycurgus, Hyperides, and Dinarchus.[134] Furthermore, the prominence of the courts is emphasized by Aristotle both in the *Constitution of Athens* and in the *Politics*,[135] and an evaluation made by a metic in historical and analytical works is not likely to be biassed in so far as the separation of powers between the agencies of government is concerned. Thus the overwhelming number of passages emphasizing the supremacy of the courts in fourth-century Athens is probably representative of what the Athenians believed, and not just a number of compliments invented by Demosthenes to flatter his audience in a forensic speech.[136] The fact, however, that the *dikasteria* often took precedence over the *ekklesia* and were called *kyria tes politeias* must not lead to the erroneous belief that the *dikasteria* now mattered much more than the *ekklesia*. Admittedly, the *dikasteria* were considered the bulwark of the democracy,[137] but when the Athenians made decisions about war, peace, foreign policy, and important individual decisions concerning domestic policy, it was still the *demos* in the *ekklesia* that was *kyrios*. *Dikasteria* and *ekklesia* were equally important for the working of the Athenian democracy.[138] Thus, as my overall conclusion I will simply quote again the general description of Athenian democracy given in Aristotle's *Ath. Pol.* 41. 2: 'all things are controlled through *psephismata* [passed in the *ekklesia*] and [by decisions made] by the *dikasteria*.'

---

[131] Dem. 3. 14–15; cf. 1. 16; 4. 20, 30, 45; 8. 32–4, etc.
[132] Dem. 13. 16.
[133] Andoc. 3. 28–32.
[134] Aeschin. 3. 1–8, 20; Lycurg. 1. 4, 79; Hyp. 3. 35–6; Din. 1. 106.
[135] Arist. *Pol.* 1273ᵇ41–74ᵃ3; *Ath. Pol.* 9. 1; 41. 2.
[136] The above argumentation was set out in less detail in Hansen (n. 28), 18.
[137] Dem. 13. 16; 24. 2, 154; 25. 6; Aeschin. 3. 7–8, 235; Din. 3. 16; Lycurg. 1. 4. It is the *dikasteria* which protect the laws: Dem. 21. 223–4; 22. 45–6; 24. 37; Aeschin. 3. 6.
[138] Cf. *AA* (n. 20), 107, 124.

10

Public Property in the City

DAVID LEWIS

THE standard books on the Greek city either have no treatment of public property at all or take it for granted in treating public finances. This is an attempt to fill some of the gap. It is concerned mostly with classical Athens and operates with a rather narrow definition, pursuing the key Greek word for 'public', *demosios*.[1] It will emerge in the course of the paper that other forms of communal ownership operate functionally in a very similar way, in that the city can exercise control of their administration and revenues.

In the Appendix, I review some current views about the history of the word *demos*, and conclude that it can, very early and certainly before the word *demosios* starts appearing, simply mean the whole citizen body with no programmatic nuance of 'lower classes' or implications of democracy.

The earliest relevant appearance of *demosios* is in Solon fr. 4, the unjust *hegemones* (leaders) who steal and snatch, sparing neither sacred nor public property (*outh' hieron kteanon oute ti demosion pheidomenoi*, 12–13). It has been suggested to me that there may be some elements of persuasive definition here, with a transition from the property of individual members of the *demos* to that of the *demos* as a whole, but I incline to think that the lines do establish the concept of public property for Solon's time, as well as the use for it of the word *demosios*; we may also recall the statement, generally passed over, that Solon's *seisach-theia* involved the abolition of debts, both private (*idia*) and public (*demosia*) (Aristotle, *Ath. Pol.* 6. 1). There is of course no reason to think the usage specifically Athenian; we can recall the athlete who might get corn from the public possessions of

I am grateful to Sally Humphreys, Robin Osborne, and the editors for help in revision.

[1] There are others, notably *koinos* (common).

the city (*sita . . . demosion kteanon ek poleos*, Xenophanes fr. 2, 8).

Solon's language happens to contrast *demosia* with *hiera*; to *hiera* we shall return. We should note that later, at least from the fifth century, *demosia* are most commonly contrasted with *idia* (private), not only adjectivally, but in the adverbs *demosiai . . . idiai*. For reasons which are by no means clear to me, when the contrast is with *hiera*, it is more normal to use *hosia* (profane) than *demosia*, both in technical and non-technical contexts.

What are the origins of public property? If we simplify the origins and purpose of the *polis*, we can perhaps give it three primitive functions.

The role of common defence may not need money/property at first (walls are more a matter of labour), but is going to involve it as soon as the cost of the equipment needed (including, for instance, both ships and mercenaries) outruns the resources of individuals.

In the religious sphere, leaving buildings on one side for the moment, we might say, moving rapidly over some very rugged ground, that the community needs resources as soon as it moves in on or adds to the cults already being performed by family groups. These resources are not sacred in their origins, but are used to supplement the existing resources of the cults. The keyword here is *demoteles*, applicable both to sacrifices and to festivals.[2] I have no example of the word earlier than the fifth century, though I suspect it existed earlier.[3] So far we have covered the two main things which the archaic state spent its money on; compare the Peisistratidai, who out of their 5 per cent tax carried on their wars and sacrificed sacrifices (Thucydides 6. 54. 5). Admittedly, they also adorned the city fairly, but public building does not, I think, rank as a primitive function of the *polis*.[4]

The third primitive function is the administration of justice.

---

[2] Sacrifices, Herod. 6. 57. 1 (Sparta), Orac. *ap.* Dem. 21. 53; festival, Thuc. 2. 15. 2 (Athens, Synoikia). See now J. K. Davies, *Cambridge Ancient History*, iv² 379.

[3] The practice could be expressed in other ways. Note the Salaminioi in 363/2 (*LSCGS* 19. 20–1, 86–7): δ'σα μὲν ἡ πόλις παρέχει ἐκ τὸ δημοσίο, . . . ξύλα ἐφ' ἱεροῖς ἡ πόλις διδωσιν ἐκ κύρβεων.

[4] Temple-building, indeed may be an interest of the collectivity, but will always have been classified as *hieron*, not *demosion*.

Except for eccentric states who found it desirable to pay their juries, this cost no money. What it surely did do was to provide one obvious way in which the *polis/demos* could acquire property. Here the history of confiscation is important.[5] In a sense, confiscation is a capital punishment, associated—as it was, for example, in the list of penalties referred to an Athenian court for the fifth-century allies—with death, exile, and loss of civic rights. Someone is being excluded from the community, and the question inevitably arises as to what happens to his property. I do not propose to spend time on the theoretical political regimes in which there may have been no private property, no alienability of land, only *genos*-property. As strictly defined as this, they are incompatible with the confiscation of the property of individuals.[6]

Confiscation-words always seem to involve the *demos*-root. *demeuo* is the commonest verb, but there are isolated instances of *demosieuo* and *demosioo*. *demosion/demosia einai/gignesthai* (be or become public) are very common indeed.

The earliest alleged instance of confiscation which I have so far managed to recall is that of the Bacchiads of Corinth in 657. In the anti-Kypselos story of Herodotus 5. 92 ε, Kypselos exiled many Corinthians, deprived many of their property and a very large number of their life. There could be other ways of describing the event, and Nicolaus (*FGr Hist* 90 F 57 §7) has 'he exiled the Bacchiads and confiscated (*edemeuse*) their property'.[7] Let us throw in a couple of sixth-century examples: Peisistratos' property was auctioned by the *demosios* (presumably a public slave acting as herald) and bought by Kallias, the only person prepared to bid (Herodotus 6. 121. 2); at Naxos, Lygdamis found no one prepared to give much for the property of those whom he had exiled, and sold it back to the exiles (Aristotle, *Oeconomicus* 1346ᵇ7 ff.; there is a great deal missing from this story).

There are clearly various possibilities. As far as Corinth is

---

[5] I am not much concerned here with the history of the fine, surely very primitive, and of course possible long before the introduction of coinage.

[6] Cf. D. M. Lewis, in *Ancient Society and Institutions: Studies Presented to Victor Ehrenberg* (Oxford, 1966), pp. 181–2.

[7] '... may be nothing more than a restatement in fourth-century terms' (J. B. Salmon, *Wealthy Corinth* (Oxford, 1984), p. 195).

concerned, Will argued,[8] without evidence, that the Bacchiad land was distributed to the landless, and the same thing has sometimes been supposed to have happened at Athens, where confiscation by Peisistratos himself is not actually attested. Such situations constitute a redistribution of land, and create no permanent accession to the city's own property. Immediate resale of confiscated property was always common, and we have detailed evidence for it at Athens, above all with the confiscated property of the Hermokopidai and the Thirty. It is doubtful whether such resales ever did much to build the capital structure of the city. Periklean Athens was abnormal in carrying capital balances over from year to year. The normal Greek attitude did not distinguish between capital and income. Resale of confiscated property was straightforward reprivatization, to allow the proceeds of confiscations to balance the income and expenditure account for the current year (cf., for fourth-century Athens, Lysias 30. 22.) And, of course, there is always a strand of Greek thinking in which the city, faced with a windfall, may simply declare a dividend to its members; for Athens and for confiscations, I can only think of the property of the mining magnate Diphilos, and the story of the distribution of his property is not all that well attested ([Plutarch], *Lives of the Ten Orators* 843 D).

The possibility most relevant to us is that the confiscating city sees for the property confiscated either an actual practical use or a means of ensuring income. A situation akin to confiscation may arise at the end of a tyranny.[9] It is probably the case that the Athenian tyrants' property in the silver mines passed to the Athenians collectively, but otherwise I do not think I know a demonstrable Athenian case, and, in our fullest fourth-century texts about the retention and leasing of confiscated property, the property is in the hands, not of a state, but of the Delian and Delphian Amphictionies.[10]

What other means were there for the state to acquire property? At Athens, there seem to have been various legal conventions,

[8] *Korinthiaka* (Paris, 1955), pp. 477–81.
[9] A tyrant's objects of practical use may go for sacred purposes (e.g. Herod. 3. 123. 1).
[10] *Inscriptions de Délos* 98 B 31 ff.; *Fouilles de Delphes* iii 5. 15–18.

the origins of which are uncertain. I do not pretend to understand the entire legal situation about the silver mines, but it seems relatively clear that the state assumed the right to lease the use of what was underground.[11] I suppose that it was the case that the state owned the major quarries, but this was not, apparently, a universal rule; the deme of Eleusis in 332/1 can lease quarries which are sacred to or belong to Herakles in Akris (*SEG* xxviii 103). The concept of ownership may be inappropriate.[12] Similarly, it is not clear what the rules were about areas which were simply vacant, with no obvious claimant (*erema*). Xenophon in the *Poroi* (2. 6) asserts that, in the 350s, there were many vacant houses and plots within the walls and recommends giving the right of land-ownership (*enktesis*) to worthy metics who are prepared to build on them; nothing is said about the nature of the state's rights in the matter or about money passing.

To this we can add those areas which had been in the public domain for so long that no question of private property could arise. The Agora, the Kerameikos, and the Pnyx are the obvious examples; the various gymnasia may fall somewhere between public and sacred property. We find all these delimited by boundary-markers (*horoi*) without the use of *demosia*. One building, the prison, is distinctive enough actually to be called *to demosion*. Another category of importance is the road-system. It seems that it was generally recognized that roads were public property. We have *horoi* demarcating them and they are constantly named as boundaries; the main text which explicitly describes a road as *demosia* is Demosthenes 55 at 13 and 16.

What other pieces of real property can we see? The fifth century does not provide very much.[13] There is the publicly-owned house (*oikia demosia*) named as a boundary for the surface water to which the lessee of the shrine of Neleus/Kodros/Basile will be entitled (*IG* i³ 84. 36; 417 BC). This was certainly in Athens, apparently just inside the city-wall to the south of the Acropolis (Travlos, *Pictorial Dictionary*, 332 with

[11] See e.g. R. J. Hopper, *BSA* 48 (1953), 200–54.
[12] On quarries, see R. G. Osborne, *Demos* (Cambridge, 1985), pp. 93–110.
[13] The public bath-house and other public property discovered by Hiller in *IG* i² 385 have disappeared in *IG* i³ 420.

fig. 435). There is some reason to think that it may have been near the law-court at the Palladion, and it was surely large enough to serve as a clear landmark, but there is absolutely no indication as to its use.

But the greatest quantity of fifth-century evidence for public property is concerned with the Piraeus. What the status of the relevant land was before the Piraeus was planned we cannot know, and we have no indication of how the state went about acquiring it to implement the ideas of Themistokles and Hippodamos of Miletos.[14] Hippodamos is extremely relevant to our subject at the theoretical level. He apparently recommended (Aristotle, *Politics* 1267^{b}33 ff.) that a city's territory be divided into three, *hiera* to provide the resources for religious observance, *demosia*, or *koine*, from which the military class could live (Aristotle does not report how these two divisions would be worked), and *idia*, for the farmers. I doubt if this is directly relevant to his operations at the Piraeus. It now seems that his main innovation there was, not the grid-system of streets with which modern scholars have associated him, but which is certainly older, but the concepts of *nemēsis* and *diairesis*, the systematic allocation of different parts of an area for different purposes. We have a large number of fifth-century *horoi* from the Piraeus. I have no very clear ideas about their date or which of them can or cannot be specifically associated with Hippodamos; there is a fair amount of literature about whether epigraphic rules about three-bar sigma and tailed rho should apply to such *horoi* and whether Hippodamos can have survived to make a town-plan for Rhodes after 408. What we do have includes texts which clearly echo language associated with Hippodamos, e.g. *achri tes hodo tesde to astu nenemetai* 'up to this road the *astu* has been assigned' (*IG* i^2 893 = i^3 1111), *achri tesde tes hodo teide he Monichias esti nemēsis* 'up to this road in this direction is the assignment of Mounichia' (*IG* i^2 894 = i^3 1113). Others mark obviously public areas, the trading area (*emporion*), ferries and roads (*IG* i^2 887 = i^3 1101; i^2 890 = i^3 1104; two of each). Others use *demosios*, the enigmatic lounges, *lescheon demosion horos* (i^2 888 = i^3 1102), a lost text, perhaps of doubtful reading, distinguishing a public mooring from others,

---

[14] On Hippodamos, see A. Burns, *Historia*, 25 (1976), 414–28.

hormo demosio horos (i² 889 = i³ 1103), and perhaps five (two not certainly from the Piraeus) defining, surprisingly, a public gateway (i² 891 + *SEG* x 379, xiv 27 = 1097, 1105–8). But land is also so defined. Two texts (i² 892 + *SEG* x 380 = i³ 1109, 1110) proclaim *apo tesde tes hodo to pros tō limenos pan demosion esti* 'from this road on the harbour side everything is public'. It is sufficiently clear that, in the planning of the Piraeus, the designation of public property was of major importance. At a guess, the point of thus designating it in the case of the last area was at least as much a matter of preventing private encroachments as of reserving it for state use.

This little efflorescence of *horoi* of public property appears to have remained unparalleled. Only one *horos* later than the fifth century seems to have used *demosios* at all, for a public road in the Roman period (*IG* ii² 2628).

It should further be noted that, as far as I can see, the area between the road and the harbour at Piraeus is the only piece of public land in Attica not designated by function. No text encourages us to think that the Athenian state ever retained, worked, or leased anything called *ge demosia* (public land). All we find are public buildings, *demosia oikodomemata*, which the council had to supervise (Aristotle, *Ath. Pol.* 46. 2). We know quite a lot about the activity of the *poletai*, the board responsible for state leasing. The language of the *Ath. Pol.* does not absolutely forbid us to suppose that they ever leased any public land or buildings, but there is no evidence in their own documents that they did. The thought did occur to Xenophon that there were possibilities here to adorn the city and increase revenues (*Poroi* 3. 12) for the construction of business dwellings and shops, presumably on a rental basis; Euboulos does not seem to have taken that precise hint,[15] though he did improve the buildings in the trading area (Dinarchus 1. 96). Archaeologically speaking, there are various places and periods where we may suspect commercial intrusion into public buildings, but, as far as I understand current doctrine, purpose-built shops start with the Stoa of Attalos in the second century.

The one case where the *poletai* lease land which is not obviously

---

[15] *Contra*, G. L. Cawkwell, *JHS* 83 (1963), 64.

sacred seems to take us into a rather different sort of situation. It comes in the document I published in 1959 (*SEG* xviii 15; Schwenk, *Athens in the Age of Alexander*, no. 17), a law of the 330s ordering them to lease an area called 'the New Land' (*he Nea*) in two sections, apparently to produce revenue for the Lesser Panathenaia. Nothing actually proves that it is being thought of specifically as public land, and it is clearly something pretty abnormal. Virtually everyone has followed Robert's suggestion[16] that *he Nea* is the newly-returned territory of Oropos. I still see some difficulties of detail in reconciling this with the evidence of Hyperides about what happened there, and more still in the light of a new text which apparently records a survey of Oropos.[17] But, accepting Robert for the moment, we must surely regard the problems of a sudden extension of state-territory as very exceptional.[18] There would be an obvious mirror-image of this transaction in what happened when Plataea was destroyed in 427 (Thucydides 3. 68. 3). After an interim period in which Megarian exiles and pro-Theban Plataeans were allowed to live in the city, it was demolished, its materials used for an inn and a temple to Hera, and confiscating (*demosiosantes*) the land, the Spartans leased it for ten years, and Thebans cultivated it. Even without contiguity such circumstances could occur. We could similarly assimilate to annexation the first Athenian solution to the future of Lesbos, also in 427 (Thucydides saw many parallels between the events). The four revolting cities were divided into three thousand lots (*kleroi*). Three hundred of these were reserved for the gods, and the remainder were leased back to the Lesbians, with the rents going to the Athenians cleruchs. It is doubtful whether that solution lasted long, but it is certain that Athens continued to claim that she had acquired property in the empire, a claim not to be given up until the states concerned joined the Second Athenian Confederacy in 377: 'the *demos* shall give up all the possessions, private or belonging to the Athenian state (*demosia Athenaion*), in the land of those who make the alliance, giving them firm assurances' (Tod ii 123.

---

[16] *Hellenica*, 11/12 (1960), 189–203. Langdon (n. 17) has a new suggestion.

[17] M. K. Langdon, *Hesperia*, 56 (1987), 47–57.

[18] For some modern confusions between extending a city's territory and extending its property, see A. H. M. Jones, *The Greek City* (1940), p. 359 n. 67.

27–31). Not all of this can have been buildings for Athenian garrisons and governors; some of it was surely agricultural land.

Before returning to other possessions of the Athenian state, we should take some kind of look at public land elsewhere, though I do not pretend to have done very much of the work necessary. My guess is that, in the classical period, Athens may not have been particularly untypical in not having the custom of holding land as state land.[19] Of course the concept exists. In an unpublished text of the early second century,[20] the Thessalian town of Skotoussa sent commissioners round its wall circuit to establish the status of the land adjacent to the walls; among the things which they determined was what land was to be public (*damossos*) and what private (*iddioustikos*). It seems to me that the object of that particular operation was to make sure that certain ground should be kept clear in order not to hamper defence. Some of the evidence takes us into a world where the conditions are to some extent different. Take the case of Zelea in Hellespontine Phrygia, where we have a substantial text (Dittenberger, *Sylloge*[3] 279), apparently from soon after the departure of the Persians. There is apparently a fair quantity of public lands (*choria demosia*, elsewhere *demosiai geai*) and a strong suspicion that individuals have encroached on them. A board, to be composed of uninvolved persons, is appointed to investigate and fix appropriate prices. For citizens three possibilities are envisaged: (1) they just pay up and keep the land; (2) they claim that they have already bought it or validly acquired it from the city (if that claim fails, they are surcharged 50 per cent); (3) they simply leave, and the board has to sell the vacant land fairly rapidly. There is provision for spending the proceeds of sale on the public temples and other needs of the city, but I do not get the impression that the main motives are financial. Whatever the previous situation had been (I suppose it is most likely that the land concerned had been owned by Persians or their sympathizers), independent Zelea does not want to keep citizen tenants. One category of public land will however remain unaffected, that held by

[19] For a different judgement on later periods, see Jones (n. 18), pp. 245–6.
[20] V. Missailidou-Despotidou, 'A Thessalian Inscription and its Topographical Implications', M.Phil. thesis, (Oxford, 1986).

Phrygians who are paying *phoros* on it; they cannot be turned into owners.

I return to Athens.[21] As military equipment became more specialized the state will have had to acquire more and more which could only be public property; I do not suppose that there were many private catapults. The horses of the cavalry were, however, private, though a sort of insurance location was paid for them.[22] But Athens' principal military property was her navy. Its buildings we have already covered by implication, but the wasting capital tied up in its hulls, equipment, and stores, was enormous. Apart from the private trireme fielded by the elder Alcibiades in 480, the triremes were of course *demosiai*. I doubt if it often occurred to anyone to make the point, but Xenophon (*Poroi* 3. 14) does, as an analogy for his proposal to acquire and lease public merchant-ships.[23] He has been reproved for that proposal;[24] was it not enough trouble to keep the navy in repair? There is a possible parallel, which would justify the criticism. When Olbia needed to transport blocks of stone around 230, it had to have recourse to private transport because *ta ploia ta demosia* were in bad condition (*Sylloge*[3] 495. 146–151).[25]

I turn now to a very different category of public property. *Demosios*, at Athens and elsewhere, develops into a noun, understanding *doulos* (slave). The public slaves of Athens have hardly been studied more than incidentally since O. Jacob's rather uneven *Les Esclaves publics à Athènes* of 1928, and it may not be all that clear what sort of size of work-force they constituted.

For readers of Aristophanes, the first constituent to come to mind will be the force of Scythian archers. Scholars used to

---

[21] I slide over various minor objects owned by the state, which were labelled *demosia*. In the earliest of these, a series of bronze weights of about 500, the label *demosia Athenaion* of course reveals as much about its official character as about its ownership. The public seal, the *sphregis demosia*, and the public coin-type, the *demosios charakter*, involve the same kind of usage.

[22] J. H. Kroll, *Hesperia*, 46 (1977), 83–140.

[23] It is hardly clear what *ta alla demosia* are.

[24] Cawkwell (n. 15), 64.

[25] I do not know why Philippe Gauthier (*Un Commentaire historique des Poroi de Xénophon* (1976), p. 108) thinks these were warships.

accept some very high figures for this police-force, running up
to 1200. I am sure that Jacob was right to point out that they
had confused the police-archers with general figures given for
the size of the force of military archers. He himself was not
inclined to go beyond 300 at the outside, and I would guess
that even that was too high. In any case, it died off; we hear of
it last in Aristophanes' *Ecclesiazusae* of 392, and its functions
seem to have been performed thereafter by less exotic persons,
perhaps simply attached to various magistrates rather than a
corps.

Having started with the administration of justice, we should
proceed first to the courts.[26] The complexities of the equipment
required for their administration were considerable, and the
Ath. Pol. from time to time refers to individuals who are clearly
slaves in its description of the operations; there is indeed a clear
reference in Plutarch's *Demosthenes* 5. 2 to the *demosioi* who open
the courts. Given that there were several courts (a fact that *Ath.
Pol.* tends to lose sight of), we should, I think, be reckoning in
terms of a staff well into three figures.

Just as the *demosion* was the goal, so the *demosios*, sometimes
the *demios*, was the public executioner. Considering various
indications in Plato's *Phaedo* and Plutarch's *Phocion*, it took a
good deal more men than him alone to run the gaol, even with
the relatively undeveloped nature of the imprisonment, tor-
ture, and execution process in classical Athens; somewhere
between ten and twenty does not seem unreasonable.

The *Ath. Pol.* mentions one or two other work-forces. The
five road-builders (54. 1) have *demosioi* workmen to repair
roads. The city commissioners (*astynomoi*) (50. 2) have all sorts
of functions which might need labour, but their only *demosioi*
assistants who happen to be mentioned are those who remove
corpses from the roads.[27] It may well be legitimate to suspect
that other boards also have them. It seems unlikely, for
example, that the superintendents of shrines, who have half a
talent a year for repairing shrines (50. 1), relied either on
working with their own hands or on hired labour.[28]

[26] Jacob, *Les Esclaves*, pp. 87 ff.

[27] Is this because roads are *demosia*? Final responsibility for burial rests with the local
demarch (Dem. 43. 57–8).

[28] I am not clear under whose authority the *andrapoda* are operating who are
demolishing the crag and working on the theatre in *IG* ii² 1629. 1010–29.

No figures can be suggested for these. For hard figures and some idea of scale, we have to turn to the Eleusis accounts, which are fortunately nice and clear. We notice first that what we are dealing with here are *demosioi*, with no sacred language about them, unlike the *hieroi paides* who turn up in the service of Apollo at Didyma (*Didyma, die Inschriften* 41. 60); their employers, the commissioners of Eleusis, are after all state officials. In *IG* ii² 1673, now tentatively dated to 333/2,[29] there were 28 *demosioi* on the strength to be clothed, shod, and fed. But a new fragment shows that 9 of these were stone-transporters, perhaps temporary accretions to the normal establishments. If we leave them out of account, the normal establishment becomes 19, comparable with the 17 well-attested for 329/8 (*IG* ii² 1672. 5, 42, 71, 117, 142).

To turn to more general administration, a fifth-century inscription from the theatre of Dionysos had long attested the existence of assistants (*hyperetai*) of the council (*IG* i² 879 = i³ 1390), but it was some years after Jacob wrote that actual names started turning up. We now have evidence starting from the middle of the fourth century for the allocation of *hyperetai* to the council on the basis of one per tribe (*Agora* xv, nn. 37, 62, 72). It is roughly at the same time (*IG* ii² 120. 12 of 353/2) that we get our first *demosios*, one Eukles, named in a public decree and ordered to come and help make a list of the contents of the Chalkotheke. A body of such high-grade *demosioi* had of course existed for some time. The Coinage Law of 375/4 (*SEG* xxvi 72), which begins by ordering the already existing public coin-tester (*dokimastes ho demosios*) to sit in the Agora, goes on to provide for a new one to sit in the Piraeus, to be selected from the *demosioi*, if possible; if not, a new one is to be bought (lines 37–41). Other references to such persons are to be found, in the *Ath. Pol.* (47. 5) and in inscriptions, and it seems unlikely that any public transaction took place without the presence of one or two, providing civil service continuity.[30]

I suspect further that actual references to these administrative *demosioi*, either by function or by name, are merely singling out cases where the slave concerned happens to be abnormally

[29] K. Clinton, *Arch. Eph.* 1971, 112.

[30] For *demosioi* in charge of Athenian weights and measures in the late 2nd cent. BC, see *IG* ii² 1013.

visible. It may be the case that, in the 320s, there was in the dockyards one Opsigonos, important enough to be quoted as the *demosios* (*IG* ii^2 1672. 197) or even, alongside Dikaiogenes the general, as 'the *demosios* Opsigonos, the one in the dockyards' (ibid 381–2), but I doubt whether the singular has any exclusive meaning. The superintendents of the dockyards had other staff as well, and were able in 357 to lend a *hyperetes* to a trierarch in search of missing naval equipment (Demosthenes 47. 35) to do odd jobs for him like screaming into the street for citizen witnesses (ibid. 36).

When the new coin-tester for the Piraeus gets going, he is to be paid from the same source as the mint workers. That in itself strengthened the existing presumption, based on a fragment of Andocides about Hyperbolos' father (schol. Aristophanes, *Wasps* 1007), that the workers in the mint were public slaves. I gather that all doubt is now removed by an unpublished law of 354/3 from the Agora (Agora I 7495).

My feeling is that it would be conservative to suggest that the Athenian state owned several hundred slaves in the fourth century, and that there would be nothing particularly surprising if the total ran into four figures. It is against this background that Xenophon's proposals (*Poroi* 4. 13 ff.) for the city to acquire *demosia* slaves and lease them for work in the silvermines can be assessed, though, on the face of it, his proposed eventual expansion to a scale of three for every Athenian citizen would involve a very considerable increase in the size of the state's holding.

There can have been in the air some feeling that it was more proper that the city should be the owner of large bodies of slaves. Whether this is connected with, for example, the fact that Spartan helots were not the private property of individuals but were in a sense *demosioi* slaves (Strabo 8. 5. 4, p. 365), I do not know. The thought had occurred to some that a city might be better off if all craftsmen were public slaves, but that was hardly practical. In noting that, Aristotle (*Politics* 1267^{b}15 ff.) does offer the view that at least those who work for the state (*tous ta koina ergazomenous*) should be *demosioi*. That, he says, was the case at Epidamnus, and Diophantos once tried to arrange it at Athens. The passage has not attracted much attention, I think, but this must be the Diophantos, who was the shadowy coeval of Euboulos. Perhaps such a phenomenon as the increase in the body of *demosioi* at Eleusis in the 330s in order to provide for stone-hauling reflects a feeling of this kind that it was better for the state to own slaves and do a job itself than to privatize and put work out to contract. The argument cannot have been purely economic.[31]

Reviewing the Athenian evidence as a whole, there would seem to be three special factors which may have influenced the growth and nature of public property. First, the tyranny. We can hardly prove that Athens inherited, say, the silver mines or the Scythian archers from the tyrants, but both are clear possibilities. Secondly, the empire, creating the need and providing the resources for a greatly enhanced public sector for warfare and administration. Thirdly, democracy. Officials appointed by lot and not particularly wealthy could not be expected to provide the equipment and personnel for many functions which may have been performed in other states by aristocrats, but the jobs still had to be done.

I have not yet been able to think of other possessions of the Athenian state, but Athens certainly did not cover the whole spectrum of possibilities.[32] We cannot be sure that Athens never bought guard-dogs, as they did at Teos (*SEG* xxvi 1306. 19–21), but she never seems to have felt the need for a National Stud and left the winning of international horse-racing prestige to individuals. The main contrast here that we know about is with Argos with its *demosios keles* winning at Olympia in 480 and *demosion tethrippon* in 468 (*Oxyrhynchus Papyri* 222). The public stable at Argos still existed around 420 (Isocrates 16. 1), and I do not suppose that it was a unique institution there. Without going all the way back to the collective victory of the Eleans of Dyspontion in 672, I would suppose that there was

---

[31] It is in the context of financial economy that a Roman governor of the 1st cent. AD recommended Ephesos to replace citizens doing servile jobs by public slaves (H. Wankel (ed.), *Die Inschriften von Ephesos, IK* 11 (Bonn, 1979), 17. 42–44 = 18. 13–18), but a social view is also present.

[32] The public flocks of Miletos, herded by public shepherds, which appear in some books, turn out to be an imaginative expansion by Haussoullier, *Études sur l'histoire de Milet et du Didymeion* (Paris, 1902), p. 250, of the public wool stolen there by Verres, according to older texts (Cic. *Verr.* 2. 1. 34(86)); there wasn't even any public wool, that I can see.

some fairly solid framework of convention behind the circumstances in which the Spartan Lichas entered his chariot at Olympia in 420 as the public property of the Boeotians (Thucydides 5. 50. 4).

This paper has not been concerned with sacred property or the property of organizations below *polis* level. Functionally, we have only considered part of the phenomenon of public property. Although the Athenians drew their distinction between *demosia* and *hiera*, even going to the lengths of charging themselves interest when they borrowed from Athena, I do not think that we can rationally support their attitude. It was they themselves, after all, who decided that Athena was going to make the loan. Similarly, the emphasis which I have laid on the fact that Athens rarely retained land for leasing as public property ceases to be very meaningful when we consider that there was. sacred land at Athens which was leased on the instructions of the Assembly by public officials. Admittedly, the proceeds were presumably used for sacred purposes, but, as I have said, sacred purposes are an integral part of state expenditure. More general purposes of the state can also be served. Xenophon's suggestion about stimulating economic activity by bringing vacant property within the walls into use may not be documentable in terms of public property, but the efflorescence of mass leases of sacred property now attested for the 340s and 330s[33] can hardly be totally unconnected.

The scale of such non-private property has been the subject of guesses by Andreyev and myself,[34] ranging from 5 to 10 per cent. If this were right, we should not be entitled to apply it beyond Attica. The scale of sacred property in Greek lands will have varied widely. More particularly, it can be expected to rise in states where cult was the most important activity. We have already seen that the Delian and Delphian Amphictyonies were capable of retaining and leasing confiscated property, and we can envisage other situations in which temple property played a more substantial part in the economy; Artemis at Ephesos is an obvious one. At this stage, the difference of scale turns into a genuine difference in the nature

[33] M. B. Walbank, *Hesperia*, 52 (1983), 100–35, 177–231.
[34] M. I. Finley (ed.), *Problèmes de la terre en Grèce ancienne* (1973), pp. 198–9.

of the society we are looking at, and perhaps this after all is the justification for having tackled public property at Athens on the more confined definition.

Many problems remain. It is by no means clear why Athens was not prepared to retain agricultural land in state ownership. The editors wonder whether there was some recognition of the inefficiency of revenue-raising by public exploitation, but no such inhibition is found in the administration of the silver-mines. Above all, a great deal of further study is needed of the operation of the other types of non-private property, whether belonging to gods or associations, both in the purely Athenian context and in contrast with other states.[35] Again, it is worth considering whether the problem we saw about the status of abandoned property is matched by that of areas which had never been effectively owned at all; much of Greece is forest, mountain, or upland grazing.[36] The question of what consti-tutes property could hardly be more sharply raised, and merges into the more difficult question of the growth of a distinction between property owned by the Athenians collectively, implied in stories about mass distribution, and property owned by the state. That touches on the most fundamental questions of the nature of the *polis*.

Appendix
Demos and Some of its Cognates

As readers of Appendix I of Whitehead, *Demes of Attica*, will be aware, the Liddell and Scott article on δῆμος is by no means satisfactory.

---

[35] To take one well-known example, Athena never lent money to states or indivi-duals as Apollo of Delos did (Tod ii 125), but the local Attic shrine of Nemesis at Rhamnous did lend to individuals (ML 53).

[36] The editors are reminded of the phenomenon of the *eschatiai* which I discussed in Finley (n. 34), 210–12. We could also consider the frequent appearance in a heavily wooded area of the word *anamphisbetos* in Langdon's new text (above n. 17); Langdon (p. 52) takes it as meaning that its status was not in dispute, but I incline to think that no one was claiming it.

Whitehead's main concern is to establish that there is nothing particularly new about Kleisthenes' use of it for his new village communities. With a slight modification, I agree, but I am a bit doubtful about some of the more general issues.

Liddell and Scott start δῆμος as '*district, country, land*' with ample epic justification. As I. 2 they sling in, on the side, 'the *people, inhabitants* of such a district', quoting *Il.* 3. 50, where Hector describes Paris' behaviour a μέγα πῆμα to his father πόληϊ τε παντί τε δήμωι, and adding two rather arbitrary references, the first to the πᾶς δῆμος which is to build a temple under the πόλις of Eleusis (*Hym. Cer.* 271). But I. 2 is evidently regarded as a false start, and we pass to II, 'hence (since the common people lived in the country, the chiefs in the city), the *commons, common people*', starting with the δήμου ἀνήρ in *Il.* 2. 198, who is certainly contrasted with the category of being a βασιλεύς or an ἔξοχος ἀνήρ ten lines earlier, but continuing with the two sons of Merops, ἀνέρε δήμου ἀρίστω, at *Il.* 11. 328, who are not, to my mind, relevant. As Whitehead has shown, II, despite its later importance, is relatively uncommon early. It seems to me that its main distinguishing mark is that it appears in contrast with βασιλεῖς or some higher body. Thus it may already be implied in Hes. *Op.* 260–1, where the δῆμος has to pay for the ἀτασθαλίας of the βασιλεῖς, and in Tyrtaeus fr. 4 West (the Rhetra fragment), the δημότας ἄνδρας and the δήμου πλῆθος are at least different parts of the body politic from the βασιλεῖς and the γέροντες.

Liddell and Scott's III, 'in a political sense, *the sovereign people, the free people*', is presented as a new start. Whitehead comments on that: 'though as a historico-political development its emergence from usage ⟨II⟩ is plain enough.' I think I disagree. The earliest instances quoted are from the *Seven Against Thebes*. That is obviously unsatisfactory, even on the narrowest definition of 'political'. The well-known sixth century text from Chios (ML 8) speaks of δήμο ῥήτρας. The earliest Attic decree (*IG* i³ 1) begins ἔδοξεν τôι δέμοι and I have claimed that *IG* i³ 105. 35 τάδε ἔδοξεν ἐλ Λυκείο τôι δ[έμοι τôι'A]θε[να]ίον is a copy of a late sixth-century text. There is no real difference between this and the seventh-century text from Dreros (ML 2) ᾱδ' ἔϝαδε πόλι. As we might well have suspected from *Il.* 3. 50, πόλις and δῆμος can be interchangeable. I see no discontinuity between that text, *Il.* 11. 328, *Hym. Cer.* 271, and the instances we are discussing, except that δῆμος is now found in contexts we should call constitutional. I see no reason to exclude the higher levels of society from these usages of δῆμος and believe them to mean 'the whole people', *populus*. Unlike Whitehead, I derive them from I. 2, not from II. In Liddell and Scott terms, there is no firm line to be drawn between their I. 2, some of the instances casually put under II, and their III. Of course, there is continued ambiguity. Students of Solon's poems will be well aware of instances, totally absent from Liddell and Scott, where uncertainty is possible whether δῆμος means *populus* or *plebs*. Andrewes has argued (*The Greek Tyrants*, 35–6) that Aristotle had found some early literary passage of constitutional relevance, where he thought that δῆμος should be understood to refer to the hoplites. The differentiation of II from this stream and the development of their I. 1 into the village sense do not concern us here. I only observe, in a way I think Whitehead has not quite done, that, although there were δῆμοι in Attica before Kleisthenes in a development of I. 1, what Kleisthenes did was to create, for example, a δῆμος τῶν Ἀχαρνέων in a sense indistinguishable from the δῆμος τῶν Ἀθηναίων classifiable as III; this is of course ground covered in Osborne's paper (ch. 11).

From δῆμος I pass to the adjectives. The linguists (I am relying on Chantraine) tell us that both δημόσιος and δημοτικός are not derived from δῆμος but from δημότης, but fortunately they concede that δημόσιος always behaves functionally as if it were derived from δῆμος, so we need not worry ourselves about that. We can also put δημοτικός on one side. Despite some nineteenth-century scholars who tried to turn Nikias into an oligarch on the strength of the assertion (Xen. *Hell.* 2. 3. 39) that neither his son nor he ever did anything δημοτικόν, we are surely now all agreed that δημοτικός is specialized, in Athens, to δῆμος II *plebs*; the only place known to me where it has any official meaning is Olbia, where there is a δημοτικὸν δικαστήριον, supposed to be contrasted with one for foreigners (Tod ii 195. 17).

The main paper's primary concern is with δημόσιος. I hope I have shown that δῆμος *populus* is of sufficient antiquity for δημόσιος to be related to it, that the use of the word need not be programmatic, that, when it starts appearing, there need not be any suggestion of the existence of institutions we might call democracy. Liddell and Scott is an imperfect guide on δημόσιος as well, omitting the four earliest appearances of it known to me. Two of these are very general, hardly differing very much from Paris's behaviour being a μέγα πῆμα to the δῆμος. Solon fr. 4 talks about the bad state of Athens in general ταῦτα μὲν ἐν δήμωι στρέφεται κακά (23), and passes to how it affects individuals οὕτω δημόσιον κακὸν ἔρχεται οἴκαδε ἑκάστωι (26). δημόσιον κακὸν also appears in the late-seventh-century epitaph ML 4, where it seems to describe the loss to the Corcyrean people of its drowned *proxenos* (it also comes in Theognis 50). That, of course, is the text where δᾶμος itself appears three times, once in the phrase πρόξενϝος δάμου φίλος, twice as the body which made the tomb, just as the Eleusinian δῆμος was to build the temple to Demeter; I stress again that there is no implication of democracy. Rather different is the appearance in the Chian text we have already alluded to; here the various appearances of δῆμος are matched, as is well-known, by the reference to the βολὴ ἡ δημοσίη, but to relate that to what I have said about δῆμος has no bearing on the main paper. It is the fourth reference, Solon fr. 4. 12–13, from which the treatment there starts.

The *Demos* and its Divisions in Classical Athens

ROBIN OSBORNE

'WE are all democrats now'. Or are we? One might pose it as a test of liberal political views whether or not a person favours direct democracy. Direct participatory democracy unquestionably presents popular power in its least compromised form, and the old disclaimer that direct democracy may be desirable but simply not possible in a modern nation state is no longer applicable. There is now no technical barrier to achieving any degree of political participation that might be deemed appropriate: all citizens could be provided with the means of observing and participating in political debates and of voting at the end of them without having to leave their armchairs. Or one could replicate the conditions of classical Athens more precisely by having one 6,000 seat first-come-first-served assembly place per 30,000 citizens or 2,400 square kilometres, as desired. For most people, however, the details don't matter; the whole idea of direct democracy is quite unacceptable. The media presuppose this in their hostile reporting of trade union meetings, and the feeling is to be found among the political left wing as well as among the oligarchic forces of the right. It is objected that decisions would be taken on the basis of bad, but emotive, arguments by people not in full command of the facts; that there would be no consistent policy and so fickle decisions would be made; that divisions within the citizen body would be highlighted and political riots would become common as large sections of society became frustrated with the gap between their paper power and their actual powerlessness.

This paper has greatly benefited from the comments of members of the seminar, in particular from David Lewis, Oswyn Murray, and Simon Price.

I raise all this not to initiate a debate on the merits and demerits of any current political constitution—although contemporary practices are indeed hard to justify on rational grounds. I raise it rather to highlight the remarkable nature of Athenian democracy, largely overlooked by both enthusiasts and detractors, ancient and modern. For classical Athens did allow all citizens (on an admittedly very narrow definition of citizen) a potential say and vote on all matters, and yet it did not make any higher proportion of demonstrably bad decisions than other regimes, ancient or modern. Oligarchic Sparta is not famous for the stability of its foreign policy, and modern governments of every political hue can be observed not only making inconsistent individual decisions but radically altering the principles on which overall policies are built with a frequency which would certainly have alarmed Plato.[1] Still more remarkably, and this is what I wish to dwell on here, classical Athens was not marked by strong divisions and political riots; the Athenian population displayed a remarkable solidarity, breached only under severe outside pressure in conditions of defeat at war. It is true that some contemporary critics complained that political decisions were dominated by the 'naval mob' who swung things in directions unacceptable to 'the better part' of the people, but this naval mob evaporates on closer analysis, and, ironically, the rhetoric which created it may in fact have helped to mask and to stifle real divisions.[2]

How and why was the Athenian citizenry so solidary a body? One traditional answer lies in apathy. If you believe that the vast majority of Athenian citizens were politically apathetic and that there was actually a positive value placed on non-involvement,[3] then it becomes not very surprising that the political temperature was low. However, since it is now evident that between a quarter and a fifth of the Athenian citizen body

[1] On the instability of Spartan foreign policy, see G. E. M. de Ste Croix, *The Origins of the Peloponnesian War* (London, 1972), pp. 151–66. For Plato's views, see *Republic* 488, 561.

[2] Cf. P. Harding, 'In Search of a Polypragmatist', in G. S. Shrimpton and D. J. McCargar (eds), *Classical Contributions: Studies in Honour of M. F. McGregor* (New York, 1981), pp 41–50; S. C. Todd, '*Lady Chatterley's Lover* and the Attic Orators', *JHS* 110 (1990).

[3] For the positive value placed on non-involvement in some circles, see L. B. Carter, *The Quiet Athenian* (Oxford, 1986).

—and not the same quarter every time!—regularly attended the Assembly (*ekklesia*), and that a clear majority of Athenian citizens served at least once in their lives on the Council (*boule*), the steering and executive committee of the Assembly, it seems unlikely that non-involvement holds the key to the success of Athenian democracy.[4] Both wealth and place of residence did influence the extent of political participation, but that the much greater difficulty of involvement in politics for men living in remote parts of Attica led to no perceptible breach between town and country residents itself indicates the solidarity of the Athenian citizen body.[5]

This paper attempts to answer the question of Athenian solidarity by looking at the anatomy of Athenian society and arguing that the citizen body (the *demos*) was united by its divisions. The first part of the paper looks at the subdivisions of the *demos* and argues that the way in which these organized themselves reinforced the organization of 'central' administration and prepared citizens for the rhetoric of the Assembly. In the second part of the paper I take a close look at one of the local communities within Attica, the village of Rhamnous, and try to show how common assumptions about group organization and the proper objects of group activities made it possible for the various people who found themselves at Rhamnous for various reasons to combine for action in *ad hoc* bodies which could act effectively even when they could not give a simple abstract description of their own membership.

I

At the beginning of the *Politics* Aristotle gives an analytical history of the *polis*. He points out how natural and necessary forces lead first to the union of male and female and the formation of the household, then to the union of households into villages, and finally to the union of villages into *poleis*. As households are all ruled by the most senior male member so

[4] M. H. Hansen, *The Athenian Ecclesia* (Copenhagen, 1983), pp. 1–23; id., *Demography and Democracy: The Number of Athenian Citizens in the Fourth Century* BC (Herning, 1985), pp. 51–64; R. G. Osborne, *Demos: The Discovery of Classical Attika* (Cambridge, 1985), pp. 42–6.
[5] Osborne (n. 4), pp. 88–92.

poleis were first ruled by kings (1252^a24–1252^b31). In this ideal history the organization of each unit is modelled on the organizations of the prior unit, and it is the organization of the family in the household which provides the type of the organization of the more complex units.

In the most influential of modern works on the ancient city, Fustel de Coulanges posits as actual history a process not far removed from that described by Aristotle. Families formed into phratries, phratries into tribes, and tribes into a *polis*, and at all stages, for Fustel, the groups were united by the bond of common cult practices—each unit had its own particular exclusive cult practices but also shared in the cult practices of the larger group or groups to which it belonged. And at every stage the organization of the groups was exactly comparable: 'Family, phratry, tribe, city, were, moreover societies exactly similar to each other, which were formed one after the other by a series of federations.'[6]

Seen against the background of such models of city organization, the organization of classical Athens is quite remarkable: far from the government of the larger unit being organized on lines derived from the government of the sub-groups, the sub-groups arguably model their organization and their deliberations upon that of the city.

In classical Athenian democracy the primary division of the *demos* (citizen body) was the *demos* (deme—village or ward). I put it like that because I want to stress the ambiguity of the word *demos* and the implications of that ambiguity more stongly than has normally been done. The demes of Attica may have already been so called during the archaic period, but it is only with the arrival of democracy after Kleisthenes, when ultimate political responsibility came to rest with the whole citizen body, that *demos* will have acquired its powerfully ambiguous overtones.[7] I am not trying to claim that there was real confusion in the use of *demos*, for even when there is no qualifier (*demos* of the Athenians, *demos* of the people of

---

[6] N. D. Fustel de Coulanges, *La Cité antique* (Paris, 1864 [Eng. trans. Baltimore, 1980]), book iii, ch. 3.

[7] D. Whitehead, *The Demes of Attica 510–250 BC* (Princeton, 1986), Appendix 1; D. M. Lewis, above, pp. 260–63. Cf. R. K. Sinclair, *Democracy and Participation at Athens* (Cambridge, 1988), pp. 15–16.

Aixone) the context of the use of the word only occasionally leaves much room for doubt. My point is rather that the use of the same referent for the whole body of citizens and for its 139 constituent parts created a strong bond of identity: the *demos* could not act without associating all the *demoi* in that action. Decisions promulgated over the name of the *demos* of the Athenians claim the support not only of all Athenian citizens as individuals but of those individuals grouped into their demes. At the basic linguistic level the *demos* and its divisions were inseparable.

As well as being used neutrally to refer to the whole citizen body, *demos* was also used with a pejorative overtone to refer to the 'common people'. In oligarchic regimes those in power could happily regard themselves as distinct from the *demos*, but there was no such possibility at Athens. No member of a deme who sat and watched Aristophanes' gentle ridicule of the character Demos in his comedy the *Knights* could dissociate himself from the attack. The basic linguistic resistance to divisions within the citizen body extends to 'class' as well as local divisions.

Deme and *demos* were not parallel in every sense.[8] The deme had no tribal subdivisions of its own, there were no deme trittyes, no deme demes. But the deme did parallel the assembled *demos* to a very high degree. Demes assembled in an agora, not an *ekklesia*, but at least one deme had a hierarchy of deme meetings headed by a 'principal agora' (*agora kyria, IG* ii[2] 1202. 1–2), just as the assembled citizen body had its principal assemblies (*kyria ekklesia*). At least some demes demanded a quorum for particular items of business (*IG* ii[2] 1183. 21), as did the citizen Assembly. Speakers in the deme agora spoke, like their counterparts in the Assembly, under oath (Dem. 57. 8).

Demes elected their own magistrates (*archai, IG* i[3] 253), of which the most important was the demarch. The demarch in fact had various responsibilities for deme participation in the activities of the central administration, and the demarch of the

---

[8] On the organization of the demes, see Whitehead (n. 7), pp. 86–148; Osborne (n. 4), pp. 72–87. For another way in which the demes were miniature *poleis*, see E. Kearns, 'Change and Continuity in Religious Structures after Cleisthenes', in P. Cartledge and F. D. Harvey (eds), *Crux: Essays Presented to G. E. M. de Ste Croix* (Exeter and London, 1985), pp. 189–207.

Piraeus was, exceptionally, selected by lot centrally (Arist. *Ath. Pol.* 54. 8). The use of the title demarch marks out this official as a local rather than a central one in central references, and in the fourth century the demes themselves invariably refer to the activities of the demarch as 'ruling in the deme' (*demarchon*). But the accounts of the temple of the goddess Nemesis at Rhamnous from the middle of the fifth century date themselves by the name of the demarch using the phrases 'in the year when X was ruling in the deme' (*demarchontos*) and 'in the year that Y was ruling' (*archontos*) interchangeably; for the writers of these accounts the demarch was clearly their local archon (ML 53).

Alongside the demarch we hear of a large number of other deme magistracies—not all of which were to be found in every deme—all having names which can be paralleled in central administration: stewards (*tamiai*), secretary (*grammateus*), recorder (*antigrapheus*), accountants (*logistai*), assessors (*paredroi*), estimator (*epitimetes*), advocates (*synegoroi*), heralds (*kerykes*), and sacristans (*hieropoioi*). Demes subjected candidates for office to an examination prior to election (*dokimasia*) and to a scrutiny at the end of their period of office (*euthyne*). The deme did not have its own equivalents of *all* central officials, and even those deme officials with central parallels often performed functions that were not parallel, but the striking thing is that with the exception of the demarch (probably the only official a deme was required to have by central authority) all the offices in the deme bear the names of central officials: the demes show no originality in nomenclature in their optional officials at all.

This parallelism contrasts strongly with both past and present local government in Britain. Back in the early modern period parish administration was largely in the hands of the church and the manor. The church acted through the Parish Vestry, with major roles played by the Churchwardens and lesser ones by the Sidesmen, and the manor acted through the Manorial Courts. Of various named officials only the Constable bears a name found also in central administration.[9]

---

[9] See e.g. J. Boulton, *Neighbourhood and Society* (Cambridge, 1987), pp. 265: 'The main burden of parochial administration fell on the church warden'; K. Wrightson and D. Levine, *Poverty and Piety in an English Village: Terling 1525–1700* (New York, 1979), pp. 103–9.

Current parish administration relies on a Council with Chairman and Clerk: these are bland and neutral titles less evocative of central government than of school governors (compare also the business-world overtones of the Chief Executive of Local Authorities).

In Athens the situation found in the demes is not exceptional. Little in detail is known of the local groupings of demes known as trittyes, but the tribes, made up of three trittyes, parallel the demes. Their meetings were called *agorai* and structured to give some principal meetings (*kyriai agorai, IG* ii^2 1141, 1165). The one official whose activities were of central importance, for military reasons, was called the phylarch, although his position with regard to the tribe seems not to be closely comparable to the position of the demarch with regard to the deme: the phylarch has no overall responsibility for the tribe, and tribal documents are not dated by the phylarch. The only other regular tribal officers are the overseers (*epimeletai*)—an all-purpose title used also in central administration.[10] The overseers had charge of tribal moneys (*IG* ii^2 1148) and served as tribal secretaries, taking responsibility for recording the honours voted by the tribe. In the early third century Erekhtheis gave its *epimeletai* the task of looking after the heiress of one particularly valued tribal member (*IG* ii^2 1165). Arrangements seem to have varied to some extent from tribe to tribe: the tribe Akamantis had a steward (*tamias*) in charge of its money at the end of the fourth century (*SEG* xxv 141).

A like situation prevailed also in the kinship groups (phratries) and priestly families (*gene*) which were not so closely bound up in the administrative structure and which were in existence long before Kleisthenes. The phratries had *agorai* which in at least one case were structured to include 'principal meetings' (*kyria agora, SEG* xxxii 150). The only regular officials are the phratriarch and the priest, but special committees may be set up, and when they are their nomenclature conforms to the pattern observed above (e.g. the advocates (*synegoroi*) of *IG* ii^2 1237). Phratry records are called 'the communal records' (*koina grammateia, IG* ii^2 1237. 8), a title also used of deme records.

---

[10] On tribal *epimeletai* see J. S. Traill, *Demos and Trittys* (Toronto, 1986), pp. 79–90.

The priestly families used the central title archon for their chief official (*IG* ii² 1232, *Hesperia*, 39 (1970), 143), and met at 'principal meetings' (*kyria agora*, *SEG* xxi 124, a second-century BC document). As well as the priests/priestesses there are heralds (*kerykes*) and various religious assistants given different names in different families, some unexampled in other groups, but some (e.g. the assessor (*paredros*) of the Kerykes, *IG* ii² 1230) sharing a name with a central secular official.

In addition to these cult groups linked by kinship and often with a long history, Athenians formed themselves into voluntary self-selecting groups for cult activities. Both groups calling themselves *orgeones* and groups calling themselves *thiasotai* will be treated together here, for the relationship between the two is complex and some groups certainly described themselves interchangeably as *thiasotai* and *orgeones* in the same document (*IG* ii² 1316 of the late third century BC). Names of officials vary from one group to another; some groups relied on a single official or group of officials to do all the routine tasks, and such officials are frequently referred to as overseers (*epimeletai*, *IG* ii² 1262), while other groups proliferated officials to a greater or lesser extent. Sometimes the title given to an official describes his particular duty, as with the priests (*IG* ii² 1273), sacristans (*IG* ii² 1261), catering managers (*hestiatores*, *IG* ii² 1259, *SEG* xxi 530), kitchen supervisors (*IG* ii² 1301), and temple attendants (*zakoroi*, *IG* ii² 1328). But in some of these groups a full range of administrative officials and structure of meetings developed, with meetings known as *agorai*, principal meetings (*agorai kyriai*), stewards for financial matters (*tamiai*), secretaries (*grammateis*), recorder (*antigrapheus*), and archivist (*grammatophylax*) for secretarial matters, and even archons (*IG* ii² 1278, *SEG* ii 9). Special committees may be set up to execute decisions (*SEG* ii 9, cf. *IG* ii² 1330), and officials submit themselves to scrutiny after holding office (*euthynai*, *IG* ii² 1263). Thus these small groups voluntarily construct for themselves a full structure of administrative paraphernalia on the model of central administration.

More remarkably still the same applies to the self-help *eranos* groups, friendly societies that served some of the functions of life assurance groups. Run, in general at least, by a 'head of the *eranos*' (*archeranistes*) these groups have stewards (*tamiai*), overseers (*epimeletai*), secretaries (*grammateis*), and sacristans (*hiero-poioi*), and in one late example they are even found meeting in a 'principal' meeting (*agora kyria, IG* ii² 1335 of 102/1 BC).

The variations in precise nomenclature among the officers of the official groups, and the use of 'official' names by groups which were purely voluntary and had no part at all to play in central administration, shows that the occurrence of 'central' terminology in these subdivisions of the *demos* is not a matter of central directives; indeed the only officials which central administration may have insisted on (the demarch and the phylarch) bear peculiar titles. Not only did the *demos* as a whole not take over family or religious terminology to express analogous possession of authority in the *polis* as a whole, but the terminology which it did adopt became the model terminology for the administration of the sub-groups, even when kinship or cult were important organizing features of the group, and even when the group pre-existed the formation of the democratic administration. The primacy of the political seems to be indicated.

But the parallelism between the *demos* and its divisions extends beyond the rhetoric of nomenclature, to the ways in which the groups framed their decisions and the types of motion which they chose to display publicly on stone. Honorific measures dominate all corporate decisions. Unlike the Athenian *demos*, but for obvious reasons, the vast majority of groups honour only their own members. This is not always the case with the demes, but though they may honour members of other demes they can never give them membership of their own deme, in the way that the *demos* could grant citizenship.[11] The closest parallel to the grant of citizenship is perhaps the local tax exemption which demes could grant.[12] Among the smaller groups membership of the group seems not to be attractive as a reward, but the Paraloi do grant one Meixigenes son of Mikon of the deme of Cholleidai in the later fourth century a share in the sacrificial meat (*IG* ii² 1254).

Demes honoured their members especially with crowns, mostly of olive, but also of ivy and of laurel as well as of gold. Gold crowns are most frequently to the value of 500 dr. but

---

[11] For which see M. J. Osborne, *Naturalisation at Athens*, 3 vols. (Brussels, 1981–3).
[12] *IG* ii² 1187. 16, 1188. 29 f., 1204. 12, 1214. 25.

some are twice as valuable; these sums are exactly comparable to those of crowns offered to citizens in central honours. Demes record gifts of crowns on stone and may announce them.[13] Some crowns are accompanied by gifts of money with which to make sacrifices, up to 100 dr. being given for this purpose (*IG* ii² 1186), or by grants of the privilege of sitting at the front at festivals. The demes announce, from an early date, that the honours are given to encourage ambition (*philotimia*) in others. All these types of honour, as well as the motivation for them, can be discovered in central honours, where the body as a whole also gave olive and gold crowns, public announcement of honours, front seats, and tax exemption. The Assembly also gave statues in some circumstances; no extant record indicates that a deme ever did this, but some of the smaller groups did so.

Tribal honours follow the same pattern: olive crowns, gold crowns, exemption from tribal liturgies, grants of money for sacrifice and dedication (*SEG* xxv 141). Phratry honours are too few to enable much to be said, but one honorific act of a priestly family is particularly interesting. A late Hellenistic inscription honouring the priestess of a *genos* whose name ends in -oinidai grants her a statue which it refers to with the term *agalma*, which is standard not for images of men, for which *eikon* is used, but for images of gods (*SEG* xxix 135). The highest form of civic honour is here taken and turned round by the *genos* to suit the particular circumstances of its grant.[14]

Thiasotai and *orgeones* not infrequently granted statues (*eikones*) in combination with crowns (*IG* ii² 1271, 1314, 1327, 1334). The Artists (*tekhnitai*) of Dionysos (*IG* ii² 1330) went still further in honouring Ariarathes V of Cappadocia: they set up two statues, an *agalma* of the king himself and an *eikon* of his wife. This honour involved an exceptional formation of a sub-committee of three men who were sent off to request the honorand to continue to bestow his benefactions (protection and tax exemption) on the group. More usually these groups limited themselves to the standard clauses expressing hope that

[13] *IG* ii² 1178, 1186, 1187, 1189, 1193, 1202, *SEG* xx 117, 120, *Arch. Eph.* 1932 Chr. 30–2.

[14] See Ph. Gauthier, *Les Cités grecques et leur bienfaiteurs* (*BCH* Supp. 12; Paris, 1985), ch. 2 and index s.v. statues.

their honorific actions will encourage *philotimia*, although occasionally there is a note to the effect that the honorand had undertaken to continue his benefactions.

One important feature of decrees from all these groups is the way in which they take up and cite public services for the whole *demos* and honorific motions first moved in the Council and Assembly. Thus the deme of Aixone honoured Demetrios of Phaleron on the grounds that he was 'good to the *demos* of the Athenians and to the *demos* of the people of Aixone' (*IG* ii² 1201. 4–5); the deme of Melite had earlier honoured one of its members, Neoptolemos, because he did whatever good he could to the *demos* of the Athens and the *demos* of the people of Melite in word and deed (*SEG* xxii 116). The garrison demes of Eleusis and Rhamnous repeatedly joined with other groups in honouring generals, garrison commanders, and the like. Citation and repetition of public praise is less common in the smaller groups, but it is not unknown: in particular fellow holders of an office seem on occasion to have clubbed together into an *ad hoc* association to honour and crown a fellow officer who had already been honoured by the Council and Assembly (*IG* ii² 1251, 1257).

The situation may be summarized in the following way. The Athenians grouped themselves into permanent or semi-permanent corporations in a number of different ways. These groups were founded on a wide variety of criteria—locality, descent, combinations of locality and descent, common occupational interests, common religious interests, mutual assistance in primarily financial matters, common military service, and so on. An individual Athenian might belong to a large number of such groups, and in these groups he would associate closely with a wide range of sorts and conditions of men. Some groups were by definition made up solely of citizens, others included metics and foreigners (or might even be dominated by them). Some included women and even slaves. Membership of these groups placed the Athenian in a wide variety of different circumstances, but in each he acted and construed his experiences and expressed his needs in basically similar ways. The structure of the groups and of the meetings of the groups was parallel to the structures of the *polis* as a whole. Offices were given similar or identical titles, power was minutely subdivided, meetings were formalized, and paper and (fortunately for our knowledge) stonework multiplied. To some extent this was all a façade, as is clearly seen in the group which had offices of secretary (*grammateus*), steward (*tamias*), and overseer (*epimeletes*), but had them all held by the same man (the Sabaziastai *eranos* group in the Piraeus, *IG* ii² 1335 of 102/1). What is important is that the façade was thought worth erecting, that these groups saw themselves as miniature *poleis* and gave themselves a fundamentally political framework. They acted as little *poleis* too, doing the same kinds of thing as the assembled *demos* and publicly advertising the same motives. The assembled *demos* could honour in ways simply not open to the smaller groups, but none of the small groups forged any form of honour peculiar to itself: the nearest that we get to originality seems to be the use of *oak* for their crowns by the worshippers of Bendis (*IG* ii² 1284). The political framework for action is even adopted by the foreign groups: the Thracian *orgeones* of Bendis head their decrees 'Gods' (*Theoi*), date them by the archon and the Athenian month, meet in principal meetings (*agorai kyriai*), have stewards (*tamiai*), secretaries (*grammateis*), and overseers (*epimeletai*), and include clauses about encouraging ambition (*philotimia*) in their decrees. All these heterogeneous groups share aims, methods, and expressed values, and although their decrees tend to be less fulsome than those of the city they do not differ in kind at all.

I have argued above that in the case of the nomenclature of officials there is some reason to believe that the central use of a name came first and that the smaller groups imitated central practice. It cannot be certain that in all instances, even of nomenclature, the influence went in this direction, and it is even less possible to be certain that the rhetoric of group honours was entirely forged in the Assembly. The first extant clause about encouraging ambition (*philotimia*) in others in an Athenian inscription appears in a decree moved by a deme, and there can be no a priori reason why this particular rhetorical strategy should not have passed from deme to Assembly.[15] What is significant is not where the initiative took

---

[15] *IG* ii² 1173 (securely restored). For a contrary opinion, see D. Whitehead, 'Competitive Outlay and Community Profit: *Philotimia* in Democratic Athens', *Classica et Mediaevalia*, 34 (1983), 55–74 at p. 62 n. 25.

place but the fact that the terminology and the rhetoric were interchangeable from the *demos* to its divisions, and that none of the groups discussed sought to distinguish itself in any way from the model of the *demos*.

This conformist behaviour is shown up in relief by the organization and behaviour of subversive groups. Clubs of various sorts existed in Athens which have left no records on stone. That in itself is testimony to their non-conformity. Some of the clubs were more or less purely social institutions, with little or no political engagement. But others were more explicitly political, and the literary sources which mention them and their activities make the assumption that these political activities were subversive of democracy.[16] The subversive element is vividly brought out by the names which these groups chose to give themselves—the Triballoi (named after a Thracian tribe), the Kakodaimonistai ('Evil Demons'), and so on—by their binding themselves together in a partnership of crime, by their deliberate flaunting of accepted practices (eating offerings put out to the goddess Hekate, feasting off the testicles of pigs used in ritual purification before meetings of the assembly) and by their violent behaviour.[17] The inversion of conventional group practices by these clubs itself bears witness to the strength of the model of organization and group expression offered by the *demos* and its divisions.

II

The importance of there being a single dominant model of group organization and activity emerges very clearly from the examination of the interaction of various groups within a local community. In the following section I shall look closely at group action at Rhamnous in north-east Attica. Precisely because a number of different groups had reason to spend time at Rhamnous, the inscriptional records from that deme are much richer than those from any other deme, with the

---

[16] See Thucy. 8. 54. 4 with Andrewes' comments in A. W. Gomme, K. J. Dover, and A. Andrewes, *A Historical commentary on Thucydides:* v. Book VIII (Oxford, 1981), pp. 128–31. See also the law in Hyperides 4. 8.

[17] The best, if highly distorted, evidence for clubs comes from Andocides 1 (especially 48–50, 61–8) and Demosthenes 54 (especially 13–23, 38–40).

exception of the comparable religious and military centre of Eleusis. Rhamnous was not typical of the demes of Attica: the presence of large numbers of non-demesmen created a situation which most other Athenian villages never faced. This does not, however, diminish its value, for the importance of the behaviour which can be seen at Rhamnous does not lie in the frequency of such actions but in the fact that such things could happen even once. The easy combination of discrete groups at Rhamnous in peculiar circumstances points to the importance of conventional group organization for the ease with which individuals moulded by membership of those groups combined regularly in the citizen Assembly.

Rhamnous was a deme, a fort, and a sanctuary, and had the most northerly harbour on the east coast of Attica, convenient for the crossing to Euboea.[18] The acropolis has two sets of fortifications, neither of which can be dated precisely on archaeological grounds, but are probably to be placed in the later fifth and middle fourth centuries.[19] On the acropolis was a temple and a theatre, and a votive deposit has yielded sixth-century pottery. Inland, and above the acropolis lies the sanctuary of the goddess Nemesis, with its two fifth-century temples, the earlier of the 480s and the larger perhaps of the last three decades of the fifth century.[20] Linking the acropolis and the sanctuary is a roadway lined with monumental tombs, and there are more tombs on the continuation of the road inland from the temples.[21] The tombs seem to be predominantly of fourth- and third-century date. Where the demesmen resided is much less clear; some, at least, may have lived south of the temples in the vicinity of the tower at Limiko, where there is a further cemetery and a cluster of classical remains.[22]

[18] For the importance of the link between Attica and Euboea see Thucy. 7. 28, 8. 95. The importance of Rhamnous varied according to the current political status of Oropos.

[19] J. Pouilloux, *La Forteresse de Rhamnonte* (Paris, 1954), pp. 39–42, 55–60; J. Ober, *Fortress Attica: Defense of the Athenian Land Frontier 404–322 BC* (Leiden, 1985), pp. 135–7.

[20] For a convenient summary of the archaeological remains see R. Stillwell (ed.), *Princeton Encyclopedia of Classical Sites* (Princeton, 1975). On the temple of Nemesis see now M. M. Miles, 'A Reconstruction of the Temple of Nemesis at Rhamnous', *Hesperia*, 58 (1989) 133–249, discussing the date at pp. 226–35.

[21] *Praktika* 1958. 28–37, 1975. 15–25, 1976. 5 ff., 22 ff., 1977. 2–24, 1978. 3 f.; *Arch. Eph.* 1979. 3–10, 17 ff.

[22] Osborne (n. 4), pp. 141, 190–1, 195.

The epigraphic evidence from Rhamnous reflects these various aspects of the community. From the fifth century come an enigmatic dedication made by 'The Rhamnousians on Lemnos' and two separate extracts from the accounts of the goddess Nemesis.[23] From the middle of the fourth century on there are decrees of demesmen, leases of land by a group of demesmen, and inscriptions which reflect, in one way or another, the presence of troops at the fort. Two features of this epigraphic evidence are remarkable: the quantity of decrees is enormous—some 50 inscriptions survive—and the variety of bodies from which the inscribed decisions emanate is very wide.

Three inscriptions record and publish honours given by the Council and Assembly to men with connections with Rhamnous. **28**[24] is a dedication by Thoukritos of Myrrhinous which records his being crowned by the Council and Assembly in four separate years around the middle of the third century for services as general over the coastal land. **29** of the 230s is a dedication by Kallisthenes of Prospalta on being crowned for services as general over the coast, and records honours received from the cavalry (*hippeis*), Council, and Assembly in one year for services as phylarch, from Council and Assembly in two years for being general, and by Council and Assembly and cavalry in another year for services as hipparch. Neither of these men was a member of the deme of Rhamnous, and the same may be true of the man honoured in the third such decree, which dates to the end of the fourth century (**10**).

In two further cases the deme joins in honouring a man also honoured by Council or by Council and Assembly. **8** of about 330 records honours given to the ephebes of the tribe Pandionis and their officers by the Council and Assembly, the Rhamnousians, Eleusinians, and men of Phyle (Rhamnous, Eleusis, and Phyle being, presumably, the three forts in which they had served their tour of duty). **11** marks a dedication to Dionysos made by the priest of the hero Archegetos on being crowned by the Council, the demesmen, and the soldiers; presumably the

---

[23] See chronological list of inscriptions from Rhamnous involving corporate bodies in Appendix A.

[24] Numbers in bold type refer to Appendix A.

demesmen are those of Rhamnous, and the soldiers those resident in the fort there in the late fourth century.

Honours given by the Council and Assembly are cited also in a third-century decree honouring Epichares for his services during the Chremonidean War (**21**). Nikostratos of Rhamnous, proposing the honour, records at the opening that when Epichares had earlier been hipparch he had served well and that the Council and Assembly had honoured him for that.[25]

In three mid-third-century cases the citation mentions not honours given by Council and Assembly but services rendered to them. The citation in **31** begins 'since Dikaiarchos took over his father's goodwill towards the *demos* of the Athenians and the corporation (*koinon*) of those stationed at Rhamnous'; **34** crowns Aischrion of Phyle for his valour (*arete*) and ambition (*philotimia*) 'which he continues to have to the Council and *demos* in the same way as to [those serving at Rhamnous]'; **35** honours Demostratos of Phlya in very similar language for his valour (*arete*) and the disposition (*eunoia*) which he continues to have towards the Council and *demos* as well as towards the Athenians serving at Rhamnous.

31 explicitly refers to the *koinon* of those stationed at Rhamnous. The very act of passing a decree and giving honours itself constituted the recognition by those involved of their corporate status, but the degree to which this recognition is explicit, and the identity of the corporate body clearly defined, varies a good deal, even in cases where the corporation has some structure and even some officers. Relatively clear-cut is the *eranos* of the Amphieraïstai (**32**) which describes itself as a *koinon* in a late third-century decree: it has an *archeranistes*, a secretary (*grammateus*), and a steward (*tamias*), none of whom are demesmen of Rhamnous. Another body which at least has funds it can claim as its own is the body of Athenians serving at Rhamnous responsible for **34** and **35**. But the claims for the existence of a *koinon* in **31** and **39**, from 236/5 and 225/4, are more involved and need to be dealt with at length, for they bring us to the most interesting feature of this body of inscriptions.

---

[25] The exact nature of the corporation passing this decree is not clear, but fragment *c* suggests that it included soldiers.

The honours for Dikaiarchos (**31**) begin with the archon date and 'The Rhamnousians decided'.[26] Without the archon date this is the formula which opens the straightforward deme decree honouring Kallippos of Melite, another commander of the Rhamnous garrison in the middle of the third century (**26**). After the list of services rendered, however, this decree has as its resumption formula 'The Rhamnousians and the other Athenians and all those living at Rhamnous decided'. This is not only a wider body than just the demesmen of Rhamnous; it is not even a body that is restricted to citizens.[27] At the end of the decree the six-word summary of the essence of the measure, placed in a crown, reads 'Those citizens living at Rhamnous [honour] Dikaiarchos'. This is a short-hand formula, and it may for that reason actually be the best guide to who those passing the decree actually thought that they were, but it is worth noting that if taken literally this formula would exclude non-resident demesmen of Rhamnous.

Exactly comparable with this split of identity in those passing the decree is a split in the corporate body which is explicitly said to be benefited and the benefactions to which are celebrated. The opening of the decree mentions Dikaiarchos' goodwill (*philia*) towards 'the *koinon* of those stationed at Rhamnous'. The passage after the resumption formula praises Dikaiarchos for his valour (*arete*) and disposition (*eunoia*) which he continues to have towards king Demetrios, the *demos* of the Athenians 'and to the *koinon* of those living at Rhamnous'. Finally, in place of the standard clause about encouraging ambition this decree declares its motive to be 'that there be a memorial to those who wish to do good to the *koinon* of Rhamnousians and those living in the fort'.

Those looking for a juridical definition of the body involved here have a field day, for the inscription itself declares, implicitly or explicitly, that it issues from the demesmen of Rhamnous, the citizens living at Rhamnous, those serving at Rhamnous, those living at Rhamnous, the demesmen and those living at the fort, and the demesmen of Rhamnous and the other Athenians and all living at Rhamnous.

---

[26] Texts and translations of **31** and **39** will be found in Appendix B.
[27] Some scholars have suggested the deletion of the second 'and' here to get rid of the non-Athenians, but this is a desperate and insensitive remedy.

Commentators talk, not exactly surprisingly, of confusion.[28] Pouilloux was inclined to attribute the confusion to the war then raging, but an exactly comparable confusion is apparent in **39** which dates from a decade later, when war raged no longer.

Like **31**, **39** is almost perfectly preserved. This is true of few of the decrees from Rhamnous, and it may be that had they been better preserved other decrees would have displayed a like confusion. **39** opens 'The Rhamnousians and those living at Rhamnous decided'. The resumption formula reads 'The Athenians sailing together in the warship (*aphractos*) decided'. The six-word summary reads: 'The Athenians sailing together [honour] Menander son of Teisander of Eitea'. The expense of the honour is charged to the *koinon* (by contrast to **31** where it is charged to the demesmen), but what *koinon*?

The beneficiaries of the actions for which Menander is praised are various. He looked after the equipment of the ship, did all that those in authority over him ordered, gave oil to the young men (*neaniskoi*) for their exercise in the gymnasium, sacrificed for the health, safety, and unanimity of those sailing together so that being saved and of one mind they might be useful to the *demos* in future, crowned the rowers, paid the fee to have the ship guarded, sacrificed to Nemesis, and provided sacrificial beasts and wine.

Of the honours given to Menander one is standard, a gold crown, but the other is unparalleled 'exemption from sailing'. As we have seen, demes could and did grant exemptions from local taxes, and Pouilloux has suggested that an exemption from duty raised on trade by sea is in question here. There are linguistic and juridical problems with this, however, as well as the consideration that permission to trade without paying dues at the tiny harbour of Rhamnous would have been a pretty otiose privilege for a rich trierarch like Menander.[29] It may be

---

[28] Pouilloux (n. 19), p. 131 writes 'La Rédaction du décret atteste une confusion juridique'; L. Moretti, *Iscrizioni storiche ellenistiche* (Florence, 1967), i. 55, similarly 'Altra cosa notevole in questo decreto è la confusione giuridico-protocollare'.

[29] For Pouilloux's suggestion see J. Pouilloux, 'Trois Décrets de Rhamnonte', *BCH* 80 (1956), 55–75, at 67. It is difficult to believe that 'sailing' (*plous*) on its own can mean 'duty raised on traffic by sea', and were the presence of the demesmen at Rhamnous in the decree solely to make legal the grant of exemption from such a tax by the fellow-sailors it would be remarkable that they are conspicuously not mentioned as the body that grants that privilege, the fellow-sailors alone being mentioned in that context.

more reasonable to see exemption from sailing as comparable to the exemption from military services attested in an Amphiktionic decree of 278/7 (*IG* ii² 1132. 14): what Menander would be given is permission not to sail with the vessel of which he is trierarch for the rest of the year. This is a privilege of considerable worth, and one that the Athenians sailing with him in the warship would both know the value of and have it in their power to grant.

But why were those who passed these decrees so confused as to their own identity? A further glance at the situation at Rhamnous in these years suggests an answer. The Athenians at Rhamnous at any one time were there for various reasons. There were the demesmen of Rhamnous, descendants of those living at Rhamnous at the end of the sixth century BC. Some of the demesmen lived there, others owned land there but lived elsewhere, and others again had no land or residence there but returned from time to time for religious, family, or political reasons. There were the worshippers at the sanctuary of Nemesis and perhaps at the healing cult of Aristomachos/ Amphiaraos. There were soldiers at the fort. The soldiers came in various groups: young men training as ephebes, non-Athenians granted the privilege of being treated as Athenians for tax purposes (*isoteleis*), foreign mercenaries who had been especially honoured for loyal service (*paroikoi*),[30] foreign mercenaries, and sailors. Resident as a garrison at Rhamnous for a more or less lengthy period, the troops made contact with the local residents in a variety of contexts, and mixed with them.

The extent of this mixing is well brought out by the decree of the *eranos* of the Amphieraïstai probably passed in the 220s (**32**). This decree shows how the visitors to Rhamnous clubbed together and formed a group centred on the cult of Amphiaraos and active in refurbishing his sanctuary. Prominent parts in this group are played by Archestratos of the deme of Erchia and Diokles of the deme of Hamaxanteia, who are two of the three-man committee set up to deal with the honours voted to Menander the trierarch in **39**. Menander himself may figure in the list of those contributing. Diokles was *archeranistes* and seems

---

[30] The meaning of *paroikoi* is not entirely certain: see the review of suggestions by Moretti (n. 28), pp. 73–4.

to have been the prime mover of the *eranos*, and Archestratos was its steward (*tamias*). But the decree of the *eranistai* was proposed by a member of the deme of Rhamnous, and the part played by another member of the deme is explicitly singled out for the record. Something of the complexity of the situation becomes apparent from the fact that the Rhamnousian proposer here, Theotimos son of Theodoros, is the recipient of honours from the privileged foreign mercenaries (*paroikoi*) in **41** for his services as general.

Far from there being a number of discrete groups relating to each other as group to group at Rhamnous in this period of the later third century, it is clear that the ever-changing community was made up of individuals who, through various circumstances, some in their own control and some beyond it, became attached to other individuals in a variety of groups. Criteria for membership, aims, and obligations varied from group to group, giving a permanent existence to some and an ephemeral one to others. The various individuals seem to have found group formation easy, and all the signs are that individual relations were marked by co-operation not antagonism. The incoherence of inscriptions such as **31** and **39** in their description of the responsible group is a mark not of tension between various organizing principles but of the difficulty that men who knew the group by its individual members had in identifying that group to the outside observer in terms of established categories.

The exceptional circumstances at Rhamnous, particularly in the latter half of the third century, give a vivid glimpse of the mixing of highly disparate individuals which must, albeit in less dramatic forms, have been a constant feature of life in classical and Hellenistic Athens. Permanent groups and temporary associations, groups with a history and groups without, groups with strict membership rules and groups with none, political and apolitical groups, all intermeshed as their members got together, whether in joint groups or in some new group. As the groups linked and reformed all lines of distinction were bent and even obliterated. One of the most striking features of this is the ease with which groups formed and took corporate action, even though the group was unclassifiable in terms of accepted social categories. In linking to act together those resident in Attica ignored, indeed flagrantly breached, the formal divisions within the population (most notably that absolute divide between citizen and non-citizen), and they breached the informal divisions too: as common soldiers and rich trierarchs join local residents in working to restore the shrine of Amphiaraos at Rhamnous, divisions of wealth, home base, and occupation all get submerged.

Part, at least, of the explanation for this remarkable situation lies in the features of group organization and action observed in the first part of this paper. The dominance of the 'political' model of group structure and the widespread adoption of the categories of action promoted by political rhetoric made for the unparalleled ease with which a group could be formed on any basis whatsoever. All the corporations, permanent or *ad hoc*, adopt a framework constructed along identical lines. None of the groups questions the categories of organization or of action and value manifested by the *polis* as a whole. Groups honour members in the same sorts of way and for the same sorts of reasons as does the *demos* in the Assembly. It is this conformity which makes for the easy subversion of the divisions set up by other, politically or religiously bounded, groups.

III

After Kleisthenes, or at least after the middle of the fifth century, it was the democrats who were the conservatives. This examination of the *demos* and its divisions has shown just how profoundly conservative the citizens of democratic Athens became, and how that conservatism even infected foreign groups more or less permanently resident in Attica. By the adoption of a single norm of organization and standard of action the divisions of the *demos* both manifested and reinforced the solidary ideology of the Athenian citizen body. The divisions rehearsed on a more or less public stage the values of the community, displayed those values and the results of putting them into practice. Conventional civic values were reinforced, conventional norms of behaviour confirmed.

The remarkable success of direct democracy in Athens can in

part be explained by the way in which this conservatism led to solidarity, but only in part. For the conservatism was not passive but active: the adoption of the political standard for group behaviour led not to apathetic repetition of old tricks in established groups but to ever innovative action in a rich flowering of new associations. The honour given to Menander the trierarch of exemption from sailing is unattested in any other Athenian document, and there is every chance that this unparalleled combination of demesmen and fellow-sailors forged an unparalleled form of honour in a unique situation. In enabling action to be taken by *any* group the political model gave all Athenians, indeed all free residents in Attica, the possibility of free expression, and ensured that the exclusiveness of existing groups erected no barriers to prevent individuals from joining in the display of their own values by their publicly inscribed actions.

Thucydides puts into the mouth of Perikles the statement that Athenians regard the politically inactive not as people who minded their own business but as useless. In fact many Athenians may have gone but rarely to the Assembly place of the Pnyx hill. But no Athenian could keep clear of all the various divisions of the *demos*. By their action in these smaller groups the Athenians not only declared their commitment to the organization and values of the direct democracy; they also had so ready a way of turning into group action any of the various social obligations they might individually acquire that they effectively forestalled incipient social tensions. Involvement in direct democratic machinery *was* essential to the health of Athenian democracy, but it was involvement in the democratic machinery of the divisions of the *demos* that was as important as, perhaps more important than, involvement in the direct democratic government of the *polis*.

Appendix A

Decisions of corporate bodies published at
Rhamnous

Date	Publications	Corporate body responsible
1. 500–480	*Ergon* 1984. 54	the Rhamnousians on Lemnos
2. Early C5	*Ergon* 1984. 55	?deme
3. 450–440	*IG* i³ 248, ML 53, Pouilloux (n. 19) 35	deme
4. 339/8	*IG* ii² 2493, *SEG* xxxii 225	*meros* of demesmen plus an individual
5. 339/8	*Hesperia Supp.* 19, 66–74	*meros* of demesmen plus an individual
6. 333/2	*IG* ii² 3105, Pouilloux 2 bis, *SEG* xxxi 162	ephebes and gymnasiarch
7. 333–330	*IG* ii² 4594a, Pouilloux 1	ephebes
8. *c.*330	Pouilloux 2, *Praktika* 1982. 161	deme (with Council and Assembly, Eleusinians and Phylasians)
9. *c.*320	*IG* ii² 2968, Pouilloux 4	the soldiers
10. *c.*300	Pouilloux 3	Council and Assembly
11. late C4	*IG* ii² 2849, Pouilloux 25	Council, demesmen, soldiers
12. C4/3	*SEG* xxxi 114	?deme
13. C4/3	*SEG* xxxi 115	?deme
14. C4/3	*IG* ii² 2861, Pouilloux 5, *SEG* xxxi 159	?
15. C4/3	*SEG* xxxiii 204	the soldiers
16. C4/3	*Ergon* 1984. 56	?
17. C3	*IG* ii² 3109, Pouilloux 6	deme
18. C3	*SEG* xxxi 111	?deme
19. C3	*Ergon* 1985. 48	deme
20. 300–250	*Ergon* 1984. 56	?
21. 264/3	*SEG* xxiv 154, *Ergon* 1985. 46	?deme and soldiers
22. 262/1	*IG* ii² 1217, Pouilloux 6	?deme
23. 250s	*IG* ii² 2977, Pouilloux 10, *SEG* xxxi 161	the soldiers stationed at Rhamnous

Date	Publications	Corporate body responsible
24. 256/5	Pouilloux 7, *SEG* iii 122, xxv 153, xxxii 152	the *isoteleis* stationed at Rhamnous
25. 256/5	*IG* ii² 3467, Pouilloux 8	deme and citizens living at Rhamnous
26. mid C3	*SEG* xxii 120	deme
27. 240s	*IG* ii² 1286, Pouilloux 11, *SEG* xxix 289, xxxi 117	the soldiers stationed under Timokrates
28. ?240	*IG* ii² 2856, Pouilloux 12, *SEG* xxxi 157	Council and Assembly
29. 230s	*IG* ii² 2854, Pouilloux 9, *SEG* xxv 205, xxxi 156	Council and Assembly and *hippeis*
30. 240–235	*SEG* xxii 129, xxxi 118	the encamped soldiers
31. 236/5	Pouilloux 15, *SEG* xxv 155	see discussion in text, p. 281
32. 220s	*IG* ii² 1322, Pouilloux 34	*eranos* of the Amphieraïstai
33. 220s	*Ergon* 1984. 56	?
34. 229	*SEG* xxii 128, xxviii 107	Athenians serving at Rhamnous
35. ?229	Pouilloux 14, *SEG* xv 111	Athenians serving at Rhamnous
36. ?229	*Ergon* 1986. 94	Athenians serving at Rhamnous
37. c.229	*SEG* xxxi 119	?*paroikoi*
38. 225–200	*Ergon* 1984. 56	*paroikoi*
39. 225/4	Pouilloux 17, *SEG* xv 112, xxi 537	see discussion in text, p. 282
40. 215/14	Pouilloux 18	the *paroikoi* stationed at Rhamnous
41. 215	Pouilloux 19, *SEG* xv 113, xix 82, xxv 158	the *paroikoi* stationed at Rhamnous
42. c.215	*SEG* xxxi 20	the citizen soldiers and those encamped at Rhamnous
43. 212/11	*Ergon* 1986. 93	the *paroikoi* stationed at Rhamnous
44. late C3	*IG* ii² 1312, Pouilloux 21, *SEG* iii 125	demos (deme)
45. late C3	*IG* ii² 1311, Pouilloux 13	Athenians serving at Rhamnous
46. late C3	*IG* ii² 1310, Pouilloux 16	the soldiers stationed under As. . .

Date	Publications	Corporate body responsible
47. late C3	Pouilloux 20	?
48. late C3	*IG* ii² 1313, Pouilloux 22	?
49. late C3	*SEG* xxxi 110	?deme
50. *c.*200	*SEG* xxxi 112	...sioi (? i.e. deme) and those stationed at the fort.
51. early C2	*SEG* xxii 130, xxxi 113	the *paroikoi* stationed at Rhamnous
52. 100/00	*IG* ii² 2869, Pouilloux 23, *SEG* xxxi 160	?

Appendix B

Texts and Translations of **31** *and* **39**

31 (text as *SEG* xxv 155)

Ἐπὶ 〚Ἐκχφάντου〛{υ} ἄρχοντος· ἔδοξεν Ῥαμνουσίοις· Ἐλπίνικος
[Μ]νησίππου Ῥαμνούσιος εἶπεν· ἐπειδὴ Δικαίαρχος πατρικὴν
[π]αρειληφὼς φιλίαν πρὸς τὸν δῆμον τὸν Ἀθηναίων καὶ τὸ
[κ]οινὸν τῶν ⟨ʿΡ⟩α⟨μ⟩νοῦντι ταττομένων, διαφυλάττει τὴν φιλί-
5 [α]ν, καί κατασταθεὶς μετὰ τοῦ πατρὸς Ἀπολλωνίου ὑπὸ το[ῦ]
〚 βασιλέ[ω]ς Ἀντιγόνου 〛 ἐπὶ τὴν φυλακὴν τοῦ φρουρίου καλ[ῶς]
καὶ φιλοτίμως ἐπεμελήθη τῆς τε φυλακῆς τοῦ φρουρίου καὶ
τῶν οἰκούντων ἐν αὐτῶι, εὔτακτον παρέχων αὐτόν τε καὶ τοὺς
στρατιώτας τοὺς ὑπὸ τὸν πατέρα ταττομένους, καὶ διὰ
10 ταῦτα αὐτοὺς ἀμφοτέρους Ῥαμνούσιοι καὶ Ἀθηναίων οἱ οἰ-
κοῦντες τὸ φρούριον ἐστεφάνωσαν χρυσῶι στεφάνωι κατὰ
τὸν νόμον· ὡσαύτως δὲ καὶ ἐπ' Ἐλευσῖνος γενόμενος ὁ πατὴρ
[αὐ]τοῦ ἐπ⟨η⟩ινέθη καὶ ἐστεφανώθη ὑπό τε Ἐλευσινίων καὶ τῶν ἄλ-
λων Ἀθηναίων τῶν οἰκούντων ἐν τῶι φρουρίωι· καὶ πάλιν αὐτὸς
15 κατασταθεὶς εἰς Πάνακτον καλῶς καὶ ἐνδόξως ἐπεμελήθη
τῆς τε τοῦ φρουρίου φυλακῆς καὶ τῆς ἄλλης χώρας τῆς Ἀττι-
κῆς· καὶ νῦν τεταγμένος ὑπὸ τοῦ βασιλέως Δημητρίου ἐν τεῖ
ἄκραι τεῖ Ἐρετριέων διατελεῖ εὔνους ὢν τῶι δήμωι τῶι Ἀθηναίων καὶ κοινεῖ πᾶσιν καὶ ἰδίαι τοῖς ὑπεκτεθημένοις τὰ βοσκή-

20 ματα διὰ τὸν πόλεμον διασώιζων καὶ βοηθῶν εἰς ὃ ἂν αὐτ[όν]
τις παρακαλεῖ· καὶ παραγενομένου τοῦ στρατηγοῦ Φιλοκή-
[δ]ου εἰς Ἐρετρίαν συνηγόρησέν τε τούτωι καὶ τῶν πολιτῶν
[ἕ]να ἀπηγμένον ἐπὶ θανάτωι ἐξ⟨ε⟩ί⟨λ⟩ετο ἐκ τοῦ [δε]σμωτηρί[ου
καὶ ἀνέσωισεν ἀποδεικνύμενος τὴν εὔνοιαν ἣν ἔχει πρὸς
25 τοὺς πολίτας· ἐπαγγέλλεται δὲ καὶ εἰς τὸν λοιπὸν χρόνον
εἰς ὃ ἂν αὐτόν τις παρακαλεῖ ἢ κοινεῖ ὁ δῆμος ἢ ἰδίαι τις τῶ[ν]
πολιτῶν χρείας παρέξεσθαι· ἔδωκεν δὲ καὶ ἱερεῖα εἰς τὴν θυ-
σίαν τῶν Νεμεσίων καὶ τοῦ βασιλέως ἐκ τῶν ἰδίων, ἐγλειπου-
[σ]ῶν τῶν θυσιῶν διὰ τὸν πόλεμον, ὅπως ἔχει καλῶς τὰ πρὸς
30 [τ]ὰς θεὰς ν Ῥαμνουσίοις· τύχει τεῖ ἀγαθεῖ δεδόχθαι Ῥαμνουσίοις καὶ τοῖς [ἄλ]λοις Ἀθηναίοις καὶ τ[οῖ]ς οἰκοῦσιν ἐν Ῥαμνοῦντι πᾶσιν ν ἐπαινέσαι Δικαίαρχον Ἀ[π]ολλωνίου Θριάσιον ἀρ[ε]-
τῆς ἕνεκα καὶ εὐνοίας ἣν ἔχων διατελεῖ εἴς τε τὸν ⟦ [βασιλέ] ⟧-
⟦ α Δημ[ήτ]ρι[ο]ν ⟧ καὶ εἰς τὸν δῆμον τὸν Ἀθηναίων καὶ εἰς τὸ
35 κοινὸν τῶν οἰκ[ού]ντων ⟨Ῥ⟩αμνοῦντα, καὶ στεφανῶσαι αὐτὸν χ[ρυ]
σῶι στεφάνωι κατὰ τὸν νόμον· ἀναγράψαι δὲ τόδε τὸ ψήφισμα τοὺς ἐπιμελητὰς καὶ τὸν δήμαρχο[ν] τὸν Ῥαμνουσίων
ἐν στήλαις λιθίναις δυεῖν, ἵνα εἶ ὑπόμνημα τοῖς βουλομένοις
εὐεργετεῖν τὸ κοινὸν Ῥαμνουσίων καὶ τῶν οἰκούντων τὸ φρού-
40 ριον, καὶ στῆσαι τὴν μὲν ἐν τῶι τεμένει τοῦ Διονύσου, τὴν δ' ἐν
τῶι Νεμεσίωι· εἰς δὲ τὴν ποίησιν τῶν στηλῶν καὶ τὴν ἀναγρ[α]-
φὴν τοῦ ψηφίσματος μερίσαι τὸν ταμίαν τὸν Ῥαμνουσίων
τὸ ἀναλωθὲν καὶ λογίσασθαι τοῖς δημόταις· ἑλέσθαι δὲ κ[αὶ]
ἐξ ἑαυ[τῶν] πέντε ἄνδρας οἵτινες συντελοῦσιν τὰ ἐψηφισ-
45 μένα ἤδη· οἵδε εἱρέθησαν· Ἐλπίνικος Μνησίππου, Λυκέας
Ἱεροκλέου, Στρόμβιχος Κλεοδωρίδου, Θρασύμαχος Ἀντιμάχου,
Λυσίθεος Διοκλέου.   *vacat*

(*in corona*)
Οἱ [οἰ]κοῦντες
τῶν πολιτῶν
50   Ῥαμνοῦντι
Δικαίαρχον.

In the year when Ekphantos was archon: The Rhamnousians decided, on the proposal of Elpinikos son of Mnesippos of Rhamnous that since Dikaiarchos had carried on his father's goodwill towards the *demos* of the Athenians and the corporation of those stationed at Rhamnous, and continues that goodwill, and when he was set in charge of the security of the fort and of those living in it by king Antigonos, along with his father Apollonios, he showed himself and those stationed under his father well disciplined, and because of this the Rhamnousians and those Athenians living at the fort crowned both of them with a gold crown according to the law; and in the same way when his father was at Eleusis he was praised and crowned by the Eleusinians and the other Athenians living in the fort; and again when he was put in charge at Panakton he looked after the security of that fort and of the rest of the Attic countryside well and gloriously; and now stationed by king Demetrios on the headland of the Eretrians he continues to be well-disposed to the *demos* of the Athenians, both to all in common and individually to those seeking refuge for their flocks because of the war, protecting them and helping in any way he is asked to; and when the general Philokedes came to Eretria he pleaded with him and had one of the citizens who had been condemned to death freed from prison and saved him, showing how well disposed he is to the citizens; and he announces that for the future he will meet the needs both of the *demos* in common and of any individual citizen as he is asked to; and he has given victims for the sacrifice to Nemesis and to the king from his own money, at a time when sacrifices had ceased because of the war, in order that the Rhamnousians should have their relations with the goddess in good order; therefore the Rhamnousians and the other Athenians and all those living at Rhamnous decided, and may they be right! to praise Dikaiarchos son of Apollonios of the deme of Thria for his valour and the good disposition which he continually shows to king Demetrios and the demos of the Athenians and the corporation of those living at Rhamnous, and to crown him with a gold crown according to the law. The *epimeletai* and demarch of the Rhamnousians are to have this decree inscribed on two stone pillars, in order that there may be a memorial to those who are prepared to do good to the corporation of the Rhamnousians and those who inhabit the fort, and are to stand one in the sanctuary of Dionysos and one in the sanctuary of Nemesis. The *tamias* of the Rhamnousians is to divide up the expense of the making of the pillars and the inscription of the decree and reckon it to the demesmen. Five demesmen are to be chosen to see to the completion of what has now been decreed. The following were chosen: Elpinikos son of Mnesippos, Lykeas son of Hierokles,

Strombichos son of Kleodorides, Thrasymachos son of Antimachos,
Lysitheos son of Diokles.

The citizens

living

at Rhamnous

honour

Dikaiarchos

39. (text as *SEG* xv 112)

Ἔδοξεν Ῥαμνουσίοις καὶ τοῖς οἰκοῦσιν τῶν πολιτῶν
Ῥαμνοῦντι · Τιμοκράτης Ἐπιγένου Ὄαθεν εἶπεν · ἐπειδ[ὴ]
Μένανδρος κατασταθεὶς τριήραρχος εἰς τὸν ἐνιαυ[τὸν]
τὸν ἐπὶ Νικήτου ἄρχοντος τῆς τε τοῦ πλοίου ἐπ[ι]-
5 σκευῆς ἐπεμελήθη καλῶς καὶ φιλοτίμως ἀναλ[ίσ]-
κων ἐκ τῶν ἰδίων ὅσα παρήγγελλον αὐτῶι οἱ ἐπὶ τού[του]
τεταγμένοι · ἔθηκεν δὲ καὶ ἔλαιον τοῖς νεανίσκ[οις]
[ἵ]να ἐπιμελόμενοι τοῦ σώματος δυνατώτεροι γίνων-
[τ]αι · ἔθυσεν δὲ καὶ τῶι Διὶ τῶι σωτῆρι καὶ τεῖ Ἀθηνᾶι τεῖ
10 [σω]τείραι περὶ ὑγιείας καὶ σωτηρίας καὶ ὁμονοίας τῶν
[συ]νπλευσάντων, ὅπως ἂν ὁμονοοῦντες καὶ σωιζόμε-
[νοι κ]αὶ εἰς τὸ μετὰ ταῦτα χρήσιμοι γίνωνται τῶι δήμωι
[καὶ] ὑπεδέξατο φιλοτίμως ἐκ τῶν ἰδίων · vac. ἐστεφάνω-
σε δὲ καὶ τοὺς ἐπὶ τοῦ πλοίου ὑπηρέτας φιλοτιμίας
15 ἕνεκεν τῆς εἰς ἑαυτούς · ἔδωκεν δὲ καὶ τὰ ναυφυλά-
κια παρ᾽ ἑαυτοῦ καὶ παραγενόμενος εἰς Ῥαμνοῦντα
ἔθυσεν τεῖ Νεμέσει μετὰ τοῦ στρατηγοῦ καὶ τῶν ἱερο-
ποιῶν τῶν αἱρεθέντων μεθ᾽ αὐτοῦ ⟦ --- ⟧ καὶ ἐπέδωκεν ἱερε[ῖ]-
α καὶ οἶνον · ὅπως δ᾽ ἂν ἐφάμιλλον εἶ τοῖς ἀεὶ καθισταμέ-
20 [ν]οις τριηράρχοις εἰδόσιν ὅτι χάριτας ἀξίας κομιοῦν-
[τ]αι ὧν ἂν εὐεργετήσωσιν · ἀγαθεῖ τύχει · δεδόχθαι
Ἀθηναίων τοῖς συνπλεύσασιν ἐν τῶι ἀφράκτωι ·
ἐπαινέσαι Μένανδρον Τεισάνδρου Εἰτεαῖον καὶ
στεφανῶσαι χρυσῶι σ[τ]εφάνωι κατὰ τὸν νόμον
25 ἀρετῆς ἕνεκα καὶ φιλοτιμίας τῆς εἰς ἑαυτούς ·
εἶναι δὲ αὐτῶι καὶ ἀτέλειαν τοῦ πλοῦ εἰς τὸ μετὰ ταῦτα ·
ἀναγράψαι δὲ τὸ ψήφισμα ἐν στήλει λιθίνει καὶ στῆσαι πρὸ[ς]
τεῖ πύλει · ἑλέσθαι δὲ καὶ τρεῖς ἄνδρας ἤδη ἐξ ἑαυτῶν οἵτινες συντελοῦσιν τὰ ἐψηφισμένα · τὸ δὲ ἀνάλωμα τὸ γεν[ό]-
30 μενον λογίσασθαι τῶι κοινῶι · οἵδε εἱρέθησαν · Τιμοκρά-

της Ἐπιγένου Ὀῆθεν, Ἀρχέστρ[α]τος Αἰσχίνου Ἐρχιεύς,
[Δι]οκλῆς Δίωνος Ἀμαξαντ[εύς].

(*in corona*)
Ἀθηναίων
οἱ συνπλεύσαντες
35 Μέναν⟨δ⟩ρον
Τεισάνδρου
Εἰτεαῖον.

The Rhamnousians and the citizens living at Rhamnous decided, on
the proposal of Timokrates son of Epigenes of the deme of Oa, that
since Menander, when he had been appointed trierarch for the year
when Niketos was archon looked after the equipment of the boat
keenly and well, spending of his own money as much as those serving
under him demanded; and he made oil available to the *neaniskoi* in
order that they might take care of their bodies and become fitter; and
he sacrificed to Zeus Soter and Athena Soteira for the health, safety,
and unanimity of the fellow sailors, in order that being safe and in
concord they might be useful for the *demos* in the future, and gave an
ambitious entertainment at his own expense; and he crowned the
rowers on the boat for their keenness among themselves; and he paid
the fee for guarding the boat and when he arrived at Rhamnous
sacrificed to Nemesis along with the general and the sacristans who
had been elected with him, and provided sacrificial victims and wine;
therefore, in order that there may be rivalry among future trierarchs
in the knowledge they will receive worthy thanks from those they
benefit, the Athenians sailing together on the aphract have decided,
and may they be right! to praise Menander son of Teisander of Eitea
and to crown him with a gold crown according to the law for his
valour and ambition shown towards them; also he is to have
exemption from sailing for the future. The inscription is to be
inscribed on a stone pillar and set up at the gate. Three men are now
to be chosen from their own number to see to the completion of what
has been decreed. The expense incurred is to be charged to the
corporation. The following were chosen: Timokrates son of Epigenes
of Oa, Archestratos son of Aischines of Erchia, Diokles son of Dion of
Hamaxanteia.

Athenian
fellow sailors
honour
Menander
son of Teisander
of Eitea

12

What is *Polis* Religion?

CHRISTIANE SOURVINOU-INWOOD

THE attempt to reconstruct, and make sense of, a religious system to which we have extremely limited access, and which is very different from those which have conditioned our own understanding of the category 'religion', demands a methodology which, as far as possible, prevents our own—culturally determined—assumptions from intruding into, and thus corrupting, the investigation. We also need to discard the layers of earlier interpretations which form distorting filters structuring the data on the basis of the assumptions and expectations of scholars of earlier generations, when it was not fully realized that all reading and interpretation, and all 'common sense', are culturally determined. Here I present highly compressed versions of selected parts of my arguments, to define the parameters within which, on my analysis, *polis* religion operated in the classical period.

The *polis* provided the fundamental framework in which Greek religion operated. Each *polis* was a religious system which formed part of the more complex world-of-the-*polis* system, interacting with the religious systems of the other *poleis* and with the Panhellenic religious dimension; thus direct and full participation in religion was reserved for citizens, that is, those who made up the community which articulated the religion. One belonged to the religious community of one's own *polis*, (or *ethnos*);[1] in the *sacra* of others, even in Panhellenic

I am very grateful to the editors for their very considerable help with the reorganization of what was originally one long article into two separate papers, the present one, and another entitled 'Further Aspects of *polis* Religion', which will be published in *Annali, Istituto orientale di Napoli: Archeologia e storia antica*, 10 (1988).

I am also very grateful to Professor W. G. Forrest, Professor D. M. Lewis, and Dr R. Parker for discussing various aspects of this paper with me. Dr Parker has also kindly commented on the original long version of the paper.

[1] I cannot consider *ethnos* religion here. The differences between *ethnos* and *polis* religion do not impinge on our investigation.

sanctuaries, one could only participate as a *xenos*. On at least
some occasions a *xenos* could take part in cult only with the help
of a citizen, normally the *proxenos* of his city, who acted as
'intermediary'.[2]

It would seem that the transgression of these rules did not
involve disrespect to the gods, that the prohibition was perceived to pertain to the human articulation of the divine world,
which was not considered inviolable. For Kleomenes, dis-
regarding the priest's ban on him as a *xenos*, had the priest
removed and performed a sacrifice on the altar at the Argive
Heraion.[3] Later, Kleomenes was believed by the Spartans—
who took religious prohibitions and other prescriptions especially seriously even when at war[4]—when he claimed that he
had obtained omens there; this suggests that his action was not
seen as liable to offend the goddess and preclude her from
sending him an omen. Furthermore, although Apollodoros in
[Demosthenes] 59 states that it was impious for Phano who was
allegedly not an Athenian citizen to have become *basilinna*, his
tone and arguments (94–107 and 110–11), and the fact that he
also brings up (85–7, 110) the accusation of adultery (a woman
taken in adultery was not allowed to attend the public rites),
suggest that it was not quite as self-evident as one might have
expected that the illegitimate officiating of a *xenos* in the most
central and secret rites of the *polis* (59; 73) was a clear-cut,
unambivalent, case of serious impiety—as opposed to being
merely an offence against the *polis*.

The idea that the transgression of the rules excluding *xenoi*
did not offend the gods is connected with another point (to
which I shall return), that the ownership of sanctuaries was
perceived as belonging to the human, not the divine, sphere,
which is why sanctuaries could change hands without it being
felt that any disrespect to the gods had been committed. This

---

[2] On *proxenoi*: C. Marek, *Die Proxenie* (Frankfurt, etc., 1984); M.-F. Baslez, *L'étranger dans la Grèce antique* (Paris, 1984), pp. 39–40, 111–25; Ph. Gauthier, *Symbola: Les étrangers et la justice dans les cités grecques* (Nancy, 1972), pp. 17–61; cf. also M. B. Walbank, *Athenian Proxenies of the Fifth Century* BC (Toronto and Sarasota, 1978), *passim*, esp. p. 2.

[3] Herod. 6. 81–2. It is unclear whether *xenoi* were totally forbidden to sacrifice, or had to sacrifice elsewhere in the precinct, or through a *proxenos*.

[4] A. J. Holladay and M. D. Goodman, *CQ* 36 (1986), 151–60. The validity of the representations encoded in the story does not depend on its historicity.

contrasts with the transgression of different types of exclusion which did offend the gods.[5] One such offence, the sacrilegious nature of which was confirmed by the Pythia, and which brought divine punishment, was Miltiades' attempt to enter the *megaron* of the Thesmophorion of Paros, from which men were excluded (Herodotus 6. 134–5). Another sacrilegious transgression was entering a sanctuary in one's *polis* while forbidden to do so after being deprived of citizen rights (e.g. Andocides 1. 71; cf. 32–3; 72). The transgression of this exclusion, which was punishable with death (Andocides 1. 33), constituted impiety and threatened the effectiveness of all the religious practices of the *polis*.

The *polis* anchored, legitimated, and mediated all religious activity. This is true even in the Panhellenic sanctuaries where the *polis* mediated the participation of its citizens in a variety of ways. At Delphi the *polis* schema articulated the operation of the oracle. The oracle's religious personnel consisted of Delphians, and the participation of non-Delphians was mediated by Delphians who acted as *proxenoi* and offered the preliminary sacrifice before consultation by non-Delphians. On regular consultation days this sacrifice was offered by the Delphic *polis* for all the enquirers; on other days it was offered on behalf of the enquirer by the *proxenos* of his city.[6] The non-Delphians, then, were treated on the model of *xenoi* worshipping at the sanctuary of another *polis*. The same dominance of the *polis* articulation occurred, it appears, in other Panhellenic sanctuaries. In the sanctuary of Zeus at Olympia *proxenoi* again played a role,[7] the judges of the Olympic Games were Eleans (Herodotus 2. 160; Pausanias 5. 9. 5), and the Eleans made decisions as to who was allowed to participate in the Games and worship at the sanctuary (cf. e.g. Thucydides 5. 50).[8]

[5] Of course, what counted as sacrilegious behaviour liable to attract divine punishment was variously perceived (cf. e.g. Andoc. 2. 15).

[6] Cf. Eur. *Androm.* 1102–3. Cf. Marek (n. 2), pp. 168–70; G. Roux, *Delphes: Son oracle et ses dieux* (Paris, 1976), p. 75; G. Daux, in *Le monde grec: Pensée, littérature, histoire, documents: Hommages à Claire Préaux* (Brussels, 1975), pp. 480–95; Baslez (n. 2), p. 40; L. Gernet and A. Boulanger, *Le Génie grec dans la religion* (Paris, 1970; first edn., 1932), p. 264; cf. also *CID* 5 (p. 17) and perhaps also nos. 4 (pp. 15–16) and 6 (pp. 18–19); cf. also p. 76.

[7] Gauthier (n. 2), pp. 41–6; Marek (n. 2), pp. 169; cf. also Baslez (n. 2), p. 40.

[8] On Dodona see Hyperides 4. 24–6; cf. 19. 26; these passages suggest that it was arguable that expensive dedications to sanctuaries should not be made by outsiders

Another manifestation of the fact that the *polis* mediated the individual's participation in Panhellenic cult can be seen in the order of consultation of the Delphic oracle.[9] Greeks came before barbarians; among the Greeks, the Delphians before all other Greeks; after the Delphians and before the other Greeks came the other ethnic groups and *poleis* who were members of the Delphic Amphictiony. Consultation by the remaining Greeks was, apparently, arranged according to some geographical order. Within this basic articulation operated the *promanteia*, a privilege which the Delphic *polis* granted to individuals, *poleis*, or other collectivities. Here again, that is, the oracle is treated as a sanctuary of the Delphic *polis* in which the latter could grant special privileges to its benefactors. The *promanteia* did not transcend categories, it only involved priority over people belonging to the same category: given to a barbarian it meant he could consult the oracle before other barbarians, not before Greeks; an Athenian could consult before other Athenians, an Amphictionic *polis* before all other Amphictionic peoples, but after the Delphians.

Another example of the mediation of the *polis* in Panhellenic religious activities is the *theoriai* sent by individual *poleis* to the Panhellenic sanctuaries and also to other *poleis*.[10] The *theoroi* of each *polis* conducted ritual acts in the Panhellenic sanctuaries in the name of that *polis* (e.g. [Andocides] 4. 29). The treasuries erected by individual *poleis* in the great Panhellenic sanctuaries are the physical expression of this mediation, the symbolic representation of the *polis* religious systems in those sanctuaries. They housed the offerings dedicated by their citizens and the ritual furnishings for the various cult activities, and were also a visual reminder of the cities which had built them, whose achievement and wealth they advertised and glorified.

A major context of inter-*polis* religious interaction, besides the Panhellenic, is that of the Amphictionies or Leagues, associations of *poleis* or *ethne*, or a combination of the two,

without the permission of the *polis/ethnos* who owned the sanctuary, which (irrespective of the underlying 'political' reasons) confirms that even in Panhellenic cultic contexts the *polis* articulation was felt to be basic.

[9] Roux (n. 6), pp. 76–9.

[10] M. P. Nilsson, *Geschichte der griechischen Religion* i[3] (1967), pp. 549–52, 826–7; Baslez (n. 2), p. 59.

which celebrated one or more festivals together and were focused on one or, as in the case of the Delphic Amphictiony, two sanctuaries. They developed their own institutions, such as the amphictionic council of the Delphic Amphictiony, the duties of which included the conduct of the Panhellenic Pythian Games and the care of the finances of the sanctuary and upkeep of the temple. Even in the case of the Panhellenic Games the Delphic *polis* was the symbolic centre: it was the Delphic *polis* that sent *theoroi* to announce the Pythian Games;[11] and the laurel for the victors' crowns was brought from Tempe in the course of a ritual (of an initiatory type) involving male adolescents from the Delphic *polis*.[12] Thus the same articulation pertains in the Panhellenic Games as in the order of the oracular consultation: the Delphic *polis* at the centre, the Amphictiony forming the inner circle, the other Greeks the outer one. Here the barbarians were excluded from competing—for this was one of the rites defining membership of the group 'Greeks'. That it is the *polis* which mediates the participation of individuals in the cult activities of the Leagues is also illustrated by a story according to which the transgression of one individual during the games of Triopian Apollo was punished through the expulsion of his city, Halikarnassos, from the religious League of Dorian cities (Herodotus 1. 144). This reveals a mentality[13] in which the individual is perceived as participating in the ritual (including the agonistic) activities in the name of his *polis*, which mediates and guarantees that participation. This made the whole *polis* guilty of impiety.

Even in international contexts cult remained *polis*-based: at Naukratis, which down to the fourth century had the double character of *emporion* and *polis*, some Greek cities singly set up sanctuaries that belonged to them and were 'their' *polis* shrines in a foreign land; others acting in combination set up a sanctuary called the Hellenion (Herodotus 2. 178). But (as is shown by Herodotus' insistence that only the *poleis* he names were involved in its foundation and had a share in it) this was

[11] e.g. *CID* 10. 45–6 (cf. pp. 118–19).
[12] A. Brelich, *Paides e Parthenoi* (Rome, 1969), pp. 387–405; C. Sourvinou-Inwood, *CQ* 29 (1979), 233–4.
[13] The historicity of the story is irrelevant; truth or invention, it is an expression of the relevant Greek perceptions.

not a supra-*polis* 'Greek' shrine, but the common sanctuary of an *ad hoc* combination of cities, in which the *polis* was the basic unit.

Greek religion, then, consists of a network of religious systems interacting with each other and with the Panhellenic religious dimension. The latter is articulated in, and through, Panhellenic poetry and the Panhellenic sanctuaries; it was created, in a dispersed and varied way, out of selected elements from certain local systems, at the interface between the (interacting) *polis* religious systems—which it then also helped to shape.[14] The Greeks saw themselves as part of one religious group; the fact that they had common sanctuaries and sacrifices—as well as the same language and the same blood, a perceived common ancestry, and the same way of life—was one of the defining characteristics of Greekness (Herodotus 8. 144. 2). This identity was cultically expressed in, and reinforced through, ritual activities in which the participating group was 'all the Greeks' and from which foreigners were excluded, of which the most important was competing in the Olympic Games (Herodotus 2. 160; 5. 22). But each person was a member of this Panhellenic group in virtue of being a member of a *polis*. It is not simply that being a citizen of a particular *polis* guarantees one's Greekness; as we saw, the *polis* mediated participation in Panhellenic cult.

The gods who were worshipped in the different *poleis* were, of course, perceived to be the same gods (cf. also Herodotus 5. 92–3). What differed was the precise articulation of the cult, its history, its particular modalities, which aspect of each deity each city chose to emphasize, which deities were perceived to be more closely connected with, and so more important to, the city, and so on. Such differences were to a very large extent perceived as relating to the past, to a deity's relationships to particular places and to the heroic ancestors of the individual cities and the cults that these had founded—which were hallowed, both by tradition and because many of these founders belonged to the heroic past in which men had a closer connection with the divine, and thus mediated between man's limitations and the unknowability of the divine. The perception that different needs gave rise to different cults was most

[14] Cf. e.g. on divine personalities C. Sourvinou-Inwood, *JHS* 98 (1978), 101–21.

unambiguous in the case of cults articulating social groups. Common cult was the established mode for expressing communality in the Greek world, for giving social groups cohesion and identity; it would therefore have been perceived as inevitable that the particular social realities of the particular *poleis* would be reflected in the articulation of their cults. This was not a matter of a 'state' 'manipulating' religion; the unit which was both the religious body carrying the religious authority and the social body, acting through its political institutions, deployed cult in order to articulate itself in what was perceived to be the natural way.

All Greeks were bound to respect other cities' sanctuaries and cults if they did not wish to offend the gods. The 'law' of the Greeks as reported in Thucydides 4. 98. 2 (cf. 4. 97. 2–3) was that whichever *polis* had control over a land also owned its sanctuaries, and they should worship as far as possible according to the rites that were customary there before the change of ownership.[15] The underlying perceptions here are that since the gods were the same, and since *polis* religion (including its sanctuaries) was part of the wider *polis* system, possession of the land naturally entailed ownership of the sanctuary; and that, since the way the gods were worshipped in any particular *polis* and sanctuary was partly a result of its past history, traditional practices, hallowed by their connections with a heroic founder and/or by custom, should be respected as far as possible; but not absolutely, since those sanctuaries and cults could not but be affected by the different religious system which they entered, by the articulation of religion in the rest of the *polis*; thus the rites practised after the conquest would be the result of the interaction between those already established and—to a lesser, but varying degree—the religious system of the *polis* that now controlled it. In my view, underlying it all is the notion that the articulation of religion through the systems of particular *poleis* is a human construct, created by particular historical circumstances and open to change under changed circumstances (Thucydides 4. 98. 3–4).

Greek religion is, above all, a way of articulating the world, of structuring chaos and making it intelligible; it is a model

[15] I. Malkin, *Religion and Colonization in Ancient Greece* (Leiden, 1987), pp. 149–50.

articulating a cosmic order guaranteed by a divine order which also (in complex ways) grounds human order, perceived to be incarnated above all in the properly ordered and pious *polis*, and providing certain rules and prescriptions of behaviour, especially towards the divine through cult, but also towards the human world—prescribing, for example, that one must not break one's oaths (e.g. Homer, *Iliad* 3. 276–80; 19. 259–60), or that one must respect strangers and suppliants who have the special protection of the gods, especially Zeus, precisely because they are most vulnerable.[16] The *polis* was the institutional authority that structured the universe and the divine world in a religious system, articulated a pantheon with certain particular configurations of divine personalities, and established a system of cults, particular rituals and sanctuaries, and a sacred calendar. In a religion without a canonical body of belief, without revelation, without scriptural texts (outside certain marginal sects which did have sacred books but are irrelevant to our present discussion), without a professional divinely anointed clergy claiming special knowledge or authority, without a church, it was the ordered community, the *polis*, which assumed the role played in Christianity by the Church— to use one misleading comparison (for all metaphors derived from Christianity are inevitably misleading) to counteract and destroy alternative, implicit models. It assumed the responsibility and authority to set a religious system into place, to mediate human relationships with the divine world.[17] Connected with this is the fact that, as we shall see, *polis* religion embraces, contains, and mediates all religious discourse—with the ambiguous and uncertain exception of some sectarian discourse. Even festivals common to different *poleis*, such as the Thesmophoria, the most widespread Greek festival, were articulated by each *polis*, at *polis* level. Hence, the same festival could take different forms in different, even neighbouring, *poleis*. For example, the Agrionia at Orchomenos was celebrated differently from the festival of the same name at

---

[16] Plato, *Laws* 729 E-730 A. Cf. Nilsson (n. 10), pp. 419–21; J. Gould, *JHS* 93 (1973), 90–4.

[17] We can observe the *polis* putting into place its religious system, and through this creating itself, its own 'centre', in the foundation of colonies (on which cf. Malkin (n. 15), *passim*, esp. pp. 1–2).

Chaironeia;[18] and at Eretria the Thesmophoria had certain unique features: Kalligeneia was not invoked, and the meats were grilled in the sun, not on the fire (Plutarch, *Moralia* 298 B–C).

Connected with the absence of revelation, of scriptures, and of a professional divinely anointed priesthood is the fact that a central category of Greek religion is unknowability, the belief that human knowledge about the divine and about the right way of behaving towards it is limited and circumscribed. The perception that the articulation of religion through the particular *polis* systems is a human construct, created by particular historical circumstances and open to change under changed circumstances, is in my view connected with this awareness of the severe limitations of human access to the divine, of the ultimate unknowability of the divine world, and the uncertain nature of human relationships to it. The Greeks did not delude themselves that their religion incarnated the divine will.

The only anchoring for the *polis'* endeavour to ensure the optimum behaviour towards the gods was prophecy, which offered the only direct means of access to the divine world in Greek religion. But this access also was flawed, because, according to Greek ideas about divination, human fallibility interferes, and the word of the gods is often misinterpreted. Nevertheless, through the Delphic oracle (above all), the *polis* could ensure some, if ambiguous, assurance of the correctness of its religious discourse.[19] Thus cities consulted the oracle to ensure that the appropriate worship was offered to the appropriate deities either on a particular occasion such as that of a portent (e.g. [Demosthenes] 43. 66) or more generally for health and good fortune;[20] a vast number of cults and rites were established at the Delphic oracle's instigation and/or on

[18] Orchomenos: A. Schachter, *Cults of Boiotia* i (London, 1981), pp. 179–81. Chaironeia: ibid. 173–4; ii (1986), p. 146.

[19] One safeguard against the flawed nature of the prophetic vehicle was to consult more than one oracle (cf. e.g. Hyperides 4. 14–15). But even this could not guarantee unflawed access to the gods. On the role of oracular divination cf. R. Parker, in P. Cartledge and F. D. Harvey (eds.), *Crux: Essays Presented to G. E. M. de Ste Croix* (Exeter, 1985), pp. 298–326.

[20] Cf. Dem. 21. 52; H. W. Parke and D. E. W. Wormell, *The Delphic Oracle*, ii. *The oracular responses* (Oxford, 1956), pp. 114–15, no. 282. Cf. Parker in *Crux* (n. 19), p. 304.

its advice or with its simple approval (e.g. *LSCG* 5. 4–5, 25–6; *LSCG* 178. 2–3; Herodotus 4. 15).[21] The introduction of new cults[22] was connected with the awareness of the fallibility of human knowledge of the divine and the appropriate forms of worship, which entailed that potentially there was always room for improvement. Especially in times of crisis or difficulties, the question 'is there some god we have neglected?', or more generally 'how can we improve our relationship with the divine?' would have arisen, generating pressures towards innovation, especially the introduction of new cults (e.g. Herodotus 7. 178–9). The oracle provided the authority for such changes; but because prophecy is flawed, the danger of getting things wrong could not be eliminated.

It is in this context that we must place the tension between conservatism and innovation in *polis* religion, which is revealed and exploited in Lysias 30, on Nikomachos' codification of the Athenian sacred calendar.[23] The most important argument for religious conservatism in this speech[24] is that the ancestral rites have served the Athenians' ancestors and themselves well, and thus should not be changed. On the desirability of the new sacrifices the speech is ambivalent—an attitude which certainly fits the rhetorical context. In classical Athens, the tension between conservatism and innovation tended to be 'resolved' with the former drifting towards the non-abandonment of old cults and the latter towards the introduction of new ones.

The Greek *polis* articulated religion and was itself articulated by it; religion became the *polis*' central ideology, structuring, and giving meaning to, all the elements that made up the identity of the *polis*, its past, its physical landscape, the relation

[21] The poets' mythological/theological articulations were not authoritative; for the Muses who inspired them often lied. Cf. Hesiod, *Theog.* 27–8; M. L. West (ed.), *Hesiod: Theogony* (Oxford, 1966), p. 163 on 28; K. J. Dover, *Greek Popular Morality in the Time of Plato and Aristotle* (Oxford, 1974), p. 130. On Greek poetry and religion, P. E. Easterling, in P. E. Easterling and J. V. Muir (eds.), *Greek Religion and Society* (Cambridge, 1985), pp. 34–49.

[22] See e.g. J. K. Davies, *Democracy and Classical Greece* (Glasgow, 1978), pp. 180–1, and below, p. 311.

[23] See especially S. Dow, *Proc. Massachusetts Historical Soc.* 71 (1953–7), 3–36; id., *BCH* 92 (1968), 177–81; id., *Historia*, 9 (1960), 270–93; K. Clinton, *Studies in Attic Epigraphy History and Topography Presented to Eugene Vanderpool* (*Hesperia*, Suppl. 19; Princeton, 1982), 27–37.

[24] I am concerned with the rhetorical strategy, which operates within the parameters of collective assumptions; the speaker's 'real' beliefs and motivations are irrelevant.

ship between its constituent parts. Ritual reinforces group solidarity, and this process is of fundamental importance in establishing and perpetuating civic and cultural, as well as religious, identities.[25] Its heroic cults in particular gave the religious system of each *polis* much of its individuality, its sense of identity and difference, which were connected with the mythical past and sanctified the connection of the citizens with that past to which they related through those cults. This is an important reason for the density of heroic cults (often for figures who appear to us insignificant) in Athenian deme religion: they helped define the deme's identity, both through the performance of distinctive rites and also through the fact that they related the deme to its territory and its mythical past. In the colonies the heroic cult offered to the founder played a similar role.[26] Religion continued to provide the one stable cohesive force in the classical *polis*, even in Athens after the development of a new Athenian self-definition—whose focus was anyway very largely religious, namely the Acropolis, the Panathenaia, Theseus as Athenian hero par excellence and good democratic king, and the burial of the war dead.[27] This was especially true in a time of crisis, when there was the danger—and sometimes the reality—of sections of the *polis* preferring ideology over country and rupturing the *polis*. This is a prime reason why the profanation of the Mysteries and the mutilation of the Herms was taken by many to be part of an oligarchic or tyrannical conspiracy, an attempt to overthrow democracy (Thucydides 6. 28. 1, 6. 60–1; cf. also Diodorus 13. 2. 3). Religion is the facet of *polis* ideology that all citizens should respect most; thus a sign of disrespect towards religion is a sign of disloyalty towards the *polis* and the *politeia*.

The central place of religion in civic life[28] is an expression of the close relationship between the two. The perception that

[25] I cannot discuss this complex notion; in the simplified form in which it is put here it goes back to Durkheim's work, but it does not depend on acceptance of the latter *in toto*. Cf. also the not-unrelated perception in Plato, *Laws* 738 D–E; 771 B–772 A.

[26] Malkin (n. 15), pp. 189–266.

[27] See esp. N. Loraux, *The Invention of Athens* (Cambridge, Mass., and London, 1986).

[28] Some instances in Athens: homicide trials were conducted in a sanctuary, *Ath. Pol.* 57. 4; sacred structures were situated in 'political' buildings, e.g. the altar in the Bouleuterion, Xen. *Hell.* 2. 3. 52, 53, 55; Antiphon 6. 45; political and social life functioned with the help of rites, prayers, oaths and curses; the election for office by lot entailed selection by the gods.

religion was the centre of the *polis* also explains, and is revealed in, a variety of stories[29] and practices.[30] It is also related to the perception that it is the relationship of the *polis* with its gods that ultimately guarantees its existence, that in the origins of the *polis* there is often (explicitly or implicitly) located a form of 'guarantee' by the gods, of a finite and relative protection, which the cultic relationships of the *polis* with the gods—above all with its principal deity—strives to maintain. Such a guarantee is surely perceived to be at the root of the oracular sanction for the foundation of colonies. Cities whose origin was perceived to lie in the mythical past expressed their divine guarantee through myth. In Athens the myths embodying, among other things, this 'guarantee' of protection are that of the earth-born king Erichthonios and, above all, that of the contest between Athena and Poseidon for Attica;[31] the gift of an olive tree by Athena brought about and was the sign sealing the relationship between Athena and Athens, and the olive-tree was thus the symbolic core of Athenian *polis* religion and the guarantee of Athens' existence.[32] This perception is expressed in the story (in Herodotus 8. 55) that this olive-tree which had been burnt by the Persians together with the rest of the Acropolis had by the next day miraculously germinated[33] a cubit-long shoot. (It is significant that Herodotus begins this story with the 'history' of the sacred olive-tree and the salt-water spring which were the tokens of the contest between Athena and Poseidon.) The fact that the olive-tree sprouted again immediately and miraculously signified that the burning of the Acropolis did not entail the end of the Athenian *polis*, for it was the sign that Athena's guarantee was still valid, and at the same time the act which renewed that guarantee and thus signalled Athens' continued existence.[34] The story of the Tro-

[29] e.g. Herod. 7. 153 (cf. F. de Polignac, *La Naissance de la cité grecque* (Paris, 1984), pp. 119–21).

[30] e.g. the important place of religion in the Athenian ephebic oath (on which cf. e.g. P. Siewert, *JHS* 97 (1977), 102–11; also the mirror-image of lines 8–9 of the oath, Lycurgus, *Leocr.* 2; the oath is cited in *Leocr.* 76–8).

[31] On Erichthonios, R. Parker, in J. Bremmer (ed.), *Interpretations of Greek Mythology* (London and Sydney, 1987), pp. 193–7; on the contest, ibid. 198–200.

[32] See also M. Detienne, in M. I. Finley (ed.), *Problèmes de la terre en Grèce ancienne* (Paris and La Haye, 1973), p. 295.

[33] Detienne (n. 32), p. 295.

[34] Whether or not Herodotus believed this event had happened is irrelevant. What

jan Palladion which Odysseus and Diomedes stole from Troy because otherwise Troy could not be taken[35] is an expression of the same perception: it had been given to Dardanos, the ancestor of the Trojans, by his father Zeus and was thus a sign of the 'divine guarantee', of the benign relationship between Troy and the gods. Its loss was a sign that the guarantee had come to an end.

As will become clear, in the classical period the *polis* had ultimate authority in, and control of, all cults, and *polis* religion encompassed all religious discourse within it.[36] *Polis* cults may be classified in broad categories on the basis of their worshipping group.[37]

One category is that in which the worshipping group encompasses the whole *polis*, the cults administered on behalf, and for the welfare, of the whole *polis*, which I shall call 'central *polis* cults'. They are varied in type. A first group of central *polis* cults is located at, and pertains symbolically to, the geographical, social, political, and symbolic centre of the *polis*. To this group belong the cults of the civic divinities who, above all, are explicitly concerned with the identity and the protection of the *polis* as one whole, and thus focus and express the *polis*-holding aspects of *polis* religion. In Athens the two main civic deities were Athena Polias and Zeus Polieus. Next to, and symbolically connected with, this pair was the pair Athena Polias and Poseidon Erechtheus. A poliad Athena was associated with Zeus Polieus elsewhere too (e.g. Kos: *LSCG* 151 A 55 ff. for

---

matters is the perception embodied in the story. The inferred departure of the sacred snake from the Acropolis at the time of the evacuation of Athens, which was taken to mean that Athena had abandoned the Acropolis (Herod. 8. 41), did not entail that she was abandoning the *polis*; it could be seen as a sign of her approval of the evacuation.

[35] Nilsson (n. 10), p. 435; Sir James Frazer (ed.), *Apollodorus: The Library* (London, 1921) ii. 226–9 n.2, with a list of the sources.

[36] Cf. below, *passim*, and also the discussion in 'Further Aspects of *polis* Religion' (see preliminary note). In my view, the *polis* had had this authority from its beginning, and the changes pertained only to who administered its authority and how. I hope to argue elsewhere against the prevailing model according to which 'the state' took over cults which had originally belonged to—as opposed to being administered on behalf of the *polis* by—the *gene* and other kinship groups.

[37] I concentrate on Athens, where the available evidence allows us to consider the system of *polis* religion as a whole; this is necessary in order to try to make sense of Greek religion.

Athena; 156 A 19–20). Athena was Polias/Poliouchos in many cities.[38] In Troezen we find a pair reminiscent of the Athenian Athena Polias and Poseidon Erechtheus, Athena Polias and Sthenias and Poseidon Basileus, whose quarrel for the sovereignty of the land ended with an agreement to share it.[39] One set of cults in this group was generally centred on the Agora, the civic and social centre which also had a religious aspect.[40] In many *poleis*, the common hearth of the *polis*, the *koine hestia*, which was also an altar-hearth for Hestia, was located in the *prytaneion*.[41] At Kos the hearth-altar of Hestia was in the Agora, clearly not in a building, and it was the focus of an important ritual during the festival of Zeus Polieus.[42] The common hearth in the Prytaneion, and Hestia's cult, was the symbolic centre of the *polis*. The common hearth of a colony was lit with fire from the *prytaneion* of the mother-city, and this was a significant act in the establishment of the new *polis*.[43] Among the cults situated in the centre were the cults of deities connected with, and presiding over, the central *polis* institutions: in Athens, Zeus Boulaios and Athena Boulaia (Antiphon 6. 45; Xenophon, *Hellenica* 2. 3. 53, 55), Zeus Agoraios,[44] Artemis Boulaia.[45] Zeus Agoraios also occurs in other *poleis*,[46] as does Zeus Boulaios, sometimes paired wth Hestia Boulaia.[47]

---

[38] F. Graf, *Nordionische Kulte* (Rome, 1985), p. 44 and n. 4; R. F. Willetts, *Cretan Cults and Festivals* (London, 1962), pp. 280–1 (cf. also 207–8, 233); L. R. Farnell, *The Cults of the Greek States* i (Oxford, 1896), p. 299.

[39] Paus. 2. 30. 6; cf. C. M. Kraay, *Archaic and Classical Greek Coins* (London, 1976), p. 100.

[40] R. Martin, *Recherches sur l'Agora grecque* (Paris, 1951), pp. 164–201, 229–48; R. E. Wycherley, *How the Greeks Built Cities*, 2nd edn. (London, 1962), pp. 51–2; F. Kolb, *Agora und Theater, Volks– und Festversammlung* (Berlin, 1981), pp. 5–15 and *passim*; cf. also G. Vallet, F. Villard, and P. Auberson, *Megara Hyblaea: i. Le quartier de l' Agora archaique* (Rome, 1976), pp. 412–13.

[41] S. G. Miller, *The Prytaneion: Its Function and Architectural Form* (Berkeley, 1978), pp. 13–14; J.-P. Vernant, *Mythe et pensée chez les Grecs* i (Paris, 1971), pp. 150, 165; P. J. Rhodes, *A Commentary on the Aristotelian Athenaion Politeia* (Oxford, 1981), p. 105 on 3. 5; W. Burkert, *Greek Religion: Archaic and Classical* (Oxford, 1985), p. 170.

[42] *LSCG* 151 A; S. M. Sherwin-White, *Ancient Cos* (Göttingen, 1978), pp. 322–3. Cf. also Nilsson (n. 10), pp. 153–4; W. Burkert, *Homo Necans: The Anthropology of Ancient Greek Sacrificial Ritual and Myth* (Berkeley, 1983), p. 138 n. 10; Vernant (n. 41), i. 155. For Hestia, Zeus, and Athena at the centre of the *polis* cf. also Plato, *Laws* 745 B, 848 D.

[43] Malkin (n. 15), pp. 114–34.

[44] R. E. Wycherley, *GRBS* 5 (1964), 162, 176; J. Travlos, *Pictorial Dictionary of Ancient Athens* (London, 1971), p. 466; Kolb (n. 40), p. 57.

[45] Travlos (n. 44), p. 553.

[46] Graf (n. 38), pp. 197–8; Willetts (n. 38), pp. 233–4.

[47] Graf (n. 38), pp. 176–7 and cf. 363.

One of the gods often associated with the civic life of the *polis* is Apollo Delphinios.[48] In some cities, as at Miletos and Olbia, his cult was at the centre of civic life; in others, as in Athens, it was less central, but also associated with important institutions. At Miletos the cult of Apollo Delphinios and the Delphinion, his sanctuary,[49] were intimately connected with the civic life of the *polis*. The Delphinion was the main sanctuary with which were associated the Molpoi, a college with religious functions which was also closely connected with the civic life of the *polis*: their leader was the annual chief magistrate of the city, and the college had responsibilities pertaining to civic law; in the Delphinion were set up the sacred laws of the Molpoi and also state treaties, proxeny decrees, and the like. At Miletos Apollo Delphinios was associated with Hekate (*LSAM* 50. 25 ff.) who apparently had a civic aspect in that city. In Athens Apollo Delphinios and his sanctuary were again associated with civic law;[50] he also had a shrine in at least some demes, certainly at Erchia (*LSCG* 18 *A* 23–30) and almost certainly also at Thorikos.[51]

Heroic cults, involving both the alleged graves of mythical heroes and those of the heroized historical founders of new cities, are an important category of cult located in the Agora.[52] Since the Athenians claimed to be autochthonous, Athens did not have a founder, but it did have founder-like figures, Theseus the synoecist, Erichthonios/Erechtheus, and Kekrops. In, or associated with, the Athenian Agora—conceivably in the Old Agora[53]—lay the shrine of Theseus, which housed

---

[48] F. Graf, *Mus. Helv.* 36 (1979), 1–22.

[49] G. Kleiner, *Die Ruinen von Milet* (Berlin, 1968), pp. 33–5; W. Koenigs, in W. Müller-Wiener (ed.), *Milet 1899–1980: Ergebnisse, Probleme und Perspektiven einer Ausgrabung: Kolloquium Frankfurt-am-Main 1980* (Tübingen, 1986), pp. 115–16; Graf (n. 48), pp. 7–8. In the archaic period the Delphinion appears to have been outside the walls (F. Graf, *Mus. Helv.* 31 (1974), 215 n. 26). After the Persian Wars the centre of the city shifted to this area (G. Kleiner, in R. Stillwell (ed.), *The Princeton Encyclopedia of Classical Sites* (Princeton, 1976), p. 578).

[50] Graf (n. 48), pp. 9–10; Travlos (n. 44), pp. 83–90.

[51] G. Daux, *Ant. Class.* 52 (1983), 150–74 (cf. Parker (n. 56), pp. 144–7 and *passim*), text of the deme Thorikos (hereafter *Thorik.*), 6, 63–5, cf. 11.

[52] Martin (n. 40), pp. 194–201; Kolb (n. 40), pp. 5–8, 19, 24–5, and esp. 47–52; W. Leschhorn, '*Gründer der Stadt*' (Stuttgart, 1984), pp. 67–72, 98–105, 176–80; Malkin (n. 15), pp. 187–260; de Polignac (n. 29), pp. 132–52; C. Bérard, in G. Gnoli and J.-P. Vernant (eds.), *La Mort, les morts dans les sociétés anciennes* (Cambridge and Paris, 1982), pp. 89–105.

[53] The location is controversial. Cf. Travlos (n. 44), pp. 1–2, and now esp. G. S. Dontas, *Hesperia*, 52 (1983), 62–3.

Theseus' alleged bones brought back by Kimon and which
played a small role in the civic life of the *polis*.[54] The shrines-
and-graves of Erechtheus and Kekrops are situated on the
Acropolis, at the Erechtheion, and are intimately connected
with the cult of Athena Polias and Poseidon.

Central *polis* festivals connected with the poliad divinities
and/or the constitution of the *polis* are, for example, the
Panathenaia, the Synoikia, the Dipoleia in Athens, the festival
of Zeus Polieus in Kos. There are very many other central *polis*
cults of different kinds in the different *poleis*, some located in the
polis centre and others not. Many were centred on shrines
located within the city but not in its central core (for example,
in Athens the Lykeion), others on peri-urban or extra-urban
shrines. Processions connected the *polis* centre with some of
these shrines. The most important sanctuaries outside the
Athenian city, ritually connected with its centre, were those of
Demeter and Kore at Eleusis and of Artemis at Brauron.
Eleusinian cult was intimately intertwined with the other
central *polis* cults; its symbolic place in the centre of Athenian
religion was given material expression in the Eleusinion in the
centre of Athens, whence began the procession to Eleusis and in
which took place rites and acts pertaining to the relationship
between the Eleusinian nexus and the Athenian *polis* (e.g.
Andocides I. 111). In Argos a very important central *polis* rite
was the procession to the extra-urban Heraion. In Sparta the
major procession was at the Hyakinthia, linking Sparta with
the sanctuary of Apollo at Amyklai.[55]

Each significant grouping within the *polis* was articulated
and given identity through cult. In Greece all relationships and
bonds, including social and political ones, were expressed, and
so defined, through cult (cf. also Plato, *Laws* 738 D). This is
why the creation of new *polis* subdivisions entailed cultic
changes. Thus Kleisthenes' reforms did not involve the subordination of cult to politics, but the ordinary creation of group
identity. The *polis* had set in place a particular organization of

[54] J. P. Barron, *JHS* 92 (1972), 20–2; cf. Dontas (n. 53), pp. 60–3 *passim*; Travlos (n.
44), pp. 578–9; cf. Plut. *Thes.* 36. 2; Paus. 1. 17. 2. 6. On other *heroa* in the Athenian
Agora, H. A. Thompson, in *Athens Comes of Age: From Solon to Salamis* (Princeton, 1978),
pp. 96–108.
[55] Argos: Burkert (n. 42), pp. 162–8; de Polignac (n. 29), pp. 41–92 *passim*, esp. 88.
Sparta: Brelich (n. 12), pp. 141–7.

polis religion; now it was changing it because the *polis* organization as a whole was changing. This change was sanctioned by the Delphic oracle: the Pythia selected the eponymous heroes for the ten tribes out of a hundred names submitted to her, and since the tribes were the new major subdivisions of the *polis*, this selection was a symbolic *pars pro toto* for all the cultic changes connected with the reorganization of the *polis*. In classical Athens the deme was the most important religious subdivision after the *polis*. The cults and rites that went into the making of the cult of these demes were undoubtedly not new; most would have been local rituals, now brought under the adminsitration of the demes. Some may have been significantly reshaped, others not.[56] Cultic innovation, we saw, was accepted without problems; Kleisthenes' reforms were clearly not perceived to have involved the abandonment of long-established practices for which there was a much greater reluctance;[57] they seem similar to the course recommended by Plato (*Laws* 738 B–C). Moreover, articulations of this type were not, we saw, perceived as sacred and unchangeable—not surprisingly, given the role of religion in the definition of sociopolitical units which themselves changed considerably over the years.

In so far as we can judge, the *polis* subdivisions had, first, cults in which only their members could participate, which helped define those groups through the exclusion of non-members; second, some at least also had cults to which out-

[56] At least some may have been phratry cults before (cf. Humphreys, cited by R. Parker in T. Linders and G. Nordquist (eds.), *Gifts to the Gods* (Proceedings of the Uppsala Symposium 1985; Uppsala, 1987), p. 138 n. 13; D. Whitehead, *The Demes of Attica* (Princeton, 1986), p. 177). If, as I believe, phratries began as local units, perhaps by the late 6th cent. phratry membership had become radically dissociated from locality, and there had been in any case a need for a new locality-bound articulation.

Some classical demes formed cultic units which appear to reflect older groupings articulated through cult, whether or not they had been exclusively cultic, variable associations of three or four demes, focused (in different ways) on religious practice: the Marathonian Tetrapolis (D. M. Lewis, *Historia*, 12 (1963), 31–2; *LSCG* 20; Dow (n. 23), pp. 174–5, 181–2; Whitehead, pp. 190–4; H. W. Parke, *Festivals of the Athenians* (London, 1977), pp. 181–2; J. D. Mikalson, *A. J. Phil.* 98 (1977), 425, 427); the Tetrakomoi (Lewis, p. 33); the League of Athena Pallenis (Lewis, pp. 33–4; R. Schlaifer, *HSCP* 54 (1943), 35–67; S. Solders, *Die ausserstädtischen Kulte und die Einigung Attikas* (Lund, 1931), pp. 13–14); and the Trikomoi (Lewis, p. 34). On these associations cf. also P. Siewert, *Die Trittyen Attikas und die Heeresreform des Kleisthenes* (Munich, 1982), pp. 118–20.

[57] *Ath. Pol.* 21. 6; cf. Rhodes (n. 41) ad. loc. (pp. 258–9); cf. E. Kearns in *Crux* (n. 19), p. 190.

siders could be admitted; finally, they had cults which pertained to their interaction with the other *polis* groupings: for
example, the demes participated in festivals which were primarily central *polis* festivals, either by celebrating them also in
the deme, or by taking part in the central *polis* rites as a deme.
The cults of the *genos* are a category of *polis* cult which
separately defined the members of each group, of each *genos*,
who had exclusive right to one or more priesthoods specific to
the *genos*. There were also in the various cities 'private' cultic
associations, based on personal choice (e.g. Isaeus 9. 30). The
cult of private associations often became part of *polis* religion.
Thus, for example, the cult of a god, almost certainly Apollo
Delios, who had hitherto had an informal cult to which
shipowners contributed a voluntary levy, became a *polis* cult
shortly before 429/8.[58]

We shall now consider the cults of the subdivisions of the
polis. In Athens the new Kleisthenic tribes had their own tribal
cults;[59] in addition, the Athenians were tribally articulated in
many activities, including cultic ones such as chorus competitions and the *ephebeia*. The connection of the old tribe G[e]-
leontes and the *phylobasileis* with the Synoikia, the festival
celebrating the birth of the Athenian *polis*, in Nikomachos'
calendar,[60] shows the continuing involvement of the old Ionian
tribes in cult and suggests an early, certainly pre-Kleisthenic,
intertwining of *polis* subdivisions and *polis* formation. Tribes
had a cultic role also in the other cities.[61] In the college of the
Molpoi at Miletos one representative from each tribe was
acting as a college official (*LSAM* 50. 1–3). In the rites for Zeus
Polieus and Hestia in Kos it was the tribes which provided the
primary articulation of the worshipping group *polis*.[62] The

[58] D. M. Lewis, *BSA* 55 (1960), 190–4.
[59] U. Kron, *Die zehn Phylenheroen* (Berlin, 1976), *passim*; R. Schlaifer, *HSCP* 51
(1940), 253–7; Gernet and Boulanger (n. 6), p. 255; Kearns (n. 57), pp. 192–9.
[60] *LSCGS* 10. 35 ff.; cf. Dow 1953–7 (n. 23), pp. 15–21, 25–7; also Rhodes (n. 41), p.
151; Dow 1968 (n. 23), p. 174; J. D. Mikalson, *The Sacred and Civil Calendar of the
Athenian Year* (Princeton, 1975), pp. 29–30. Cf. also L. Deubner, *Attische Feste*, 3rd edn.
(Vienna, 1969), pp. 36–8; Parke (n. 56), pp. 31–2; E. Simon, *Festivals of Attica*
(Madison, Wisc., 1983), p. 50.
[61] Gernet and Boulanger (n. 6), p. 255; D. Roussel, *Tribu et cité* (Paris, 1976), pp. 207
n. 38, 216.
[62] *LSCG* 151 A 5–15, on which see Sherwin-White (n. 42), pp. 322–3. Cf. also
Roussel (n. 61), pp. 207 n. 38, 261.

tribes' participation in the cults of the civic deities is comparable to their connection with the formation of the Athenian *polis* through the Synoikia: they and other *polis* subdivisions participated in the cults symbolizing the unity of the *polis* because this reinforced that unity and defined the subdivisions as parts of a symbolically potent whole. The Kleisthenic *trittyes* also had a cultic role,[63] and so did the old pre-Kleisthenic ones, even after Nikomachos' reforms.[64]

In terms of cult the deme was the most important *polis* subdivision in classical Athens. A few deme calendars have survived.[65] The first category of deme rites consists of rites performed in the deme. It includes: (*a*) local celebrations of central *polis* festivals and cults which were also—and sometimes predominantly—*polis* cults such as that of the poliad deities; (*b*) cults and rites which were specific to the specific demes, above all of local heroes and heroines, including that of the eponymous hero; and (*c*) major festivals celebrated only in the demes, of which the most important was the Rural Dionysia. The second main category of deme ritual activity involved the participation of the demes as demes in the central *polis* cults. This second category and the type (*a*) of the first category represent the two main ways in which deme and central *polis* cults were interwoven.

The Erchia calendar offers an example of type (*a*), that is, of a deme cult involving rites and offerings in the deme to deities which functionally above all pertained to the central *polis* nucleus, on days which were ritually significant in the central *polis* calendar. Zeus Polieus, Athena Polias, Kourotrophos,

---

[63] Lewis 1963 (n. 56), p. 35; cf. esp. *IG* i³ 255. In *IG* i³ 258 the deme of the Plotheians makes contributions to the festivals of the Epakreis, probably the *trittys* to which they belonged—though we cannot exclude that it may have been a religious association of neighbouring demes. (Cf. Lewis, pp. 27–8; Siewert (n. 56), pp. 15 n. 67, 102 n. 91, 112–13, n. 140; Parker (n. 56), p. 140; cf. also R. J. Hopper, *BSA* 56 (1961), 217–19.) Epakria may also have been the name of a pre-Kleisthenic *trittys* (cf. Siewert, pp. 15 n. 67, 112–13 n. 140).

[64] The Leukotainioi, one of the *trittyes* of the Geleontes, (*LSCGS* 10 A 35 ff.; cf. Dow (n. 23), p. 26; Siewert (n. 56), p. 15 n. 67; Rhodes (n. 41), p. 68; W. S. Ferguson, in *Classical Studies Presented to Edward Capps on his Seventieth Birthday* (Princeton, 1936), pp. 151–8, esp. 154–7) are involved in a sacrifice associated with the Synoikia (cf. Mikalson (n. 60), p. 29).

[65] On deme religion, Whitehead (n. 56), pp. 176–222; Parker (n. 56), pp. 137–47; R. Osborne, *Demos: The Discovery of Classical Attika* (Cambridge, 1985), pp. 178–81; Kolb (n. 40), pp. 62 ff.

Aglauros, and Poseidon (and perhaps also [Pandrosos])
received sacrifices on the Erchia Acropolis on the third Skiro-
phorion, which was almost certainly the day of the Arrhephoria in Athens.[66] Athena Polias and Zeus Polieus were
concerned with the *polis* as a whole; their local worship in the
demes expressed ritually the interdependence between demes
and *polis*; another symbolic strand in this complex interweaving
of the whole *polis* (symbolized through its centre) and the
subdivisions that constitute it and their cults was the Erchia
deme's sacrifices to Zeus Polieus (*LSCG* 18 *Γ* 15–18) and to
Athena Polias (*LSCG* 18 *Δ* 13–17) in the acropolis in the *asty*.
Poseidon was associated with Athena Polias at the cultic centre
of the city and the two represent an alternative poliad pair.
Aglauros and Pandrosos were part of the same central *polis*
cultic nexus and were also associated with the Arrhephoria[67] —
in which Athena was the main deity. The cult of Aglauros and
Pandrosos were associated with that of Kourotrophos: all three
were served by the same priestess.[68] Kourotrophos, who was
concerned with the *polis* in so far as she was concerned with the
growth of the children that will make up the *polis*, also received
many other offerings at Erchia. Her cult was important in
other demes too[69] and was thus an important common element
between the demes and the centre. The celebration of the
central *polis* nexus in the demes helped articulate the cohesion
of the *polis*.

Another form of interconnection of type (*a*) involved local
celebration of central *polis* festivals. The Hieros Gamos/Theo-
gamia was celebrated in Athens on 27 Gamelion, and on this
date the Erchia calendar lists sacrifices to Hera, Zeus Teleios,
Kourotrophos, and Poseidon in the sanctuary of Hera at
Erchia, which indicate a local celebration of the same rite.[70] At

[66] *LSCG* 18 *A* 57–65, *B* 55–9; *Γ* 59–64; *Δ* 55–60. Cf. M. Jameson, *BCH* 89 (1965),
156–8; Whitehead (n. 56), p. 179.

[67] Burkert (n. 41), pp. 228–9; Simon (n. 60), pp. 45–6. On the cult of Aglauros cf.
also Dontas (n. 53), pp. 48–63.

[68] On Kourotrophos, W. Ferguson, *Hesperia*, 7 (1938), 1–74, inscription (363/2 BC)
of the *genos* Salaminioi with the cult regulations, ll. 12, 45–6 and p. 21; *Suda* s.v.
kourotrophos, paidotrophos, cf. e.g. *LSCGS* 10 A 24. Cf. Th. Hadzisteliou-Price, *Kourotrophos* (Leiden, 1978); Nilson (n. 10), p. 457.

[69] *Thorik.* (n. 51), 20–3, 42–3; Tetrapolis calendar: *LSCG* 20 B 6; B 14; B 31; B 37; B
42; B 46; A 56. Cf. also Parker (n. 56), p. 146.

[70] 18 *B* 32–9; *Γ* 38–41; *Δ* 28–32. Cf. F. Salviat, *BCH* 88 (1964), 647–54; Mikalson (n.
56), p. 429; Parker (n. 56), pp. 142–3.

Thorikos there were sacrifices for Athena and Aglauros at the Plynteria (*Thorik.* [n.51] 52–4), celebrated on a different date from that of the central *polis* festival.[71] This may have allowed the demesmen to participate in both local and central *polis* celebration if they so wished, and suggests that the local rite and the central one were seen as complementary, the purifications and washing of the local statue of Athena being a counterpart to (and perhaps also symbolically dependent on) that of the ancient image of Athena Polias. The cult of Zeus Herkeios was practised in the demes[72] and in the central *polis* cult nexus, as well as in the *oikos* with which it is symbolically associated.[73]

The participation of the demes as demes in the central *polis* cults (e.g. *IG* i^3 258. 25–7; cf. 30–1), in the *asty* and elsewhere, is the second main way in which the relationship between the central *polis* cults which pertain to the whole *polis* and those of the *polis* subdivisions is expressed. Among the central *polis* festivals in which the demes participated as demes was the Panathenaia, in which the meat of the sacrificial victims was distributed deme by deme, among the participants sent by each deme.[74] The deme of Skambonidai at least is known to have participated in the Synoikia (*LSCG* 10 C 16–19), which, as we saw, celebrated the formation of the *polis* and with which the old tribes and the old *trittyes* were also associated. The absence of religious activities in Erchia during some major *polis* festivals may be indicative of a general tendency, suggesting that the demesmen attended the rites at Athens (or Eleusis).[75] This 'complementarity' is another sort of interconnection between the Athenian central *polis* cult and those of the demes. Another category of festival was celebrated both in Athens and in some at least of the demes. The Thesmophoria and a group of closely related women's rites, particularly the Skira, probably belong to this class.[76] The Plotheia decree suggests that there may have

[71] Deubner (n. 60), pp. 17–22; Parker (n. 56), pp. 152–5; R. Parker, *Miasma* (Oxford, 1983), pp. 26–8.

[72] *Thorik.* (n. 51), 22 and left and right side (cf. Daux, 157–60).

[73] I discuss the significance of this fact in 'Further Aspects of *polis* Religion' (see preliminary note).

[74] *LSCG* 33 B 25–7; cf. 10 A 19–21; Mikalson (n. 56), p. 428; Parke (n. 56), p. 48; Osborne (n. 65), p. 180; Parker (n. 56), pp. 140–1.

[75] Mikalson (n. 56), p. 428.

[76] Cf. Parker (n. 56), p. 142. The deme Eleusinia are, in my view, comparable to the deme Thesmophoria. The central *polis* nexus pertaining to the Eleusinian cult was

been also a third category of cult, participation in the cult of the *trittys*.[77]

In so far as we can judge, in other *poleis* too there was similar participation of the subdivisions in central *polis* cults. We glanced at tribal participation above, and we shall consider some aspects pertaining to phratries below. Here I shall say something very briefly about the Spartan religious system. The same type of cultic interconnections between the *polis* and its subdivisions is also seen in Sparta. In the celebration of the extremely important festival of the Karneia an articulation by phratries came into play (Demetrius of Skepsis *ap*. Athenaeus 141 E–F), while another articulation was involved in the selection of the Karneatai for the liturgy of Apollo Karneios.[78] There is also unambiguous, if fragmentary, evidence showing that girls' choruses were organized according to the *polis* subdivisions, by tribe and/or by *obe*.[79] Cults associated with the subdivisions of the Spartan *polis* are not attested in the classical period, but given the paucity of evidence that is perhaps due to chance.[80]

Phratries[81] everywhere appear to have had cults common to all the phratries of the *polis*, of the gods who were the protectors

focused above all on Eleusis and the *asty* Eleusinion. I hope to discuss this cult elsewhere.

[77] Unless the Epakreis were a religious association comparable to the Tetrapolis (above n. 56). Guarducci (*Historia*, 9 (1935), 211) suggested that the *penteterides*, the third category of sacrifices to which the Plotheians contribute in ll. 25–8, besides deme and central *polis* cults, may have been celebrated by the Epakreis, for they correspond to the Epakreis category in the tripartite articulation of ll. 30–1; Mikalson (n. 56), p. 427, believes they are analogous to the Marathonians' biennial sacrifices. Parker (n. 56), p. 140 n. 32, noted that the central *polis penteterides* are another possibility.

[78] Hesychius s.v. *Karneatai* tells us that five unmarried youths were selected from each [= tribe? obe?] for this *leitourgia* (cf. Brelich (n. 12), pp. 149–50).

[79] C. Calame, *Les Choeurs de jeunes filles en Grèce archaique* (Rome, 1977), i. 273–6, 382–5.

[80] R. Parker, 'Spartan Religion', in A. Powell (ed.), *Classical Sparta: Techniques behind her Success* (London, 1989), pp. 142–72.

[81] On phratries see esp. A. Andrewes, *JHS* 81 (1961), 1–15; S. C. Humphreys, *Anthropology and the Greeks* (London, 1978), pp. 194–8, cf. 206–8; Roussel (n. 61), pp. 93–157; most recently, M. A. Flower, *CQ* 35 (1985), 232–5. On phratry cults and ceremonies, J. Labarbe, *Bull. de l' Académie royale de Belgique*, Classe des Lettres, 5th ser., 39 (1953), 358–94; C. Rolley, *BCH* 89 (1965), 441–83; Roussel, 133–5; M. P. Nilsson, *Cults, Myths, Oracles and Politics in Ancient Greece* (New York, 1972, 1st edn. 1952), pp. 162–70; cf. Graf (n. 38), 32–7; cf. *CID*, pp. 28–88 *passim*; also Latte in Pauly–Wissowa, *Realencyclopädie*, s.v. *Phratrioi theoi*.

of the phratries in that city and were also worshipped at the central *polis* level, and also to have all celebrated, each phratry separately, certain *polis* festivals. One of these was the main festival of the phratries at which new members were admitted; this was known as the Apatouria in most Ionian cities and was, in Athens at least, celebrated by each phratry in its own local centre (cf. *IG* ii² 1237. 52 ff.)—and as the Apellai in the Dorian–North-West Greek world.[82] These were central *polis* festivals.[83] Another group of phratry cults were cults which were distinctive and exclusive to each phratry, which thus helped define it as a group.[84]

In Athens the main deities of all the phratries were Zeus Phratrios and Athena Phratria, who had a temple in the Agora and also another shrine with an altar but no temple.[85] Apollo Patroos may conceivably also have been worshipped by all the phratries; he also had a temple in the Agora.[86] Andrewes suggested that his cult was in the custody of the *gene* but all members of the phratry were perceived as sharing in it. This may well be right. The fact that, as *Athenaion Politeia* 55. 3 shows, having a cult of Apollo Patroos was a prerequisite of archonship[87] does indeed suggest that by that time at least there was a direct connection with (citizenship through) the phratries. In my view, it was perceived as a cult of the phratries which was administered by the *gene* at the centre of each phratry—and also a cult of the *polis* as a whole. This was perhaps not seen as radically different from the priesthood of Zeus Phratrios being held by the *genos* at the centre of the phratry.[88]

---

[82] Rougemont in *CID*, pp. 46–7, suggests that only the *apellaia*, the sacrifice at a male's achievement of majority, had to be offered on the day of the Apellai, and that the sacrifices for infants and weddings did not have a fixed date. In Athens, in special circumstances, one could be presented to the phratry at another festival, such as the Thargelia (Cf. Isaeus 7. 15).

[83] According to schol. Aristoph. *Acharnians* 146 the Apatouria is a '*demoteles*' festival.

[84] Nilsson (n. 81), pp. 162–4.

[85] X. de Schutter, *L'Antiquité classique*, 56 (1987), 116; Nilsson (n. 81), pp. 165–7; Kearns (n. 57), pp. 204–5; Travlos (n. 44), pp. 96, 572–5.

[86] de Schutter (n. 85), p. 104, cf. 108; Roussel (n. 61), p. 73; Kearns (n. 57), p. 205; Travlos (n. 44), p. 96.

[87] Rhodes (n. 41) ad loc. (pp. 617–18); Andrewes (n. 81), pp. 7–8.

[88] As e.g. it is surely implied in Andoc. 1. 126 that Kallias did. A comparable custodianship may have been the background to the move of the common *hiera* from private houses to a common house of the Chiot phratry Klytidai (cf. *LSCG* 118; Graf

The fact that all the phratries in Athens had the same main deities suggests that their most important cults resulted from a central articulation of cult, an articulation of the *polis* given symbolic expression and cohesion through cult. The cults of Zeus Phratrios and Athena Phratria, a central *polis* cultic nexus almost certainly created at the formation of the *polis*, expressed the phratries' communality and their identity as constituent elements of the city. The latter was signalled especially strongly because the two Phratrioi deities were also the two poliad deities. Thus the protection of the *polis* includes the protection of the phratries that make it up; and the protection of the phratries contributes to the protection of the *polis*. The hypothesis that there was a connection between this cultic nexus, the phratries, and the act of constitution of the *polis* is supported by the fact that a sacrifice was made to Zeus Phratrios and Athena Phratria at the Synoikia.[89] Again, the fact that this sacrifice was made on the authority of the law of the *phylobasileis* and was associated with the old Ionian tribe Geleontes suggests that this cultic connection with the formation of the *polis* was old, certainly pre-Kleisthenic. In Kos also Athena and Zeus were both Phratrioi and Polieis.[90]

But of course the situation was not as tidy everywhere—as is to be expected when the pantheon of each city was a different system which could vary considerably in each case. At Erythrai it was Poseidon who was worshipped as Phratrios while Athena was Polias; the epithet of Zeus more directly connected to the *polis* as a central unit was Agoraios.[91] Zeus Patroos seems to be the—or at least one of the—phratry god[s] also at Chios (*LSCG* 118) where Athena is *poliouchos* and where we lack evidence for Zeus in the type of '*polis*-holding' persona considered in this connection.[92] Despite the variety between the *phratrioi* gods of

(n. 38), pp. 428–9 (I. Ch. 3), and cf. also pp. 32–7; Forrest, *BSA* 55 (1960), 179–81)—if they are indeed a phratry and if the private individuals in whose houses the *hiera* had been kept before were *gennetai* holding the priesthoods. The fact that annually elected priests in central *polis* cults sometimes also kept the statue of the god in their house (cf. Paus. 4. 33. 2; 7. 24. 4) suggests that 'keeping the statue/other *hiera* in one's house' is symbolically correlative with 'being in charge of the administration of' and does not necessitate possession through a hereditary connection. The privileged position of the *genos* within the classical phratry cannot be doubted (cf. Andrewes (n. 81), pp. 3–9).

[89] *LSCGS* 10; cf. Nilsson (n. 81), p. 166; Mikalson, (n. 60), pp. 29–30.
[90] Sherwin-White (n. 42), pp. 158, 293, 295, 298–9.
[91] Graf (n. 38), pp. 207, 209 ff., 197–9.   [92] Cf. Graf (n. 38), p. 141.

the different *poleis*, the forms of the relationship between phratry and central *polis* cults seem constant.

Another manifestation of this close relationship between the two, and of the fact that the phratries' cult is dependent on, and derives its authority from, the central *polis* religion, is seen in Thasos, where the altars of the *patrai* (here equivalent to the phratries) were set up in what is almost certainly the Thesmophorion.[93] This arrangement also expresses the links between the different phratries, especially since some of them may have shared an altar—with each group who sacrificed there having a boundary stone of their own. Each of the *patrai* had a different divinity whom they called Patroos/Patroa. Several have Zeus, some Athena, some the Nymphs, some other divinities without the epithet Patroos, and one Demeter Patroa Eleusinia. In this case—though not usually—'Patroos' seems equivalent to 'Phratrios' in other *poleis*.[94] The fact that these altars were situated in the sanctuary of Demeter may perhaps suggest that Demeter was a major protector of the *patrai*, as well as being a goddess who, in the same sanctuary, was closely connected with the centre, and with the foundation, of the *polis*.[95]

The oath of the commanders (*tagoi*) of the Delphic phratry of the Labyadai invokes Zeus Patroos (*CID* 9 A 21–2), while the oath taken by the assembly of all the Labyadai before voting—that they will vote fairly, according to the laws of the Delphians—invokes Apollo,[96] Poseidon Phratrios, and Zeus Patroos (B 10–17). Side D of the Labyadai inscription deals with festivals and other cultic matters. First the regulations specify that in a series of central *polis* festivals (D 3–11) all the Labyadai had to participate in the common banquet of the phratry.[97] Then the inscription lists certain contributions made to the Labyadai by others who consulted the Delphic oracle— that is, by those participating in the Panhellenic cult, here treated on the model of *xenoi* participating in a *polis* cult.[98] The

[93] Rolley (n. 81); id., 'Le Sanctuaire d' Evraiokastro: Mise à jour du dossier', forthcoming in the Proceedings of the Colloquium in memory of D. Lazaridis.

[94] Cf. Rolley (n. 81), pp. 458 f; id., forthcoming.

[95] Rolley (n. 81), p. 483; id. forthcoming.

[96] The most important Delphic god, and also especially concerned (W. Burkert, *Rhein. Mus.* 118 (1975), 1–21) with the Apellai and the youths' initiation and achievement of maturity, and thus of full phratry membership.

[97] *CID*, ad loc., esp. p. 64.

[98] *CID*, ad loc., esp. p. 80; Ch. Kritzas, *BCH* 110 (1986), 611–17.

'sacrifices of the Labyadai' listed in ll. 43–9[99] are clearly phratry rites. Dionysos receives a sacrifice in the month Apellaios, Zeus Patroos receives a sacrifice at the Boukatia, and on the same occasion Apollo receives the first fruits. The phratry of the Labyadai was a subdivision of the Delphic *polis*. It regulated admissions to the phratry, participation in the central *polis* festivals, and all interactions with the *polis*, including the Panhellenic sanctuary. It also issued funerary regulations (*CID* 9 C 19 ff.). It functioned like a mini-*polis*—though interacting with, and under the authority of (e.g. B 15–17), the Delphic *polis*. It can be argued that it combines functions similar to those of both the Athenian phratry and the Athenian deme. No village-like subdivisions comparable to the Athenian demes are known in the *polis* of Delphi, which was of course very much smaller than Athens. (The coexistence of phratries and village-like subdivisions was not limited to Athens; there were, for example, phratries and obes in Sparta, and phratries and demes at Locri Epizephyrii.)

In the classical period priests and priestesses[100] functioned under the authority and control of the *polis*. Each served one (or sometimes more than one) deity and could not officiate in cults beyond their prescribed domain. Even within the same cultic nexus each priest had definite prescribed ritual duties and was not entitled to perform any other ritual acts (e.g. [Demosthenes] 59. 116–17). Some priesthoods were limited to the members of a particular *genos*.[101] Non-gentilicial priesthoods were open to all the citizens (Isocrates 2. 6) who were of the appropriate sex, and, where appropriate, age group and status (virgin, for instance), provided that they were physically unblemished[102], and had not performed an action which made them ineligible; for example, a man who prostituted himself was debarred from holding certain offices, including priest-

---

[99] Cf. *CID*, pp. 59, 62, 82–5.

[100] Burkert (n. 41), pp. 95–8; E. Sinclair Holderman, in G. Arrigoni (ed.), *Le donne in Grecia* (Rome–Bari, 1985), pp. 299–330. In Athens: R. Garland, *BSA* 79 (1984), 75–8; J. Martha, *Les Sacerdoces athéniens* (Paris, 1882); D. D. Feaver, *Yale Class. Stud.* 15 (1957), 123–58; on Eleusinian sacred officials: K. Clinton, *The Sacred Officials of the Eleusinian Mysteries* (Philadelphia, 1974). On the categories of religious roles in Athens, Humphreys (n. 81), p. 254; cf. also Garland, pp. 75–123.

[101] On *gene* see esp. Humphreys (n. 81), pp. 196–7.

[102] Burkert (n. 41), pp. 98 and 387 n. 48.

hoods (Aeschines 1. 19–21). Such priests were appointed by the community or elected by lot—which allowed the gods to choose; from the later fourth century onwards in particular geographical areas priesthoods were increasingly frequently sold. Priestly perquisites varied. Some priests and priestesses served for life, others for a set period, usually a year. They were not obliged to dedicate themselves exclusively to priestly duties (*LSCG* 69. 1–6 for one example of the minimum amount of time a priest had to spend in the sanctuary in one cult). There were certain requirements of ritual purity during the period of office.[103] They had liturgical and administrative duties (e.g. for the latter *LSCG* 115. 7–8; 69. 5 ff.; 37). Sometimes some of these administrative duties were hived off to others. Aristotle (*Politics* 1322[b] 11–12) notes that in some places, for example in small cities, the superintendence of cults is concentrated in the priesthood, while elsewhere it is divided among several offices, such as *hieropoioi*, *naophylakes*, and *tamiai* of the sacred monies. The *neokoros* was warden of the sanctuary, and in some cases at least (e.g. *LSCG* 69. 6–8) the priest had the responsibility to compel him to take care of the sanctuary and its visitors. There were varying numbers of other administrators in the different sanctuaries in the different periods, often with different names in the different *poleis*.[104] There were also colleges of religious officials concerned with the administration of certain rites, such as the *hieropoioi* in Athens;[105] the finances of the sanctuaries were overseen by committees, such as the *tamiai* in Athens, or *hierotamiai* in some other places, the treasurers of the various gods.[106]

Limitations of space force me to stop here. I discuss some aspects of the role and function of priests and priestesses and their relationship to the *polis* in another paper, which is complementary to the present one (cf. preliminary note, above, p. 295) and where I also discuss some other questions which pertain to, and are facets of, the phenomenon '*polis* religion'. Two of these are the financing of cults and the openings and

---

[103] Parker (n. 71), pp. 87–94, 52–3, 175.

[104] See e.g. B. Jordan, *Servants of the Gods* (Göttingen, 1979), p. 22, cf. 23–8.

[105] *Ath. Pol.* 54. 6–7; cf. Rhodes (n. 41) ad. loc. (pp. 605 ff.). On administrative religious offices in Athens cf. also Garland (n. 100), pp. 116–18.

[106] Jordan (n. 104), p. 66; Burkert (n. 41), pp. 95–6.

closures of the religious system of the *polis*, the inclusions and exclusions of various categories of outsiders. A third concerns an important aspect of Greek religion: I argue that it is not the case that Greek religion is a 'group religion' in the sense that group worship was the norm and individual cultic acts somehow exceptional; it was the individual who was the primary, the basic, cultic unit in *polis* religion, and not, for example, a small group such as the *oikos*. Finally, I argue in that paper that in the classical period *polis* religion encompassed, symbolically legitimated, and regulated all religious activity within the *polis*, not only the cults of *polis* subdivisions such as the demes, but also cults which modern commentators are inclined to consider private, such as, for example, *oikos* cults.

I hope to have shown in the present paper that, and how, the *polis* provided the fundamental, basic framework in which Greek religion operated. I also set out the complex ways in which the Greek *polis* articulated, and was articulated by, religion, and I proposed certain reconstructions of ancient religious perceptions pertaining especially to the articulation of *polis* religion. The role of the *polis* in the articulation of Greek religion was matched by the role of religion in the articulation of the *polis*: religion provided the framework and the symbolic focus of the *polis*. Religion was the very centre of the Greek *polis*.

I3

Saving the City

EMILY KEARNS

WHEN the Eleans were fighting the Arcadians, the story runs, a woman came to the commanders with her baby son, saying that she had been told in a dream to give him to fight for the city. The generals put the child at the front of their ranks, and when the enemy charged the child became a snake, so that they fled in terror and confusion. The story was told to account for the cult at Elis of a divine or perhaps heroic figure called Sosipolis ('city-saving').[1] Modern students of the past, heir to the Thucydidean scorn for 'the mythlike',[2] would tend to draw a more or less firm line between such picturesque stories and what 'really' happens when the city is in danger and crisis, even if they recognize that some supposedly historical events in fact contain strong elements of myth. It would be idle to deny that the distinction between historical events and myth is in some respects an important, indeed vital, one. Yet it is at last becoming more widely recognized that myths, too, are relevant to history, and not only as distorted mirrors of 'historical events'. It seems unlikely that aetiological and above all patriotic stories like that of the child-snake Sosipolis should bear little relation to the thought-patterns of the period in which they were first told; the study of such apparently unpromising material may rather throw some light, albeit from an oblique angle, on Greek views of the city and of the crises which beset it. In particular I hope to demonstrate that the strangeness and paradox which is the central point of many such stories lends a special importance in this context to elements located on the city's fringe, those who in a sense belong to the city yet are not exactly citizens. In most cities, the obvious examples of such marginal groups are women,

---

[1] Paus. 6. 20. 4–5.   [2] Thuc. 1. 22. 4 (to mythodes).

children, slaves, and foreigners; the degree and type of marginality varies between the different groups and between cities,
but it may still be legitimate and helpful to consider them in
connection with each other. Although (from a rather different
point of view) the similarities between such groups were
recognized by Aristotle, who treats at least women and slaves as
parallel, in recent years much of the credit for developing and
analysing the parallelism between these groups and their
relation to society as a whole must go to Pierre Vidal-Naquet,
whose work on 'women, slaves and artisans', as well as on
adolescents, has shed much light on the outer reaches of the
Greek city.[3] In this study, along with the human marginal
groups of the Vidal-Naquet type, I shall also be considering
gods and heroes as comparable groups. In any Greek *polis*,
representatives of these two superhuman categories are intimately connected with the communal life and well-being of the
city, which cannot prosper without their special protection; yet
they are not in a normal sense part of the city, but rather form
a divine superstructure.

The concept of *soteria* may relate to various types of situation. That which is saved may be individual or community;
that which is doing the saving may be human or divine. The
importance of the agent is suggested in the word itself, which as
the Greeks were presumably aware derives not directly from *sos*
(safe), but from the noun denoting the personal agent, *soter*,
saviour. The word, then, carries a suggestion of an act performed by someone, and common to all situations where it
occurs is an implied threat: *soteria* implies safety *from* something.[4] Even when the word appears to imply a permanent
state of safety, we should probably think in terms of the
weathering of repeated crises, actual or potential; just as, in the
concept of Solon and Herodotus, no-one can be called 'happy'
(*olbios*) till he dies,[5] so no individual and no group can ever

---

[3] Aristotle: see below, n. 22. P. Vidal-Naquet, *The Black Hunter* (Baltimore, 1986),
esp. chs. 7–11; see also 4–6.

[4] In Athens, *soteria tes poleos* seems also to have had a technical meaning, giving
priority to a particular matter for deliberation and removing some of the normal
constitutional safeguards in such matters; the phrase must originally have been used in
times of crisis. See P. J. Rhodes, *The Athenian Boule* (Oxford, 1972), add. note C, pp.
231–5.

[5] Herod. 1. 32. 5–7.

really be safe in the sense of being situated beyond threat. (So English 'deliverance' is usually a better equivalent than 'safety'.) Such threats, in their basic form, are very limited in number: to the individual, death, disgrace, illness, injury, and poverty; to the city, defeat, plague, famine, civil disturbance, and natural disasters. The picture is so general as to be much the same whether we concentrate on myth or on what we take to be history. The type of remedy found appropriate may of course differ in the two cases, but the patterns are close enough to suggest that both may have a bearing on some Greek modes of thought.

The natural reaction to the prospect of disaster, once initial despair and paralysis are over, is to seek help, probably from several directions at once. Gods and mortals both have a part to play, and both may be called *soteres*. In either case, the help given, the eventual saving action, may operate either in a straightforward, plausible way, or more indirectly and unexpectedly. With human action, it is easy to see the ways in which straightforward saving action occurs: it is positive qualities of courage, endurance, strength, and prudence, which qualify a man to be a saviour, or a whole group of men (such as those who fought at Marathon) to be accorded special reverence. The gods too on occasion give help of a straightforward, direct kind, usually in answer to prayer: thus to take the case of an individual (but it need be no different with cities) Chryses in *Iliad* 1 prays to Apollo for help, and Apollo intervenes directly. Complications arise when the help comes in the form of advice or instruction—the inevitable form when an oracle is consulted. This type of saving action is much more complex and usually involves some element of the unexpected. Further, as in the case of an individual who is told in a dream what will cure him, so with a city whose representatives are given an oracle, human action is necessary to complement the divine. Thus if we look in detail at the case of Sosipolis, it becomes clear that not just one event but three or four are necessary to *soteria*. Help comes first of all from the gods—vaguely conceived—as shown in the woman's dream. The human agents, the woman and the generals, each make the correct response. They cannot themselves be called *soteres*, but they have the potential to accept or reject the proffered *soteria*. Finally, and most spectacularly, the child-snake, neither quite human nor unambiguously divine, puts deliverance into actuality and wins the title of City-Saviour. In this pattern, the divine instructions are rarely easy to follow or even apparently sensible. So here *soteria* comes from a highly improbable method and source: from the aggressive power of the being least able to defend itself. Somehow, what was marginal to the city has become central. This kind of topsy-turviness is clearly associated with the gods, whose mode of operation is notoriously often at odds with that of human beings. But it relates not only to the god who gave the nonsensical-sounding oracle or who sent the dream, but to the divine or heroic being who was the direct agent of *soteria*.

Figures like Sosipolis or the saving victims of human sacrifice may then be seen as paradoxical because of the role of the divine. But from another point of view they could be seen as themselves generating the paradox. Gods are not the only beings more powerful than mortals; from the point of view of the city a special importance is due to the hero, and figures of the type under discussion either stand very close to heroes or are actually described as such. While every city has its own protecting deity, the god cannot be unique to that city, and indeed his or her sympathies might conceivably lie quite elsewhere. The problem is already highlighted in the *Iliad* (6. 297–311) when the women of Troy bring gifts to the Athena of the Acropolis, the city's Athena Polias, addressing her as *rhysiptolis*, city-saviour; the goddess favours the Greeks, and averts her eyes from the gifts brought by the Trojan women. Heroes were less susceptible to divided or alienated sympathies. In their lifetime they had belonged to a particular city, and provided that the city had treated them well, and that after their death no enemies intervened successfully to steal their allegiance, you could expect that they would continue as heroes to favour their city's interests. The ways in which heroes help their cities are manifold. Heroes were often seen as the middle term of a series: 'gods, heroes, human beings',[6] and indeed they can act both like gods and like ordinary mortals. In the cult paid to them after death, we see them acting essentially like

---

[6] Antiphon 1. 27: see J. -P. Vernant, *Mythe et société en Grèce ancienne* (Paris, 1974), pp. 117–8 (= *Myth and Society in Ancient Greece* (Brighton, 1980), p. 107)—rather overstating the case—and E. Kearns, *The Heroes of Attica* (forthcoming), ch. 7.

gods, intervening from a clearly superhuman level. In the myths and narratives of their lives, they act on a human level, it is true—in theatrical terms they are a human protagonist, not a *deus ex machina*—but at the same time the deeds reveal a paradox which seems to mark them out as more than human.

The cult aspect is more straightforward than the mythic. Like gods, heroes may be approached by prayers and sacrifice in times of crisis: thus for instance the Aiakids, as well as 'all the gods', were approached before the battle of Salamis (Herodotus 8. 64). If in response to this they are often seen fighting in the ensuing battle, so too are gods. Of course, the intervention announces victory, and in either case the apparition shows that something more than human is occurring, and yet the mode of action is direct, plausible, and human. Heroes and gods who appear helping in this way are generally those who have the closest connection with the city or the land where the battle takes place. Their motivation, also, is plausible and human: they fight for their own.

A number of cases show, however, that there were ways of using cult to break the natural link between hero and city, and these go some way to forming an index of the importance and influence of that link. Plutarch (*Solon* 9) reports—with what reliability is is hard to gauge—that in the struggle to wrest Salamis from Megara Solon won the favour of the Salaminian heroes Kychreus and Periphemos, previously one supposes pro-Megarian, by secret sacrifices. Euripides shows that this was a mode of thought at least recognizable in the 420s, with his warning that if enemies manage to sacrifice to the heroines known as Hyakinthides they will be victorious and bring trouble on Athens.[7] It would be very interesting to know exactly on what level such ideas mattered. Clearly a city would not lose by sacrificing punctiliously to its own heroes, but did it seriously hope to win wars by sacrificing to those of other people? Perhaps it was worth a try. The various sixth- and fifth-century episodes of the removal of heroic bones seem to represent (at least partially) a similar phenomenon, the wish to tie a hero (your own or someone else's) to your city by ensuring his physical presence. As Herodotus tells the episode of the bones of Orestes, almost as much of the point lies in the

---

[7] Eur. *Erechtheus* (C. Austin, *Nova fragmenta euripidea*, fr. 65. 78 ff.).

removal of the bones from Tegea as in their arrival at Sparta; even though unrecognized and unworshipped by the Tegeans, the hero had been their protecting talisman.[8]

There was, then, a significant group of heroes whose cult and existence as heroes was particularly concerned with the city and with its safety, and this connection seems to have been felt seriously. But most heroes have a myth as well as a cult, a myth which presents the hero in his lifetime as a human being, usually but not always in the ancient past, and which shows him as behaving in a remarkable way. Several of these myths relate the hero's saving of the city, and like the cult phenomena they can give us a route to Greek ideas and practice on the subject. Relatively few heroic myths narrate the straightforward saving of a city by brave or well-planned fighting alone. There are a few examples: Theseus and the Athenians fighting off the Amazons, and from certain points of view some of the labours of Herakles. The heroic fighter-saviour persists in historic times: the appearance of Brasidas as a kind of 'founding hero', a *heros ktistes*, in Amphipolis is well-known—Thucydides tells us that he was considered the city's founder, but he also goes on to say that the Amphipolitans considered him their 'saviour'.[9] This takes us one step further: seeing that the hero is essentially a dead person, the pattern becomes much more satisfactory if the death can actually occur as part of the saving action—as Brasidas died in Thrace. Thus, those who died at Marathon become the objects of heroic cult:[10] those who survived, though accorded respect, did not suddenly become heroes when they died quietly in their beds.

But the importance of the death of the *soter* is illustrated even more strikingly in the conspicuous group of stories in which it is not linked with the direct action of annihilating the threat to the city. Thus at Athens, in a story of unclear origins, the king Kodros saves his city from the Dorians not by leading his

[8] Herod. i. 66–8. Comparable in many ways are the bones of Theseus, brought back by Kimon to Athens in 475 (Plut. *Cimon* 8. 5–6). See E. Rohde, *Psyche*, 9th and 10th edns. (Tübingen, 1925), i. 160–3; F. Pfister, *Der Reliquienkult im Altertum* (Giessen, 1909), pp. 188–211, 510–14.

[9] Thuc. 5. 11, where *nomisantes* probably carries the implication of a customary cult title. Characteristically Thucydides adds another, more cynical, motivation.

[10] *IG* ii² 1006. 26, 69. This is a late second-century BC inscription, but it seems inconceivable that cult did not begin in the fifth century, as with the dead at Plataea (Thuc. 3. 58. 4).

troops in the attack, but by resorting to disguise in order to get himself killed in an undignified skirmish. The story may have been polished up a little after Leonidas, though it can hardly originate there,[11] but it takes the saviour one step further in self-abnegation. This is not a 'do and die' suicide mission, as with Leonidas or the Roman generals' practice of *devotio*, but a substitution of 'dying' for 'doing': for what is considered a glorious death in battle, with all the honours due to a military leader, is substituted a death that is certain, ignominious, and—apparently—useless. Very often the saviour figure is not a leader of men at all; deliverance is procured through the willing sacrifice of a young boy, or much more often a young girl or girls. Despite the mythical flavour of this variant, such stories were often taken seriously; the well-known example of the daughters of Erechtheus, subject of a Euripidean tragedy, can be used by the fourth-century orator Lycurgus as an *exemplum* for the here-and-now.[12] In this scheme the saviour, whose action is now completely indirect, can save the city from the whole range of disasters, not only military defeat or destruction by monsters. But though within the story this type of heroic saviour is a human being, not a god, the means by which salvation is procured are, in the normal way of thinking, completely unlikely and paradoxical. Such events do in fact seem to occur only in response to divine instruction, only within the context of a divinely sanctioned inversion of norms, and this more-than-humanness is signalled also by the heroic status of the saviour; after the event, further divine instruction reveals that she must be worshipped as a heroine. Heroization also generally occurs with the saviour who is a more conventional leader of men, whether the Kodros or the Herakles/ Brasidas type, and so the story of the saving action is, among other things, an *aition* for the cult. The myth of the deliverance of the city by a hero in his or her lifetime, then, merges into the myth of deliverance through divine instruction. Both types

[11] Pherecydes, *FGrHist* 3 F 154; Hellanicus, ib. 323a F 23. The story may be not a great deal older than this: see H. W. Parke and D. E. W. Wormell, *The Delphic Oracle* (Oxford, 1956), i. 296–7.

[12] Lycurgus, *Against Leocrates*, 98–101. On the theme in tragedy, esp. Euripides, see J. Schmitt, *Freiwilliger Opfertod bei Euripides* (Giessen, 1921); E. A. M. E. O'Connor-Visser, *Aspects of Human Sacrifice in the Tragedies of Euripides* (Amsterdam, 1987); N. Loraux, *Tragic Ways of Killing a Woman* (Cambridge, Mass., 1987), pp. 31–48.

involve the consultation of an oracle—help from outside the city itself—and both typically end in the institution of a cult.

It is not perhaps a surprising conclusion that both gods and heroes do paradoxical things, although the division between human action on the one hand, divine and heroic on the other, does not entirely correspond to the likely/unlikely divide. Victories won in a perfectly normal way, plagues survived without extraordinary measure, can still be credited to divine intervention. On the other hand, the distinction in mode can sometimes be seen by structural correspondences which under- line the difference in action between heroic-mythic model and human copy. A case in point is the Athenian myth of Aglauros, the daughter of Kekrops, who in one version fell off the Acropolis to her death, not in an accident caused by disobe- dience, but deliberately in order to save the city. In cult, Aglauros has close links with the ephebes, who take their oath in her sanctuary, and in her name before any other. The martial connections of Aglauros are strengthened both by the ephebic oath and by the recently published inscription which finally locates the Aglaurion; both underline her mythical association with Ares by cult links.[13] Aglauros, then, who as a heroine continued to have a special interest in victory, had given her life for the city; the ephebes, young and unmarried like her, had to be prepared to do the same. The youth, and therefore the status as in some ways marginal to the city, is the same. The mode of deliverance is entirely different, the indir- ect, implausible suicide versus the direct, likely method of hacking the enemy to pieces; the area of action is different, the heart of the city as opposed to its borders; and of course the sex is different, for normally it is males who possess the necessary strength to save. No doubt it is relevant to this last point that elements of transsexuality are characteristic of transitional age- states like that of the *ephebeia*, but this is not the only thing that can be said about the gender of their patroness. Praxithea, the mother of another princess-victim, makes the girl-boy parallel explicit in Euripides' version, and professes to be glad to give her daughter for her city as she would give a son:

If instead of females there were a male crop in the house, and the

---

[13] *Ephebeia*: P. Siewert, *JHS* 97 (1977), 102–11. Inscription: G. S. Dontas, *Hesperia*, 52 (1983), 48–63.

enemy's fire had hold of the city, would I not, fearing death, send them out to battle? May I have children such as will fight and distinguish themselves among men, and not ciphers, born in the city to no avail.[14]

Yet much as the theme seems to have appealed to Euripides, in real life a girl—far more marginal to the city than a boy— would be extremely unlikely to save her city in any way, except the still more indirect one of changing her status by marriage and bearing male children to grow up and fight.[15] The difference is that within the myth we are not in the sphere of the human, but in that of the heroic, where norms are reversed. The Aglauros story is an injunction to the ephebes, but it speaks its own mythical language: to read the injunction, the mythical improbabilities must be translated into the terms of normal life.

Of course this example is too neatly schematic to stand for the whole truth, not least because in Greek history it is often difficult to distinguish myth from 'real life': the one has a way of modelling itself on the other. And just as *soteria* myths *can* narrate a straightforward means of deliverance, so in what seems to be history, where gods and heroes cannot immediately be discerned, unlikely agents may be the means of salvation. In what follows I propose to treat 'mythical' and 'historical' accounts together and examine the relationship of both 'likely' and 'unlikely' ways of saving to the city itself.

One approach to this question is to examine the role and status of the saviour with regard to the city. Where the deliverance of the individual is concerned, there is a clear difference in the story according as he/she is saved by friend, enemy, or neither-in-particular. In the case of the city, the possibilities are more complex. In particular, we can see that the likely/unlikely distinction, in so far as it concerns the identity of the saviour, will show some overlap with another important distinction: that between help that comes from within the city, and help from outside. The city, being a plural form, is able more easily than an individual to save itself, in that one person or group within it may be able to save the

---

[14] Eur. *Erechtheus* (n. 7), fr. 50.
[15] That this is as real a contribution to a 'war effort' as any man's is the famous argument of Lysistrata, Aristoph. *Lysistrata* 588 ff.

whole community. This perhaps is the most likely mode of deliverance, having convincing psychological roots: one fights more keenly for a city because it is one's own. And what makes it one's own? The Athenian answer is given by Euripides' Praxithea, in the same speech in which she argues for giving daughters, like sons, in the struggle against the enemy: Athenians fight more determinedly for their city than do other Greeks because they are autochthonous. The importance of the connection between autochthony and patriotism has been demonstrated by Loraux,[16] and from our point of view Praxithea's statement expresses what is likely, help from within; 'within-ness' is taken to its ultimate conclusion in the concept of springing from the earth itself.

The 'saviour-from-within' role of a Miltiades, a Themistocles, or Aratus is taken also by some heroes, those who like Theseus at Marathon or the four Delphic heroes in 279[17] are observed leading their people to victory. More generally, the hero-leader, the *archegetes*, continues to give help and leadership to his people after death as he did in life. Is there anything similar in divine aid? When Poseidon appears fighting for Mantineia, or Hermes for Tanagra, or Athena more generally bestows protection on Athens, it is a clear case of the god protecting his own, and yet it is not quite right to say that 'help has come from within.' In one sense, the particular gods of a city are often very much within it: with some exceptions, notably Hera-sanctuaries, their temples are placed on the acropolis, at the inmost heart of the city. Ancient chained cult-images perhaps bear witness to at least a half-belief that their presence there was as physical as any other. Yet at the same time the gods are something different, something outside; they cannot entirely be constrained, they are not subject to ordinary physical laws—they can hear wherever they may be—and though they may have a special connection with a city this is not usually significant (there are a very few exceptions) in defining their overall nature. They would hardly in normal usage be termed a member of a city, a native, even in the sense

[16] N. Loraux, *Les Enfants d'Athéna* (Paris, 1974), esp. pp. 35–73; *The Invention of Athens* (Cambridge, Mass., 1986), pp. 148–50.

[17] Plut. *Theseus* 35; Paus. 10. 23. 3. See W. K. Pritchett, *The Greek State at War* iii (Berkeley and Los Angeles, 1979), pp. 11–46.

that the 'local heroes', *epichorioi heroes*, are native. Divine help, then is always in one sense help from outside, and one of its messages would seem to be that the city, for all its strength and plurality, is not actually self-sufficient.

But heroic saviours may also come from outside: beside the ranks of those *archegetai* who continue to protect the city they championed in life, is a group of protecting heroes who are foreigners, even enemies. Foreign heroes do not usually save the city in their lifetime, apart from a few special examples such as Herakles, benefactor of mankind. More commonly an event of their life might explain their unexpected allegiance, though their function as saviours begins only after their death and their clear heroic status. Thus a foreigner and an enemy becomes a protecting hero in Herodotus' account (5. 114) of the story of Onesilos, killed besieging Amathous in Cyprus. His head was stuck on a city gate where it soon began to swarm with bees. The story is not difficult to complete: an oracle was consulted, and the reply was to worship Onesilos, whose name means 'benefactor of the people', as a hero. The detail of the gate is significant. Onesilos belongs in a largish group of heroes situated at gates, but in his case it is entirely appropriate that the enemy, situated just *outside* the transitional point and trying to force an entrance, should be transformed into the protector, for whom the gate rather represents the movement from inside to out, defence coming from within aimed at the aggressor outside. It sums up his ambivalent position as enemy-protector, while the cult guarantees his benevolence and confirms his new status as 'belonging'.

Dramatists seem to be particularly fond of the foreign protector-hero, often supplying an explanation in mythical terms for the change of allegiance. Oedipus will save Athens from the Thebans, because he has repudiated his wicked sons; the Argive Eurystheus will protect Attica against Dorian invasion, because of his ancient feud with the children of Herakles. At the point of death the defeated Eurystheus speaks of his coming status: he will lie under the earth forever as a *metoikos*. Like the metic, the foreign hero is within the *polis*, but not of it: he both belongs and does not belong. The help given by a metic in this play contrasts strongly with Praxithea's argument on autochthony. If non-Athenians do not truly belong to the cities where they were born, still less can metics belong to the cities of their adoption, cities where they are physically but not constitutionally situated. Eurystheus, in a play of surprises, promises unlikely help, from a source not entirely outside the city, but not fully within it either.

To the status of metic—part inside, part outside—with which our foreign heroes in some measure correspond, may be added others which contrast with the usual picture of the full or normal citizen. Slaves, women, and children are obvious examples of people living in the city who in differing ways lack the fullness of belonging, and who therefore by the principle, if not the actual conclusion, of Praxithea's argument, might be expected to contribute less to the city's well-being. In many cities, we should add groups like *perioikoi* and helots, who are recognized natives but excluded from full citizenship. If paradox is in some measure important, we might then expect to find city-saviours also among these groups, and to some extent this does occur. But the groups are not all equally represented. Although some late traditions name various eminent Spartans as *mothakes* (sons of a Spartiate father and a helot mother),[18] it seems that neither in Sparta nor elsewhere are there any stories—at least, surviving stories—of helots or people of similar status whose actions save the *polis*. Slave saviours too are thin on the ground. It is not uncommon to find domestic slaves, along with free women, defying the enemy in the last desperate stages of a siege—a reassuring type of story, but one in which the slaves are normally secondary to the women. They receive a little more emphasis than usual in Plutarch's account of the siege of Chios by Philip V (*Moralia* 245 B–C): Philip offered the slaves of the Chians, if they would come over to him, their freedom and the chance to marry their owners; meaning, as Plutarch thinks it necessary to explain, the wives of their masters. In answer to this both women and slaves pelted him with stones from the city walls until his forces gave way.[19]

Though strict realism is hardly a necessary quality in *soteria-*

---

[18] Athenaeus 6. 271 E–F; Aelian, *Varia historia* 12. 43.

[19] From Chios we have also the tradition of the slave Drimakos, later heroized under the name Eumenes, who in his lifetime helped out the city by negotiating between the citizens and bands of marauding slaves (Athen. 6. 265 D–66 E); but if Drimakos is a saviour, he saves the city from his own kind, and the story's main point seem to be 'set a slave to catch a slave'.

stories, the lack of slave and helot saviours does to some extent reflect a realistic perspective. Slaves (with the possible partial exception of domestic slaves) and groups considered inferior and incomplete citizens, are likely enough—though it is not inevitable—to feel open hostility towards their masters or dominators, the true *politai*; the wives and children of citizens, though they may on occasion half-consciously resent the family's structure of authority, will not experience anything on the same scale. The relationship of mutual hostility and fear which exists in the first category obviously leaves its mark on the narration of events, especially if elements hostile to the ruling classes have had a hand in shaping the tradition.

As for saviours who come from a less sharply defined, but still clearly 'inferior', marginal section of society, the situation seems even less promising. Such areas do, however, provide a sort of inverse saviour in the form of the scapegoat (*pharmakos*), a figure in some ways the saviour's opposite, but also oddly akin: it is his expulsion which constitutes a saving action.[20] Normally, the scapegoat is picked from the outermost reaches of society; he is poor, a beggar, destitute, disreputable, a criminal, or all of these. His expulsion is commonly seen as a purification, the city ridding itself of unclean and dangerous elements, and he himself as the 'offscourings' (*peripsema, katharma*). But another common strand of thought is that the city, like Polykrates (Herodotus 3. 40–3), must throw away something valuable in order not to lose everything. When this viewpoint becomes dominant, we at once have a problem: how can the expulsion of such a worthless human being be of assistance?

The problem can be solved by a further paradox. If marginality in the city is a normal feature of the scapegoat, it sometimes happens that centrality is implied as well, as for instance at Massalia (Marseilles) where the destined man was fed in the *prytaneion* for a year before his expulsion; he is thus both honoured as a public benefactor and symbolically identified with the city itself, at the end of the year coming forward from its most central point, its hearth. This gives him something in common with the foreign, 'metic' saviour-hero,

[20] Xen. *Hell.* 3. 3. 4 explicitly opposes *soter* and *apotropaios*. On scapegoats, see J. M. Bremmer, *HSCP* 87 (1983), 299–320 and R. Parker, *Miasma* (Oxford, 1983), pp. 257–71.

who is both inside and outside the *polis*. The pattern is also comparable with the story of king Kodros, who disguised himself as a poor woodman in order to get himself killed and so to save Athens. To some extent, it is the motif of false appearances which is important here—a king conceals his true identity by taking on a humble disguise, as gods also very often do. What was commanded by the oracle was the death of the king, not of a woodman. But taken in connection with the scapegoat of Massalia, the apparent marginality of the saviour-victim becomes more important: the scapegoat, starting from the outermost point, is drawn to the centre of the city, both physically and figuratively, while Kodros, as king, begins from the centre and journeys to the circumference (again, physically as well as figuratively, for as a woodman he is situated outside the city walls.)[21] A difference is now apparent between Kodros and the scapegoat on the one hand, and slaves and helots on the other; where the latter group stand simply on the city's outer circles, the position of Kodros and the scapegoat is ambivalent. Can it be that both centrality and marginality in the city are qualifications for saving it, and that the most satisfactory pattern combines the two?

To answer this question, we may turn to perhaps the most remarkable of the 'unlikely' and in some senses marginal groups from which saviours commonly are drawn: women. This group of course cuts across most other divisions, so that women may be of noble or royal birth, of middling status, or poor and humble. They may also be slaves or foreigners. These distinctions are important, but none the less—and this is obvious—women of whatever social rank also stand partly outside the male-dominated structures of *polis* society. Their presence is, of course, essential biologically, and this necessity is reflected in various *polis*-based religious rituals in which only women—frequently only citizen women—may take part. A woman, then, is linked to a city, but whether she is actually a citizen is less easy to determine. Aristotle seems undecided: women are 'half the city', and he can speak of a mother as a

[21] It will be seen that my analysis is close to that of Bremmer (n. 20), but at this point I must disagree. The king is not a 'marginal at the top [of society]' (p. 304); rather, his position is conspicuous because he is at the centre of society. The relation between the king and the beggar is like that between *soter* and *apotropaios*: their position at opposite ends of the spectrum gives them much in common.

citizen, but in a stricter sense a citizen is defined as one who participates in the administration of justice and the holding of office—which clearly excludes women.[22] Loraux points out that there is no true feminine of *Athenaioi*, but merely *Attikai gynaikes*, descriptive of a local situation rather than the status of actually belonging to a *polis*.[23] It would not be going too far to say that in this respect—if not in others—women are perceived as it were like animals, sharing man's living space almost by accident, insignificant in the divisions of society which really count.

But this is only a very partial perception. The dual position of a woman, both as set apart as a member of the group of females, and as having also some particular status applicable also to men, is nicely demonstrated in the most typical myth of the female saviour. It is the king's daughter or daughters who give their lives to save the city: the king gives centrality, the girls marginality. Even more neatly than with the scapegoat or with Kodros, because no element of pretence is involved, both saviour-rich areas of society are drawn on simultaneously.[24] As virgins, the girls are not only untouched and whole for sacrifice, they are also without any part in even the limited contribution of the woman to the *polis*, that of bearing children. Under normal circumstances, an unmarried girl is only of potential, not actual, use to the *polis*. She is also one of the most obviously vulnerable members of society, needing the protection of others rather than supplying protection herself. Not only are women, and especially girls, not central in a general sense, they represent also an inert element, a liability, when the city is under attack. Even descriptions of plagues

---

[22] Arist. *Pol.* 1269ᵇ18; 1275ᵇ23; 1275ᵃ22–3. The definition in the last passage excludes also children and the old, as Aristotle points out; he does not think it necessary to mention women explicitly in this context.

[23] Loraux (n. 16), pp. 124–5.

[24] Robert Parker points out to me that another way of looking at the story is to put the emphasis on the king's action in giving his daughters, as Aeschylus presents Agamemnon offering up Iphigeneia. This works well with some variants of the story, such as the *aition* for the cult of Artemis Mounychia, where the father, Embaros, represents the cult's priest, but elsewhere this idea seems less dominant. Although Euripides was particularly fond of the idea of willing self-sacrifice, he did not draw it out of thin air: it is a general principle that a sacrificial victim (human or animal) should consent to be sacrificed (see K. Meuli, *Gesammelte Schriften* ii (Basle, 1975), pp. 993–6), and in most cases the story is told to account for the cult of heroines, putting the emphasis firmly on the girls.

stress the particular vulnerability of women in crisis: they become infertile, suffer miscarriages, and die giving birth, all disasters affecting both city and individual. As for war, 'it is men (*andres*) who are the city, and not walls or empty ships'. It is not the spirit of the citizenry which the commonplace opposes to material armaments, but specifically the fighting power of men.[25] Implicit is the identification of citizenship with the ability to defend the city; the *polis* is then quintessentially itself when it is legitimating its existence in war. In this context the role of a woman in saving the city is perhaps the biggest paradox of all.

Then can the myth of the human *soteira* have any relation to any normal experience involving women? I suggested earlier that a myth like that of Aglauros corresponds to real-life demands on the ephebes by substituting, within the framework of a patriotic story, improbable, fantastic elements for normal ones, and the heroine's sex is of course one of these elements: she would seem to be a model for males, not females. On the other hand, when girls like her or like the cult group of the Hyakinthides, identified with the daughters of the warrior-king Erechtheus, give their lives for their city, they become heroines, and their cult, it seems, is still concerned with *soteria*. Here too the element of paradox is much reduced, as their superhuman status allows them a power which even male mortals do not enjoy. Is then the paradox of womanhood confined to significance as a term in the world of myth, simply one variable in the translation of events from likely to unlikely, and vice versa? To begin to answer this, we may look at a different kind of story presenting women as saviours. This is one which presents women in a more active role, rather than in the negative and paradoxical sacrifice, and it is one which seems to be situated rather closer to historical reality than the death of the king's daughters. The enemy is close at hand and may even have entered the city, or there is fighting between two groups in the

---

[25] Thuc. 7. 77 is the most famous formulation, but the idea occurs already in Alcaeus fr. 112. 10 (Lobel–Page, *Poetarum Lesbiorum Fragmenta*), and Sophocles, *Oedipus Tyrannus* . 56–7; also Eur. fr. 828 Nauck². A much later, somewhat contrived, version in Dio Cass. 56. 5. 3 shows a completely changed meaning: here it is not *andres* but *anthropoi* who form the city, and they are contrasted not with ships and walls but with houses, stoas, and agoras: fighting capability is no longer an appropriate criterion under the *pax romana*.

city, and in a last-ditch defence the women have gone up to the
rooftops and hurl down tiles on their enemies. In contrast to
my previous example, this is clearly a natural and practical
response, and in purely naturalistic terms it may be effective, at
least in a limited way. Often the scene is mentioned as a detail
in a longer narrative of fighting, and not as the turning-point
and bringer of safety. Thus in Thucydides' account of the *stasis*
at Corcyra we are told (3. 74. 1) that the women of the
democratic families joined in the fighting from the rooftops,
'daringly' and 'standing their ground beyond their nature', but
their intervention was not critical.[26] The scene, then, is not
inherently unlikely or mythical, but real incidents can easily be
elaborated to exaggerate the degree of help given by the
women's intervention; the picture can also be transferred to
events in which the action is quite unhistorical. Thus the story
of Telesilla and the Argive women warding off the Spartan
attack on the city takes the familiar pattern and uses it to
explain an oracle, an honorific statue of Telesilla, and a festival
in which each sex dresses in the clothes of the other.[27] The city's
customs are explained in terms of the city's history. A further
function of all such traditions is of course to say 'Even our
women are better than their men'. One version of the Telesilla
story in fact has a rider which looks as though it is added by
pro-Spartan tradition in order to nullify this point: the Spartans withdrew because of the disgrace that would attach to
them if it became known that they had been fighting women.
The same point applies to the male groups who are commonly
found fighting alongside women, composed of those who are
excluded from regular fighting forces: house-slaves, and of the
free, those who are too old or too young to fight. All these
categories are listed in Pausanias' Telesilla account, and all can
be more or less opposed to the *andres*, the men who are the city's

[26] Another example in Thucydides is at 2. 4. 2, when the Plataeans ('themselves and
their women and their slaves'—see below, p. 343) thus defeated the Thebans. Further
examples, many with a more 'mythical' flavour, abound; they are discussed in D.
Schaps, *Class. Phil.* 77 (1982), 195–6, F. Graf, 'Women, War and Warlike Divinities',
ZPE 55 (1984) 245–54, and N. Loraux, 'La cité, l'historien, les femmes', *Pallas*, 32
(1985), 7–28.
[27] The oracle, which predicts among other things that 'the female will overcome the
male', is first attested by Herodotus (6. 77), who does not, however, mention Telesilla
or the story connected with her. The story is given in Plut. *Mor.* 245 D–E and Paus. 2.
20. 8.

'tower of war', in Alcaeus' words.[28] But women are the most
conspicuous among these groups, because the most definitively
and permanently opposed to the normal fighting group: the
women of the Corcyraean *demos* resisted 'beyond their nature',
says Thucydides.[29]

But I think there are further reasons for the appeal of the
story of women as successful defenders. The centrality–marginality paradox is not confined to the king's daughters, but in
another sense applies to all women: it is a curious feature of
Greek women that while in one sense they are on the city's
margins—not so much citizens as wives and daughters of
citizens—in another sense their position is *inside*, in contrast to
men who of course suffer trials and tribulations outside the city.
Proverbially the woman is 'seated inside.'[30] When she does
venture out, trouble may be expected to follow, whether it is
the unacceptable face of maenadism—the agitation of Pen-
theus in the *Bacchae* surely expresses anxieties not confined to
him—or more prosaically (but no less threateningly) the
beginning of an adulterous affair, as narrated in the first speech
of Lysias. Most intriguingly, in opposition to the 'women on
the rooftops', we find another group of stories occupying much
the same area of myth, history, and mixture of the two: the
women who go to celebrate a festival at an out-of-town
sanctuary, and who are carried off as an act of aggression by an
enemy group.[31] Here no blame can attach to the women, who

[28] See above, n. 25.

[29] The story-type is a persistent one, and its paradoxical side comes out even more
clearly in the death of Pyrrhus at Argos, killed in Plutarch's account (*Pyrrhus* 34) by a
poor old woman hurling a tile to protect her son, thus enabling another man to deliver
the fatal blow. (In another version (Zonaras 8. 6) a woman trying to see what was
going on lost her balance and fell on top of Pyrrhus, so killing him.) The paradox here
is largely of the personal, not the civic, level: the powerful ruler falls victim to a woman
of lowly status, not even in her prime. Nevertheless, the woman's action helped her city
as well as her son, so that her categorization as in every way an unlikely saviour is
important. Outside the Greek world, there is a similar story from a state not unlike the
Greek *polis*, in the Venetian tradition of the defeat of Baiamonte Tiepolo's revolt in
1310: Tiepolo's standard-bearer was hit by a mortar hurled by an old woman leaning
out of her window, and in the subsequent confusion the forces loyal to the doge gained
their advantage. The woman's status as saviour was ratified in the story by permission
to hang the banner of the Republic from the fatal window on the anniversary of the
event. (She also received a promise that her rent would never be increased.) See
Cambridge Medieval History, vii. 30.

[30] Aesch. *Choephoroe* 919; Page, *Poetae Melici Graeci*, 848. 15.

[31] Examples in Herod. 6. 138. 1, Paus. 4. 16. 9; cf. Plut. *Solon* 8. 4, Paus. 4. 17. 1.

have gone to celebrate a perfectly legitimate, indeed necessary, festival: it is simply their nature as women which makes them vulnerable and hence a liability to the city, and this vulnerability is exposed when they go outside—in this case, outside the easily defended town area. The rooftops story, on the other hand, shows women inside the town (this is true even in the variant of Telesilla and her followers, who defend the walls of Argos), and in most cases if not in their houses at least on them; it is the protective covering of the house itself which they tear up for a defence against the enemy. Women outside are attacked and violated, women inside, on the other hand, themselves attack and are often successful, reversing apparent norms. So in the equivalence Aglauros–ephebes, the ephebes typically occupy the borders of Attic territory, while the princess's saving action takes place in the very heart of the city. These are the correct places for men and women. Though in each there are many other elements, on one level the 'rooftops' and 'festival' stories, and to some extent no doubt reality, complement each other and affirm that society has got it right: in a successful city, men go out and women stay in.

So from one point of view a story of paradox and implausibility can be seen to be reinforcing social norms. In order to save the city women, standing outside the normal circle of fighter-citizens, remain physically 'inside'. A similar reversal of the male function occurs in the rather more fantastic story of the virgin sacrifice; the woman's role in saving is a passive one, while men—more typically but not exclusively—save their city by active means. All the same, the sacrificed princesses are given a far more definitive role in saving their country than any young male soldier is likely to have,[32] and the unexpected is still an important element in the idea of women as fighters and especially as fighting saviours.

The type of the unlikely saviour has an obvious story-telling appeal: well-known stories from other cultures feature children or even animals in the role. But we have seen that there is more to say about women as saviours—whether throwing rooftiles or being sacrificed—than that they are unlikely. These

---

[32] Thus Praxithea, justifying her consent to her daughter's sacrifice: 'Men who die in battle receive a common tomb and equal glory with others; but when my daughter dies, this city will give one garland to her alone.'

saviours of the *polis* have a particular and significant relationship with that *polis*. It is not quite clear whether women—in common with some of the other groups we have been considering—belong to the city or not: women in particular, excluded though they are in a sense, are also characterized in some narratives by elements implying centrality, proximity to the centre of belonging. The 'rooftile' story-pattern is in some ways a reassuring one: it humiliates the enemy, and within the *polis'* own society it separates the sexes and keeps each in its proper place. But this does not destroy the paradox that if the women succeed in their defence, if the girls consent to be sacrificed, the city owes its salvation to women. (The same of course applies to other marginal or non-fighting groups: slaves, the very young, and so on.) This paradox is *not* really reassuring, since its necessary corollary is that the men (free men of fighting age) who are said to compose the city are not in actual fact its saviours. Within the paradox, then, is contained a serious question, central to the city's perception of itself: what, or who actually composes the city in these most critical moments?

The answers given by the various stories are not all equally surprising. I have suggested that all the groups outside that of free, *helikioi andres*, are not in fact equally represented in the traditions of unlikely saviours. It may be that (male) slaves feature less than women for what we might call realistic reasons—because they are really less likely to care for the city's survival—or equally that women are more prominent than slaves for the sake of the paradox, the fact that their physical strength is less than that of men. A further factor, as I have suggested, would seem to be that women far more than slaves show a combination of centrality and marginality. It is likely that if we had more evidence we would find different *poleis* displaying variations on the theme, indicating differing concepts about who is a citizen or, more vaguely, who really belongs.

In order to analyse this further, we can compare two methods of subdividing the *polis*. In any Greek city the divisions of the population (men, women, slave, free, foreign, native-born, 'the good', 'the many') form a strong contrast with the many equally overlapping divisions of the citizen body which are such a remarkable feature of the classical *polis*: tribe,

deme, phratry, *genos, obe* ... Those divisions are a major and
distinctive feature of Greek society, but there are other and
perhaps more radical ones well-known to the political philosophers. Modern popular critiques of ancient democracies,
claiming that systems excluding women and slaves do not
deserve the name of democracy, may seem to the ancient
historian to beg the question, but they do remind us that even
in a democracy *polis* and population are not coincident. In
describing one of the episodes where the city is defended by
women, Thucydides needs to emphasize the fact that all the
inhabitants of Plataea took part in its defence; the phrase he
uses, in conformity with linguistic norms, is 'themselves, their
women, and their slaves'. 'The Plataeans', *hoi Plataieis*, does not
mean 'the inhabitants of Plataea', not even 'the native inhabitants', but the group which participates in deliberation and
fighting. In this sort of terminology, the masculine gender
signifies males alone and is not inclusive of others. Again, we
may debate whether, and in what sense, women in Athens
could be, or usually were, phratry members,[33] but there can be
no doubt that all groups of the phratry type were perceived as
structures primarily relevant to males. Phratries, demes, and so
on—bar a few jokes—are all more or less equal; when serious
inequalities are observed in the tribal structure, this normally
reflects a perception that some are less citizens than others.
Divisions between citizens and non-citizens (or less-citizens)
can be equally complex and much more ambivalent, but they
reflect a very clear inequality. It is perhaps this difference
above all that makes the one system of divisions so much more
significant than the other where the act of saving is concerned.
The importance of a particular phratry does not need stressing;
its existence is defined by the fact that it is indisputably part of
the citizen body, and membership of that body is in part
defined by it. It does not save, any more than it can be saved
(for it is clearly nonsense to speak of the saving of a phratry or
a deme). It is the groups formed by the other system of
divisions, those outside the clearly-defined centre of belonging,

[33] J. P. Gould contends that it was only exceptionally that girls were introduced into
the phratries (*JHS* 100 (1980), 40–2), but his views have not found general acceptance;
they are contested most recently by M. Golden, *CQ* NS 35 (1985), 9–13.

which so often come forward to save the city and assert their claim to form part of it.

Yet this is a claim which is always held at arm's length. If the city is saved by unlikely means, that suggests the unpredictability usually associated with the divine, an unpredictability which actually reaffirms the norms which are to be followed by human beings and which supports the effectively unequal organization of society. If the challenge, implicit at one level in the stories, to the more exclusive concept of the city were to be taken to its conclusion, the paradox of the unlikely saviour itself would be rendered impossible. Story and society are mutually dependent.

D

The Decline of the City

14

Doomed to Extinction: The *Polis* as an Evolutionary Dead-End

W. G. RUNCIMAN

I

THIS chapter is an exercise in comparative sociology, not in the history of classical Greece. I say this not merely to excuse the ignorance of detail which specialist readers are likely to detect, but also to emphasize that it is addressed not to the question (interesting as it is) 'how did Macedon become the dominant power in Greece?' but to the question 'with or without the rise of Macedon, could the *polis* have survived?'. In arguing that it could not, I am (so far as I can discover) within the general consensus of specialists. But there does not appear to be a consensus about why not, and my own answer may well be regarded by some readers as sensible but obvious and by others as intriguing but misconceived. The theoretical perspective from which it is arrived at is, as the title of the chapter implies, evolutionary, but not in either a Marxian or a Weberian sense; that is to say, I assume neither that changes in forms of social organization are the outcome of contradictions between the forces and social relations of production nor that they exemplify a process of cumulative rationalization. I assume no more than that they are generated by continuing competition for power—whether economic, ideological or coercive—within and

I am grateful both to the editors and to the members of the Oxford seminar for constructive comments on earlier drafts.

between societies, but without there being any predetermined
direction which they are bound to follow on that account.[1]

But what is a *polis*? For my purpose, a *polis* is a type of society
for which the proper label is not 'city-state' but 'citizen-state'.
It does not have to have an urban centre dominating a rural
hinterland (which would exclude Sparta for a start). Nor does
it have to be small enough for a Stentorian herald to be heard
by all its members. Nor does it have to cover any and all of the
cases to which the Greeks themselves applied the term *polis*
(particularly since even Aristotle is inconsistent in his use of
it).[2] Two necessary conditions are paramount. First, a *polis*
must be juridically autonomous in the sense of holding a
monopoly of the means of coercion within the territory to
which its laws apply. Second, its form of social organization
must be centred on a distinction between citizens, whose
monopoly of the means of coercion it is, who share among
themselves the incumbency of central governmental roles, and
who subscribe to an ideology of mutual respect, and non-
citizens, the product of whose labour is controlled by the
citizens even if the citizens do the same work (when not under
arms). The *poleis* which survived and indeed flourished in the
Hellenistic and even Roman periods were, therefore, *poleis* in
name only: they were urban communities with a life of their
own, but not 'citizen-states' in the sociological sense.

It follows from this definition that the distinction between
democracies and oligarchies is a distinction within a common
mode. It also follows that a hereditary tyranny is not a *polis*,
any more than is the Roman principate or an Italian *signoria*
(or for that matter an Islamic garrison town headed by an
independent *amir*), but that the appointment of a temporary
aisymnetes, like a Roman dictator or an Italian *podestà*, is
perfectly consistent with the definition. Nor does it matter
whether the non-citizens whose labour is controlled by the
citizens are slaves, serfs, debt-bondsmen, share-croppers, or
helots: it only matters if they are wage-workers in a formally
free labour market, or junior kinsmen, or free tenants or

[1] This perspective is outlined in my 'On the Tendency of Human Societies to Form
Varieties', *Proc. British Academy*, 72 (1986), 149–65.
[2] See J. A. O. Larsen, *Greek Federal States: Their Institutions and History* (Oxford, 1968),
p. 17.

smallholders who are not, however, entitled to carry arms. And finally, it follows that the Weberian distinction between a 'patrician city' (*Geschlechterstadt*) and a 'plebeian city' (*Plebejerstadt*)[3] cuts across that between a *polis* and an aristocratic warrior-state in which the relations between patrons and armed retainers, or commanders and professional troops, or knights enrolled in military orders and lay brothers or servants, are more important than those between citizens and non-citizens.

Then what is a dead-end? A type of society, or mode of the distribution of the means of production, persuasion, and coercion, is not a dead-end if it is an intermediate stage in a continuing endogenous evolution. Nor, on the other hand, is it a dead-end if it is a set of roles and institutions which reproduce themselves unchanged because and for as long as their ecological and sociological environment remains unchanged, as is the case with a number of hunter-gatherers and nomadic pastoralists documented in the historical and ethnographic record. A dead-end is where institutional evolution stops although the environment is changing, and the type of society in question becomes extinct through incapacity to adapt to that change. In saying this, I am well aware that the notion of adaptation is not uncontentious in sociological, as in biological, evolutionary theory. But I mean by it no more than an increase, or at least retention, of economic, ideological and/or coercive power by a society relative to others with which it is in not only contact but competition.

One last preliminary point needs to be made. The incidence of *stasis* was not (in my view) material either way to the failure of the *poleis* to adapt to their changed environment. No doubt it is true that the destruction of lives and property resulting from prolonged and severe internal violence makes any society less able to resist an alien predator than it might otherwise have been. But it is not *stasis* which of itself drives any given type of society into extinction. There are many examples in the historical and ethnographic record of societies whose exceptionally high level of internal violence did not prevent their institutions from reproducing themselves quite stably enough.

[3] Max Weber, *Economy and Society*, ed. Guenther Roth and Claus Wittich (New York, 1968), ii, ch. 16, sections ii–iv.

Korea is one; Mamluk Egypt is another; Haiti is a third. The most which can be said is that relief from *stasis* may be one of the motives which helps to secure acquiescence once evolution to another mode has occurred: Rome after the victory of Augustus and Japan after the victory of Tokugawa are two obvious instances. Whether, therefore, as some specialists believe (but others dispute) *stasis* was more frequent and perhaps also more intense in the fourth century BC than it had been in the fifth,[4] this does not alter the fact that for other reasons the Greek *poleis* had by then shown themselves unable to make the evolutionary modifications necessary for their survival as independent societies of a distinctive common type.

II

If the world had consisted of nothing but *poleis* (and perhaps a few remote tribal *ethne*) clustered, in Plato's simile, round the shores of the Mediterranean like frogs round a pond, then perhaps they could have reproduced themselves indefinitely without competition either between or within them forcing an evolution to another mode; tyrannies would no doubt have reappeared here and there, but only for a time and without developing the institutions of monarchical absolutism on the Near Eastern model; wars would have been won and lost, alliances formed and dissolved, democracies overthrown by oligarchies and oligarchies by democracies, and secessions, rebellions, and *coups d'état* have succeeded or failed, but in a sort of perpetual Brownian motion without any fundamental institutional change. But the world did consist of other types of society too; and as it turned out, the form of social organization which the *poleis* had evolved out of the confusion and depopulation which had followed the collapse of the Mycenaean system was positively disadvantageous in the wider environment which they themselves had helped to create. What is more, the disadvantages are equally apparent whether it is the

---

[4] Contrast the view of A. Fuks, 'Patterns and Types of Social-Economic Revolution in Greece from the Fourth to the Second Century BC', *Ancient Society*, 5 (1974), 59 with that of Andrew Lintott, *Violence, Civil Strife and Revolution in the Classical City* (London, 1982), p. 252.

mode of production, persuasion, or coercion which is given greater attention.

Let me start with the mode of production. It seems now to be generally accepted that what may be called the Weber–Hasebroek–Finley view of the ancient Greek economy is broadly correct—that is, that the *poleis* had no economic policies as such and that their economic institutions, such as they were, were inextricably bound up with and subordinated to their political institutions (and attitudes). In part, this was because of the low esteem in which not only manual labour (other than some healthy outdoor farmwork) but trade, artisanship, and the whole range of banausic occupations were held: the literary sources seem unanimous in the view that only politics, soldiering, and estate management are fit occupations for a gentleman, that working for somebody else is incompatible with the ideal of freedom, and that anybody who needs work done compels somebody else—helot, bondsman, captive or bought-in chattel-slave (or wife)—to do it for him. But this was not the decisive constraint, since these attitudes did not preclude the use of other people's labour to generate wealth. Xenophon was no Adam Smith. But he was perfectly well aware of the need for investment to show a profit (*to lusitelein*) and of the value of an economic surplus (*periousia chrematon*). What is more, his ideas about expanding the output of the silver mines by employing state-owned slaves, building up a state-owned merchant fleet to be chartered out, and building good hotels in the Piraeus to attract more foreign traders are, whether or not politically practicable, eminently sensible in economic terms.[5] The reason for which none of the Greek *poleis*, even Athens, achieved sustained economic growth is not that the idea of it was either inconceivable or distasteful to them. It was, rather, that their mode of production prevented them from seeing that profit (unlike a balance of payments) is not zero-sum: one person's gain need not be entirely at another's expense.

It would be going too far to suggest that fifth- and fourth-century Greeks were unconscious—let alone conscious—mercantilists. But their economic behaviour was a function both of

---

[5] See the comments of Philippe Gauthier, *Un commentaire historique des Poroi de Xénophon* (Geneva and Paris, 1976), esp. pp. 107–8 (on the merchant fleet proposal).

the physical facts of ecology and technique and of the sociological facts of the organization of production and trade. The *poleis* were organized in the first instance for autarky as the concomitant of political autonomy in a world of near-continuous warfare. The citizen-militiaman is concerned above all with the defence of his community. His needs are for arms and armour, an assured supply of food, and sufficient communal resources in money, raw materials, and dependent labour for the maintenance of the tangible and intangible basis of the institutions which define his role as citizen. He may incidentally practise a craft or trade, but this does not involve him in any form of collective social organization: his membership of the citizen body is what counts, and if he is deprived of it through debt or disgrace or being on the losing side in an outbreak of *stasis* this is incidental to the relation of his occupational role to the means of production. He is not a taxpayer in the modern sense, although he may be liable to a liturgy or an emergency levy if he is deemed to be of sufficient means. He may be involved in trade, and if it is as an *emporos* rather than a *kapelos* he may lose no social prestige by doing so;[6] but he is more likely to leave such things to be done by foreigners or metics. He will expect to benefit from, and perhaps to participate in, raids for booty carried out against other *poleis* (or *ethne*, or barbarian, i.e. non-Greek, territories), but such booty will be used either for donatives or for public works, not for investment in productive assets. He may well own imported articles of pottery or clothing, consume oil and wine not necessarily home-grown, and perhaps be dependent (as the Athenians in particular were) on foreign grain, but the scale of his purchases is likely to be modest at best: if he is one of the rich and fortunate few, he will probably use his wealth to buy jewels and slaves (and perhaps to risk some of it in a bottomry loan or invest in a workshop manned by servile artisans). I put all this in the ethnographic present in full awareness of the diversity of the *poleis* and the institutional differences between them. But I do so in order to convey the overwhelming impression which the standard sources leave of a world in which making a profit, whether by force or guile, was

[6] See Victor Ehrenberg, *The People of Aristophanes: A Sociology of Old Attic Comedy* (Oxford, 1943), p. 90.

just as much of a preoccupation as anywhere else, but the conception of productive growth was totally alien.

Against this background, the change in the mode of coercion from militia to mercenaries which all commentators agree to be significant could hardly fail to work more against the adaptation—that is, augmentation of power—of the *poleis* than in favour of it. As the scale of war increased, the transition from '*ville-foyer*' to '*ville-bastion*'[7] could perhaps have been expected to work to the advantage of whichever *poleis* were richest and therefore best able to afford the new style of warfare and therefore likeliest to grow richer still on the proceeds of victory. But this is not what happened. The advantages were purely temporary (notably the brief hegemony of the Phocians after their expropriation of the treasures of Delphi). The trouble with the mercenaries was that there were so many of them—or rather, so many in relation to the resources with which to support them. It seems clear from the sources that their pay was minimal—they were expected to get their rewards from successful campaigns.[8] But these campaigns were destructive of precisely the resources on which they, like everyone else, needed to live. Nor was colonization any longer an option. The solution, as Isocrates saw, was to send an army against Persia. But how were the *poleis* ever going to do it? They could neither get rid of their (or each other's) surplus hoplites nor pool them for common use; and as the number and size of mercenary armies increased, so the citizens with assured livelihoods from sources other than soldiering became progressively demilitarized. The result was that the *poleis* became less capable, not more, of defending themselves against an invader of a more formidable kind.

This in turn leads on to the mode of persuasion—that is, to the need to unite the citizens of the *poleis* in adherence to a common ideology of legitimacy and prestige. It was only in those parts of Greece where the *ethnos*, not the *polis*, was the dominant form of political organization that federations came into being in which allegiance was more than defiantly parochial. What is more, the obstinate attachment of the *poleis* to their distinctive symbols of independence—cults, coins, and

[7] Yvon Garlan, *Recherches de Poliorcétique Grecque* (Paris, 1974), p. 277.

[8] W. K. Pritchett, *The Greek State at War* (Berkeley and Los Angeles, 1974), ii. 101–4.

calendars alike—was coupled with an extreme institutional conservatism of which the *graphe paranomon* is the limiting expression. There are to be found no innovations in constitutional theory, no extension of the criteria of citizenship, no mergers of autonomy within a common Hellenism, no binding alliances, and no ideology of subordination beyond recognition of *de facto* sovereignty and the obvious need to preserve the safety of the *koinonia*. Nor was there ever internal consensus on a value-system entitling either the rich or the well-born to deference from their inferiors. Aristotle implies that those whose forebears had *arete* as well as money have some justification in thinking themselves superior, but his *Politics* (and every other literary source known to me) testifies overwhelmingly to their failure to persuade those whom they designated as *kakoi* to share that view. The sentiment which Plato in Book 8 of the *Republic* puts into the mouth of the poor hoplite seems authentic enough: the rich are only rich because the poor are not brave enough to have a go at them. And even when a tyrant succeeded in acquiring, with the help of his followers, a monopoly of the means of coercion, this never carried with it the aura of legitimacy enjoyed by the Egyptian pharaohs or the monarchs of Babylonia or Persia. It was only, perhaps, in periods of extreme *stasis* that the internal world of the *poleis* became truly Hobbesian. But neither, on the other hand, was there ever any doctrine of legitimate accretion of power at the expense of fellow-Greeks. Attachment to the *polis*, yes—both as love of one's own and as approval of it as a form of social organization, to be favourably contrasted with Persian monarchy on the one hand and, on the other, the pre-political life in which each patriarchal head of a separate *oikos* lays down *themis* for his own. But justification of anything more than the initial *synoikisis*, no—every *polis* is as entitled as every other to defend its interests, and every citizen within it likewise.

As always, the relative importance of the modes of production, persuasion, and coercion respectively is impossible to disentangle with precision. But more to the point is the extent to which, as so often, they reinforced one another. Just as, in the archaic period, the switch from stock-rearing to arable farming, the beginnings of a new style of warfare, and the development of a civic ideology symbolized by monumental temple-building mutually accelerated the accretion of power of all three kinds which made the emergence of the *poleis* possible,[9] so in the classical period the constraints on productivity, the burdens of an increasingly different style of warfare, and the lack of an ideological justification for hegemony mutually inhibited the further accretion of power on which their survival depended. Without the financial resources, how could a *polis* build the fortifications and hire the mercenaries? But until the mercenaries could find some other livelihood than war, how could they be prevented from depleting the resources of an overwhelmingly agricultural community? And unless they could be enlisted in the service of a tyrant capable of establishing a securely legitimated monarchy for which they could furnish the standing army, how could they be prevented from drifting from one paymaster to another and, as Isocrates complained, assaulting whoever they ran into on the way?[10]

From the perspective of the comparative sociologist, it is a paradigm case of a mode of the distribution of power on which environmental pressure has the effect of generating maladaptive responses. In Athens, Demosthenes bewailed the Macedonians' unsporting use of peltasts and horsemen in year-round campaigning, and the military training of the ephebes was reorganized. But the aim of policy was still, as attested by Aristotle,[11] the efficient operation of a citizen army (with the sons of the rich trained as necessary in light—as well as heavy—infantry warfare); and the poorer citizens continued to rely, as attested by Demosthenes,[12] on distributions from a public treasury now increasingly incapable of providing them. Likewise in Sparta, the dominant concern was to arrest the

---

[9] See my 'Origins of States: The Case of Archaic Greece', *Comparative Studies in Society and History*, 24 (1982), 351–77.

[10] Isocrates, *Philip* 120, where as in other of his writings he proposes the solution that they should be settled in *poleis* on territory in Asia Minor 'sliced off' from the Persian *basileia*.

[11] The assumption that citizen rights go with the bearing of arms and that citizens need to be good soldiers runs through the *Politics*: the need for training in light-infantry warfare (but with *stasis* rather than defence against an aggressor in mind) is discussed at 1321[a].

[12] *Philippic IV*, 10. 41, where he adds (45) the revealing comment that by this means a small *polis* becomes a large one and a large one 'preserves itself'—not, notice, expands further into an empire.

decline in the number of *Homoioi* (whether caused by low fertility, casualties in war, or overconcentration of landed property through female inheritance), but without any change in the criteria of admission. In all this, I am well aware of the risk of either, on the one hand, selecting items of evidence which may not be typical of the Greek world as a whole or, on the other, constructing an ideal type of an anachronistic *polis* incorporating all the features least adaptive to the selective pressures of the mid fourth century. But let the argument be put the other way round: there is not one of the *poleis*, whether more or less oligarchic or democratic, which did in fact adapt its institutions in the way which, with hindsight, can be seen to have been necessary if they were to survive as a type of independent society. It may sound a little rhetorical to speak of them as 'doomed' to extinction. But I have still to say: even if they weren't, they reacted to their changed environment as though they were.

But (someone may want to object) is there really a problem here at all? Have I not just summarized a set of familiar obstacles which, whatever differences there may be among specialists on points of nuance and detail, make it categorically impossible for institutions suitable for these small, would-be autarkic communities to be adapted for survival in a world of imperial powers? Isn't the citizen-state as a mode of the distribution of power incapable almost by definition of augmenting its economic, ideological, and coercive resources sufficiently to hold its own in competition with extended, populous, warlike, patrimonial or absolutist monarchies? The answer, however, is no. In the first place, it is by no means self-evident that a *polis* (or temporary coalition of *poleis*) which had defeated Persia should necessarily be defeated by Macedon: Chaeronea was, after all, quite a close-run thing. And in the second, it is possible to point to well-documented cases where societies in the same mode of the distribution of power *did* adapt their institutions and augment their resources with unarguable success. I have two in particular in mind. In the first, adaptation was primarily political and military, and in the second, economic and commercial. Both evolved, in due course, into another mode but not until after they had successfully reproduced themselves over many generations within what were still the institutions of a citizen-state. They are, as readers will no doubt have guessed, Rome and Venice.

The early history of Roman institutions is notoriously obscure. But three characteristics important for comparison with the Greek *poleis* seem generally agreed: the strength of vertical ties between patrons and clients; the extension of citizenship to selected adult males in other Italian territories; and the frequent manumission of slaves who thereupon acquired free citizen status. All three do, no doubt, have to be qualified. Patron–client relations were not unknown in the Greek world—witness Plutarch's account of Kimon;[13] citizenship could occasionally be granted to a foreigner or metic; and some Greek slaves, notably the banker Pasion, might enjoy dramatic upward social mobility. But the difference in degree was fundamental. It may be that the pervasiveness of *clientela* in Roman society has sometimes been exaggerated. But whether or not ties of *fides* were transmitted from father to son to quite the extent that they were traditionally supposed by scholars to be, there can be no doubt of the existence of the availability to powerful patrons of (in Cicero's phrase) 'men with small means and no jobs',[14] nor about the extent and scope of inequality within the citizen body which was both generated and perpetuated thereby. Likewise, manumission fed into the citizen body a steady stream of new recruits who, as well as being for the most part both able and industrious, were, although of inferior status to those born free, more grateful for their freedom than resentful of their inferiority. And the selective enfranchisement of Latins and allies had a similar effect in adding to the citizen body men who, although they might be sneered at as *inquilini*, were well aware of the privileges they now enjoyed and were consistently loyal to the *senatus populusque Romanus*. Rome's successful expansion within what were still the institutions of a citizen-state was possible because and only because those institutions were at the oligarchic extreme within that mode—far more so than any

---

[13] *Cimon* 10, reports him as using the booty from his campaigns to allow poor citizens free access to his fields and to provide them (if, according to Aristotle, they were members of his own deme) with a free dinner every day. But this is still far short of *clientela* on the Roman model.

[14] *Pro Murena* 70: '*tenuiorum amicorum et non occupatorum est ista adsiduitas, quorum copia bonis viris et beneficis deesse non solet*'.

'oligarchic' Greek *polis* (and least of all Sparta where the *Homoioi*, although by no means strictly equal,[15] were much nearer to each other in wealth, prestige, and political-cum-military power than the citizens of Athens). But it is not just restating the obvious to say that the 100,000 *assidui* of the early second century BC whose service with the legions had made Rome the dominant Italian and indeed Mediterranean power were citizens. However few of them actually exercised their vote, their magistrates were elected; however incompetent those magistrates, they were never deposed by a tyrant or replaced by a king; however reluctant the citizens of call-up age were (and they increasingly were[16]) to be conscripted for fresh campaigns, they were never displaced by mercenaries and were never deprived of the right to bear arms; and however impoverished many of them were as a consequence of the effects of near-continuous warfare, they were never depressed below the critical dividing-line between slave and free (although debt-bondage probably survived its formal abolition in 326 BC, and a poor citizen might well find himself at risk of illegal enslavement). The conclusion is inescapable: a *polis can* expand to be (in the sense appropriate to the times) a world power.

In the case of Venice, expansion of resources within the institutional framework of a citizen-state was not, as Doge Andrea Dandolo later affected to believe, the outcome of a voluntary *synoikisis* in the late seventh century,[17] but, as in the case of early Rome, the replacement of a patrimonial monarchy by a communal republic in the first half of the eleventh. By then geography and politics between them had created an expansionist naval power in which merchants as well as landowners were of high status and subordinate territories were worked either by dependent tenants without citizen rights or by slaves (particularly on the Cretan plantations). In due course, whereas Rome evolved from citizen-state to monarchy without a change in the mode of production, Venice

[15] See G. E. M. de Ste Croix, *The Origins of the Peloponnesian War* (London, 1972), pp. 124 ff., arguing in support of Plutarch's view of Sparta as an 'aristocratic oligarchy' (*Mor.* 826 f.).

[16] See William V. Harris, *War and Imperialism in Republican Rome 327–70 BC* (Oxford, 1979), p. 48, who dates this reluctance from the mid-2nd cent. BC.

[17] See Frederic C. Lane, *Venice: A Maritime Republic* (Baltimore, 1973), pp. 87–8.

evolved from citizen-state to (for want of a better term) 'bourgeois' institutions through a change in the mode of production which left the mode of coercion intact. But in the intervening period it survived as a *polis* without either lapsing into tyranny or succumbing to a would-be imperial invader. The citizens were organized by parishes, and assessed by their *capi* for forced loans and for military (or naval) service. The fiscal system was based on liturgy rather than tax; citizens, not mercenaries (although there were some), were the basis of the armed forces; and the few bureaucratic functions were performed by elected committees whose members held office only for a few years at most. The economic resources which made not only survival but expansion possible came predominantly (although not exclusively) from trade. The anonymous extensor of the mid-eleventh-century document known as the *Honorantiae Civitatis Papiae* who wrote of Venice '*illa gens non arat, non seminat, non vindemiat*' was exaggerating. But imagine the same thing written of Athens![18] Venetian sea-power was used not only, as was Athenian, for war and plunder or to safeguard the supply of grain and strategic raw materials, but to profit directly from the expansion of East–West commerce; and occupied territories were not only used as strategic bases but economically exploited both systematically and on a large scale. Again, the conclusion is inescapable: a *polis can* expand to be a world power without ceasing to be a *polis*.

IV

But now, perhaps, I am inviting a more damaging objection from the other flank. Granted (it might be said) that a *polis can* expand and thus survive in a world of would-be imperial powers, is it not a purely contingent matter that Athens did not do so in the manner of Venice, or Sparta in the manner of Rome? But the answer is again no; both in turn, when the opportunity presented itself, failed to take it for reasons not of historical mischance but as a direct consequence of the

[18] Or imagine there being in any Greek *polis* a role of *consul mercatorum*, such as in late 12th-cent. Florence and Modena was occupied by a member of the nobility: Daniel Waley, *The Italian City-Republics* (London, 1969), p. 24.

character of their own institutions and the constraints within which they functioned.

It can hardly be disputed that Athens was, as Thucydides says, the strongest naval power in Greece, and whatever the right answer to the question how far the members of the Delian league resented, tolerated, or (if democratically governed) welcomed Athenian hegemony, the hegemony itself was an acknowledged fact. What is more, the geographical extent of the Athenian state, its substantial population, its area under cultivation, and its revenues from the silver mines of Laurion gave it a potential for expansion through sea-power relatively equal (one would suppose) to Venice. But it is clear from the policy of Perikles as reported to us by Thucydides that such expansion was neither achieved nor even sought.[19] The tribute from the allies was deliberately thesaurized in order to be available to be melted down for military expenses, and much ready cash was in any case needed for the construction and maintenance of the triremes and the oarsmen to crew them (not all of whom were Athenians); nor could the triremes be used as merchant ships. Sea-power was, to be sure, used to protect strategic imports—notably Black Sea grain—but not for conquest and exploitation of the Venetian kind. No doubt it was exploitative that allied wealth should be diverted to paying Athenian citizens to hold public office, that tolls should be levied purely for the benefit of Athens from seaborne trade, that well-off Athenian citizens should be able to buy land outside of Attica and poorer ones to have it given to them, and that access to Athenian ports and markets should be withheld in defiance of treaty obligations. But this is a world away from systematic and exorbitant poll or land taxes or levies in kind, loans at usurious rates, coerced labour services, or even (to borrow a nice descriptive detail from Strabo) Caesar's colonists in Corinth digging up old graves for vases and bronzes to ship back to the burgeoning Roman antique market.[20]

Likewise, the settlement of colonists or cleruchs, or the appointment of *archontes* or *epimeletai* to allied *poleis*, was not

---

[19] This seems a reasonable inference from Thuc. 2. 13 where Perikles' advice to his fellow-citizens about the conduct of the coming war presupposes a defensive strategy financed by the *periousia chrematon* drawn from the allies.

[20] Strabo 8. 6. 23.

part of an attempt at imperial expansion of a Roman or Venetian kind. *Archontes* were sent out to keep other *poleis* democratic and pro-Athenian, not as proconsuls with missions of further annexation; and cleruchs, although they remained available to the Athenian cause in time of war, did no more than create new little *poleis* for themselves, complete with their own assembly and magistrates on the Athenian model.[21] Expulsions, to be sure, were a normal instrument of policy, as in Aegina and later in Samos, but not of a policy of conquest. Indeed, the main motive would seem to have been the opportunity to settle Athenian citizens for whom there was not enough land in Attica. Once again, we are a world away from expansion such as Roman consuls or Venetian doges would have conceived of it.

But if Athens lacked the resources and the will to expand through sea-power, might not Sparta have had the resources and the will to expand through the deliberate use of a fighting force as formidable on land in its day as the Roman legionaries were in theirs? But the Spartans were, after their initial conquest of Messenia, even less disposed to imperial aggrandizement than the Athenians. The literary sources give an impression more moralistic than sociological of the Spartans' innate conservatism and their inability to cope with the gold, luxury, and exposure to foreign influences which the victory over Athens brought them. But it is true that they were far less well adapted for growth through conquest than the Romans were. They were, indeed, deeply suspicious of foreign influences; they were acutely conscious of the continuing need to keep tight coercive control over their Helots; they were totally unwilling to extend citizen status to foreigners (or even to more than a selected few *neodamodeis* of their own);[22] and they were quite right to fear that an influx of wealth would

---

[21] Indeed, they may have done less. If the suggestion put forward by P. A. Brunt is correct, 'the cleruchies were simply groups of lot-holders, often non-resident, in allied territories, who did not form communities with "municipal" status': 'Athenian Settlements Abroad in the Fifth Century BC', in *Ancient Society and Institutions: Studies Presented to Victor Ehrenberg* (Oxford, 1966), p. 87.

[22] By the time of Kleomenes III and Nabis, it was obvious, as they recognized, that restoration of anything like the Lycurgan system would require not merely a redistribution of land but enfranchisement of Helots (or at any rate *perioikoi*) to occupy it. But it was by then far too late.

undermine the basis on which their distinctively, albeit not thoroughly, egalitarian structure and culture were constructed. Their one major colonial enterprise, at Heraclea Trachinia, was a failure. Thucydides implies that the Spartans were not much good at running this kind of a show,[23] and although it would no doubt be a mistake to attribute their non-imperialism, as it were, simply to the failings of individual harmosts, it was not a role for which their peculiar upbringing had trained them. It was not just political mischance which prevented Sparta from expanding into the vacuum left by its defeat of Athens, and it was not its own defeat at Leuktra which put an end to a process which had never, in fact, got under way. Still less than in the case of Athens would it be plausible to argue that Sparta was capable of an evolution to great-power status but was thwarted by accidental contingencies.

Athens and Sparta were not, to be sure, the only *poleis* in Greece, and the fact that they are the two best-documented in our sources is not a reason to concentrate on them to the exclusion of all the rest. But there is no other which came nearer, or even as near, to breaking out of the constraints imposed by its legal and customary institutions into an accretion of resources on a Roman or Venetian scale. Perhaps the strongest potential candidate was Corinth, with its early *synoikisis*, its strategic position on the Isthmus, its stable oligarchy,[24] its tradition of naval supremacy,[25] and its exceptionally tolerant attitude to the practitioners of handicrafts.[26] But there is no evidence that any of this furthered a seriously, let alone successfully, expansionist policy after the fall of the tyranny.[27]

---

[23] Thuc. 2. 92, where the Spartan *archontes* are alleged to have frightened most of the inhabitants away by governing harshly (*chalepos*) and at times unfairly (*ou kalos*).

[24] J. B. Salmon, *Wealthy Corinth: A History of the City to 338 BC* (Oxford, 1984), p. 236, attributes this stability to the 'broadly moderate' character of the oligarchy, by which he means that 'however decisions were taken they were reached with a careful eye to what the citizens in general could be persuaded, rather than forced, to accept'.

[25] Specialists are divided over the date of the Corinthian 'thalassocracy', and it is by no means certain that the Corinthians were the first Greeks to build triremes; but there seems no reason to doubt that Corinth did become, at least for a time, the dominant naval power in Greece. See Salmon, pp. 222–3.

[26] Herod. 2. 167. 2 ('*hekista de Korinthioi onontai tous cheirotechnas*').

[27] Periander, whom Aristotle calls '*polemikos*' (*Pol.* 1315[b]), may well have entertained imperial ambitions. But if he did, and the oligarchs who took over after the killing of his successor and nephew (ibid.) did not, the conclusion that the Greek *poleis* could only

If Corinthian trade, particularly in pottery, was both extensive and profitable, it still did not alter the traditional priority accorded to political and military institutions: no dominant class of manufacturers or merchants evolved which might have influenced Corinthian policy in the direction of imperial expansion for commercial ends. And although the Corinthians did attempt to use their fleet to extend their political influence in North-West Greece during the decades following the Persian Wars, this never amounted to anything approaching the Athenians' domination of the Aegean. If any further evidence is called for to show how far Corinth fell short of a Roman- or Venetian-type evolution, it is provided by the history of its relations with its colonies. Even if, as seems questionable, some of them may have been founded with commercial and/or strategic purposes partly in view, rather than simply as a response to population increase and a shortage of cultivable land, they remained to a similar degree to the Athenian colonies independent little *poleis* whose relations with their mother-city were conducted in much the same way as those between *poleis* generally.[28]

Examples which would tell against my argument might still be found outside of mainland Greece. But the area where the potential for imperial expansion can best be demonstrated— Sicily—turns out to tell strongly in favour of it. Not only was it the tyranny of Dionysios in Syracuse which came nearest to establishing an effective rule over Sicily as a whole, but the subsequent attempt of Timoleon to revive the Sicilian *poleis* in their earlier institutional form only served to show how much of a dead-end that form had indeed become. It is true that during the period between the Deinomenids and Dionysios, Syracuse had been able as an autonomous citizen-state not only

transcend the limitations of their institutions by becoming monarchies instead of citizen-states is reinforced yet again.

[28] It may be that the relation between Corinth and its colonies was closer than this implies: A. J. Graham, *Colony and Mother City in Ancient Greece* (Manchester, 1964), p. 152, concludes that it was 'somewhere between autonomy and absorption in the state of Corinth'. But his claim that 'the colonies were sufficiently closely connected to Corinth to be regarded as a means of extending Corinth's power abroad' (p. 142) is undermined by his earlier admission that 'the evidence of some independence in foreign policy, if no other, proves that the colonies had a separate existence from the mother city' (p. 139).

to hold its own against other Sicilian *poleis* but also to beat off the ill-fated Athenian expedition. But it was only under Dionysios that its power was augmented on a major scale; and Timoleon's restoration, if it can be so called,[29] broke down almost at once. In any case, Timoleon himself was a professional *condottiere* who relied on mercenaries to just the same extent as his opponents,[30] and his resettlement of Greek Sicily was carried out in a manner altogether more reminiscent of Dionysios than of Kleisthenes. The rapid breakdown of stability which followed it and the subsequent return of Syracuse to tyranny under Agathokles may not have been predictable in advance, but they are not surprising in retrospect. In Finley's words, 'The autonomous, self-governing Greek city was beyond redemption even in old Greece, and there was surely no hope for it in Sicily where it had never grown strong roots.'[31]

V

What, then, was it about the Greek *poleis* which prevented any of them from breaking out of the evolutionary dead-end up against which they found themselves? If there is any single inference to be drawn from the comparison with Rome and Venice, it is simply that the *poleis* were all, without exception, far too democratic. Some, of course, were more oligarchic than others. But this meant only that their government was in the hands of a relatively smaller number of relatively richer citizens rather than a relatively larger number of relatively poorer ones. In terms of a close concentration of economic, ideological, and coercive power in the hands of a compact, self-reproducing élite, no Greek *polis* ever came anywhere near the degree of oligarchy which characterized the institutions of both Rome and Venice during the period of their achievement of world-power status. In no Greek *polis* did there ever form a

---

[29] Plut. *Timoleon* 39. 3 reports that in the decree read out at his funeral he was credited with 'giving the Sicilians back their laws', which is a palpable exaggeration. Diodorus (16. 82. 5) puts it more cautiously in terms of the offer of a place to settle and a share in the *politeia* of Syracuse (cf. 19. 2. 8).

[30] R. J. A. Talbert, *Timoleon and the Revival of Greek Sicily* (Cambridge, 1974), p. 65.

[31] M. I. Finley, *Ancient Sicily*, 2nd edn. (London, 1979), p. 101.

nobility or patriciate with an effective monopoly of the means of production, persuasion, and coercion and the capacity to transmit that monopoly to its chosen successors. There was no lack of individual leaders of outstanding ability and ambition: Perikles and Kimon in Athens, Pausanias and Lysander in Sparta, or Epaminondas in Thebes all towered above their allies and rivals alike. But they never commanded the scale of economic, ideological, or coercive resources controlled by the leading families of Rome or Venice, whose large fortunes, undisputed prestige, and privileged access to high political and military office enabled their abilities and ambitions to be channelled into a progressive augmentation of the power of their citizen-states as such.

The objection might be raised at this point that during the fourth century BC inequalities were widening dramatically within the *poleis*, not only in Athens (where the literary sources document a mounting resentment of the rich by the poor) and Sparta (where an abortive conspiracy was mounted against the *Homoioi* by one of the *Hypomeiones* in 397 BC),[32] but, for example, in Argos where, according to Diodorus, the *demos* instigated an outbreak of 'club-law' (*skytalismos*) in which the demagogues themselves as well as the oligarchs were killed before the *demos* 'recovered their senses'.[33] But all this was, so to speak, polarization of the wrong kind. It all took place within institutional constraints which permitted an alternation between 'oligarchy' and 'democracy' as the Greeks defined them but ruled out the possibility of effective and sustained concentration of power at the top. In fourth-century Greece, this could only be achieved by a monarchy: it is not purely coincidental that the career of Philip of Macedon at one corner of the Greek world should find a parallel at the opposite corner in the career of Agathokles in Syracuse, who, having re-established the tyranny overthrown by Timoleon, was then

[32] Xenophon does not explicitly say that Kinadon was one of the *Hypomeiones*, merely that he was not one of the *Homoioi* (*Hell.* 3. 3). But the presumption must be that he was a Spartiate who either had no *kleros* or could not pay his dues to the *syssitia*. Aristotle (*Pol.* 1306^b) cites him as an example of a bold (*androdes*) man excluded from 'honours' (*timai*).

[33] Diod. 15. 58. 4 (*ho de demos pausamenos tes luttes eis ten proüparchousan ennoian apokateste*).

able to win recognition for himself as one among other Hellenistic kings.[34]

This prompts me to end by re-emphasizing the importance of ideological in addition to economic and commercial and/or political and military constraints. Their relative importance may, as I have conceded already, be impossible to apportion precisely. But the ideology of the Greek *poleis* was not only strongly anti-monarchical—so, after all, was that of both Rome and Venice—but strongly populist: it was, that is to say, hostile to the concentration of power in the hands of any single person, family, or group except for limited periods and for limited purposes as endorsed by the citizen body as a whole. It is, no doubt, risky to place too much reliance on anecdotal evidence. But the attitude of the Athenians to Perikles at the beginning of the Peloponnesian War and the attitude of the Spartans to Lysander at the end of it both testify to a spirit of collective jealousy which consistently put the curbing of the ambitions of an individual leader above the growth of the power of the *polis* itself to which the fulfilment of those ambitions would have contributed.[35] As has often been observed, it was the Greeks who invented ostracism, but the Romans who invented the triumph. It goes, I hope, without saying that no value-judgement is implied by this comparison: whether it was a good thing or a bad thing that no Greek *polis* evolved as Rome (or Venice) did is up to you. But if any Greek *polis* was to survive as an independent citizen-state in competition with one or more would-be world powers, it had to become capable of being a world power itself. This none of them ever did, and the explanation lies in their constitutional inability to augment their ideological as well as their economic and coercive resources to the necessary degree.

---

[34] Diodorus begins his account of Agathokles' career with a symptomatic comment on the policy of some *poleis* of depriving their leading politicians of the outward forms of power in order to avert the risk of monarchy (19. 1. 1). Finley (n. 31), p. 106, doubts whether Agathokles' 'new titulary' marked any significant change, and Diodorus (20. 54. 1) attributes it to the example of the Diadochi; but if nothing else, it is still evidence of the additional status which the diadem was thought to confer.

[35] It may be worth noting in passing how Sallust gets it wrong in attributing to the Athenians and Spartans imperial aims of a Roman kind: 'in Graecia Lacedaimonii et Athenienses coepere urbis atque nationes subigere, lubidinem dominandi causam belli habere, maxumam gloriam in maxumo imperio putare' (*Cat.* 2. 2).

I accordingly conclude that the title which I have given to this chapter has been vindicated in a double sense. Not only is the language of evolutionary sociological theory appropriate to the argument which I have advanced, but the facts which I have adduced in support of it convincingly dispose of any counter-factual hypothesis to the effect that if individual personalities or contingent events had been other than they were, one or more Greek *poleis* would have survived as autonomous citizen-states in what we now call with hindsight the Hellenistic as opposed to the Hellenic world.

Index